Mind the Gap

ECPR Press

ECPR Press is an imprint of the European Consortium for Political Research. It publishes original research from leading political scientists and the best among early career researchers in the discipline. Its scope extends to all fields of political sci-ence, international relations and political thought, without restriction in either approach or regional focus. It is also open to interdisciplinary work with a predominant political dimension.

ECPR Press Editors

Editors

Peter Kennealy is Deputy Director of the European University Institute library in Florence, Italy.

Alexandra Segerberg is Associate Professor at the University of Stockholm, Sweden.

Associate Editors

Ian O'Flynn is Senior Lecturer in Political Theory at Newcastle University, UK.

Lanra Sudulich is Senior Lecturer in Politics and International Relations at the University of Kent, UK. She is also affiliated to Cevipol (Centre d'Etude de la vie Politique) at the Universite libre de Bruxelles, Belgium.

Mind the Gap

Political Participation and Representation in Belgium

Edited by Kris Deschouwer

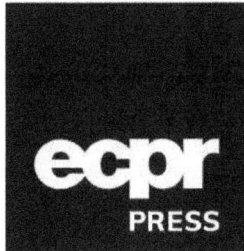

ecpr PRESS

Published by the European Consortium for Political Research, Harbour House, 6-8 Hythe Quay, Colchester, CO2 8JF, United Kingdom.

British Library Cataloguing in Publication Data
A catalogue record for this book is available from the British Library

ISBN: HB 978-1-78660-541-2 PB 978-1-78661-305-9

Library of Congress Cataloging-in-Publication Data

Names: Deschouwer, Kris, editor.
Title: Mind the gap : political participation and representation in Belgium / edited by
   Kris Deschouwer.
Description: London : ECPR Press, [2017] |
   Includes bibliographical references and index.
Identifiers: LCCN 2017039926 (print) | LCCN 2018000314 (ebook) | ISBN
   9781786605429 (electronic) | ISBN 9781786605412 (cloth : alk. paper) | ISBN
9781786613059 (paper : alk paper)
Subjects: LCSH: Representative government and representation—Belgium. |
Democracy—Belgium. | Political participation—Belgium. | Elections—Belgium. |
Voting research—Belgium. | Belgium—Politics and government.

Classification: LCC JN6301 (ebook) | LCC JN6301 .M56 2017 (print) | DDC
   323/.04209493—dc23
LC record available at https://lccn.loc.gov/2017039926

ecpr.eu/shop

Contents

Abbreviations

ALDE	Alliance of Liberals and Democrats for Europe
BPPS	Belgian Political Panel Survey 2006–2011
CD&V	Christen-Democratisch en Vlaams (Flemish Christian democratic party)
cdH	Centre Démocrate Humaniste (francophone Christian democratic party, formerly Parti Social Chrétien)
CVP	Christelijke Volkspartij (Christian Democratic and Flemish formerly, Christian People's Party)
DéFi	Démocrate Fédéraliste Indépendant (Brussels-based party for francophone defence – formerly FDF)
EGP	European Green Party
EPP	European People's Party
FDF	Front Démocratique des Francophones (Brussels-based party for francophone defence – now DéFi)
FN	Front National (francophone radical right party)
GDP	Gross domestic product
ISPO	Institute for Social and Political Opinion Research
LDD	Lijst Dedecker (Flemish radical liberal party)
MEDW	Making Electoral Democracy Work
MP	Member of parliament
MR	Mouvement Réformateur (francophone liberal party)
N-VA	Nieuw-Vlaamse Alliantie (Flemish autonomist party)
OECD	Organisation for Economic Co-operation and Development
OLS	Ordinary least squares
Open VLD	Open Vlaamse Liberalen en Democraten (Flemish liberal party)
PCA	Principal component analysis
PIOP	Pole Interuniversitaire Opinion publique et Politique

PLP   Parti de la Liberté et du Progrès (Party of Liberty and Progress)
PP   Parti Populaire (francophone radical right party)
PR   Proportional representation
PS   Parti Socialiste (francophone socialist party)
PSC   Parti Social Chrétien
PTB   Parti du Travail de Belgique (radical left party – PvdA in Dutch)
PvdA   Partij van de Arbeid (radical left party – PTB in French)
PVV   Partij voor Vrijheid en Vooruitgang
S&D   Socialists and democrats
SES   Socio-economic status
SP.a   Socialisische Partij Anders (Flemish socialist party)
VAA   Voting advice application
VB   Vlaams Belang (Flemish radical right and separatist party – until 2003 Vlaams Blok)

Figures

Tables

Acknowledgements

The research on which this book is based has been made possible in the first place by the Belgian Federal Science Policy and its research programme for Interuniversity Attraction Poles. The PartiRep network was financed under phase VI (2007–2012) and phase VII (2012–2017). Without the scale created by this programme, the research – and especially the large data-gathering activities – would simply not have been possible.

All the universities that were part of the network have also contributed to the financing of the work. We would like to express our gratitude to the Vrije Universiteit Brussel, the Université libre de Bruxelles, the KU Leuven, the Université catholique de Louvain, the Universiteit Antwerpen, the Universiteit Leiden and the Universität Mannheim.

Several researchers and several projects in the PartiRep programme have been financed by the Belgian science foundations. We are grateful for the ample support provided by the Fonds voor Wetenschappelijk Onderzoek and the Fonds de la Recherche Scientifique.

Introduction

The many gaps in Belgian politics

Kris Deschouwer

THE BELGIAN GAPS

Some elections are identified as 'critical' (Evans & Norris 1999). It means that their results are deviating from normal and predictable patterns. They show, for instance, high levels of volatility, contain important surprises like the sudden rise or sudden decline of one or a few parties, lead to innovative governmental coalitions and – very importantly – mark a turning point. Critical elections are landmarks in the electoral history of a country. The elections of 24 November 1991 were, for Belgium, without any doubt critical elections, and they were labelled as such as soon as the results came in. Election Day was referred to as 'Black Sunday', pointing in the very first place at the success of the radical right party Vlaams Blok, which had gathered almost 7 per cent of the votes with a programme that contained the typical 'Le Pen' cocktail of nationalism, law and order and xenophobia. A party called Rossem – after its founder and leader – polled 3 per cent of the votes with a strong anti-establishment discourse (and while Jean-Pierre Van Rossem himself was in jail after being accused of major fraud). The two largest party families of Belgium – Christian democrats and socialists – both lost heavily and for the first time their combined votes added up to merely 50 per cent, down from 58 per cent in 1987 (and still no less than 79 per cent in 1961). The two still had a majority of the seats in parliament and did again form a coalition, but only after difficult negotiations that took more than three months.

These were critical elections indeed, and all these electoral shifts were soon interpreted as one major call, as one loud and clear 'signal of the voter'. That voter appeared to be unhappy and clearly willing to voice this feeling at the polls. There was a general consensus on the fact that there was a 'gap' between citizens and politicians, that their agendas did not match, that

1

representation was not functioning properly, that parties had lost the ability to keep in touch with the real problems of the people and that therefore action was needed. It triggered discussions about the way in which parties should be organised and about the way in which elections could better capture the will of the people. Some seized this opportunity to defend the abolishment of compulsory voting, others believed that an electoral threshold to keep smaller parties out of parliament might help and still others thought that preference voting should be encouraged to allow voters to really choose their representatives. A 'new political culture' was also needed that included, among others, a reduction of clientelist practices and of cumulating of political mandates.

These were critical elections for Belgium, but the centre of the post-election debate was actually not Belgium as a whole but mainly Flanders, the Dutch-speaking region in the north of the country. The radical right party Vlaams Blok did indeed only present candidates in Flanders, being originally a party defending the independence of Flanders. In Flanders it had polled 10 per cent of the votes. The party Rossem was also a Flemish phenomenon only, polling 5 per cent of the votes in the region. In the francophone south of Belgium, the Christian democrats and socialists had also lost votes, but together still controlled more than 60 per cent of the electorate. A small radical right party Front National (FN) had booked some success (2 per cent), but the major surprise came from the green party Ecolo that doubled its score to nearly 14 per cent.

These different electoral results in north and south were not at all new in 1991. They have been there ever since elections were held in Belgium. They are one of the indicators of a much older 'gap' in Belgium politics, that is, the gap between the two language groups, between the French speakers of the south (Wallonia and Brussels) and the Dutch speakers of the north (Flanders and Brussels) (McRae 1986). This gap had in the 1950s become so deep, putting north and south against each other both on preferred policy choices and on the institutional future of the country, that all major parties fell apart into two unilingual parties, presenting candidates only to voters in their own language group. It was exactly a conflict between north and south on the distribution of competencies between central state and regional authorities that brought down the government and led to early elections in November 1991.

The gap between north and south has been responsible for many political crises in Belgium. One that did not pass unnoticed to the world started after the federal elections of 2010. Once again a conflict on the institutional organisation of the country had ended the federal coalition and early elections were called. Parties in Flanders almost unanimously agreed that a new federal government could only be formed on the condition that a major constitutional reform granting more powers to the substates would be agreed on. Francophone parties, on the contrary, had promised their voters that they would not yield to these demands and would not enter a coalition if that would involve agreeing on constitutional reforms. The result was a government formation process that lasted eighteen months – 541 days exactly – to form in the end a grand coalition of the three traditional party families: Christian democrats, socialists and liberals (six parties).

During these eighteen months, life in the country went on more or less as usual (Hooghe 2012). Substate governments installed after elections in 2009 kept on functioning, the outgoing coalition went on as a caretaker government and Belgium chaired the European Union (EU). Even more remarkable though was the almost complete absence of any popular discontent with what was happening. International media were showing concern about the viability of Belgium, asking even whether it would be worth the while trying to make it survive at all. And while the Belgian political leaders were angrily staring at each other across the language border and refused to move an inch away from their original electoral pledges, there was no sizeable mobilisation of the people to support their political leaders in their battle, and there were only some very friendly actions urging the political elites to become sensible and to just govern the country together. The regional 2009 and federal 2010 electoral campaign had focused a lot on these institutional matters, but electoral research afterwards showed that the institutional issue was not very salient for most of the citizens (Deschouwer et al. 2010). Even many supporters of parties defending in the short or longer term the full independence of Flanders were not in agreement with the radical proposals of the party platforms. This is yet another intriguing 'gap' in Belgian politics, which is quite similar to what can be seen at the European level. In matters of institutional reform the party elites hold much more radical views than their rank and file. Party elites have run ahead of their voters in defending European integration, and in Belgium they furthermore defend more devolution while their voters actually prefer the national status quo.

Belgium is not the only country that can now look back at almost three decades of discussions about the quality of representative democracy. Both in public debates and in political science the dominant tone in debates about democracy is currently one of concern (e.g. Alonso, Keane & Merkel 2011; Mair 2013; Hay 2007; Keane 2009). There are many now well-known indicators that all suggest that traditional patterns of political participation and representation are eroding. Electoral behaviour has become volatile, reflecting weakening ties between voters and parties; voter turnout gradually and sometimes even spectacularly declines; party membership numbers have been plummeting; trust in political parties and more generally in representative institutions is very low. Explanations for these changing patterns and low levels of legitimacy are, among others, the fading of the old cleavage lines, the increased complexity and differentiating of society, the speed of communication and the blurring of the lines of representation and account-ability in a world where power is no longer concentrated in the national state and at the central state level.

The thirteen chapters of this book all deal with topics that are related to this discussion about the evolution and the quality of democratic politics, from perceived norms of citizenship over multilevel politics to electoral personalisation. They all talk explicitly to the literature and explore the evolutions in the case of Belgium. The country is in many respects a very 'normal' country, displaying the classic features of a parliamentary democracy and witnessing the same evolutions in societal structure, electoral behaviour and party organisation as other modern democracies. Yet Belgium is also a country that displays a number of peculiar and even exceptional characteristics that make it interesting and often a strong 'case in point' for analysing specific developments. One of these peculiarities is the extreme complexity of the political institutions. Belgium is a federal country with two types of substates: three territorial regions (Brussels, Flanders and Wallonia) and three language communities (Dutch, French and – a very small – German). These two types of substates partially but not completely overlap and relate in a different way to each other in each of the language communities (Deschouwer 2012). This transformation of the Belgian state was not a calm and smooth process since political elites from Flanders and from francophone Belgium thoroughly disagreed – and still do – on the internal boundaries and on what should be the building blocks of the federation. The disagreement broke the political parties in two unilingual pieces in the 1960s and the 1970s, leaving Belgium as a country with – very uniquely – a totally split party system. There are indeed no statewide parties in Belgium, except for a relatively small radical left party. And not only parties are split along the language divide but also all media and therefore also the public opinion. Belgium is a country with a divided demos and with political debates and political campaigns running in two different and separate spheres. If one adds to this the membership of the EU where important powers have been not only pooled but also remain shared with both the substate and the federal authorities, one can truly say that Belgium is a political system with a very low level of clarity. Tracing back the chains of representation and accountability is extremely difficult in this multilevel labyrinth.

The way in which the federal system functions is also rather peculiar. Decision-making at the federal level requires cooperation and a common agreement between the Dutch-speaking and the French-speaking community. The Belgian federation is a textbook example of a consensus democracy (Lijphart 2012) where powers are shared and where multiple veto players lead to either the absence of decision-making – which does happen regularly – or incredibly creative compromises that allow for a de-blocking of the system but that leaves at the same time all major actors deeply dissatisfied and frustrated. The consensus logic is not new for Belgium. Actually, the institutional pacification of the language divide only built on a tradition of consociationalism that had already been present since the early twentieth century for the dealing with the class and religious conflicts (Huyse 1981). The long tradition of power-sharing, of package deals, of elite collusion that combined a high degree of autonomy for each of the societal *pillars* (Rokkan 1977) and of proportional allocation of the spoils has spilled over to the organisation of the federal state. It has left the political parties and their auxiliary organisations very much in control of all important sectors of policymaking and of all public organisations and authorities that are involved in delivering the state services to the citizens. This is called *partitocracy*, and Belgium certainly is a good example of it (De Winter & Van Wynsberghe 2015).

Zooming in on the electoral system also reveals a number of specific and again rather unique features of Belgium. Since 1893, voting is compulsory. That is, all voters have to present themselves at the polling station, although they can then decide to cast a blank vote. Debates on whether this compulsory voting should be kept alive do pop up once in a while, but the principle is written in the constitution and therefore requires a very broad consensus to remove it (Hooghe & Deschouwer 2011). Seats in the different parliaments at all levels are distributed in a proportional way. Belgium was actually the first country to introduce proportional representation (PR) in 1900. More important, however, is the ballot structure. The lists presented by the political parties are semi-open or 'flexible'. This means that voters can either cast a vote for the list as such or cast one or more preference votes within the list of the choice. The question of whether electoral politics have become more personalised can therefore nicely be analysed in the Belgian context.

PLAN OF THE BOOK

This book builds on one decade of collaborative work conducted by the PartiRep research programme, an inter-university network focussing on changing patterns of participation and representation in modern democracies. The programme has mobilised since 2007 several dozens of political science researchers from the Vrije Universiteit Brussel, the Université libre de Bruxelles, the KU Leuven, the Université catholique de Louvain and the Universiteit Antwerpen. The University of Leiden and the Mannheim Centre for European Social Research were associated with the network and also contributed actively to the research. A wide variety of aspects and dimensions of political participation and representation were scrutinised and reports were published widely. The thirteen chapters of this book present several highlights of the findings and reflect on the way in which and the degree in which the overall developments in democratic government are visible in Belgium and, at the same time, raise the question to what extent the very specific and sometimes exceptional context of the Belgian political system has led to specifically or typically Belgian outcomes.

In the first four chapters the norms and expectations about democratic governance are central. In chapter 1, Jan W. van Deth searches for the way in which young adults support norms of citizenship. These are norms that define what a 'good' citizen in a democratic polity should be and should do, like being politically and socially active or obey the laws. Using a panel study that has followed young adults during five years (see later) he finds more than expected a strong support for law-and-order norms. The age of eighteen appears to be an important threshold making youngsters clearly more aware of the importance – and in the Belgian context the obligation – to turn out to vote. Overall, however, the attitudes towards citizenship norms do not evolve a lot between the age of sixteen and twenty-one, suggesting that these norms have already been internalised before reaching the age of adolescence.

In chapter 2, Camille Kelbel, Giulia Sandri and Emilie van Haute zoom in on the perception and the image of parties in Belgium. In modern democracy, in general, and in partitocratic Belgium, in particular, the political parties do not have a good press. The authors want to unravel these feelings by taking neither the public nor the party as single and unitary actors. They differentiate between different categories of the population (citizens, party activists, candidates and members of parliament [MPs]) and between the different faces of the parties. They do find a nuanced and varied picture, with actors in Flanders being less critical of parties than those in Wallonia and with citizens being more critical than elites candidates and MPs. Audrey André, Sam Depauw and Rudy B. Andeweg wonder in chapter 3 what citizens expect from their representatives, not so much in terms of policies, but with respect to how they fulfil their representational roles. They distinguish between local promoters, welfare officers, policy specialists and generalists and compare the preferences of the citizens with the preferences of the candidates at the 2014 elections. What they find is a profound mismatch – yet another gap – between the citizens' and the elites' views on how representation should work. Citizens rather prefer representatives who take care of the needs of their local area, while politicians prefer being policy specialists. This gap between the expectations of the citizens and the politicians is larger among the citizens who are less wealthy and who are less partisan and less politically sophisticated.

In chapter 4, Didier Caluwaerts, Benjamin Biard, Vincent Jacquet and Min Reuchamps further explore expectations about democratic governance by looking at models of democracy and at the degree in which citizens actually want more space for other than just the representative model. Citizens with lower levels of education are generally more supportive of all types of democracy. Their much stronger support for other than the representative model suggests that they dislike the current situation most. Higher educated citizens, on the contrary, tend to trust the political institutions more and are indeed less likely to support alternative models. And while there is – as often – a gap between the higher and the lower educated citizens, there is also a gap between north and south: Flanders seems to prefer more elitist forms of democracy, while in Wallonia there is stronger support for deliberative democracy.

Chapter 5 focuses on the Belgian split parties and party system. The absence of one single-party system and of statewide parties that can engage in a dialogue with all the citizens is often mentioned as a shortcoming of Belgian democracy. Kris Deschouwer, Jean-Benoit Pilet and Emilie van Haute analyse to what extent the unilingual parties that have the same ideological label as a party in the other language group can truly (and still) be seen as members of the same party family. They do find quite some convergence on ideological positions and see that sister parties in north and south cater for very similar electorates. Yet at the same time they consciously behave as different parties, with different names and labels and with different strategies. An interesting similarity across the language border is that party elites appear to be much more in favour of institutional changes – both further decentralisation in Belgium and further integration at the European level – than their voters.

Dave Sinardet, Lieven De Winter, Jérémy Dodeigne and Min Reuchamps look in chapter 6 at these Belgian institutional debates and explore the way in which linguistic identities affect institutional preferences and voting behaviour. They find surprisingly little evolutions over time in the territorial identifications, in which the Belgian level continues to be on top. They also confirm the limited division of the public opinion on matters of state reform, unlike the divisions at the elite level. It is especially within Flanders – where some parties defend quite radical separatist solutions – that voters are divided. And those who favour much more autonomy for Flanders do tend to vote for the parties that mobilise for this institutional change.

The way in which citizens deal with different levels of government – the regional, the federal and the European – is analysed in chapter 7 by Soetkin Verhaegen, Louise Hoon, Camille Kelbel and Virginie van Ingelgom. They want to unravel the reasons why one level is for some policies preferred over the other. They compare utilitarian motivations, identity and trust in political institutions and find that the latter – the more emotional sources – play the most important role. Comparing systematically the three levels of government they are able to show how attachment to a Belgian identity enhances the reluctance to both internal devolution and European integration.

In this complex and multilevel system, the lines of representation and accountability are not easy to trace. Ruth Dassonneville, Marc Hooghe and Marc Debus therefore wonder in chapter 8 whether patterns of economic voting can be discerned in Belgium. And despite the low-clarity setting, their results suggest that the state of the economy and economic considerations are nevertheless affecting voting behaviour in Belgium, and that this is not restricted to the highly sophisticated voters. Belgium might be extremely complex and governed by parties that in electoral campaigns do not cross the language border, but the voters apparently are still able to see the forest for the trees.

This does not mean however that making a choice at the polls is an easy thing. Evident links between voters and parties have been loosened, and this increases the potential importance of electoral campaigns. In chapter 9, Stefaan Walgrave and Christophe Lesschaeve test whether people change and adapt their policy preferences during an electoral campaign. For the 2014 campaign, the results are quite clear: the campaign does matter and make people adapt their preferences to bring them more in line with the party of their choice. More sophisticated voters appear to be already closer to their party at the beginning of the campaign and stick to their choice more than voters with a lower level of education.

This hesitation during the electoral campaign is also at the centre of chapter 10, in which Ruth Dassonneville, Pierre Baudewyns, Marc Debus and Rüdiger Schmitt-Beck focus on the timing of decision-making of the voters. Looking at figures going back to the 1990s they see that – like in other countries – the Belgian voters tend to gradually postpone their final decision. This is an indicator of declining partisanship, and voters who are less attached to a political party or less interested in politics decide later than others. And for these late deciders the classic theories for explaining voting behaviour explain less well how and why they make their final choice. Interestingly, voters casting a preference vote for one or more candidates are more numerous among the early deciders. Opting for a candidate rather than for a party is apparently not a quick late solution but a more conscious choice.

This option for choosing either for the party list or casting one or more preference votes for candidates is a peculiar aspect of the Belgian electoral system. The flexible list system offers different forms of voting and allows researchers to disentangle the personal from the partisan vote. The last three chapters all deal with preference voting and make use of the mock-ballot technique to analyse in detail the voting for parties and candidates. Silvia Erzeel, Sjifra de Leeuw, Sofie Marien and Benoît Rihoux in chapter 11 wonder whether voters are more likely to cast preference votes for candidates of their own gender. Party lists must in Belgium have an equal number of male and female candidates, which has increased the number of female MPs. Yet since parties tend to place female candidates on less-eligible list positions, a preference vote for the female candidates might further increase their numbers. The results show, however, that gender-based voting by female voters is a limited phenomenon, and that same-gender voting is more frequent among male voters. The Belgian voters are clearly not very strategic in this respect and not very gender-conscious.

In chapter 12, Audrey André, Sam Depauw and Jean-Benoit Pilet investigate the degree in which a preference vote for candidates can also be interpreted as a truly *personal* vote that is more motivated by the candidate than by the party of that candidate. They show in the first place that assimilating preference votes to personal votes is not correct. For many voters, their choice for a candidate is well nested in their party choice. Those who do cast a personal vote are citizens with a weaker partisanship and late deciders with a high degree of sophistication. Overall, personal voting is rather limited. The share of the electorate that can be convinced to cross party lines for a specific candidate is very small.

In chapter 13, Peter Thijssen, Bram Wauters and Patrick van Erkel look at preferential voting at the regional level and at the local level, suggesting that different mechanisms are at work at different levels of government. At the local level, more preference votes are cast, and they are given more frequently to those other than the first candidate on the list. Voting for candidates further down on the list is less frequent at the regional level and is related to political sophistication, that is, it is a more demanding type of vote. Yet proximity makes up for a lack of political resources. In local elections, voters with less political knowledge can compensate for this with the fact that they know the local candidates better.

DATA

The chapters in this book use different sets of data that have been gathered by the PartiRep network. Present in almost all the chapters is the *2014 PartiRep Voter Survey*. This was a two-wave panel study based on a random sample of the voters in the regions of Flanders and Wallonia, who were interviewed, respectively, in Dutch and in French. For a number of practical and related financial reasons the bilingual Brussels region (with 7.5 per cent of the Belgian voters) was not included. The first wave consisted of a one-hour face-to-face interview and reached 1,008 respondents in Flanders and 1,011 in Wallonia. It was in the field during the two months preceding the federal, regional and European elections of June 2014. All respondents were at the end of the interview invited to participate in a second post-electoral interview in which we wanted to register among other things the exact voting behaviour at the three levels of government. For measuring this in the most accurate way, and especially also for being able to trace back exactly the (multiple) preference votes cast for individual candidates, we have sent all participants three mock ballots. They all received three booklets reproducing exactly the lists and all the candidates for the electoral district in which there were voting. We have asked them to fill in the booklets immediately after casting their vote. When they were contacted again for the post-electoral wave, they could inform us about all the details of their voting behaviour. The second wave resulted in 826 Flemish and 702 Walloon interviews. All results using this *2014 PartiRep Voter Survey* have been weighted to recalibrate the sample for gender, age and level of education.

Next to this face to face and telephone survey in Flanders and Wallonia, the PartiRep team also joined in 2014 the Making Electoral Democracy Work (MEDW) project. This involved the organisation of a two-wave pre-electoral and post-electoral online survey in Flanders, Wallonia and also Brussels, using the standard questionnaire of MEDW and adding several questions on the specific Belgian situation. The sample size was 1,026 and 755 in Flanders, 1,035 and 603 in Wallonia and 757 and 518 in Brussels. When these data are used, they are referred to as *MEDW 2014*.

A few chapters also use the *2009 PartiRep Voter Survey* that was organised for the regional and European elections of June 2009. This was a three-wave panel survey, with two pre-electoral waves – one face to face and one by telephone – and a third post-electoral telephone survey. It was also based on a random sample of the voting population in Flanders and Wallonia and reached 2,331 respondents in the first wave, 1,845 in the second and 1,698 in the third. Results reported are always weighted for gender, age and level of education. When older electoral survey data are reported, they refer to the data gathered by the Institute for Social and Political Opinion Research (ISPO) of the KU Leuven and by the Pole Interuniversitaire Opinion Publique et Politique (PIOP) of the Université catholique de Louvain.

On the occasion of the local elections in October 2012, the team was in the field with an exit poll. These data – referred to as the *2012 PartiRep Exit Poll* – were gathered in forty local municipalities, resulting in a sample of 4,591 local voters, representative of the Belgian voting population. The 2012 exit poll was used to try out – successfully – the technique of the mock ballot for registering exactly the way in which the people voted. Since many and multiple preference votes are cast in local elections (see also chapter 13), this mock ballot was a necessary and also very useful tool.

Researchers of the PartiRep team took care in 2014 of the Belgian part of the Comparative Candidate Survey. It has sent out questionnaires to all candidates on all lists for the elections at the federal level and at the regional level. This has resulted in 1,816 responses, of which 102 came from candidates who were elected. Where these data are used, they are referred to as the *2014 Belgian Candidate Survey*.

One final dataset that is used is some chapters is the *PartiRep MP Survey*. This contains data based on interviews conducted between 2009 and 2011 with MPs at the statewide and substate level in fifteen countries and seventy-two assemblies (Deschouwer & Depauw 2014). This adds up to 2,096 MPs who responded to the questionnaire.

In the first chapter on norms of citizenship Jan van Deth uses the *Belgian Political Panel Survey 2006–2011* (BPPS). This is a survey in three waves among young people in Belgium, aiming at measuring a variety of political orientations and the way in which they develop. The respondents were interviewed at the age of sixteen in 2006, and then again at the age of eighteen and at the age of twenty-one. Of the 6,330 youngsters who participated in the first wave, 3,025 also participated in the third wave.

REFERENCES

Alonso, S., Keane & Merkel, W. (eds) (2011) *The Future of Representative Democracy*. Cambridge: Cambridge University Press.

De Winter, L. & Van Wynsberghe, C. (2015) 'Kingdom of Belgium: Partitocracy, Corporatist Society, and Dissociative Federalism'. In: Wolfgang Rensch & Klaus Detterbeck (eds) *Dialogues on Political Parties and Civil Society in Federal Countries*. Oxford: Oxford University Press, 40–69.

Deschouwer, K. (2012) *The Politics of Belgium. Governing a Divided Society*. London: Palgrave Macmillan.

Deschouwer, K. & Depauw, S. (eds) (2014) *Representing the People. A Survey among Members of Statewide and Substate Parliaments*. Oxford: Oxford University Press.

Deschouwer, K., Delwit, P., Hooghe, M. & Walgrave, S. (2010) *De stemmen van het volk. Een analyse van het kiesgedrag op 7 juni 2009 in Vlaanderen en Wallonië*. Brussels: VUB Press.

Evans, G. & Norris, P. (1999) *Critical Elections. British Parties and Voters in Long-term Perspective*. London: Sage.

Hay, C. (2007) *Why We Hate Politics*. Cambridge: Polity.

Hooghe, M. (2012) 'Does Multi-Level Governance Reduce the Need for National Government?' *European Political Science*, 11(1), 90–95.

Hooghe, Marc & Deschouwer, K. (2011) 'Veto Players and Electoral Reform in Belgium', *West European Politics*, 34(3), 626–43.

Huyse, L. (1981) 'Political Conflict in Bicultural Belgium'. In: A. Lijphart (ed), *Conflict and Coexistence in Belgium. The Dynamics of a Culturally Divided Society*. Berkeley: Institute of International Studies, University of California, 107–26.

Keane, J. (2009) *The Life and Death of Democracy*. New York: Simon & Schuster.

Lijphart, A. (2012) *Patterns of Democracy. Government Forms and Performance in Thirty-Six Countries*. New Haven, CT: Yale University Press.

Mair, P. (2013) *Ruling the Void. The Hollowing of Western Democracy*. London: Verso Books.

McRae, K. (1986) *Conflict and Compromise in Multilingual Societies*. Belgium, Ontario, Canada: Wilfrid Laurier Press.

Rokkan, S. (1977) 'Towards a Generalized Concept of "Verzuiling". A Preliminary Note', *Political Studies*, 25, 563–70.

Chapter 1

Norms of citizenship

Jan W. van Deth

CITIZENSHIP AND DEMOCRACY

Probably no society can exist on the basis of power and control only – without some minimum level of acceptance of its basic arrangements by its members, the future of any society is endangered. With their reliance on consensus, peaceful settlements and respect for minorities in particular, the persistence of democracy depends on citizens' support of basic virtues. Democratic virtues are usually associated with the image of a 'good' citizen, that is, with the notion of an ideal citizen in a world deprived of practical limitations. Such a 'good' citizen is, for example, considered politically and socially engaged, obeying the laws or caring for less-fortunate fellow men. Each aspect of this idealised citizen can be easily formulated as a norm of citizenship. For the persistence of democracy, the crucial question, then, is not whether citizens are always active, obedient and solidary, but rather the extent to which they support these norms. Not without reason David Easton emphasised long ago that for the persistence of political systems 'the existence of covert support, or supportive states of mind, is far more important than its actual expression in overt behaviour' (1965: 161).

Several norms of citizenship appear to be widely shared in established democracies. Data from the Citizenship, Involvement, Democracy project and from the European Social Survey show high levels of support especially for law obeying, solidarity and individual autonomy. Between 70 and 90 per cent of the populations in European countries consider these three aspects 'very important' features of a 'good' citizen. A similarly high level of support can be revealed for the norm to cast a vote in public elections. Much lower, however, is the support for the norm to be active in voluntary organisations (Roßteutscher 2004; van Deth 2007, 2013; Denters et al. 2007; Bolzendahl and Coffé 2013). The Tocquevillean idea that engagement in voluntary associations is an important aspect of being a 'good' citizen is supported by about one out of every four respondents only. Even more remarkable is the clear lack of support for the idea that a 'good' citizen should be active in politics: only 10 per cent of the people support the norm that a 'good' citizen is – generally speaking – a politically active citizen. Schudson's description of the rise of 'monitorial citizens' in modern democracies who 'tend to be defensive rather than proactive' and are reluctant to get involved in public and political affairs beyond voting seems to fit this image nicely (1998: 311).

Apparently, many citizens have a clear notion of the most important features of an ideal, 'good' citizen and they differentiate their support for distinct norms of citizenship accordingly (van Deth 2007). The consistent differences in support for various aspects of a 'good' citizen and the evident cross-national differences in these distributions suggest that support for norms of citizenship is fairly persistent and relatively unaffected by individual or contextual factors. Yet no empirical evidence is available to corroborate these expectations. As Denters and van der Kolk remark, 'A clear picture on the sources of citizenship is lacking' (2008: 155). In this chapter the images of a 'good' citizen and the development of these orientations among adolescents and young adults in Belgium over a five-year period are explored. First, support for several norms of citizenship is described and summarised in three main types: politically, socially and duty-based citizenship. Second, both the main antecedents and the predictors for these three types are determined. By dealing with these two points, the spread and development of images of a 'good' citizen among young Belgians during their transition from adolescence to adulthood are revealed. The main conclusion is that the two engaged types of citizenship are incorporated in attitudinal syndromes with recursive associations instead of relationships with clear causal paths. Besides, support for duty-based citizenship is relatively difficult to explain although especially these norms are strongly supported by young people in Belgium.

SUPPORTING NORMS OF CITIZENSHIP

The concept 'citizenship' defines the relationships between citizens and the state in terms of their respective rights and duties. Political philosophers from Aristotle and Plato to Michael Walzer and Benjamin Barber have dealt with these relationships and debated accompanying definitions of rights and duties. In democracies people have to meet the requirements of democratic life, which include, for example, that they participate in public and political affairs, are willing to accept responsibility for public tasks and decisions, be tolerant and solidary and defend individual rights and equal opportunities. In fact, the very recognition of these requirements transforms people living in some society or state into citizens living in a democratic polity. Understood in this way, citizenship, by definition, is democratic citizenship. Although one could think of people living under non-democratic regimes as citizens without rights and duties, the concepts democracy and citizenship are mutually dependent and presume each other (van Deth 2007).

Even if we restrict citizenship to democratic citizenship, many types of rights and duties have been distinguished (see Janoski 1998). The most important aspects of citizenship can be summarised by defining norms or ideals that an imaginary 'good' citizen is expected to fulfil in order to foster democracy. Which norms characterise such a 'good' citizen? Very interesting information about the ways people think about citizenship and the language they use to articulate normative ideas is provided by Pamela Johnston Conover and her collaborators (Conover et al. 1991, 1993, 2004). The results of their extensive discussions with British and American focus groups show that a 'good' citizen understands his or her rights mainly as civil rights (United States) or social rights (Britain) and does not consider political rights to be equally important (both countries). Duties are mainly conceived as responsibilities required to preserve civil life. A 'good' citizen surely values social engagement and active involvement in community matters, but citizens do not agree about the main reasons for these activities. Moreover, sophisticated arguments about the need for social concern and collective actions are frequently mentioned. Survey research among representative samples of the populations of various countries cannot uncover motivations and arguments of people as focus group discussions allow us to do. Yet the results of several large cross-national surveys corroborate the main findings of these discussions and, more importantly, show that many citizens have clear ideas about the norms that a 'good' citizen is expected to meet in a democracy (Roßteutscher 2004; van Deth 2007; Denters et al. 2007; Dalton 2008b; Bolzendahl and Coffé 2013).

Structured responses to questions about support for distinct norms of citizenship suggest that ideas about a 'good' citizen are persistent and relatively unaffected by individual or contextual factors. The genesis and development of these norms, however, are still largely white spots on the map of attitudinal requirements for a vibrant democracy. The Mannheim study of political orientations among young children in their first year in primary school shows that children at age six or seven are already able to express clear ideas about desirable aspects of a 'good' citizen with high levels of endorsement for socially desirable qualities such as helpfulness, hard work and law-abidingness (van Deth et al. 2011: 156; Abendschön 2010: 119–22; see also Hess and Torney 1967: 37–38; Moore et al. 1985). Apparently, support for distinct norms

of citizenship is already available at a very young age and meaningful patterns can be detected in these orientations long before children start to think
of themselves as citizens. Somewhat older children and youngsters probably
will reconsider their normative orientations when their cognitive skills and
competences are enhanced and the impact and relevance of societal and
political arrangements becomes more evident. These expectations are impres-
sively corroborated by Oser and Hooghe (2013) in their analyses of support
for norms of citizenship among fourteen-year-old students in Scandinavia.
What still seem to be missing, however, are empirical findings for the transi-
tory phase from adolescence to young adulthood. Especially this period – the
transformation to full citizenship – can be expected to show a re-evaluation
and confirmation of normative orientations acquired earlier in life.

The Belgian Political Panel Survey 2006–2011 (BPPS) is a three-wave
panel survey of Belgian youngsters (from both the French and Dutch-
speaking communities; see Hooghe et al. 2011) who were interviewed at ages
sixteen, eighteen and twenty-one. In the first wave, a representative sample of
6,330 young people in secondary school (fourth year of secondary school or
tenth grade), representative of the academic tracks in each school participated
in the study. A total of 3,025 respondents were interviewed in all three waves,
enabling us to follow the political orientations among young people during
a critical phase in their life. As in several other studies, support for norms of
citizenship is measured in the BPPS by presenting a number of qualities that
an ideal, 'good' citizen is expected to have:

'In a democracy being a good citizen means:
      1) Supporting people who are less fortunate than yourself
      2) Casting a vote
      3) Obeying laws
      4) Volunteering in some organisation
      5) Being active in politics
      6) Reporting a crime if you see one
      7) Following political news
      8) Committing yourself to the neighbourhood'.
Responses range from 'completely unimportant' (0) to 'very important' (5).

Mean levels of support for the eight aspects of being a 'good' citizen
youngsters in the three waves of the BPPS are depicted in figure 1.1. Several conclusions can be drawn from these results. First, the level of support
is clearly different for various norms of citizenship, ranging from very high
levels for law-abidingness and reporting crime (averages above 3.5) to rather
low levels for volunteering and being politically active (averages about 2 or
lower). Young people do not attach much importance to social and political
activities beyond voting – obedience and solidarity are much more important

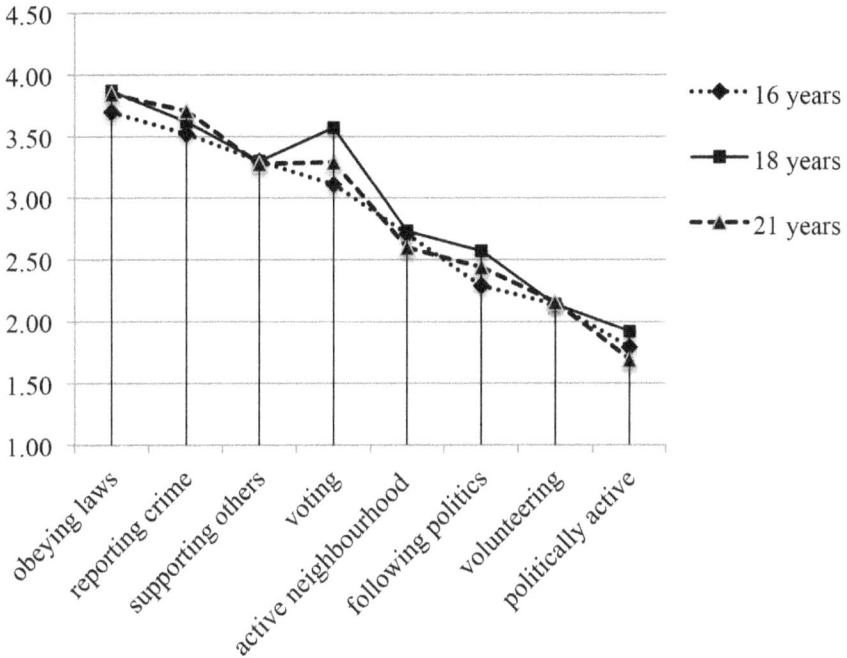

Figure 1.1. Support for aspects of a 'good' citizen (means 0–5)

to characterise a 'good' citizen. This finding is clearly in line with results of studies among adults (see van Deth 2007). Apparently, support for different norms of citizenship varies among the population, and young people are no exception when it comes to attributing less importance to volunteering and political activities. Second, average levels of support for most aspects of a 'good' citizen are almost identical in each of the three waves, suggesting that norms of citizenship barely change during the transition to adulthood. Yet one item noticeably deviates from this pattern: whereas the importance attached to casting a vote increases clearly when young people obtain the right to vote at age eighteen, the support for this norm largely returns to its initial level in the next few years. The acquisition of suffrage seems to establish a major event in the development of political orientations among young people that results in a strong upgrading of the importance of voting as an aspect of a 'good' citizen. The subsequent decline underlines the novelty of having the opportunity to cast a vote for the first time in life that incites the clear increase at age eighteen.

DIMENSIONS OF NORMS OF CITIZENSHIP

A 'good' citizen probably can be characterised by a large number of aspects, and the eight items used in the BPPS cover various important norms. These items might reflect one or more underlying dimensions of norms of citizenship that could reduce the available information in the eight items in a theoretically meaningful way. Briefly reviewing the literature on citizenship Denters, Gabriel, and Torcal notice that there is 'a considerable overlap among competing conceptions of good citizenship' (2007: 92) and that, more importantly, main aspects can be covered by a relatively low number of items. Several authors presented such underlying structures and dimensions of norms of citizenship. In their seminal work on citizenship in Sweden, Petersson and his colleagues (1998: 129–30) used a large set of items covering four dimensions: participation, deliberation, solidarity and law-abidingness. For European countries Denters, Gabriel, and Torcal (2007) presented a common pattern of three dimensions: 'Law-abidingness' (paying taxes, obeying the law), 'solidarity' (help others, think of others) and 'be self-critical' (form own opinion, be self-critical). As expected, these dimensions clearly overlap in many countries, but only the norm 'to be self-critical' loaded frequently on other dimensions as well (Denters et al. 2007: 93). The questions about norms of citizenship included in the first wave of the European Social Survey has been generally interpreted as covering two dimensions, but different authors prefer different tagging and item selection. Whereas Roßteutscher (2004: 187) labels her two dimensions 'representative citizenship' (casting a vote, obeying law, form own opinion, support people worse of) and 'participatory citizenship' (volunteering, active in politics), Denters and van der Kolk (2008: 141) delete the indistinct item (support other people) from their factor analyses and depict the two dimensions as 'liberal' and 'classical' conceptions of citizenship, respectively. Particularly the analyses of US data by Dalton (2008a, 2008b) have stimulated the debate on citizenship and its main dimensions. In his study of aspects of a 'good' citizen he clearly reports two dimensions, which are labelled 'citizen duty' and 'engaged citizen'. The first dimension reflects traditional notions of citizenship understood as the responsibilities of a citizen-subject and is based on the support for such norms as casting a vote, paying taxes, obeying the law, watching the government and serving in the military. The second dimension reveals a pattern of an engaged citizen who claims the right to bring in his or her own ideas, who is willing to act on his or her own principles, who is aware of others and who is willing to challenge political elites (Dalton 2008b: 27–28). Specifically, an 'engaged citizen' supports such norms as following his or her own opinions, helping people worse of, being active in politics and voluntary groups and choosing products deliberately. Although the available sets of items are not identical the distinction between the two types of citizenship presented by Dalton also underlies the two dimensions Roßteutscher and Denters et al. detected. It does not come as a surprise, therefore, that Coffé and van der Lippe (2010) were able to reproduce measures for engaged and duty-based citizenship in another analysis of the first wave of the European Social Survey.

In spite of the broad empirical corroboration of the idea that norms of citizenship can be summarised in a low number of more general aspects or dimensions some studies report complications with data reductions and, therefore, stick to the analyses of norms of citizenship separately (Bolzendahl and Coffé 2013: 65 and 69). To explore the opportunities for data reduction and dimensions of citizenship in the BPPS data, a factor analysis (principal component analysis [PCA]) of the scores for the eight items is performed. The results of these computations are summarised in table 1.1 revealing a clear – and very similar – three-dimensional structure in each of the three waves of the panel with acceptable levels of explained variance (R^2) and measures of sampling adequacy (Kaiser-Meyer-Olkin Test [KMO]). Apparently, not only the levels of support for the distinct norms of citizenship appear to be remarkably persistent (see figure 1.1), but also the structure underlying these scores remains more or less the same during the transition from adolescence to early adulthood. Furthermore, rather straightforward labels are suggested for each of the three dimensions. The first dimension covers all three political items and can be labelled as the 'politically engaged' type of citizenship. Since the three items on the second dimension refer to social activities dealing with volunteering or helping neighbours and other people, this type is labelled the 'socially engaged' type of citizenship. Finally, law-abidingness and reporting crime clearly establish a 'duty-based' type of citizenship that is reported in many studies about aspects of a 'good' citizen. The distinction found among young Belgians between two types of engaged citizenship, on the one hand, and a duty-based type, on the other, clearly is in line with available empirical findings as summarised in the previous paragraph for population studies. In addition, Oser and Hooghe (2013) using latent-class analyses instead of PCAs for a large number of specific norms of citizenship among Scandinavian students, evidently demonstrate the distinction between engaged and duty-based citizenships. However, the results for the BPPS show much clearer a partition of engaged citizenship in political and social types among young people.

The average levels of support for the three types of norms of citizenship are depicted in figure 1.2. Since duty-based citizenship consists of the two items receiving the highest levels of support (see figure 1.1), it does not come as a surprise that support for this type of citizenship is also relatively high. In fact, the level of support for the two engaged types is much lower, with politically based citizenship consistently closing the ranks. Table 1.2 summarises the development of support for the three types of norms of citizenship in a few key indicators. The autocorrelation coefficients all indicate significant but modest dependencies with credible lower strengths for the longest time of five years span (age sixteen to twenty-one). Whereas small

Table 1.1.   Dimensions of norms of citizenship (factor loadings – PCA; varimax rotation; only factor loadings >0.40 reported)

	16 years			18 years			21 years		
	Politically engaged	Socially engaged	Duty-based	Politically engaged	Socially engaged	Duty-based	Politically engaged	Socially engaged	Duty-based
Following politics	0.793			0.798			0.809		
Voting	0.663		(0.486)	0.748			0.787		
Politically active	0.811			0.749	(0.415)		0.754		
Volunteering		0.730			0.760			0.781	
Active neighbourhood		0.731			0.764			0.760	
Supporting others		0.720			0.682			0.721	
Obeying laws			0.829			0.802			0.805
Reporting crime			0.681			0.717			0.786
Explained variance (%)	66.4			67.2			66.7		
KMO	0.759			0.748			0.736		
N	2,796			2,939			2,943		

Table 1.2.   Development of support for politically, socially and duty-based citizenship (Pearson's r; t-tests for matched samples; pairwise deletion of missing values)

	16–18 years			18–21 years			16–21 years		
	Pearson's r	Mean diff.	T	Pearson's r	Mean diff.	T	Pearson's r	Mean diff.	T
Politically based	0.482***	0.06	-14.1***	-0. 486***	-0.04	1.09***	0.380***	0.01	-3.1***
Socially based	0.429***	0.00	-0.5	0.434***	-0.01	2.6**	0.339***	-0.01	1.8
Duty-based	0.393***	0.03	-7.3***	0.338***	0.00	-1.2	0.243***	0.03	-7.5***

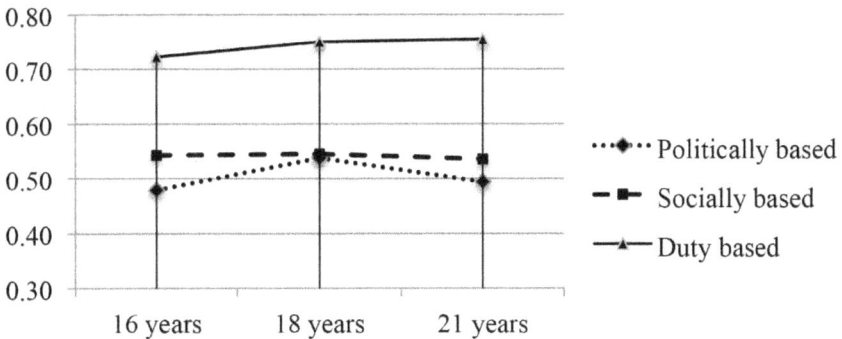

Figure 1.2. Development of support for politically, socially, and duty-based norms of citizenship (means 0–1)

and non-significant average differences are found for socially based citizenship, the two consecutive measures of politically and duty-based citizenships show relatively large differences in the first two waves. The remarkable peak in the level of support for politically based citizenship among the eighteen-year-olds reflects the already-mentioned novelty of having the opportunity to cast a vote for the first time in life. Although Oser and Hooghe (2013: 34) found that duty-based norms had become 'more prevalent' among Scandinavian students between 1999 and 2009, the rise in support for duty-based citizenship among Belgian youngsters is surprising. Especially Dalton (2008b) emphasised a shift in citizenship from duty-based to engaged norms – a shift that should be particularly visible among younger people who are 'reshaping American politics'. Yet Belgian adolescents and young adults do not only show high levels of support for duty-based norms of citizenship, but they also clearly do not turn away from these norms when they grow older.

ANTECEDENTS OF NORMS OF CITIZENSHIP

Norms of citizenship are linked to a number of attitudinal, social and socio-demographic factors. Since the analytical 'distance' between citizenship norms and other normative political orientations (for instance, post-materialism) is rather limited, we focus on social and socio-demographic antecedents of norms of citizenship. Three broad categories of these antecedents can be distinguished. First, the support for various aspects of a 'good' citizen varies across different social groups. Dalton (2008b: chapter 3) shows that the 'social basis' of these norms can be defined by age, education, income, gender, race, religious practices and party attachment: older, male, higher educated, higher paid people, frequent church visitors and voters for Conservative parties are more likely to support prosocial norms stronger than other people do (see also Denters et al. 2007: 103; Coffé and Lippe 2010: 489–92). Usually the explanations for the impact of these factors follow the conventional line of argument referring to resources and opportunities. In this approach especially the socio-economic status (SES) of citizens is relevant to account for differences in normative orientations: a high SES implies the availability not only of time and money but also of cognitive skills, competences and networks, which all reduce the opportunity costs of dealing with social and political issues. Hence, the very same people will be more willing to support norms of citizenship – all emphasising the need for social and political engagement – than people with less resources and opportunities. With its focus on adolescents and young adults the BPPS provides a limited number of social and socio-demographic variables. Obviously, in each wave all respondents are of the same age and especially in the first two waves many of them have not yet completed full-time education. As important antecedents of the level of support for norms of citizenship we select four indicators from the BPPS: gender, level of education (or educational goal), church attendance and nationality.

A second broad category of antecedents of norms of citizenship is based on the revival of neo-Tocquevillean and communitarian ideas in the early 1990s (Etzioni 1996; Putnam 1993). In these approaches institutionalised networks (mainly voluntary associations) are expected to encourage support for prosocial norms because the importance of cooperating and reciprocity becomes directly palpable in recurring contacts with other people. Besides, engagement in group activities also implies the exposure to social pressures to cooperate and to comply. Especially approaches under the label social capital combine structural aspects (networks) and cultural aspects (social trust) to account for prosocial norms: more integrated and more trustful people are more likely to support norms of citizenship than other people do (Denters et al. 2007: 97–102; Denters and van der Kolk 2008: 144). The BPPS covers various aspects of social capital. As an important antecedent of the level of support for citizenship norms, the total number of memberships in voluntary associations is used as an indicator of the extend of the formal network of a respondent. The range of the informal networks is measured with a direct question on the number of 'good friends' one has to speak about important problems. In addition to these two measures of structural aspects of social capital, for the cultural aspects the level of personal trust is specified by combining the responses to the statements that 'most people can be trusted' and that 'people are helpful'.

Indicators for political engagement constitute the third main category of antecedents of various norms of citizenship. Since these norms all refer to public and political affairs people more engaged in politics will be more familiar with the rather abstract idea of a 'good' citizen. Politically engaged citizens will also be more familiar with the necessity of prosocial behaviour as a precondition for a vibrant democracy and, therefore, attach more importance to norms of citizenship. The BPPS contains two straightforward indicators of political engagement that can be used as antecedents of support for citizenship norms: the level of subjective political interest and the frequency of following news in the media. Besides, the third wave also includes a direct measure of the left-right placement of the respondents. Since a positioning more to the left is associated with a stronger wish for social and political change (Lipset et al. 1954: 1135), it can be expected that such a position also indicates a stronger emphasis on political engagement than among respondents preferring a position more to the right side of the scale.

Relatively high scores on the various indicators for SES, social capital and political engagement increase the general likelihood to support norms of citizenship. However, the impact of these factors clearly differs for the main types of citizenship distinguished. For instance, Dalton (2008b: 51) demonstrates that several aspects of SES (education, religious involvement) are positively related to both 'citizen duty' and 'engaged citizen', whereas the direction of the impact of other aspects (age, income, gender, race, party identification) depends on the specific mode of citizenship discerned. Similar findings are reported for the impact of social capital varying between modes of citizenship (Denters et al. 2007: 99–101). By including three blocks of antecedents for three main types of support for norms of citizenship for each of the three waves of the BPPS, we are able to test general expectations as well as further specifications related to particular modes of support.

The estimates for several regression models for the support of politically, socially, and duty-based modes of citizenship are summarised in tables 1.3a, 1.3b and 1.3c, respectively. For each of the three waves Model 1 shows the results for cross-sectional relationships. In order to test the genuine impact of the antecedents selected, autocorrelation effects for the three modes of citizenship are added to the models for the second wave (Model 2a) and for the third wave (Models 2a, 2b, and 2c). The importance of distinguishing between the three modes of citizenship is immediately clear from the three tables: the impact of not a single one of the ten selected antecedents reaches an acceptable level of statistical significance in each of the eighteen models computed. The picture, however, is slightly more encouraging if we deal with the three modes of citizenship separately. First, the results for politically and socially based support show consistent relationships between attitudinal and behavioural measures for both types, that is, in each model support for politically based norms of citizenship appears to be clearly related to interest in politics and social trust, whereas support for socially based norms is related to associational involvement and social trust. Apparently, social and political engagement is an important antecedent of normative orientations: the impacts of political interest on politically based citizenship and of membership and trust on socially based norms as indicated by the (standardised) regression coefficients in tables 1.3a and 1.3b are relatively high (and not very much lower than the autocorrelation coefficients for the two types of citizenship). Since the effects of the other indicators included in the models either do not reach acceptable levels of significance or are relatively weak, it appears that politically based citizenship is most strongly related to the level of political interest: higher levels of interest come with stronger support for this type of citizenship. In a similar way, socially based citizenship is related to associational involvement and trust. Yet for this type of citizenship several additional features appear to be relevant: women, frequent churchgoers and people with a more right-wing stand support socially based citizenship significantly stronger than man, less religious people and leftists do. Finally, it is clear that support for duty-based citizenship is rather difficult to explain. The regression coefficients for this type of citizenship are relatively low and do not show a consistent pattern for all six models. Only the impact of gender reaches an acceptable level of significance in all models, indicating that women systematically show stronger support for duty-based norms of citizenship than men do (but see the contradictory results presented by Oser and Hooghe [2013: 339–40]). Besides, a more left-wing stand increases the support for this type of citizenship in the third wave. Yet as the very low measures for the fit of the various models indicate, it remains rather difficult to pinpoint important antecedents for duty-based norms of citizenship.

PREDICTORS OF NORMS OF CITIZENSHIP

The addition of autocorrelation effects to the factors included in the three main blocks of antecedents (Models 2a, 2b, 2c) does not change the impact of the main antecedents identified in the previous section. In this way the genuine impact of these antecedents is demonstrated. Conversely, the autocorrelation coefficients can be interpreted as indicators for the persistence of support for norms of citizenship in the period from adolescence to young adulthood. With respect to the widely presumed relative stability of normative orientations (Kluckhohn 1951; van Deth and Scarbrough 1995), the autocorrelation coefficients are rather modest (ranging from a maximum of 0.399 for a two years' time lag to 0.313 for a five years interval) and clearly lower than the bivariate autocorrelations presented in table 1.2. In spite of the more or less stable levels of support found for single items and for the three types of citizenship (see figures 1.1 and 1.2), the autocorrelations for the multivariate models indicate that support for each of the main types of citizenship is moderately stable at the individual level during the transition from adolescence

Table 1.3a. Determinants of politically based citizenship (linear regression; standardised coefficients)

| | 16 years | 18 years | | 21 years | | | |
	Model 1	Model 1	Model 2a	Model 1	Model 2a	Model 2b	Model 2c
SES:							
– Gender	– 0.010	0.065**	0.062**	0.034	0.043	0.013	0.024
– Education	0.135***	0.137***	0.093***	0.069**	0.049*	0.036	0.030
– Church attendance	0.005	–0.006	0.003	0.057**	0.049*	0.055**	0.050**
– Nationality	–0.013	0.003	–0.004	0.015	–0.003*	0.010	–0.004
Social capital:							
– Voluntary ass.	0.012	–0.025	–0.017	0.023	0.022	0.023	0.024
– Friends	–0.025	–0.023	–0.031	0.007	0.017	0.009	0.017
– Social trust	0.062**	0.050*	0.043*	0.072***	0.066***	0.057**	0.058**
Political engagement:							
– Political interest	0.261***	0.323***	0.247***	0.316***	0.270***	0.233***	0.226***
– Following news	0.105***	0.103***	0.075***	0.018	0.012	0.003	0.003
– Left-right placement	–	–	–	–0.027	–0.011	–0.008	–0.001
Autocorrelations:							
– Score at 16 years	–	–	0.372***	–	0.313***	–	0.172***
– Score at 18 years	–	–	–	–	–	0.399***	0.319***
Variance expl. (corr. %)	14.4	18.8	31.8	13.2	23.0	28.0	30.6
N	2,719	2,029	1,906	2,154	2,039	2,121	2,009

Notes: Level of significance: *p < 0.05; **p < 0.01; ***p < 0.001.

• Gender: male (1), female (2)
• Education: sixteen and eighteen years: educational goals 'no secondary' (1), 'secondary' (2), 'higher education' (3) and 'university' (4); twenty-one years: 'secondary' (1), 'non-academic higher' (2), 'university' (3) and 'adult education' (4)
• Church attendance: ceremonies attended past year: 'never' (1) to 'more than once a week' (5)
• Nationality: Belgian nationality (1), other (2)
• Voluntary associations: number of voluntary associations
• Friends: number of good friends 'none' (1) to 'fifteen or more' (7)
• Social trust: mean score of 'most people can be trusted' and 'people are helpful' (0–10)
• Political interest: 'not interested' (1) to 'very interested' (4)
• Following news: frequency 'never' (0) to 'daily' (5)
• Left-right placement: scale from 'left' (0) to 'right' (10)

Table 1.3b. Determinants of socially based citizenship (linear regression; standardised coefficients)

	16 years	18 years		21 years			
	Model 1	Model 1	Model 2a	Model 1	Model 2a	Model 2b	Model 2c
SES:							
– Gender	0.172***	0.212***	0.144***	0.167***	0.114***	0.105***	0.084***
– Education	0.037	-0.039	-0.052*	-0.038*	-0.058**	-0.041**	-0.056**
– Church attendance	0.076***	0.067***	0.030	0.086***	0.060**	0.064***	0.048
– Nationality	-0.007	0.015	0.017	0.010	0.015	0.000	0.009
Social capital:							
– Voluntary ass.	0.047**	0.146***	0.124***	0.142***	0.132***	0.108***	0.110***
– Friends	-0.022	-0.024	-0.012	-0.013	-0.007	-0.011	-0.011
– Social trust	0.174***	0.210***	0.154***	0.208***	0.185***	0.174***	0.167***
Political engagement:							
– Political interest	0.058**	0.072**	0.063**	0.008	0.005	0.001	0.000
– Following news	0.030	0.031	0.026	0.014	0.007	0.004	0.003
– Left-right placement	–	–	–	-0.211***	-0.190***	-0.160***	-0.159***
Autocorrelations:							
– Score at 16 years	–	–	0.388***	–	0.291***	–	0.176***
– Score at 18 years	–	–	–	–	–	0.364***	0.291***
Variance expl. (corr. %)	8.6	14.1	27.9	17.3	25.8	29.4	32.1
N	2,730	2,030	1,915	2,154	2,046	2,122	2,016

Notes: See table 1.3a.

Table 1.3c. Determinants of duty-based citizenship (linear regression; standardised coefficients)

	16 years	18 years		21 years			
	Model 1	Model 1	Model 2a	Model 1	Model 2a	Model 2b	Model 2c
SES:							
– Gender	0.061**	0.070**	0.051**	0.102***	0.080***	0.077***	0.069***
– Education	0.102***	0.080**	0.036	–0.007	–0.007	–0.021	–0.017
– Church attendance	0.047*	–0.001	–0.017	0.035	0.019	0.026	0.015
– Nationality	–0.005	–0.011	–0.006	0.029	0.015	0.031	0.018
Social Capital:							
– Voluntary ass.	–0.067**	–0.027	–0.012	–0.034	–0.034	–0.024	–0.028
– Friends	–0.046*	–0.027	–0.020	–0.037	–0.022	–0.024	–0.015
– Social trust	0.073***	0.073**	0.041*	0.056	0.033	0.049*	0.037
Political engagement:							
– Political interest	0.090***	0.122***	0.097***	–0.012	–0.029	–0.023	–0.033
– Following news	0.112***	0.068**	0.054**	0.028	0.042	0.014	0.026
– Left-right placement	–	–	–	0.100***	0.083***	0.084***	0.077***
	–	–	–	–	–	–	
Autocorrelations:							
– Score at 16 years			0.382***		0.259***		0.147***
– Score at 18 years	–	–	–	–	–	0.334***	0.276***
Variance expl. (corr. %)	5.7	4.5	18.7	1.9	8.3	12.8	14.5
N	2,725	2,028	1,915	2,158	2,041	2,126	2,013

Notes: See table 1.3a.

to early adulthood. Since panel data for older people are lacking, it is unclear whether these shifts in support are characteristically for young people or point to a more general lack of persistence for these orientations.

In spite of the fact that the autocorrelation coefficients reach modest levels only, it is clear that the support for each type of citizenship depends most clearly on the previous level of support. Yet various factors – interest, trust and associational involvement – show consistent and substantial effects. The unique character of the BPPS as a three-wave panel study allows us to assess the probability of the direction of causal effects, that is, to test whether, for instance, political interest results in support for politically based citizenship or, conversely, support for that type increases the level of political interest. For the main antecedents of politically and socially based citizenship identified in the previous section, time-lagged correlations corrected for gender, education and church attendance are computed (see table 1.4). Since left-right placement is only available in the third wave, similar computations are carried out for duty-based support and the level of political interest as the next most consistent and relatively strong antecedent. By comparing the rows for each of the six pairs of relationships in table 1.4, the relative strength of the various effects becomes clear.

The results in table 1.4, once again, underline the differences between politically and socially based citizenship, on the one hand, and duty-based citizenship, on the other. For the first two types, the findings show consistent patterns for each of the three pairs of waves and the antecedents selected. Starting with politically based citizenship, it is clear that this normative orientation is more likely to be the cause of interest and trust than the other way around (i.e. the coefficients in the second and fourth rows in table 1.4 are higher than those in the first and third rows, respectively). Whereas for social trust, the picture is rather clear (trust being a consequence and not a cause of citizenship orientations), the results for political interest suggest a relatively strong recursive relationship with norms strengthening interest and interest strengthening norms. Apparently, support for politically based interest and interest in politics are parts of the same syndrome and reinforce each other. For socially based citizenship all twelve coefficients reach an acceptable level of significance. The results for voluntary association membership appear to corroborate the Tocquevillean idea that support for norms is a consequence of associational involvement. Yet the recursive effects here are relatively strong too, indicating that people supporting socially based norms are also more likely to get involved in associations (self-selection effect). For social trust the recursive relationships are underlined by the fact that the relative size of the effects is different for the first two waves (with stronger effects initiating from socially based citizenship) than for the two other comparisons.

Table 1.4. **Main determinants and effects of politically, socially and duty-based citizen-ship (linear regression coefficients)**

	16–18 years		18–21 years		16–21 years	
	unstand.	*stand.*	*unstand.*	*stand.*	*unstand.*	*stand.*
Politically based citizenship:						
Interest (t₁) → Pol. based cit. (t₂)	0.062	0.238***	0.076	0.287***	0.058	0.210***
Pol. based cit. (t₁) → Interest (t₂)	0.858	0.225***	0.972	0.231***	0.651	0.153***
Trust (t₁) → Pol. based cit. (t₂)	0.001	0.010	0.007	0.055**	0.003	0.023
Pol. based cit. (t₁) → Trust (t₂)	0.369	0.361***	0.616	0.070***	0.354	0.042*
Socially based citizenship:						
Vol. ass. (t₁) → Soc. based cit. (t₂)	0.011	0.093***	0.021	0.170***	0.013	0.108***
Soc. based cit. (t₁) → Vol. ass. (t₂)	0.559	0.070***	0.949	0.115***	0.487	0.061***
Trust (t₁) → Soc. based cit. (t₂)	0.009	0.090***	0.018	0.169***	0.013	0.118***
Soc. based cit. (t₁) → Trust (t₂)	1.384	0.148***	1.050	0.105***	0.888	0.092***
Duty-based citizenship:						
Interest (t₁) → Duty-based cit. (t₂)	0.031	0.121***	0.007	0.031	–0.001	–0.005
Duty-based cit. (t₁) → Interest (t₂)	0.286	0.069***	0.300	0.061**	0.099	0.023
Trust (t₁) → Duty-based cit. (t₂)	0.003	0.034	0.005	0.045*	0.005	0.048*
Duty-based cit. (t₁) → Trust (t₂)	0.492	0.056**	0.168	0.016	0.252	0.027

Notes: Level of significance: $*p < 0.05$; $**p < 0.01$; $***p < 0.001$. Controlled for gender, level of educational goals and church attendance at age sixteen.

Here, too, the likelihood of a specific causal relationship is unclear – in other words, social trust and socially based citizenship influence each other continuously. Finally, the results for duty-based citizenship are rather difficult to summarise since almost none of the coefficients involving the third wave reaches an acceptable level of significance. Only for the first two waves the results show – as with politically based citizenship – that, although political interest precedes support for norms, these effects are part of an evidently recursive relationship. Moreover, the results for the first two waves also show that social trust is rather more likely to be a consequence of support for duty-based citizenship than a cause.

The findings for the determinants of the three types of norms of citizenship clearly enable a much more interesting specification than offered by the results for antecedents presented in the previous section. Although the relationships between the three types of citizenship and important factors such as political interest, social trust and associational involvement are established in both approaches, the results of the panel analyses show that the impact of political interest and of associational involvement are parts of syndromes with recursive relationships. Yet both interest and associational involvement are more likely to be causes than consequences of norms of citizenship. For social trust, however, the results are less ambiguous and suggest that higher levels of support for the three types of citizenship result in a higher level of social trust.

CONCLUSION AND DISCUSSION

The empirical analyses of the support for distinct norms of citizenship among adolescents and young adults in Belgium show a few remarkable findings. First, attitudes towards specific aspects of a 'good' citizen vary considerably with much stronger support for law-abidingness and reporting crime than for volunteering and political activities. Although these differences are very similar to results obtained for the populations of many countries, the strong support for law-and-order norms is not in line with the idea of a 'younger generation reshaping politics', as Dalton (2008b) reported for the United States. Among young people in Belgium support for duty-based norms of citizenship is strong and increases slightly during the transition from adolescence to adulthood. Second, whereas population studies usually report a distinction between duty-based and engaged types of citizenship, support for various norms of citizenship among young people shows a clear and persistent distinction between politically and socially based norms of citizenship, on the one hand, and duty-based citizenship, on the other, probably due to the acquirement of suffrage support for politically based citizenship reaches a peak at age eighteen but remains at a relatively low level in each of the three waves. Third, the differences between engaged and duty-based types are also reflected in the antecedents for the three main types of citizenship distinguished here, with relatively strong effects obtained for political interest, trust and associational involvement for the two engaged types, and gender as the most consistent antecedent for duty-based citizenship. Finally, the results show that support for norms of citizenship is moderately stable at the individual level. Besides, political interest and associational involvement clearly show recursive relationships with, respectively, support for politically based and socially based citizenship (although they both act somewhat clearer as consequences than causes). For social trust, the evidence suggests that higher levels of support for the three types of citizenship result in a higher level of social trust.

Especially the results for the repeated cross-sections and the panel analyses shed new light on old debates. Contrary to implicit but widely shared presumptions among students of young people, adolescence and young adulthood are evidently *not* the phases in life in which norms of citizenship are developed and internalised. On the contrary, at age sixteen, Belgian young people are definitely able to distinguish between various norms and to combine these orientations in meaningful ways – apparently, the 'crystallization' of these orientations was already finished before the first interview was concluded. Moreover, support for types of citizenship is part of attitudinal syndromes with recursive relationships and differentiated causes and consequences. Studying support for norms of citizenships among adolescents and young adults, then, did not result in clues for the genesis of these orientations. These norms – and probably the syndromes detected here – seem to be generated and shaped in a(n) (much) earlier phase of life.

In the past two decades many authors have pointed to the relevance of social capital for the development of prosocial norms. By showing that associational involvement is an important antecedent and determinant of socially based citizenship, our findings corroborate an important aspect of especially neo-Tocquevillean interpretations in this area. Yet it is clear that associational involvement is not only a cause but, to a somewhat lesser degree, also a consequence of support for norms of citizenship. Whether the fact that social trust most likely is a consequence of support for norms of citizenship rather than a cause is more burdensome for neo-Tocquevillean ideas is difficult to assess. Regrettably, no unambiguous expectations about the casual relationships between these two cultural aspects of social capital are available. With respect to the prominent position of social trust in many approaches, however, social trust seemingly is considered more important – that is, social trust should be conceptualised as a cause and not as a consequence of other orientations as found here. The explanation of prosocial norms on the basis of available social capital, then, should focus on associational involvement and much less on social trust.

Citizens attribute by far the highest level of support to duty-based norms of citizenship and Belgian adolescents and young adults to not diverge from this pattern. The relatively poor performance of the models to explain duty-based citizenship and the development of these norms is the most unsatisfactory result of our analyses. Apart from the conclusion that girls/women are much more likely than boys/men to support duty-based citizenship, none of the other factors considered plays a consistent role. Since shifts in the support for duty-based citizenship will be the most likely change among citizens in democratic societies, this type of citizenship should play a major role in further research in this area.

REFERENCES

Abendschön, S. (2010) *Die Anfänge demokratischer Bürgerschaft. Sozialisation politischer und demokratischer Werte und Normen im jungen Kindesalter*. Baden-Baden: Nomos.

Bolzendahl, C. and Coffé, H. (2013) 'Are "good" citizens "good" participants? Testing citizenship norms and political participation across 25 Nations', *Political Studies*, 61: 63–83.

Coffé, H. and van der Lippe, T. (2010) 'Citizenship norms in Eastern Europe', *Social Indicators Research*, 96(3): 479–96.

Conover, P. J., Crewe, I. M. and Searing, D. D. (1991) 'The nature of citizenship in the United States and Great Britain: Empirical comments on theoretical themes', *Journal of Politics*, 53(3): 800–832.

Conover, P. J., Crewe, I. M. and Searing, D. D. (2004) 'Elusive ideal of equal citizenship: Political theory and political psychology in the United States and Great Britain', *Journal of Politics*, 66(4): 1036–68.

Conover, P. J., Leonard, S. T. and Searing, D. D. (1993) 'Duty is a four-letter word: Democratic citizenship in the liberal polity', in Marcus, G. E. and Hanson, R. L. (eds) *Reconsidering the Democratic Public*. University Park: Pennsylvania State University Press: 147–71.

Dalton, R. J. (2008a) 'Citizenship norms and the expansion of political participation', *Political Studies*, 56(1): 76–98.

Dalton, R. J. (2008b) *The Good Citizen: How a Younger Generation Is Reshaping American Politics*, Washington, D.C.: CQ Press.

Denters, B. and van der Kolk, H. (2008) 'What determines citizens' normative conceptions of their civic duties?' in Meulemann, H. (ed.) *Social Capital in Europe: Similarity of Countries and Diversity of People?* Leiden: Brill: 135–57.

Denters, B., Gabriel, O. and Torcal, M. (2007) 'Norms of good citizenship', in van Deth, J. W., Montero, J. R. and Westholm, A. (eds) *Citizenship and Involvement in Europe: A Comparative Analysis,* London: Routledge: 88–108.

Easton, D. (1965) *A Systems Analysis of Political Life*, Chicago: University of Chicago Press.

Etzioni, A. (1996) *The New Golden Rule: Community and Morality in a Democratic Society*, New York: Basic Books.

Hess, R. D. and Torney, J. V. (1967) *The Development of Political Attitudes in Children*, Chicago: Aldine Publishing.

Hooghe, M., Havermans, N., Quintelier, E. and Dassonneville, R. (2011) *Belgian Political Panel Survey (BPPS) 2006–2011. Technical Report*, Leuven: K. U. Leuven.

Janoski, T. (1998) *Citizenship and Civil Society. A Framework of Rights and Obligations in Liberal, Traditional, and Social Democratic Regimes*, Cambridge: Cambridge University Press.

Kluckhohn, C. (1951) 'Values and value-orientations in the theory of action: An exploration in definition and classification', in Parsons, T. and Shils, E. A. (eds) *Toward a General Theory of Action*, Cambridge, MA: Harvard University Press: 388–433.

Lipset, S. M., Lazarsfeld, P. F., Barton, A. H. and Linz, J. (1954) 'The psychology of voting: An analysis of political behaviour', in Gardner, L. (ed.) *Handbook of Social Psychology*. Cambridge: Addison-Wesley: 1124–76.

Moore, S. W., Lare, J. and Wagner, K. A. (1985) *The Child's Political World: A Longitudinal Perspective*, New York: Praeger.

Oser, J. and Hooghe, M. (2013) 'The evolution of citizenship norms among Scandinavian adolescents, 1999–2009', *Scandinavian Political Studies*, 36(4): 320–46.

Petersson, O., Hermansson, J., Micheletti, M., Teorell, J. and Westholm, A. (1998) *Demokrati och Medborgarskap. Demokratiradets Rapport 1998*, Stockholm: SNS Förlag.

Putnam, R. D. (1993) *Making Democracy Work. Civic Traditions in Modern Italy*, Princeton, NJ: Princeton University Press.

Roßteutscher, S. (2004) 'Die Rückkehr der Tugend?' in van Deth, J. W. (ed.) *Deutschland in Europa. Ergebnisse des European Social Survey 2002–2003*, Wiesbaden: VS-Verlag: 175–200.

Schudson, M. (1998) *The Good Citizen. A History of American Civic Life*, Cambridge, MA: Harvard University Press.

van Deth, J. W. (2007) 'Norms of citizenship', in Dalton, R. J. and Klingemann, H.-D. (eds) *The Oxford Handbook of Political Behavior*, Oxford: Oxford University Press: 402–17.

van Deth, J. W. (2013) 'Citizenship and the civic realities of everyday life', in Print, M. and Lange, D. (eds) *Civic Education and Competences for Engaging Citizens in Democracies*, Rotterdam: Sense Publishers: 9–21.

van Deth, J. W. and Scarbrough, E. (eds) (1995) *The Impact of Values*. Oxford: Oxford University Press.

van Deth, J. W., Abendschon, S. and Vollmar, M. (2011) 'Children and politics: An empirical reassessment of early political socialization', *Political Psychology*, 32(1): 147–73.

Chapter 2

Who framed the party? The perception of political organisations

Camille Kelbel, Giulia Sandri and
Emilie van Haute

INTRODUCTION

Belgium is characterised by profusion and centrality of parties. The Belgian party system is split in two, it is highly fragmented and the effective number of parties has increased drastically through the years, largely due to the multiplication of cleavage politics (Delwit 2012). Parties are also central social and political actors, to the point that Belgium has been described as an ideal type of pillarisation and partitocracy (Deschouwer 2002; van Haute et al. 2013). They control various aspects of the political life, including the policymaking process. Party agreement and party discipline are high in parliament (Deschouwer and Depauw 2014; Close and Nunez 2017). Yet, as elsewhere, Belgian party organisations suffer from a lack of trust (Henry et al. 2015), the proportion of citizens who are party members has lowered (van Haute et al. 2013) and voter turnout is in decline despite compulsory voting. These are clear signs of a *désamour* between the public and parties.

However, when analysing the public image of parties, the 'public' is usually taken as a homogenous entity. Yet the perception of parties' role could vary on the basis of the socio-demographic profiles of citizens, as several studies have demonstrated (Marien 2011; Norris 2011; Webb 2013), but also be a function of political attitudes and behaviours, and more specifically on the basis of individual relationship with (and thus proximity to) parties.

This chapter therefore aims at better understanding the perception and image of parties in Belgium. The question that this chapter addresses is: is there too much party and if so, who thinks so? Using data from the 2014 PartiRep Voter Survey and the 2014 Belgian Candidate Survey, this chapter investigates the gaps in the perception of the weight of parties in the policymaking process across various groups. More specifically, we investigate the determinants of these opinions at three levels: the macro-level (between Flanders and Wallonia), the meso-level (across parties) and the individual level (proximity to parties and views on democracy). Looking more in depth into this question brings us insights as to who thinks there is too much party and where the lines of division lie. It ultimately contributes to a better under-standing of the functioning of representative democracy in Belgium and more generally to the debate on the crisis of party democracy (Dalton and Weldon 2005).

The chapter is structured as follows. First, we present the literature and the main hypotheses. Second, we present the methods and data used. Third, the chapter explores the various gaps in how parties are viewed and evaluated in Belgium. We present the main findings and then offer concluding remarks.

PERCEPTIONS ON PARTY DEMOCRACY: SOME THEORETICAL EXPECTATIONS

Recent studies have pointed at the increased dissatisfaction with political parties and the deterioration of the public image of parties in advanced indus-trial democracies (Ferrin and Kriesi 2016). Evidence of this dissatisfaction is found in declining membership figures (van Haute et al. 2017), lower elec-toral turnout (Dassonneville and Hooghe 2016), weaker party identification (Dalton 2014), lower trust in parties (Zmerli and Hooghe 2013) or the rise of populist parties (Mudde and Kaltwasser 2017).

These combined trends point to a general questioning of party democracy (Dalton and Weldon 2005; Poguntke et al. 2016). Political parties are no longer recognised as (the sole) legitimate actors for mediating political rep-resentation, and they are responding to these challenges by introducing new opportunities for citizens' participation both in the system (Bengtsson and Mattila 2009; Altman 2010) and within their organisation (Sandri et al. 2015), which may further alter their legitimacy.

This literature largely assumes that the general public is critical of parties, but often assumes both 'the public' and 'the party' to be homogeneous enti-ties. This chapter wants to bring a more nuanced view.

First it distances itself from a unitary conception of political parties. Rather, we differentiate between various faces: the party in central office, the party in public office and the party on the ground (Katz and Mair 1994). We assume that references to 'too much party' implicitly target the party in central office specifically and its weight in representative democracy and the policymaking process.

Second, various studies have pointed at the heterogeneity of public prefer-ences for models of (intra-party) democracy (Bowler et al. 2007; Bengtsson and Mattila 2009; Webb 2013; Close et al. 2017). Accordingly, there is no reason to assume homogeneous attitudes towards political parties. Therefore, we want to investigate the gaps in the perception of the weight of parties in the policymaking process, across various groups: across polities, across parties and between individuals.

First, we expect differences in the perception of parties across polities. The Belgian political landscape presents a unique characteristic because two separate party systems coexist (Deschouwer 2002). Therefore, one may expect variations in how parties are perceived in these two separate systems since voters are exposed to two different political settings. The party system in Flanders was deeply shaken by the Black Sunday in 1991 that saw the surge of a radical right party Vlaams Blok (now Vlaams Belang [VB]). This electoral earthquake has generated a reaction among the mainstream parties. The Flemish liberals called for a depillarisation of society, which has been partly heard in Flanders. Many parties have changed names (see chapter 5 in this volume). The party system has become more volatile, with flash parties, party splits, temporary electoral alliances and mergers. By contrast, the party system in French-speaking Belgium is characterised by much more stability. Name changes and party splits are rare, and seats are mainly divided between four actors (Delwit 2012). This stability gives more grips to parties over the social and political life. Accordingly, we expect to find more criticisms of the weight of parties in French-speaking Belgium than in Flanders.

Hypothesis 1: The perception that parties weigh too much on the policymaking process is higher among the French-speaking than the Dutch-speaking polity.

Second, we expect differences across parties. More specifically, we investigate the effect of party ideology and organisation on the perception that parties weight too much.

Party ideology is one central criterion used in classifying parties in families (Mair and Mudde 1998). Both Close (2016) and Gauja (2015) argue that a given party family carries a specific identity, particular values and its own culture, embodied in a model of democracy. It is expected that a party's public (from voters to legislators) for a large part agrees with and shares these values.

For instance, liberal parties are associated with individual freedom and the rejection of political authority and hierarchy, the latter characteristics being also shared by green parties (Kitschelt 1989; Cross and Katz 2013). Liberals and greens would then be more critical of the role of parties as organisations and would prefer relying on the individual work of their representatives for policymaking, hence giving 'value to the self-affirmation and independence of parliamentarians against the authority of the party organisation' (Close

2016: 2). Conversely, other party families such as the radical right or radical left emphasise discipline and the respect of hierarchy embodied by the party leader (Mudde 2007; Art 2011). These parties would see favourably the control of the policymaking by parties.

In between, the Social democrats and the Christian democrats emphasise the role of the social groups and a sense of solidarity or community that puts the individual in collective action. These parties would then not be too critical of the weight of parties in the policymaking process.

Typically, in Belgium, this would oppose on a continuum the greens (Ecolo/ Groen) and the liberals (Mouvement Réformateur [MR]/Open Vlaamse Democraten en Liberalen [Open VLD]) to the radical left (Parti du Travail de Belgique [PTB]/Partij van de Arbeid [PvdA]), radical right and regionalists (VB, Parti Populaire [PP], Lijst Dedecker [LDD], Nieuw-Vlaamse Alliantie [N-VA], Front Démocratique des Francophones [FDF]), with the socialists and the Christian democrats somewhere in the middle.

The concept of party family not only taps into ideology but also taps into organisational features of parties. Katz and Mair (1995) have stressed the evolution of party organisations and of their internal procedures. In a process of cartelisation, some parties have adopted procedures that take away the power of the middle-level elites and grant more direct rights to rank and file. It diffuses power to all party members and thereby reinforces centralisation and the power of the party in central office to the detriment of the party on the ground (Sandri and Pauwels 2011). The result is an increased division of labour between the party elites who hold strong decision-making powers and the party members who keep a legitimisation function but are endowed with an increasingly retrenching position. Sandri and Pauwels (2011) have shown that some parties in Belgium are characterised by a blurred party membership and a stratarchical relationship between members and elites (Carty 2004), ranking higher on the cartelisation index than other parties. Given the negative externalities generated by highly organisationally cartelised parties, we expect this process of cartelisation to generate criticisms over the weight gained by party elites, *a fortiori* the leader. Again, this roughly opposes the greens and liberals to the radical right and Conservatives, with the Christian democrats and – to a lesser extent – the socialists in the middle.

Therefore, we expect the perception that parties weigh too much to vary across party families due to the interactive effect of ideology and organisation:

Hypothesis 2: The perception that parties weigh too much on the policymaking process is lower among Conservatives, Social democrats, and Christian democrats than among the greens or the liberals.

Third, empirical studies tend to see the public as homogeneous. Few studies compare the degree of dissatisfaction with the weight of parties across different social groups. Yet it seems obvious to assume that partisanship affects opinions on parties: citizens who hold political or party mandates evaluate parties differently than citizens who are highly involved in politics or who are overall indifferent to party politics (Sandri and Amjahad 2015). By partisanship, we mean the proximity of an individual to a political party, from mere voter to activist to candidate to elected representative.

We expect a curvilinear relationship between partisanship and the perception that parties – understood as parties in central office – weigh too much on the policymaking process. As in May's law (1973) of curvilinear disparity of ideological radicalism based on the party strata, we expect voters and MPs to be more critical of the weight of parties, and activists and candidates less so. If candidates and MPs are indeed closer to the party in central office (Jenny et al. 2014; Deschouwer and Depauw 2014), MPs, however, as elected representatives, may feel constrained in their work by the party in central office: 'Party representatives in public office are ultimately the agents of the extra – parliamentary party organisation', and the latter thus plays a crucial role in determining attitudes and behaviours of the former (Müller 2000: 309). The extensive rules elaborated by Western European parties for managing the principal-agent relations with their representatives in public office and for ensuring cohesion in parliamentary behaviour shape the opinions of elected representatives on the extra-parliamentary party organisation (Müller 2000).

Hypothesis 3: There is a curvilinear relationship between partisanship and the perception that parties weigh too much on the policymaking process. Voters are most critical of the role of leadership in decision-making. Activists and candidates are the least critical, with MPs adopting intermediary views.

The literature has recently explored the drivers of preferences between alternative models of democracy (Close et al. 2017). It emphasises that preferences are not homogeneous and that there are clear divisions between what some call 'critical' citizens or 'dissatisfied democrats' (Webb 2013) and alienated or disaffected citizens (Dalton et al. 2001). Opinions on models of democracy and on the role of parties are closely related (Miller and Listhaug 1990). Dalton and Weldon (2005) have, for instance, shown how trust in parties is correlated to satisfaction with democracy.

Parties are central actors of representative democracy. Therefore, we expect that those who evaluate representative democracy positively are less likely to think that parties weigh too much in the policymaking process.

Conversely, we expect that those who support more participatory democracy advocate more autonomy from the party for elected representatives.

Hypothesis 4a: The higher the individuals value representative democracy, the lower is their perception that parties weigh too much on the policymaking process.
Hypothesis 4b: The higher the individuals value participatory democracy, the lower is their perception that parties weigh too much on the policymaking process.

DATA AND METHOD

This research draws on two different datasets: the *2014 PartiRep Voter Survey* and the 2014 Belgian Candidate Survey. Because the two surveys were elaborated by PartiRep researchers, a number of similar questions have been asked. They provide us with the unique opportunity to directly confront responses of citizens and elites. The single point in time at which the two surveys were conducted (2014) allows maximising comparability.

In both surveys, respondents were asked their opinion on the influence of the party leader on the MPs. The exact wording of the question was: 'Do Parliamentarians give too much or too little attention to the following groups and actors?' (to be evaluated on a 0–10 scale) with one item under examination being the party leaders. Of course, one may evaluate the role of the party in central office through other instances than its leadership. But in a party democracy such as Belgium where party leaders are the face of the extra-parliamentary organisation, we assume that opinions on the role of leadership largely reflect opinions on the role of the party in central office as a whole.

Since Belgium has two unilingual party systems, we distinguish between Dutch-speaking respondents and French-speaking respondents based on their language (mother tongue).

To measure party family, we recoded the vote intention in the *2014 PartiRep Voter Survey*, and the party affiliation in the 2014 Belgian Candidate Survey into sets of binary variables: greens (Groen, Ecolo), liberal parties (Open VLD, MR, Partei für Freiheit und Fortschritt [PFF], Vivant), Social democrats (Socialisische Partij Anders [SP.a], Parti Socialiste [PS]), Christian democrats (Christen-Democratisch en Vlaams [CD&V], Centre Démocrate Humaniste [cdH]) and radical right (VB, PP, FN), radical left (PvdA, PTB) and regionalist parties (N-VA, FDF, Pro Deutschsprachigen Gemeinschaft [ProDG]).

Next, we look at the partisanship or party strata of the respondents. We measure partisanship by differentiating between four categories of respondents. We use the candidate survey to distinguish non-elected candidates and elected MPs. We use the voter survey to differentiate between voters and party activists. To reflect the fact that party borders are becoming increasingly porous (Scarrow 2015), we identify party activists as those who report to have been or to be active in a party (whether they were/are officially members or not). We are thus left with four different strata: MPs, (non-elected) candidates, activists and ordinary voters.

To measure opinions on representative democracy we use the question on whether MPs' opinions are good reflections of what voters think, as representative democracy precisely rests on the assumption of congruence between voters and their representatives (Pitkin 1967; Eulau and Karps 1977). Those who believe that opinions of MPs are a good reflection of what the voters think were considered to hold a positive view on representative democracy.

To measure opinions on participatory democracy, we use the question of whether citizens are offered adequate opportunities to participate in political decisions. Those who disagreed were considered as favouring participatory democracy (Geissel and Newton 2012; Kern and Hooghe 2017).

Finally, we control for socio-demographic characteristics of the respondents (age, gender and education).

DISCUSSION AND ANALYSES

Descriptive analyses

We first look at the distribution of our dependent variable. We compare the perception of the weight of parties on policymaking in Belgium to the perceived weight of other actors. Figure 2.1 shows that Belgian voters think that their representatives give too much attention to parties. Only two actors are perceived as weighing too much on the policymaking work of MPs: the media and party leaders. Conversely, the other categories of actors are perceived as weighting enough for the majority of the respondents. Respondents rarely think that the listed actors should weigh more, with the notable exception of voters (from the party or the region): about 20 per cent of the respondents think that voters should weigh more in the MPs' decision-making process.

Overall, it tends to confirm the idea of a negative perception of parties and of their weight in the policymaking process in Belgium.

Next, we turn to bivariate analyses, looking at how these perceptions of the weight of parties vary across polities, parties and individuals.

Figure 2.2 looks at the differences in perception between French- and Dutch-speaking respondents. The differences are small but go in the expected direction. While Flemish respondents take the upper hand in the lower categories, French speakers are over-represented in the most critical categories

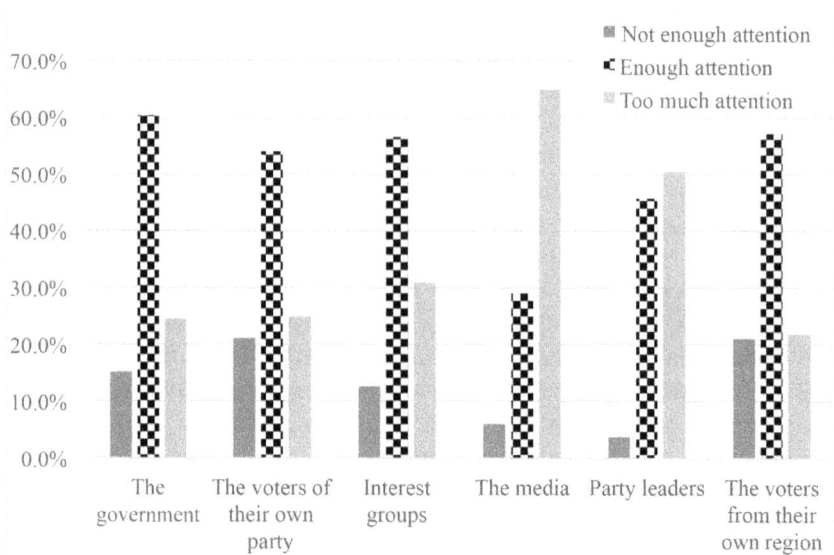

Figure 2.1. **Voters' opinion on the attention granted by MPs to different actors (%)**

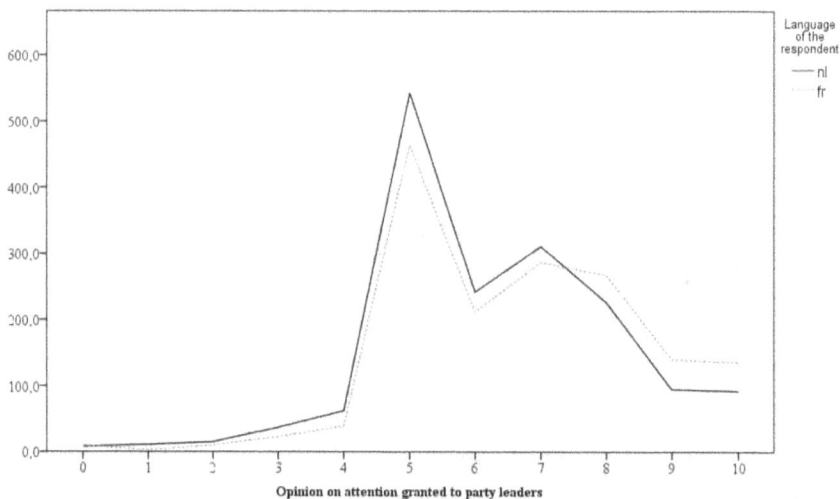

Figure 2.2. **Perceptions of the weight of parties among French and Dutch speakers. Source: 2014 PartiRep Voter Survey.**

Note: 0–10 scale (0 = not enough attention; 10 = too much attention)

thinking that parties have too much weight over the policymaking process (8–10 on the scale). Overall, French-speaking respondents display a higher average (6.67) than Dutch-speaking ones (6.29).

Table 2.1 displays the differences in perception across parties. The differences partially go in the expected direction. Surprisingly, partisans (citizens

Table 2.1. Perceptions of the weight of parties across party families (%)

	Not enough attention	Enough attention	Too much attention	N
Greens	2.1	53.8	44.1	487
Regionalists	4.9	50.9	44.2	432
Radical right	7.7	45.6	46.7	182
Christian democrats	3.2	50.7	46.2	507
Socialists	3.0	47.1	49.9	639
Liberals	2.6	46.9	50.5	497
Radical left	2.7	36.3	61.0	223

Source: 2014 PartiRep Voter Survey; 2014 Belgian Candidate Survey.

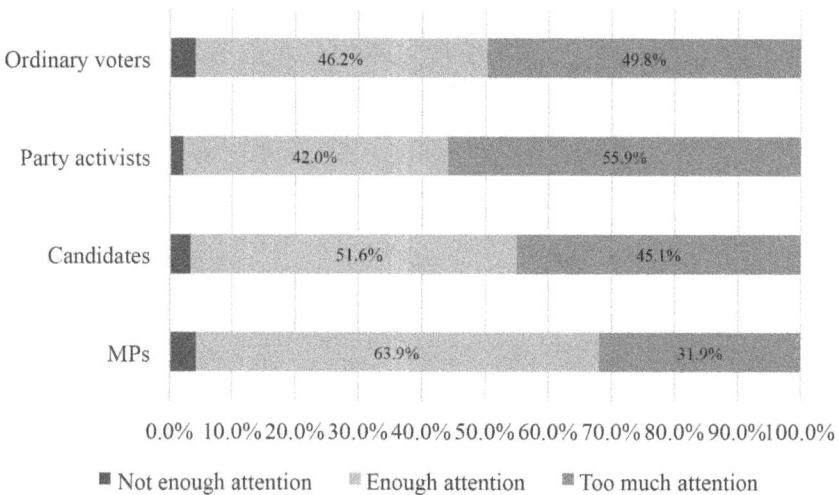

Figure 2.3. Perceptions of the weight of parties by partisanship (%). Source: 2014 PartiRep Voter Survey; 2014 Belgian Candidate Survey.

and elites taken together) of radical left tend to be the most critical towards the weight of parties, followed by the liberals. Supporters of the greens, radical right and regionalists, by contrast, are those presenting the most favourable views about parties' intervention, with the Christian democrats and socialists somewhere in the middle.

Figure 2.3 looks at the differences in perception across various types of partisans, from voters to MPs. There is a clear gap between citizens (voters and activists) and elites (candidates and MPs).

Party activists and ordinary voters are the most critical towards the weight of parties, which partially run contrary to our expectations (for the activists). A majority of activists (55.9 per cent) even think that too much attention is granted to the party leader. This goes against our expectations based on May's law. It could be interpreted as a strong criticism of centralisation in the extra-parliamentary party.

By contrast, most candidates and MPs adopt a more nuanced view and opt for the intermediary categories (giving scores between 4 and 6). Contrary to our expectations, MPs themselves are not critical of the weight of the extra-parliamentary party on their work. They are the least critical category of partisans.

Overall, the difference between the four groups is significant (p value < 0.001). It tends to point towards two gaps: between citizens and elites, and within the extra-parliamentary party, between the activists and the party leaders.

Last, figure 2.4 illustrates the relationship between the perception of parties and preferences for models of democracy. When it comes to representative democracy, the relation goes in the expected direction: the more respondents think MPs' opinions reflect the opinions of voters, the more they view positively the weight of parties. This arguably reflects an integrated approach to representative democracy: individuals who are satisfied with the way representative democracy functions are also favourable to more input from parties in this democratic model.

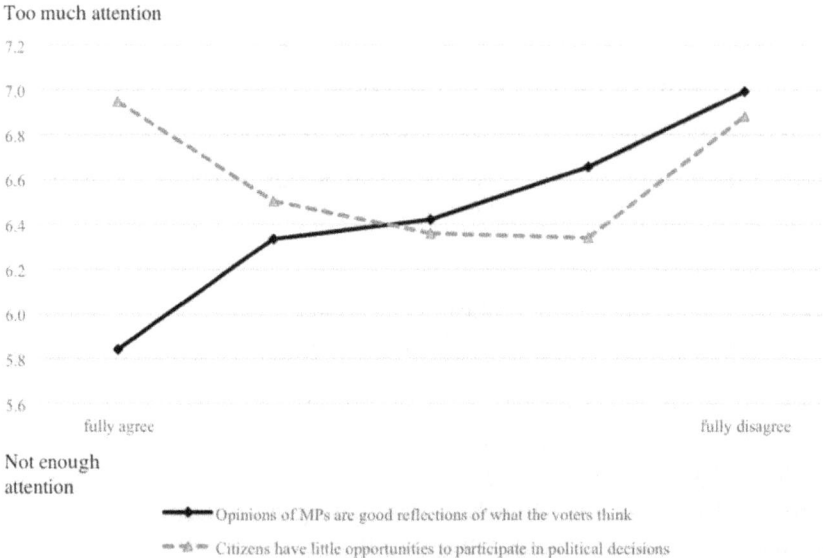

Figure 2.4. Perceptions of the weight of parties and attitudes towards models of democracy. Source: 2014 PartiRep Voter Survey.

By contrast, our expectations are only partially met when it comes to participatory democracy. Respondents who think voters do not have enough opportunities to participate also think that parties have too much weight in the policymaking process, but there is also a category of respondents who think that parties weight too much and that citizens have a lot of participatory opportunities.

Multivariate analyses

Since our dependent variable is measured as a scale (degree of attention granted to party leaders by MPs), we use linear regressions to identify the influence of our independent variables on their perception of the weight of parties in the policymaking process. We ran two models: the first includes only our independent variables as predictors; the second also includes several control variables. We base our interpretations on Model 2.

First, the language of the respondent appears as a strong predictor of their opinion on the weight of parties in policymaking. As expected, French-speaking respondents are significantly more critical about the role of party leaders than Dutch-speaking respondents, confirming our first hypothesis (hypothesis 1). There is a clear gap between the two communities as to how political parties are perceived. The role of the distinct party systems and the party offer is probably at play here.

At the meso-level, we find weak support for our hypothesis. Party family is a weaker predictor of views on the weight of parties. Partisans from radical left parties are more critical of the weight of parties in the policymaking process, which goes against our expectation. This finding could be due to technical reasons (the small number of cases). It could also be interpreted in line with their protest and 'anti-system' profile.

The other party families (socialist, green, radical right and regionalist) seem to hold rather similar views on the weight of parties as the Christian democrats. Despite not being statistically significant, the coefficients are pointing in the expected direction: liberal and green parties tend to be more critical of the weight of parties than the Christian democrats, while radical right and regionalists tend to be less critical. The socialists are also slightly more critical, and this could be linked to clear organisational differences within the socialist party family in Belgium in terms of level of cartelisation (Sandri and Pauwels 2011).

As such, hypothesis 2 is thus only partly confirmed. The attitudes towards the weight of parties oppose liberal and post-materialist parties in favour of personal freedom and individual participation (opposed to the representative model of party democracy) to regionalist and radical right parties that are less critical of the status quo.

Next, the level of partisanship does influence perceptions on the role of parties. Candidates and (even more so) MPs do hold more positive opinions towards the weight of parties in the policymaking process than citizens do. MPs who embody the party in public office are thus not critical of the weight of the party in central office over their work. This may be a sign of loyalty and gratitude of MPs towards the extra-parliamentary party. After all, MPs have won the intra-party battle for a (good) place on the list and for seats.

Contrary to our expectations, voters and activists hold similar critical views of the weight of parties. In fact, party activists appear to be even more critical than voters, which goes against our expectation of them supporting the supervision of MPs' work by the extra-parliamentary party. Rather, it seems to point towards a clear criticism of the centralisation of the party in central office. There is thus a clear gap between citizens and elites as to how much party they want. Overall, hypothesis 3 is only partially confirmed. Our results oppose citizens to political elites, and the party on the ground to the higher party strata.

Table 2.2. Explaining perception of the weight of parties (linear regressions)

	Model 1	*Model 2*
Control variables:		
Age		0.000 (0.002)
Gender		−0.191 (0.068)**
Level of education		0.095 (0.043)*
Independent variables:		
Language	0.335 (0.070)***	0.361 (0.071)***
Party family (ref: Christian democrats)		
Socialists	0.172 (0.108)	0.177 (0.110)
Radical right	−0.013 (0.160)	−0.019 (0.163)
Regionalists	−0.017 (0.120)	−0.011 (0.121)
Greens	0.057 (0.116)	0.030 (0.118)
Liberals	0.214 (0.114)#	0.177 (0.115)
Radical left	0.557 (0.152)***	0.653 (0.155)***
Partisanship (ref: voters)		
Party activists	0.257 (0.129)*	0.198 (0.129)
Party candidates	−0.043 (0.074)	−0.132 (0.081)#
MPs	−0.380 (0.219)#	−0.481 (0.223)*
Opinion on representative democracy	0.155 (0.037)***	0.134 (0.038)***
Opinion on participatory democracy	−0.053 (0.032)#	−0.051 (0.032)
Constant	5.905 (0.173)***	5.847 (0.239)***
N	3,233	3,233
R^2 (adjusted R^2)	0.029	0.033

Note: Dependent variable: 0 = not enough attention; 10 = too much attention granted to party leader. Non-standardised coefficients. Standard errors in parentheses. Sign: # $p < 0.1$; * $p < 0.05$; ** $p < 0.01$; *** $p < 0.001$.

Finally, those who hold more positive views on representative democracy also think that parties do not surpass their mandate. This confirms our bivariate analysis. Clearly, respondents who do not show confidence in the ability of MPs to reflect voters' opinions are also questioning the linkage role of political parties in representative democracy. Hypothesis 4a is thus confirmed.

Conversely, those who hold more positive views on participatory democracy tend to view negatively the weight of parties on MPs' decisions. Such views can be interpreted as a criticism of representative democracy as a whole, including a criticism of intermediary actors between citizens and politics such as political parties. However, the relation fails to achieve the conventional level of significance. After all, one may be in favour of more participatory initiatives without entirely dismissing representative democracy. Hence, we cannot fully confirm hypothesis 4b.

Last, and interestingly, age does not seem to affect the perceptions of the weight of parties. Younger generations are not significantly more critical of the weight of parties than older generations. By contrast, men are more critical of the weight of parties than women. Finally, criticisms towards the weight of parties also increase with the level of education. This seems to contradict the idea that less-sophisticated citizens are more critical of representative democracy and tends to support the thesis of the 'dissatisfied democrats' (Webb 2013) rather than that of alienated or disaffected citizens (Dalton et al. 2001).

CONCLUSION

Recent trends of growing disenchantment with party democracy have the role of parties in representative democracy at the centre of the debate. Drawing on previous literature on the public image of parties, our study aimed at analysing the perception of the weight of parties in representative democracy. This chapter aimed at disentangling what 'the public' and 'the party' means. We have looked at various publics and faces of parties.

The descriptive analyses developed in the chapter allowed exploring the perceptions of parties as organisations, and more specifically to examine how the role of the party in central office is viewed in Belgium, embodied by the party leader. The multivariate analyses tested various factors to explain variations in the perception of parties across polities (Flanders and French-speaking Belgium), party families, party strata and individuals.

All in all, our study offers a partial account of these variations in opinions on the weight of parties in representative democracy. We have shown that there is clearly too much party for some segments of the Belgian population, whereas party democracy is seen as far less problematic for others. We have identified three gaps: across the two communities (with Flanders being less critical of parties), between citizens and elites (emphasising the disconnect between citizens and elites) and within parties between rank-and-file activists and the central extra-parliamentary organisation (pointing towards a clear criticism of centralisation and of the iron law of oligarchy).

The identification of these gaps is crucial for a better understanding of the problems and criticisms that representative democracy is facing in Belgium today. Acknowledging these gaps is a first step towards thinking about bridging them.

REFERENCES

Altman, D. (2010) *Direct Democracy Worldwide*, Cambridge: Cambridge University Press.

Art, D. (2011) *Inside the Radical Right: The Development of Anti-Immigrant Parties in Western Europe*, Cambridge: Cambridge University Press.

Bengtsson, Å. and Mattila, M. (2009) 'Direct Democracy and Its Critics: Support for Direct Democracy and "Stealth" Democracy in Finland', *West European Politics*, 32(5): 1031–48.

Bowler, S., Donovan, T. and Karp, J. A. (2007) 'Enraged or Engaged? Preferences for Direct Citizen Participation in Affluent Democracies', *Political Research Quarterly*, 60(3): 351–62.

Carty, R. K. (2004) 'Parties as Franchise Systems: The Stratarchical Organizational Imperative', *Party Politics*, 10(1): 5–24.

Close, C. (2016) 'Parliamentary Party Loyalty and Party Family: The Missing Link?' *Party Politics*, Online First: http://journals.sagepub.com/doi/abs/10.1177/1354068816655562.

Close, C. and Nunez, L. (2017) 'Preferences and Agreement in Legislative Parties: Testing the Causal Chain', *The Journal of Legislative Studies*, 23(1): 31–43.

Close, C., Kelbel, C. and van Haute, E. (2017) 'What Citizens Want in Terms of Intra-Party Democracy: Popular Attitudes towards Alternative Candidate Selection Procedures', *Political Studies*, 65(3): 646–64. Online First: http://journals.sagepub.com/doi/10.1177/0032321716679424.

Cross, W. P. and Katz, R. S. (eds) (2013) *The Challenges of Intra-Party Democracy*, Oxford: Oxford University Press.

Dalton, R. (2014) 'Interpreting Partisan Dealignment in Germany', *German Politics*, 23(1–2): 133–44.

Dalton, R. and Weldon, S. (2005) 'Public Images of Political Parties: A Necessary Evil?' *West European Politics*, 28(5): 931–51.

Dalton, R., Burklin, W. P. and Drummond, A. (2001) 'Public Opinion and Direct Democracy', *Journal of Democracy*, 12(4): 141–53.

Dassonneville, R. and Hooghe, M. (2016) 'Indifference and Alienation: Diverging Dimensions of Electoral Dealignment in Europe', *Acta Politica*, Online First: https://link.springer.com/article/10.1057%2Fap.2016.3.

Delwit, P. (2012) *La vie politique en Belgique de 1830 à nos jours*, Brussels: Editions de l'Université de Bruxelles, coll. UBLire, 2nd edition.

Deschouwer, K. (2002) 'Falling Apart Together. The Changing Nature of Belgian Consociationalism', *Acta Politica*, 37: 68–85.

Deschouwer, K. and Depauw, S. (eds) (2014) *Representing the People*, Oxford: Oxford University Press.

Eulau, H. and Karps, P. D. (1977) 'The Puzzle of Representation: Specifying Components of Responsiveness', *Legislative Studies Quarterly*, 2(3): 233–54.

Ferrin, M. and Kriesi, H. (2016) *How Europeans View and Evaluate Democracy*. Oxford: Oxford University Press.

Gauja, A. (2015) 'The Individualisation of Party Politics: The Impact of Changing Internal Decision Making Processes on Policy Development and Citizen Engagement', *The British Journal of Politics & International Relations*, 17(1): 89–105.

Geissel, K. and Newton, B. (eds) (2012) *Evaluating Democratic Innovations: Curing the Democratic Malaise?* London: Routledge.

Henry, L., van Haute, E. and Hooghe, M. (2015) 'Confiance, satisfaction et comportement électoral dans un état fédéral', in K. Deschouwer, P. Delwit, M. Hooghe, P. Baudewyns and S. Walgrave (eds) *Décrypter l'électeur. Le comportement électoral et les motivations du vote du 25 mai 2014*. Louvain: Lannoo Campus, 213–34.

Jenny, M., Müller, W. C., Eder, N., Bradbury, J. and Ilonszki, G. (2014) 'MPs' Inter-Party Contacts and the Operation of Party Democracy', in K. Deschouwer and S. Depauw (eds) *Representing the People: A Survey among Members of Statewide and Substate Parliaments*. Oxford: Oxford University Press, 137–65.

Katz, R. S. and Mair, P. (1994) 'The Evolution of Party Organizations in Europe: The Three Faces of Party Organization', *American Review of Politics*, 14: 593–617.

Katz, R. S. and Mair, P. (1995) 'Changing Models of Party Organization and Party Democracy. The Emergence of the Cartel Party', *Party Politics*, 1(1): 5–28.

Kern, A. and Hooghe, M. (2017) 'The Effect of Direct Democracy on the Social Stratification of Political Participation: Inequality in Democratic Fatigue?' *Comparative European Politics*, Online First.

Kitschelt, H. (1989) *The Logics of Party Formation: Ecological Politics in Belgium and West Germany*, Ithaca, NY: Cornell University Press.

Mair, P. and Mudde, C. (1998) 'The Party Family and Its Study', *Annual Review of Political Science*, 1: 211–29.

Marien, S. (2011) 'The Effect of Electoral Outcomes on Political Trust. A Multi-Level Analysis of 23 Countries', *Electoral Studies*, 30(4): 712–26.

May, J.D. (1973) 'Opinion Structure of Political Parties: The Special Law of Curvilinear Disparity', *Political Studies*, 21(2): 135–51.

Miller, A. H. and Listhaug, O. (1990) 'Political Parties and Confidence in Government: A Comparison of Norway, Sweden and the United States', *British Journal of Political Science*, 20(3): 357–86.

Mudde, C. (2007) *The Populist Radical Right in Europe*, Cambridge: Cambridge University Press.

Mudde, C. and Kaltwasser, R. (2017) *Populism: A Very Short Introduction*. Oxford: Oxford University Press.

Müller, W. C. (2000) 'Political Parties in Parliamentary Democracies: Making Delegation and Accountability Work', *European Journal of Political Research*, 37(3): 309–33.

Norris, P. (2011) Democra*tic Deficit: Critical Citizens Revisited*, Cambridge: Cambridge University Press.

Pitkin, H. F. (1967) *The Concept of Representation*, Berkeley: University of California Press.

Poguntke, T., Scarrow, S. E., Webb, P., Allern, E. H., Aylott, N., van Biezen, I., Calossi, E., Costa Lobo, M., Cross, W. P., Deschwouer, K., Enyedi, Z., Fabre, E., Farrell, D. M., Gauja, A., Pizzimenti, E., Kopecky, P., Koole, R., Müller, W. C., Kosiara-Pedersen, K., Rahat, G., Szczerbiak, A., van Haute, E. and Verge, T. (2016) 'Party Rules, Party Resources and the Politics of Parliamentary Democracies. How Parties Organize in the 21st Century', *Party Politics*, 22(6): 661–78. Online First: http://journals.sagepub.com/doi/abs/10.1177/1354068816662493.

Sandri, G. and Amjahad, A. (2015) 'Party Membership and Intra-Party Democracy: How Do Members React to Organizational Change within Political Parties? The Case of Belgium', *Partecipazione & Conflitto*, 8(1): 190–214.

Sandri, G. and Pauwels, T. (2011) 'Party Members in Belgian and Italian Parties: A Cross-National Analysis', in E. van Haute (ed.), *Party Membership in Europe: Exploration into the Anthills of Party Politics*, Brussels: Editions de l'université de Bruxelles, 129–46.

Sandri, G., Seddone, A. and Venturino, F. (eds) (2015) *Party Primaries in Comparative Perspective*, Farnham and Burlington: Ashgate.

Scarrow, S. (2015) *Beyond Party Members*, Oxford: Oxford University Press.

van Haute, E., Amjahad, A., Borriello, A., Close, C. and Sandri, G. (2013) 'Party Members in a Pillarised Partitocracy. An Empirical Overview of Party Membership Figures and Profiles in Belgium', *Acta Politica*, 48(1): 68–91.

van Haute, E., Paulis, E. and Sierens, V. (2017) 'Assessing Party Membership Figures: The MAPP Dataset', *European Political Science*, Online First: https://link.springer.com/article/10.1057/s41304-016-0098-z.

Webb, P. (2013) 'Who Is Willing to Participate? Dissatisfied Democrats, Stealth Democrats and Populists in the United Kingdom', *European Journal of Political Research*, 52(6): 747–72.

Zmerli, S. and Hooghe, M. (2013) *Political Trust. Why Context Matters*, London: ECPR Press.

Chapter 3

Public and politicians' preferences on priorities in political representation

Audrey André, Sam Depauw
and Rudy B. Andeweg

INTRODUCTION

Whether elected representatives live up to the public's expectations is a fundamental question for any representative democracy. By now, there is a vast literature on the degree to which the policy preferences of elected representatives reflect those expressed by their voters and on the factors that may account for the variation in what is usually referred to as policy congruence (Miller et al. 2000; Powell 2000; Golder and Stramski 2010). However, important as policy responsiveness may be, it is but one component of responsiveness (Eulau and Karps 1977) and even within policy representation various styles and foci have been discerned (Wahlke et al. 1962). Such aspects of representation are less well studied.

While we know a great deal about the various aspects of their job on which elected representatives in various contexts put more emphasis (André et al. 2015; Dudzińska et al. 2014; Harden 2013), our understanding of what voters want from their representatives remains vastly underdeveloped. Do ordinary citizens want their representatives to concentrate on representing their views on national issues and the making of public policy? Do they prefer someone who will look after the local area? In recent years there has been a modest growth of studies of public preferences with regard to the focus and/or style of representation (Bowler 2017; Carman 2006; Doherty 2013; Lapinski et al. 2016; Vivyan and Wagner 2016; Bengtsson and Wass 2011). But there are still hardly any studies on the degree of correspondence between the public and their representatives pertaining to the different components of responsiveness (exceptions are André and Depauw 2017; von Schoultz and Wass 2016; Andeweg and Thomassen 2005; Méndez-Lago and Martínez 2002; Converse and Pierce 1986: 687–90).

This is regrettable as the representational relation, theorists remind us, is interactive (see Mansbridge 2003). The degree to which the job description is left to the discretion of the representative is startling (Searing 1994). One member may want to be an education policy specialist, another may seek to attract businesses to the local area and a third may focus on the redress of constituents' grievances, all seemingly without taking voter preferences into account. However, it is not only important that representatives' policy positions correspond to public opinion but also that they prioritise those aspects of the job the public considers as most important. If their priorities are found to be persistently at odds, citizens may feel their representatives are directing their efforts to the wrong tasks – even if they do not oppose the representatives' policy positions (see also Reher 2016). As such a persistent mismatch may well result in widespread dissatisfaction not only with the individual representatives but also with democratic institutions and the political process in general (Andeweg and Thomassen 2005: 520–23).

Combining evidence uniquely tailored to this fundamental question from the *2014 PartiRep Voter Survey* and the 2014 Belgian Candidate Survey, we gauge the degree of correspondence between politicians and ordinary citizens with regard to the tasks and duties an elected representative should prioritise. Do the representational priorities of those running for election match what the public wants from them? For whom is representational priority congruence low? Are voters who experience lower degrees of priority congruence less likely to turn out at elections?

In answering these questions, we offer several contributions to the literature. Foremost, the results contribute to the scholarly search for the determinants of political disengagement (see Dalton 2004). Thus far, scholars' preoccupation with policy congruence has disregarded the heterogeneous expectations that voters have of their representatives. Bridging two literatures that thus far have developed in isolation, we find that, just as politicians have opinions on which duties and tasks they put more emphasis, people have meaningful priority preferences. In addition we find that the degree of correspondence between the two varies across individuals in plausible ways. If ordinary citizens continue to experience a mismatch between the duties they want their representatives to perform and the duties actually performed by their elected representatives, their political involvement will likely suffer and, ultimately, they will withdraw from politics altogether. As such, second, we add to the debate about the attitudinal and behavioural consequences of (in)congruence between ordinary citizens and their representatives. These findings also have important implications for our understanding of political inequalities. Third, this study is also methodologically innovative. We improve on previous research by measuring citizens' and elites' preferences independently. We do not compare attitudes vis-à-vis abstract notions of representation that few have effectively pondered. Rather, we offer a more objective measure, confronting the salience to legislators of real-life legislative duties with what citizens want them to focus on.

WHAT VOTERS WANT

Given the many functions attributed to legislatures across the globe (Packenham 1970), it is only natural that different task conceptions emerge among their members. While there is growing evidence that ordinary citizens have meaningful, yet different, views about the sort of relationship they prefer to have with their elected representatives, we have a less well-developed sense of the degree, and the determinants, of correspondence between the two.

Citizens across the United Kingdom, Carman (2006) found, vary in predictable ways as to the style of representation they want from their representatives (see Wahlke et al. 1962). Andeweg and Thomassen (2005) argued that what is underpinning different styles of representation is a distinction between representation as the bottom-up translation of citizens' exogenous opinions into public policy and representation as a top-down process whereby representatives put their political views to the public for approval (see also Esaiasson and Holmberg 1996). The distinction is also mirrored in the growing number of studies contrasting support for representative versus participatory democracy (Hibbing and Theiss-Morse 2001; Allen and Birch 2015). Most notably, the degree of discretion that individuals are prepared to allow their representatives in representing their policy views differs not only across sophisticates and non-sophisticates but also across the majority and minorities in society (Carman 2007; see also Bowler 2017; Campbell and Cowley 2014).

Other studies have focused on citizen views with regard to the focus, not the style, of representation. Citizens in Finland, von Schoultz and Wass (2016) found, by and large want their representatives to focus on representing the nation (59 per cent), rather than the district, the party or some special interest. Despite differences in the electoral system, citizens in Spain (Méndez-Lago and Martínez 2002) and the United States (Lapinski et al. 2016) similarly value representatives who represent them on the salient national issues of the day. Using an experimental design, Vivyan and Wagner (2016) by contrast found UK citizens to gravitate more towards favouring a constituency focus (see also Doherty 2013 with regard to US citizens). Citizens as a whole, Griffin and Flavin (2011) conclude, do not value different foci of representation equally; there are important group differences in preferences that are likely rooted in their divergent life experiences.

As such this burgeoning literature has largely concentrated on what ordinary citizens think about foci and styles of representation – abstract notions that only few are likely to have purposefully pondered (see Carman 2006). Even within the legislative literature, the evidence as to the sources of these twin role concepts, as well as their effects, has been fragmentary if not downright contradictory (see Andeweg 2014). For this reason, legislative scholars increasingly turn towards studying roles that are defined in terms of what legislators do and that as such 'exist in the minds of most politicians' (Searing 1994: 12). By contrast, inquiries into what ordinary citizens want have yet to follow this shift in attention towards the various real-life tasks and duties on which they want their representatives to put more emphasis.

In recent decades the legislative role orientations that have attracted most attention are the ones identified by Searing (1994), even if others have identified roles that closely resemble Searing's typology (see Andeweg 2014). In Searing's study of the House of Commons, the greatest numbers of backbenchers are *policy advocates*, focusing on representing citizens' policy preferences and seeking to influence public policy. Among them, *specialists* who concentrate on a particular policy area outnumber *generalists* three to one. Generalists, by contrast, prefer to partake in the grand debates of the day, taking on whatever issue is uppermost at the time. In addition, Searing (1994) distinguished two sub-roles of *constituency members*. Welfare officers favour service responsiveness, offering constituents assistance in their dealings with public agencies, whereas local promoters focus on attracting public funds to the local area and on defending its economic needs. Albeit by other names, the roles of the policy advocate and the constituency member also feature in the works by Strøm (1997) and Andeweg (1997), as well as in Scully's and Farrell's (2003) study of the European Parliament and thus are the natural starting point to move beyond policy congruence to the correspondence of citizens' and elites' task conceptions of the good representative.

While a number of studies have noted a veritable chasm between citizens' preferences and their perceptions of what their representatives do (see Kimball and Patterson 1997), the studies that have actually contrasted elites' to citizens' views are few and far between. Representatives in Belgium (André and Depauw 2017) and the Netherlands (Andeweg and Thomassen 2005), for instance, have very different views from ordinary citizens with regard to representation, emphasising the top-down nature of the relation. In Spain, Méndez-Lago and Martínez (2002) indicated, citizens and their representatives differ most with regard to the importance of representing the constituency, citizens even more than politicians favouring representatives who represent their opinions on the national issues. The gap in this regard is narrower in Finland, as von Schoultz and Wass (2016) observed, both citizens and politicians favouring national representation. Such a gap in preferences for political representation, finally, André and Depauw (2016) demonstrated, negatively impact citizens' satisfaction with democracy. In a similar vein, if the tasks that representatives focus on in the legislative arena are not what citizens want them to do, as this chapter will demonstrate, the mismatch bodes ill for citizens' political engagement and participation.

DATA

Analysing representational priority congruence requires information about citizen and elite conceptions of the primary task of a representative during the same time period. Citizens' opinions are taken from the *2014 PartiRep Voter Survey*. Elite opinions are drawn from the 2014 Belgian Candidate Study. To obtain more reliable estimates of the party priorities, we combine the responses of incumbents and non-incumbents. As they make up less than 8 per cent of the sample, focusing on the incumbent MPs alone dramatically reduces the number of observations and would further exclude the parties who failed to win a seat in the previous election (i.e. PvdA-PTB). Including non-incumbents constitutes a more conservative test of our argument, moreover: if anything, doing so will work against finding significant differences between candidates and ordinary citizens (see von Schoultz and Wass 2016).

Representational priorities at the level of the electorate and the elite were captured using the exact same question wording:

'Members of Parliament perform their many duties in different ways. Can you rank-order the following tasks in order of importance to you?

(1)   Advising and assisting people in their contacts with public authorities
(2)   Influencing policy in a specific area
(3)   Looking after the social and economic needs of the local area
(4)   Contributing to the societal debate on current affairs'.

Following Searing (1994), we distinguish between welfare officers (item 1) and local promoters (item 3) among the constituency members. Policy specialists (item 2) and generalists (item 4) make up the policy advocates. In this manner, we purposefully do not contrast citizens' preferences to their perceptions of what politicians are doing. Instead, we offer a more objective measure that is further removed from any attitudinal and behavioural consequences the gap may have, methodically contrasting what politicians themselves say they do to what citizens want them to do.

What do citizens want from their elected representatives? For each of the four tasks, table 3.1 reports the proportion of the electorate in Flanders and Wallonia who think legislators should prioritise it. First, there is considerable heterogeneity in citizens' expectations. Different people want representatives to focus on different tasks. Second, we find that on average citizens

Table 3.1.   Most important task among citizens and candidates

	First choice citizens, %	First choice candidates, %	Sequence candidates	Difference in sequence
Local promoter	42.2	23.7	2	− 1
Welfare officer	22.8	12.4	4	− 2
Policy specialist	21.3	44.6	1	+ 2
Generalist	13.7	19.3	3	+ 1

Note: The table displays the percentage of citizens and candidates ranking a particular task as the first and foremost important.

value representatives who concentrate on local issues. About 42 per cent want their representatives first and foremost to defend the local area, while 23 per cent prefer welfare officers who offer staunch constituency service. By contrast, a sizeable minority values representatives who focus on national issues, that is, who either specialise in a specific policy area (21 per cent) or who debate and exercise their judgement on the issue uppermost at the time (14 per cent).

The predominance of local orientations among Belgian voters contrasts with recent findings abroad (but see Doherty 2013). Both the American (Lapinski et al. 2016) and Finnish (von Schoultz and Wass 2016) electorates prefer their representatives to focus on the national issues. This local orientation among the electorate is also in stark contrast with the views held by politicians in Belgium, resulting in a low degree of correspondence. The latter, on average, put more emphasis on national policymaking. Despite the electoral incentive in place to nurture personal votes, 45 per cent of the respondents of the 2014 Belgian Candidate Survey state as their primary duty influencing public policy in a specific policy area. Yet in voters' appreciation policy specialists come third, well behind local promoters and welfare officers. Only 24 per cent of the candidates prioritise defending the local area, whereas this task conception is favoured by the largest number of voters. And 19 per cent focuses on the big issues of the day, while 12 per cent, finally, concentrates on assisting individual constituents.

The extent of the citizen-elite mismatch becomes even clearer when looking beyond the mere first priority. Figure 3.1 presents a particularly vivid illustration of the low degree of correspondence. The two lines depict the cumulative frequency of candidates and voters ranking a particular task as most, second, third and least important. There is a gaping distance between the duties that politicians prioritise and what the voters want from them. The candidate line systematically lies below that of citizens in the top two panels. This pattern is reversed in the bottom two panels suggesting that, on average, citizens prefer good constituency members while candidates want to leave their mark on public policy. Of course, aggregate analyses of this kind might

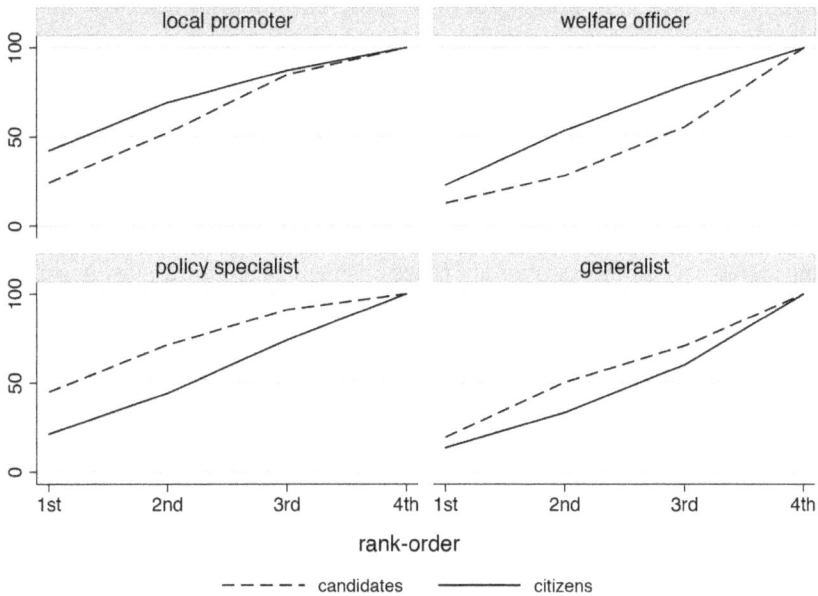

Figure 3.1. Cumulative percentage of respondents ranking a particular task first, second, third or last

be misleading. A lack of correspondence at the aggregate level might not bode ill for political engagement if there proves to be a close match between an individual citizen's representational priorities and those of the political party he or she voted for.

Representational priority congruence indicates to what extent a voter's conception of the duties that elected representatives should prioritise is shared by his or her preferred party's candidates. Following Golder and Stramski (2010), we conceptualise congruence as a one-to-many relationship. In list-PR systems like the flexible list system that is used to elect the members of the federal and regional parliaments in Belgium, mechanisms of accountability are primarily collective, not individual, and operate through political parties. Congruence is therefore measured as the match between an individual citizen's priorities and those of his or her preferred party's candidates. A citizen's party vote is commonly used as the best indication of his or her preferred party. Because the key question tapping into representational priorities is measured in the first wave of the Voter Survey, the analysis relies on the observation of citizens' preferred party at that time, making use of their voting intentions rather than their actual voting behaviour recorded in the post-electoral wave. To boost the reliability of the estimated party priorities, we draw on the information available from both the federal and regional levels of

government. The chi-squared test of the difference in priorities between candidates at the regional and the federal level proved statistically insignificant,
indicating that priorities hardly differ across levels of government.

Following Reher (2015), each of the four duties' salience among a party's
candidates is calculated as the relative frequency with which it was ranked
first, second, third and fourth. The proportion of the party's candidates
is weighted by the duty's importance using a 3-2-1-0 weighting scheme,
whereby the duty considered most important counts three times and the duty
considered second most important twice as much as the third most important
duty. After dividing their sum by the sum of the weights (i.e. 6), for any one
party these weighted proportions sum to one. As such we take into account
the entire distribution of preferences among the candidates. The party priority
scores are reported in table 3.2. There are very important differences between
the political parties, table 3.2 indicates, as to the emphasis their candidates put
on different duties. In eight parties the largest number of candidates favours
the policy specialist, while in five the local promoter is preferred (there is
one tie). In addition, priority scores range widely between the parties by 20
(local promoters), 16 (generalists), 14 (specialists) and 13 percentage points
(welfare officers). The green parties, in particular, concentrate most on policy
advocacy and least on local matters.

To measure an individual's priority congruence, he or she is given his or her
preferred party's priority scores using the same 3-2-1-0 weighting scheme:
that is, the four-party priority scores are averaged giving more weight to the
duties ranked as more important by the voter. Consider the example of a
CD&V voter who wants the representatives to be local promoters first and

Table 3.2. Priority scores by political party

Welfare officer		*Local promoter*	*Policy specialist*	*Generalist*
Flemish parties				
CD&V	0.17	0.29	0.37	0.19
Open VLD	0.21	0.30	0.30	0.19
SP.a	0.20	0.20	0.36	0.26
Groen	0.08	0.18	0.42	0.32
N-VA	0.12	0.29	0.36	0.24
VB	0.22	0.30	0.28	0.21
PvdA	0.14	0.18	0.36	0.32
Walloon parties				
cdH	0.20	0.32	0.31	0.19
MR	0.17	0.36	0.31	0.18
PS	0.22	0.29	0.33	0.17
Ecolo	0.09	0.23	0.40	0.28
FDF	0.19	0.33	0.31	0.18
PTB	0.19	0.29	0.30	0.26
PP	0.20	0.38	0.28	0.16

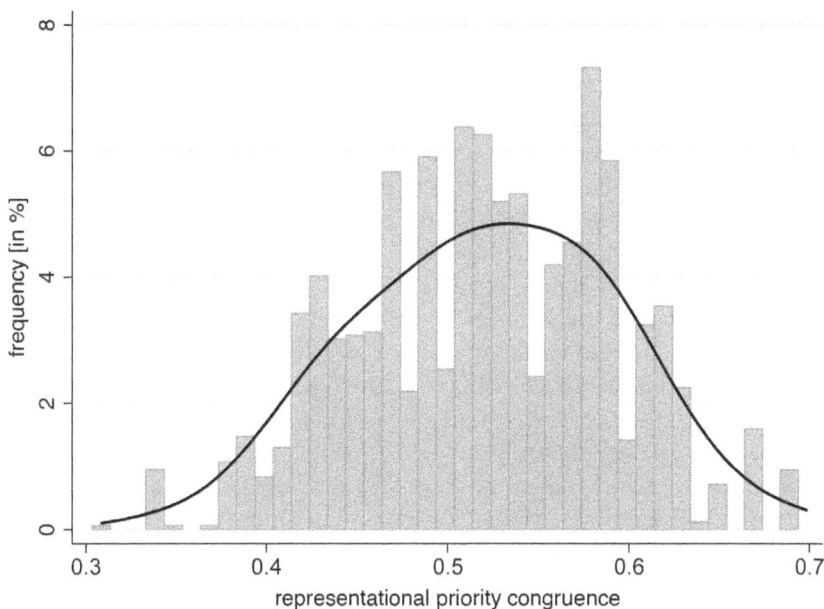

Figure 3.2. The distribution of the individual-level priority congruence measure

Note: The bin width has been fixed at 0.01 for presentational purposes.

subsequently, in descending order of importance, welfare officers, policy specialists and, finally, generalists. The voter's representational priority congruence will be $(3 \times 0.29 + 2 \times 0.17 + 1 \times 0.37 + 0 \times 0.19)/3 = 0.53$. Theoretically, priority congruence scores are bounded by 0 and 1. The observed distribution of the variable is depicted in figure 3.2. In our sample, priority congruence ranges from 0.31 to 0.70 with a mean of 0.52 and a standard deviation of 0.07. Whereas the priorities of the Flemish green party electorate are most in agreement with their representatives' (mean = 0.56), those of the Flemish socialist party electorate are least in agreement (mean = 0.49). Thus, even when carefully matching citizens to the candidates of their most preferred party at the individual level, clear evidence of a mass-elite gap in representational priorities remains. Figure 3.2 emphasises, however, that there is important variation among citizens to the extent of the mismatch, variation that is worth exploring more in depth.

FOR WHOM IS PRIORITY CONGRUENCE LOW?

In seeking to explain the differences in congruence between citizens, we use fractional regression models. This modelling strategy takes into account that the values of the dependent variable, priority congruence, are truncated between 0 and 1, thereby ruling out expected values that are out of bound. Using the logit transformation of the dependent variable provides a more conservative test than ordinary least squares (OLS) regression – although we determined that OLS regression would lead to identical conclusions.

More specifically, indications from the literature on policy congruence and that on citizens' preferences for political representation have led to the expectation that priority congruence should be especially low among unsophisticated voters, non-partisans and the least wealthy. First, we know from previous research that policy congruence is lower among unsophisticated voters than among the sophisticates (Dolný and Baboš 2015; Hill and Hinton-Anderson 1995). Sophisticated voters have more cognitive resources at their disposal and, by virtue of their political interest and involvement, more political information than the least sophisticated. Whereas many voters have only vague and amorphous political views, the opinions of sophisticated voters, including their opinions on what they want from their representatives, are more developed. Certainly, previous studies suggest that sophisticated voters and non-sophisticates differ in their views on the process of representation and what they want from their elected representatives (Bengtsson and Wass 2011; Carman 2006). The opinions of sophisticated voters are also more structured in line with party ideologies better enabling them to vote correctly for the party that best represents their opinions (Jewitt and Goren 2016; Lau et al. 2014). As such we can expect that priority congruence is also lower among unsophisticated voters than among the sophisticates.

Second, those voters who lack a strong party identification should also experience lower degrees of priority congruence. Rohrschneider and White-field (2012) argue that parties everywhere face the strategic conundrum of representing both party identifiers and non-partisans – even though their numbers clearly vary across countries. They find that party identifiers are more likely to agree with the policy positions of their party, taking their cue more readily from the party to decide on an issue (see Dalton 2004). Non-partisans, by contrast, are more appreciative of legislators who break party ranks and those focusing on constituency service (Kam 2009). Given that the relative proportions of party identifiers and non-partisans among party voters influence a party's style of representation (Önnudóttir 2016), it can be reasoned that non-partisans are also less likely to be in agreement with the party when it comes to the legislative duty on which to put more emphasis.

Third, a number of recent studies have demonstrated that public policy is more responsive to the wealthy and ignores the views of the poor (Bartels 2008; Bernauer et al. 2015; Gilens 2005, 2012). Because the wealthier have higher political participation rates and communicate their preferences more, there is a greater degree of policy congruence among the wealthy than among the poor. Politicians are also more likely to share their affluent background

Table 3.3. Accounting for individual-level variation in representational priority congruence

	Bivariate		Model 1		Model 2		Model 3	
	b.	s.e.	b.	s.e.	b.	s.e.	b.	s.e.
Female	−0.030	(0.016)#	−0.003	(0.014)	−0.005	(0.014)	−0.002	(0.014)
Age	−0.002	(0.000)***	−0.001	(0.000)#	−0.001	(0.000)#	−0.001	(0.000)
Education	0.080	(0.007)***	0.063	(0.007)***	0.064	(0.007)***	0.059	(0.008)***
Political knowledge	0.040	(0.005)***	0.024	(0.006)***	0.022	(0.006)***	0.019	(0.006)***
Ideological extremity	0.020	(0.006)***	0.014	(0.005)**	0.013	(0.005)**	0.012	(0.005)*
Party identification	0.023	(0.006)***	0.014	(0.005)**	0.014	(0.005)**	0.017	(0.005)**
Family income	0.026	(0.003)***	0.008	(0.003)*	0.009	(0.003)**	0.009	(0.003)**
Flanders	−0.043	(0.016)**			−0.042	(0.015)**		
Party-fixed effects			*omitted*		*omitted*		*included*	
constant			−0.203	(0.035)***	−0.184	(0.035)***	−0.219	(0.041)***
N	1,483		1,483		1,483		1,483	
Wald χ^2 (df)			244.59	(7)***	269.39	(8)***	381.72	(20)***

Note: Entries are the parameter estimates and robust standard errors (s.e.) (in parentheses) of fractional logit regression models as well as the models' Wald test.

#$p \leq 0.10$, *$p \leq 0.05$, **$p \leq 0.01$, ***$p \leq 0.001$, using two-tailed t-values.

and lifestyle (Schlozman et al. 2013). Not only do the wealthy and the poor differ in their policy preferences, most notably with regard to redistribution and the welfare state. In addition, the literature has long argued that there are clear differences across income groups, for instance, with regard to the demand for constituency service (Ellickson and Whistler 2001; Johannes 1980; Norris 1997) and voter preferences for good constituency members (André et al. 2013). As such we can also expect representational priority congruence to be greater among the wealthy than among the poor.

Table 3.3 first presents the results from the bivariate analyses; Model 1 combines the different explanatory variables. Model 2 explores possible differences between the regions in the country and Model 3 adds party fixed-effects. All four modelling strategies firmly support our expectations. First, priority congruence is lower among the non-sophisticates. This is true whether we capture political sophistication by a voter's level of education or political knowledge – which is widely argued to be the best yardstick of political sophistication in the survey setting (Delli Carpini and Keeter 1996; Zaller 1992). The coefficient of education in the first column is positive and highly significant. Even after controlling for basic socio-demographics and alternative explanations, the coefficient continues to be positive and significant in Models 2 and 3. Having attained a higher level of education, voters are more likely to share the views of their preferred party's representatives as to what a representative should focus on. Voters who have more political information are also more likely to experience higher levels of priority congruence. Moreover, the two have an additive effect: while, clearly, a voter's basic political knowledge is related to his or her cognitive resources, in general, both contribute to priority congruence in their own right.

Second, the evidence in table 3.3 supports the expectation that priority congruence is lower among non-partisan voters. Again, the coefficient of party identification is positive and significant. Voters who feel very close to a party are significantly more likely to share their party representatives' views as to what duties to put more emphasis on. By contrast, there is a wider mismatch between what voters want who do not feel at all close to any party and what the party prioritises. This is true for both voters on the left and on the right. In fact, voters on either extreme of the political spectrum experience higher priority congruence than voters in the centre. But even after controlling for their policy preferences, party identification continues to affect citizen-elite congruence in Models 2 and 3.

Third, priority congruence is higher, as table 3.3 confirms, for the wealthy than for the less affluent. There are ample indications that political parties are more responsive to the wealthy and we find that the legislative duties representatives prioritise are no different in this respect. In line with the Belgian political elites, wealthier citizens are markedly more inclined to prioritise national policymaking responsibilities and rank local duties as less important. As a result, the higher a voter's net family income, the greater is the correspondence between his or her priorities and those of their preferred party's representatives. The coefficient, as table 3.3 attests, is positive and significant in all model specifications.

Model 2, moreover, tentatively suggests that priority congruence is somewhat lower in Flanders than in Wallonia. Both citizens and politicians in Wallonia put more emphasis on defending local interests, compared to Flemish citizens and politicians. But the gap between the two is smaller. About 17 percentage points, for instance, separate the citizens and politicians who most favour a local promoter in Wallonia, compared to 20 percentage points in Flanders. In this sense, the debate on a New Political Culture, resulting in the ethical code passed by the Flemish Parliament in 1998 to ban clientelist practices, may have contributed to a growing process gap in the north, though not in the south of the country. Even more importantly, such regional differences do not detract from the substantive impact of political sophistication, partisanship and wealth on priority congruence.

These findings become even more telling when considered against the history of compulsory voting in Belgium. From other contexts, we know that those who are less informed, less wealthy and non-partisans are less likely to turn out to vote (Blais 2006). Given that parties tend to pay more attention to voters than to non-voters, legislators will continue to prioritise national policymaking and the mismatch in legislators' behaviour will likely continue to grow more important.

DOES PRIORITY CONGRUENCE IMPACT POLITICAL (DIS)ENGAGEMENT?

There is frequently a mismatch, we found, between what citizens want from their representatives and the duties that representatives prioritise. But we have yet to show the attitudinal and behavioural consequences for political disengagement of such a mismatch. To this effect we compute a measure of an individual's external political efficacy, tapping into their perceived ability to influence public officials and feelings of empowerment. The efficacy scale includes nine items and has a Cronbach's alpha of 0.8 (see appendix). It ranges from 1 to 4.7 with a mean of 2.7. Table 3.4 reports the results from the bivariate and multivariate OLS regression analysis. To better isolate the effect of the measure of priority congruence that now enters the regression equation on the right-hand side, all covariates that enter the models perfectly reflect those in table 3.3. In this manner Model 1 controls these known covariates and alternative explanations of priority congruence; Model 2 explores regional differences and Model 3 adds party fixed-effects.

Table 3.4 emphatically confirms the postulated positive relationship between citizens' priority congruence and external efficacy. Those whose representational priorities match the preferences of the party they voted for, the bivariate analysis indicates, are more confident that they are able to affect public officials. The coefficient is positive and highly significant. By contrast, the wider the mismatch grows with regard to representational priorities, the more the political engagement suffers. Model 1 attests that political sophistication, party identification and affluence all increase political efficacy. Model 2 further indicates that, on average, political efficacy is slightly greater in Flanders than in Wallonia. But even after controlling for these determinants and after including party-fixed effects (in Model 3), we continue to find a statistically significant effect of priority congruence.

Because voting is compulsory in Belgium, it is not possible to compare actual turnout across individuals. The *2014 PartiRep Voter Survey* does, however, capture an individual's *willingness* to vote, if voting were no longer compulsory. More specifically, respondents are asked how often they would participate in elections in that case. Four answer categories were offered: (1) never, (2) on occasion, (3) most of the time and (4) always. About 22.2 per cent estimate they would never vote, 10.2 per cent only on occasion, 14.1 per cent most of the time and 53.5 per cent would always vote. Given the categorical nature of the dependent variable, ordered logistic regression models are used to gauge the impact of citizens' representational priority congruence on electoral participation. Table 3.5 presents the parameter estimates and robust standard errors of the bivariate and multivariate specifications.

In line with the turnout literature, we find that those who are better informed, wealthier and partisan are more likely to always vote. Education and political knowledge both have a positive and significant effect on their willingness to go out and vote – whether party-fixed effects are omitted (model 1) or included (model 3), as does an individuals' party identification. The inclusion of party-fixed effects does reduce the impact of an individual's economic affluence, but the effect is in the expected direction and continues to be significant at the 10-per cent level. In line with previous studies (Hooghe et al. 2011), Model 2 further indicates that, on average, citizens' willingness to participate in elections is smaller in Flanders than in Wallonia. More importantly, even after we control for basic socio-demographics and an individual's political information, affluence and party identification, an individual's priority congruence has a direct positive effect on his or her willingness to participate in elections. Those who experience a wider mismatch, we find, between the duties, they themselves feel that their representatives should put most emphasis on and the duties those representatives prioritise are significantly less likely to turn out on Election Day.

Table 3.4. The impact of priority congruence on citizens' political efficacy

	Bivariate		Model 1		Model 2		Model 3	
	b.	s.e.	b.	s.e.	b.	s.e.	b.	s.e.
Priority congruence	1.673	(0.253)***	0.573	(0.265)*	0.654	(0.261)*	0.689	(0.269)*
Female			-0.013	(0.033)	-0.005	(0.032)	-0.011	(0.032)
Age			-0.005	(0.001)***	-0.005	(0.001)***	-0.006	(0.001)***
Education			0.079	(0.017)***	0.075	(0.017)***	0.071	(0.017)***
Political knowledge			0.032	(0.012)**	0.040	(0.012)**	0.041	(0.012)***
Ideological extremity			0.002	(0.013)	0.005	(0.013)	0.013	(0.012)
Party identification			0.056	(0.012)***	0.056	(0.012)***	0.055	(0.012)***
Family income			0.020	(0.007)**	0.018	(0.007)*	0.020	(0.007)**
Flanders					0.134	(0.033)***		
Party-fixed effects			omitted				included	
Constant	1.791	(0.134)***	2.120	(0.143)***	2.022	(0.141)***	2.267	(0.150)***
N	1,483		1,483		1,483		1,483	
R^2	0.04		0.13		0.15		0.18	

Note: Entries are the parameter estimates and robust standard errors (s.e.) (in parentheses) of OLS regression models. The dependent variable measures respondents' political efficacy.

*p≤0.05; **p≤0.01; ***p≤0.001, using two-tailed t-values.

Table 3.5. The impact of priority congruence on citizens' willingness to participate in elections

	Bivariate b	s.e.	Model 1 b	s.e.	Model 2 b	s.e.	Model 3 b	s.e.
Priority congruence	5.808	(0.800)***	2.390	(0.876)**	2.216	(0.872)*	2.128	(0.890)*
Female			−0.276	(0.119)*	−0.290	(0.120)*	−0.283	(0.120)*
Age			0.003	(0.004)	0.004	(0.004)	0.003	(0.004)
Education			0.330	(0.067)***	0.341	(0.067)***	0.321	(0.067)***
Political knowledge			0.205	(0.046)***	0.188	(0.047)***	0.172	(0.047)***
Ideological extremity			0.083	(0.046)#	0.075	(0.046)	0.099	(0.048)*
Party identification			0.218	(0.042)***	0.219	(0.042)***	0.229	(0.043)***
Family income			0.051	(0.025)*	0.057	(0.025)*	0.047	(0.025)#
Flanders					−0.294	(0.120)*		
Party-fixed effects			Omitted		Omitted		Included	
μ_1	1.722	(0.423)***	2.024	(0.482)***	1.815	(0.483)***	2.000	(0.529)***
μ_2	2.259	(0.423)***	2.620	(0.484)***	2.412	(0.485)***	2.607	(0.531)***
μ_3	2.874	(0.425)***	3.295	(0.486)***	3.090	(0.487)***	3.293	(0.533)***
N	1,483		1,483		1,483		1,483	
Wald χ^2 (df)	52.62	(1)***	151.65	(8)***	163.63	(9)***	183.05	(21)***

Note: Entries are the parameter estimates and robust standard errors (s.e.) (in parentheses) of ordered logistic regression models as well as the models' Wald test. The dependent variable is the 4-point scale measuring respondents' willingness to participate in elections.

#p≤0.1; *p≤0.05; **p≤0.01; ***p≤0.001, using two-tailed t-values.

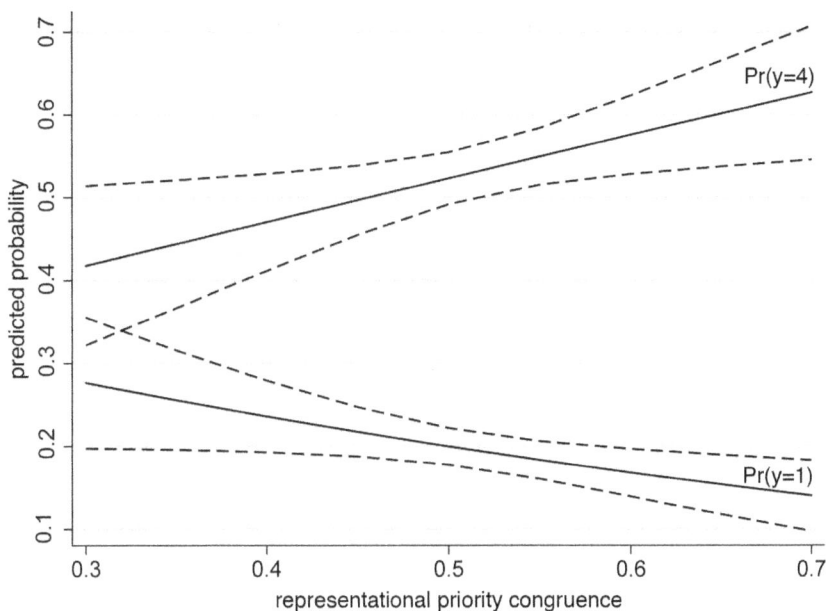

Figure 3.3.   Predicted probability of voters' willingness to participate in elections

Note: The predicted probabilities are based on Model 3 in table 3.5. The dashed lines indicate the 95 per cent confidence intervals. All other variables included in the models are held constant at their mean values.

Figure 3.3 illustrates the magnitude of the effect. It plots the predicted probabilities for those who would always vote – Pr($y = 4$) – and those who would never vote – Pr($y = 1$) – for a meaningful range of values of priority congruence. When priority congruence is minimal, the two groups can hardly be separated. But as congruence increases, the probability that an individual would withdraw from participating in elections altogether decreases fast. In fact, the probability decreases by 14 percentage points, from 0.28 to 0.14. By contrast, as congruence increases, the probability to always vote grows by 21 percentage points, from 0.42 to 0.63. That is, when citizen and elites' priorities closely match and congruence is maximal, those who would always vote outnumber those who would never vote 3:1. Taken together, these results handsomely confirm our theoretical expectations and point to the importance of our findings.

CONCLUSION

Our findings point to a profound mismatch in Belgium between citizens' and elites' views on what constitutes the job of an elected representative. While

the greater number of citizens want someone who focuses on being responsive to the needs of the local area, most politicians put more emphasis on
being policy specialists in the context of partisan representation. In addition,
priority congruence is particularly low among political non-sophisticates,
non-partisans and the least wealthy. This mismatch in priorities only adds to
the general observation that these disadvantaged groups are less likely to have
their opinions heard by policymakers (Bartels 2008).

Is the gap we observe evidence of a democratic deficit? Three arguments
may be offered as to why it should be taken in stride. First, citizen-elite differences may be inherent to the process of delegation. Certainly, there is an
important element of self-selection involved: relative to ordinary citizens,
politicians are more knowledgeable, more partisan and more affluent – all
traits, our findings suggest, that likely make them more policy-oriented
to begin with. Second, citizens' views may be egocentric, clamouring for
greater responsiveness to their own benefit even to the detriment of the
common good. Third, citizens may simply take for granted the components
of responsiveness that are typically provided by the particular institutional
context they live in and overstate in the survey setting their support for
those components that are not. If so, the ensuing gap would hardly amount
to a democratic deficit and citizens' preferences could be easily discarded as
either undesirable or impossible to meet.

The regional differences we observed between Flanders and Wallonia certainly raise intriguing questions regarding the impact of context. Ultimately,
future research will have to inquire into the variation of public preferences
across a wider range of institutional contexts. What little evidence there is
tentatively suggests that citizens' expectations vary across countries, and
even regions, arguing against the gap being either entirely inherent to the process of delegation or completely due to the public's egocentrism. Longitudinal designs may be used to further explore citizens' support for particularism
in times of economic growth and times of austerity. Yet, clearly, the dearth of
national election studies that question citizens in any detail on their views vis-
à-vis representation has hampered our understanding of this important topic.
Not only is it important to have a better grasp of where congruence is high
and where it is low, but it is also necessary to expand the scope of research
if we are to understand how contextual and individual-level determinants
interact in shaping representational congruence.

Whatever its origins, finally, we find that priority incongruence by itself
begets political disengagement. The wider the citizen-elite mismatch, we
find, the more the external efficacy suffers and the less likely the citizens
will turn out and vote on Election Day. As such priority incongruence has the
ability to deepen and perpetuate political inequalities, causing those already
disadvantaged to further withdraw from politics. While there is a growing

interest in institutional engineering as a means to bring elected representatives more in line with the public (see Norris 2004), such efforts will not be able to escape the normative question as to the propriety of the public's preferences. Is it advisable to engineer a legislature composed entirely of constituency members in an effort to restore political trust? Or will doing so merely create a public backlash against excessive particularism and poor public-service provision (Shugart 2001)? At least in Belgium, ever since the 1990s public debate about a New Political Culture, our findings suggest that the public continues to be deeply divided and ambiguous about the question (see also André et al. 2013).

REFERENCES

Allen, N. and Birch, S. (2015) 'Process Preferences and British Public Opinion: Citizens' Judgements about Government in an Era of Anti-Politics', *Political Studies*, 63(2): 390–411.

Andeweg, R. B. (1997) 'Role Specialisation or Role Switching? Dutch MPs between Electorate and Executive', *Journal of Legislative Studies*, 3(1): 110–27.

———. (2014) 'Roles in Legislatures', in S. Martin, T. Saalfeld and K. Strøm (eds) *The Oxford Handbook of Legislative Studies*, Oxford: Oxford University Press, 267–85.

Andeweg, R. B. and Thomassen, J. J. A. (2005) 'Modes of Political Representation: Toward a New Typology', *Legislative Studies Quarterly*, 30(4): 507–28.

André, A. and Depauw, S. (2017) 'The Quality of Representation and Satisfaction with Democracy: The Consequences of Citizen-Elite Policy and Process Congruence', *Political Behavior*, 39(2): 377–97. doi:10.1007/s11109–016–9360-x.

André, A., Depauw, S. and Martin, S. (2015) 'Electoral Systems and Legislators' Constituency Effort: The Mediating Effect of Electoral Vulnerability', *Comparative Political Studies*, 48(4): 464–96.

André, A., Depauw, S. and Sandri, G. (2013) 'Belgian Affairs and Constituent Preferences for "good Constituency Members"', *Acta Politica*, 48(2): 167–91.

Bartels, L. M. (2008) *Unequal Democracy: The Political Economy of the New Gilded Age*, New York: Russell Sage Foundation.

Bengtsson, Å. and Wass, H. (2011) 'The Representative Roles of MPs: A Citizen Perspective', *Scandinavian Political Studies*, 34(2): 143–67.

Bernauer, J., Giger, N. and Rosset, J. (2015) 'Mind the Gap: Do Proportional Electoral Systems Foster a More Equal Representation of Women and Men, Poor and Rich?' *International Political Science Review*, 36(1): 78–98.

Blais, A. (2006) 'What Affects Voter Turnout?' *Annual Review of Political Science*, 9(1): 111–25.

Bowler, S. (2017) 'Trustees, Delegates, and Responsiveness in Comparative Perspective', *Comparative Political Studies*, 50(6): 766–93. doi:10.1177/0010414015626447.

Campbell, R. and Cowley, P. (2014) 'What Voters Want: Reactions to Candidate Characteristics in a Survey Experiment', *Political Studies*, 62(4): 745–65.

Carman, C. J. (2006) 'Public Preferences for Parliamentary Representation in the UK: An Overlooked Link?' *Political Studies*, 54(1): 103–22.

———. (2007) 'Assessing Preferences for Political Representation in the US', *Journal of Elections, Public Opinion & Parties*, 17(1): 1–19.

Converse, P. E. and Pierce, R. (1986) *Political Representation in France*, Cambridge, MA: Harvard University Press.

Dalton, R. J. (2004) *Democratic Challenges, Democratic Choices: The Erosion of Political Support in Advanced Industrial Democracies*, Oxford: Oxford University Press.

Delli Carpini, M. and Keeter, S. (1996) *What Americans Know about Politics and Why It Matters*, New Haven, CT: Yale University Press.

Doherty, D. (2013) 'To Whom Do People Think Representatives Should Respond: Their District or the Country?' *Public Opinion Quarterly*, 77(1): 237–55.

Dolný, B. and Baboš, P. (2015) 'Voter – Representative Congruence in Europe: A Loss of Institutional Influence?' *West European Politics*, 38(6): 1274–304.

Dudzińska, A., Poyet, C., Costa, O. and Weßels, B. (2014) 'Representational Roles', in K. Deschouwer and S. Depauw (eds) *Representing the People*, Oxford: Oxford University Press, 19–38.

Ellickson, M. C. and Whistler, D. E. (2001) 'Explaining State Legislators' Casework and Public Resource Allocations', *Political Research Quarterly*, 54(3): 553–69.

Esaiasson, P. and Holmberg, S. (1996) *Representation from above: Members of Parliament and Representative Democracy in Sweden*, Ashgate: Dartmouth.

Eulau, H. and Karps, P. D. (1977) 'The Puzzle of Representation: Specifying Components of Responsiveness', *Legislative Studies Quarterly*, 2(3): 233–54.

Gilens, M. (2005) 'Inequality and Democratic Responsiveness', *Public Opinion Quarterly*, 69(5): 778–96.

———. (2012) *Affluence and Influence: Economic Inequality and Political Power in America*, Princeton, NJ: Princeton University Press.

Golder, M. and Stramski, J. (2010) 'Ideological Congruence and Electoral Institutions', *American Journal of Political Science*, 54(1): 90–106.

Griffin, J. D. and Flavin, P. (2011) 'How Citizens and Their Legislators Prioritize Spheres of Representation', *Political Research Quarterly*, 64(3): 520–33.

Harden, J. J. (2013) 'Multidimensional Responsiveness: The Determinants of Legislators' Representational Priorities', *Legislative Studies Quarterly*, 38(2): 155–84.

Hibbing, J. R. and Theiss-Morse, E. (2001) 'Process Preferences and American Politics: What the People Want Government to Be', *American Political Science Review*, 95(1): 145–53.

Hill, K. Q. and Hinton-Anderson, A. (1995) 'Pathways of Representation: A Causal Analysis of Public Opinion-Policy Linkages', *American Journal of Political Science*, 39(4): 924–35.

Hooghe, M., Marien, S. and Pauwels, T. (2011) 'Where Do Distrusting Voters Turn If There Is No Viable Exit or Voice Option? The Impact of Political Trust on Electoral Behaviour in the Belgian Regional Elections of June 2009', *Government and Opposition*, 46(2): 245–73.

Jewitt, C. E. and Goren, P. (2016) 'Ideological Structure and Consistency in the Age of Polarization', *American Politics Research*, 44(1): 81–105.

Johannes, J. R. (1980) 'The Distribution of Casework in the U. S. Congress: An Uneven Burden', *Legislative Studies Quarterly*, 5(4): 517–44.

Kam, C. J. (2009) *Party Discipline and Parliamentary Politics*, Cambridge: Cambridge University Press.

Kimball, D. C. and Patterson, S. C. (1997) 'Living Up to Expectations: Public Attitudes toward Congress', *The Journal of Politics*, 59(3): 701–28.

Lapinski, J., Levendusky, M., Winneg, K. and Jamieson, K. H. (2016) 'What Do Citizens Want from Their Member of Congress?' *Political Research Quarterly*, 69(3): 535–45.

Lau, R. R., Patel, P., Fahmy, D. F. and Kaufman, R. R. (2014) 'Correct Voting across Thirty-Three Democracies: A Preliminary Analysis', *British Journal of Political Science*, 44(2): 239–59.

Mansbridge, J. (2003) 'Rethinking Representation', *American Political Science Review*, 97(4): 515–28.

Méndez-Lago, M. and Martínez, A. (2002) 'Political Representation in Spain: An Empirical Analysis of the Perception of Citizens and MPs', *The Journal of Legislative Studies*, 8(1): 63–90.

Miller, W. E., Pierce, R., Thomassen, J., Herrera, R., Holmberg, S., Esaiasson, P. and Webels, W. (2000) *Policy Representation in Western Democracies*, Oxford: Oxford University Press.

Norris, P. (1997) 'The Puzzle of Constituency Service', *The Journal of Legislative Studies*, 3(2): 29–49.

———. (2004) *Electoral Engineering: Voting Rules and Political Behavior*, Cambridge: Cambridge University Press.

Önnudóttir, E.H. (2016) 'Political Parties and Styles of Representation', *Party Politics*, 22(6): 732–45.

Packenham, R. (1970) 'Legislatures and Political Development', in A. Komberg and L. D. Musolf (eds) *Legislatures in Developmental Perspective*, Durham, NC: Duke University Press, 521–82.

Powell, G.B. (2000) *Elections as Instruments of Democracy: Majoritarian and Proportional Visions*, New Haven, CT: Yale University Press.

Reher, S. (2015) 'Explaining Cross-National Variation in the Relationship between Priority Congruence and Satisfaction with Democracy', *European Journal of Political Research*, 54(1): 160–81.

———. (2016) 'The Effects of Congruence in Policy Priorities on Satisfaction with Democracy', *Journal of Elections, Public Opinion and Parties*, 26(1): 40–57.

Rohrschneider, R. and Whitefield, S. (2012) 'Institutional Context and Representational Strain in Party – Voter Agreement in Western and Eastern Europe', *West European Politics*, 35(6): 1320–40.

Schlozman, K. L., Verba, S. and Brady, H. E. (2013) *The Unheavenly Chorus: Unequal Political Voice and the Broken Promise of American Democracy*, Princeton, NJ: Princeton University Press.

Scully, R. and Farrell, D. M. (2003) 'MEPs as Representatives: Individual and Institutional Roles', *Journal of Common Market Studies*, 41(2): 269–88.

Searing, D. (1994) *Westminster's World: Understanding Political Roles*, Cambridge, MA: Harvard University Press.

Shugart, M. S. (2001) 'Electoral "Efficiency" and the Move to Mixed-Member Systems', *Electoral Studies*, 20(2): 173–93.

Strøm, K. (1997) 'Rules, Reasons and Routines: Legislative Roles in Parliamentary Democracies', *Journal of Legislative Studies*, 3(1): 155–74.

Vivyan, N. and Wagner, M. (2016) 'House or Home? Constituent Preferences over Legislator Effort Allocation', *European Journal of Political Research*, 55(1): 81–99.

von Schoultz, Å. and Wass, H. (2016) 'Beating Issue Agreement: Congruence in the Representational Preferences of Candidates and Voters', *Parliamentary Affairs*, 69(1): 136–58.

Wahlke, J. C., Eulau, H., Buchanan, W. and Ferguson, L. C. (1962) *The Legislative System: Explorations in Legislative Behavior*, New York: Wiley.

Zaller, J. (1992) *The Nature and Origins of Mass Opinion*, Cambridge: Cambridge University Press.

Appendix

Operationalisation and summary statistics of the explanatory variables

Variable	Operationalisation	Summary statistics				
		N	min.	max.	mean	s.d.
Female	Coded '1' for women; '0' for men	1,483	0	1	0.49	0.50
Age	Measured in years	1,483	19	85	50.19	17.20
Education	Scale ranging from no education to university degree	1,483	0	5	2.89	1.24
Political knowledge	Number of correct answers on five political knowledge questions	1,483	0	5	2.25	1.38
Ideological extremity	Eleven-point left-right self-placement scale folded at its midpoint of 5 ranging from 0 'moderate' to 5 'extreme'	1,483	0	5	1.51	1.46
Party identification	Feeling of closeness to a party ranging from not at all close to very close	1,483	0	4	1.91	0.46
Family income	Eleven-category scale ranging from a net monthly family income of under €1,000 to over €6,000	1,483	0	10	4.40	2.53

Scale for political efficacy

The following nine items are part of the scale:
(1) In elections one party promises more than the other, but ultimately it makes little difference.
(2) There is no point in voting, political parties do whatever they want.
(3) If enough people like me would voice their opinion, politicians will take this into account.
(4) Elections are no longer appropriate to really influence public policy.
(5) Influencing politicians is useless because they are not able to do anything anyway.
(6) Political leaders are capable of lying to the people if this suits them.
(7) When a politician sticks to his or her ideals and principles, he or she will not get far in politics.
(8) I believe politicians are genuinely concerned about the well-being of the people.
(9) Almost all politicians are prepared to break their promises if they can achieve more power that way.
  Respondents scored each item between '1' totally agree and '5' totally disagree. Items (3) and (8) have been reversed to reflect the direction of the scale.

Chapter 4

What is a good democracy? Citizens' support for new modes of governing

Didier Caluwaerts, Benjamin Biard,
Vincent Jacquet and Min Reuchamps

From the beginning of the 1990s onwards, political analysts in all Western countries discovered the contours of a widespread crisis of democratic representation. The alleged decline of political trust and public participation, the increasing dissatisfaction with the functioning of democracy and the rise of electoral volatility pointed out that the gap between politicians and citizens had never been wider. This idea of a deep-rooted crisis of democratic legitimacy offered an excellent breeding ground for critical reflection on the role, shape and function of democracy in modern societies.

It is in this turbulent period that a quest for new ways of governing have arisen (Geissel and Newton 2012). Established conceptions of democracy were challenged, and innovative democratic disruptors – be it deliberative, direct or participatory modes of governing – entered the political marketplace. Even though each of these challengers claimed to be capable of generating political decisions that receive broad public support, even when there is strong disagreement on the aims and values a polity should promote, we know surprisingly little about the actual support among the citizenry for these new modes of governing.

In this chapter, we look at these profound democratic transformations from the perspective of citizens. More specifically, the research question of this chapter is: Who supports these new (deliberative and participatory) and old (representative, technocratic and business) models of democracy or modes of governing? And can these preferences be explained by differences in individuals' attitudes and resources?

We will answer these questions with the data of the *2014 PartiRep Voter Survey*. Belgium is a particularly interesting country to study citizens' preferences for different models of democracy for two reasons. On the one hand, Belgium, with its strong consociational characteristics, has been a very elitist type of democracy since the 1950s. Because of its deep ethno-linguistic divides, its democratic infrastructure is shaped on the two premises of prudent elites and deferent citizens (Lijphart 1968). In other words, it is a democracy in which the demos generally play second fiddle (Caluwaerts and Deschouwer 2014). On the other hand, Belgium has also witnessed a strong political debate on the state of democracy since the early 1990s, but no fundamental changes to the political system have been implemented, and Belgium's closed political system has hindered the implementation of democratic innovations (Caluwaerts and Reuchamps 2014; 2015). As such, it is interesting to study the preferences of Belgian citizens on new and old types of democracy.

Our findings suggest that citizens hold very complex preferences when it comes to democracy, and that these preferences are strongly related to levels of educational attainment and political trust.

CITIZENS AND DEMOCRACY

Western representative democracies are nowadays put under pressure. For three decades, political science analysts have continuously highlighted the growing distrust of citizens in standard institutions of representative democracy (Dalton 2004, 2005; Norris 1999; Rosanvallon 2006). In fact, actors at the heart of the representative mechanism – elected officials and political parties – enjoy increasingly lower trust from their constituents. In addition, a steadily increasing number of citizens does not identify with most political parties, which find it increasingly difficult when it comes to attracting supporters (Mair and van Biezen 2001; Wattenberg 2000). In short, if one believes these indicators, confidence in the players and the institutions of representative democracy is shrinking.

Given this situation, a series of theorists and activists have been promoting new ways of conducting politics. These alternatives are numerous and it would be misleading to gather behind a single and specific notion. However, the first set of alternatives clearly emphasises the need for more participatory institutions (Barber 1984; Pateman 2012). They revisit the republican ideal emphasising the importance of active citizenship of all members of the community. Other researchers suggest regaining democratic legitimacy through deliberative democracy (Chambers 2003; Cohen 1989; Elster 1998). Unlike the standard procedure in an election of aggregating individual preferences, deliberative democracy is considered a discursive process, that is an exchange of arguments and justifications in the process of shaping public policy (Manin 1985). Basically, policies should be based on decisions following the deliberations of all (or a diverse subset of) members of the community (Cohen 1989: 67). Both are essential here: the deliberative nature of interactions and decision-making methods, on the one hand, and the inclusion of all stakeholders in the decision, on the other.

In recent years, the theoretical ideal of deliberative democracy has been put into practice throughout the world (Fung 2006a, 2006b), with the most standardised procedures being deliberative polls (Fishkin 2009), participatory budgeting (Baiocchi 2005; Herzberg, Röcke and Sintomer 2005), planning groups (Garbe 1986), consensus conferences (Joss 1998) or more recently constitutional assemblies (Reuchamps and Suiter 2016). In each case, the aim is to allow a great diversity of citizens to meet, exchange views and give their opinion on a public problem, bring new problems to the agenda or even adopt binding decisions. The purpose of these initiatives varies greatly from one experiment to another, ranging from just informing the public to decision-making as well as communication and consultation (Arnstein 1969; Rowe and Frewer 2005).

Paralleling the rise of the deliberative model of democracy, we also witnessed a growing appeal for direct democratic mechanisms, which allow citizens to vote for one decision or another, or to put issues on the agenda via a popular initiative. The development of the Internet has also helped to establish mechanisms for citizens to have greater input in discussions on virtual platforms (e.g. Janssen and Kies 2005; Smith et al. 2009).

Because of this injection of innovations, contemporary democracies can be characterised by a process of hybridisation, where direct citizen participation and indirect processes of representation have to find new ways of productively coexisting. However, it is obvious that this process of hybridisation has mainly been implemented in a top-down manner by officials wishing to involve citizens in matters of public interest. Processes of hybridisation thus reflect more what elites desire of democracy, and how much power they are willing to transfer, than what citizens actually want from their democracy. This leads us thus to the question as to what kind of democratic models the citizens want.

Research in political science has brought forward some answers to this question. In the United States, the work of Hibbing and Theiss-Morse (2002) opened the discussion with the following provocative thesis: 'The last thing people want is to be more involved in political decision making: They do not want to make political decisions themselves; they do not want to provide much input to those assigned to make their decisions; and they would rather not know all the details of the decision-making process' (Hibbing and Theiss-Morse 2002: 1).

Through surveys and focus groups, the authors claim that citizens are in favour of a 'stealth democracy' – that is, that they want a democracy with mechanisms of minimal control that make elected officials accountable to the people but this should be a last resort when the rulers have lost the trust they once enjoyed. For these authors, the growing distrust of parties, politicians, parliaments and governments is mistakenly interpreted for a call for direct participation. Even though citizens did develop a strong distrust towards politicians, this should not be interpreted as a call for citizens to step in their place. Instead of the current situation where citizens believe elected officials act for their own agenda or under the influence of private lobbies, the ideal system would be to give power to more empathetic, less lazy people closer to the population and who act in the interest of the highest number (Hibbing and Theiss-Morse 2002). By creating an antagonistic view of society between the people and the elite, populist leaders propose to embody these 'ideal politicians' (Mudde 2007).

Hibbing's and Theiss-Morse's study encouraged the development of other research with often contradictory results. For instance, Neblo and his colleagues (2010) argue that a much larger share of the population wishes to deliberate than what is claimed by Hibbing and Theiss-Morse. However, this desire is conditional. After all, citizens want a genuine say in politics but are now reluctant to take part in deliberative experiences due to their distrust of politicians and the limited opportunities that are available to them.

Some European studies (Bengtsson and Mattila 2009; Bornand et al. 2017; Donovan and Jeffery 2006; Font, Wojcieszak and Navarro 2015; Webb 2013) also attempted to measure the levels of support for different models of democracy. Webb (2013) has shown that different democratic models are not considered mutually exclusive and that British citizens support different – often contradictory – models of democracy at the same time. He also shows that many people support the transfer of power to a range of different actors (experts, elected officials, business leaders). This might seem contradictory from the democratic theory perspective, but these diverse preferences make sense in a general climate of distrust towards traditional democratic institutions. These often contradictory results beg the question of what Belgian citizens' preferences for democratic models are, and whether they also hold complex views of different democratic models.

SUPPORT FOR VARIOUS MODELS OF DEMOCRACY

Inspired by previous work we constructed five indicators corresponding to five possible models of democracy with each one corresponding to a question asked to respondents in the voter survey.

1. Direct democracy: The government should seek the opinion of its population much more often.

2. Technocratic democracy: Important decisions should be left to experts.
3. Deliberative democracy: Male and female politicians must often make decisions based on discussions among citizens.
4. Representative democracy: Since politicians are the ones responsible, they have to make the decisions themselves.
5. 'Business' democracy: The government would work better if decisions were made by people who have succeeded in business.

For each question respondents were asked to position themselves on a 5-point Likert scale ranging from 'strongly disagree' to 'strongly agree'.

The appreciation for these five models of democracy is shown in table 4.1. Immediately, we notice strong support for more direct forms of democracy as 84.4 per cent of the population studied is in favour of this option. Citizens would widely welcome their opinion being taken more often into account by the government. Further, a majority – albeit slightly smaller – also agree with a technocracy with no less than 62.5 per cent of respondents believing that independent experts would be better able to make good decisions. The deliberative option, meanwhile, also seems to interest a large part of the Flemish and Walloon citizens. About 77.3 per cent of them would like politicians' decisions to be more strongly rooted in discussions held between citizens. This type of democracy aims, for instance, for the creation of citizen panels or organised areas that would give them the opportunity for discussion. However, the final decision would remain in the hands of political authorities. A small majority (52.7 per cent) supports representative democracy namely supporting the idea that decisions should be made by politicians given that they are effectively the ones responsible. Finally, only a minority supports a business model of democracy where businessmen make the decisions. This model studied by

Table 4.1. Opinion of the Walloon and Flemish population in relation to the five models of democracy

	Direct democracy	Technocratic democracy	Deliberative democracy	Representative democracy	Business democracy
Strongly agree	42.5	19.1	27.5	12.2	8.6
Agree	41.9	43.4	49.8	40.5	24.2
Neither agree nor disagree	8.9	22.0	14.5	23.6	36.4
Disagree	6.1	12.4	7.5	19.9	28.2
Strongly disagree	0.8	3.2	0.8	3.7	8.6
Total	100	100	100	100	100

Hibbing and Theiss-Morse, based on the idea that the strategic management of corporate managers could inspire policymaking processes, found little backing among the Flemish and the Walloons. In fact, only 32.8 per cent of the citizens surveyed support this proposal.

These results show that the highest support goes, in the first place, towards more participatory democracy and, second, to deliberative democracy. This might indicate a demand for more participatory types of democracy. However, it seems important to emphasise that our results do not mean that citizens would want to participate in citizen panels or participatory budgets when faced with concrete opportunities. It is not because a person wants more consultation with citizens that he or she will show enthusiasm towards concrete acts of political participation (McHugh 2006). After all, the survey measured the abstract attitude of individuals towards possible democratic orientations and not their actual willingness to actively participate.

DIFFERENT MODELS OF DEMOCRACY?

The first interpretation of the results seems to point out that citizens overwhelmingly support a diverse set of democratic models. This raises the question of whether the support for the different models of democracy is mutually exclusive. In other words, do citizens back several models at the same time or can groups clearly be distinguished? One answer to this question is given by an analysis of the correlation between the supports for different democratic models (table 4.2). This analysis offers the possibility to determine whether the backing of models is negatively or positively interconnected. Whereas some links may seem conceptually obvious – such as the fact that the more a person supports direct democracy, the more he or she will support a form of deliberative democracy – others are more unusual. For example, support for the business model is positively correlated with all other models. Additionally, no negative correlation was observed between the different models.

Table 4.2.   Spearman's correlations among the five democratic models

	Direct	Technocratic	Deliberative	Representative	Business
Direct	1	0.082***	0.531***	−0.016	0.141***
Technocratic	0.082***	1	0.039	0.162***	0.250***
Deliberative	.531***	0.039	1	0.028	0.075***
Representative	−0.016	0.162***	0.028	1	0.179***
Business	0.141***	0.250***	0.075***	0.179***	1

Note: ***. The correlation is significant at 0.001 (bilateral).

This leads to a multilayered approach to the support of the various models of democracy. While political science textbooks generally have different models based on distinct philosophical traditions (Held 2006), it is clear from the analysis of the correlations that this segmentation is not found in citizens' preferences. Citizens support different democratic models that can conceptually and theoretically appear as opposites. Therefore, it is not possible to clearly distinguish groups of citizens who would support only clear and precise type of democracy. Indeed, 69.1 per cent of the electorate studied supports at least three models of democracy and 36.9 per cent supports at least four models. This is not new in the literature on democratic preferences (Coffe and Michels 2014; Donovan and Jeffery 2006; Webb 2013), but previous studies have often studied this phenomenon in terms of inconsistency and contradiction. However, as shown by other authors democratic preferences can be understood in terms of dimensions that are potentially independent from each other (Font, Wojcieszak and Navarro 2015). A pluralistic view of the support for various modes of democracy must thus be developed by identifying trends and orientations present in society and not exclusive categories of democratic models of preferences (Jacquet and Reuchamps 2016). For example, one person may wish that citizens have more influence on the political system while emphasising the importance of making certain decisions based on the verdicts of experts.

HYPOTHESES

To explain which citizens hold which democratic preferences and why, we will look at the impact of individual-level resources and attitudes. Previous studies have shown that the most highly educated and privileged individuals in society are the ones who take part in politics, especially when the method of participation requires a significant investment of time and effort (Verba, Schlozman and Brady 1995). Moreover, research on changing values and attitudes of citizens (Dalton 2005; Inglehart and Catterberg 2002) shows that the most advantaged social groups are also the ones who are most critical of traditional political authorities and demand a more direct involvement of their part. This is the combined effect of cognitive mobilisation and change in post-materialist values described by Inglehart (1997), which explains the reason behind the support for this model. This first body of research allows the assumption that it is the most socially privileged who develop greater political interest and are more confident in their ability to act in the political arena. These individuals are more demanding of a more participatory democracy. The first hypothesis is therefore that support for more participatory types of democracy (direct and deliberative) will be higher among citizens with higher SES (socio-economic status).

A counterhypothesis, however, is that the desire for a more participatory governance is mainly the result of a feeling of discomfort towards the traditional political world and feelings of ineffectiveness of the mechanisms of a representative government. According to Neblo et al. (2010), the most deprived people are the ones who do not identify with traditional politicians and who are more likely to seek a direct participation of citizens. Support for a more participatory model is then the result of social exclusion. The most disadvantaged categories, critical of conventional modes of participation, tend to call for the use of a more direct model of participation. This second hypothesis suggests that support for more participatory types of democracy is higher among lower SES groups. There are thus two conflicting hypotheses about the relationship between education and citizens' preferences for democratic models (Coffé and Michels 2014). One assumes that the most privileged want more direct citizen participation; the other suggests that this is the case of the most vulnerable groups. This chapter should attempt to bring light on that question.

Regarding the support for more delegate-type models emphasising the importance that decisions are made by elites (representative, technocratic and business models), the literature provides fewer hypotheses. According to Hibbing and Theiss-Morse (2002), the motivation for participation comes from the most advantaged social categories, who are not interested in politics and does not want to take up a more active role in the political process. They prefer to delegate this authority. We can therefore put forward the hypothesis that the people least interested in politics, who are less confident in their personal capacity to intervene in politics and who have the most confidence in the elites are the ones who will support representative, technocratic and business models of democracy.

VARIABLES

To determine whether political resources and attitudes impact citizens' preferences for democratic models, we conducted multivariate analysis in the form of five binomial logistic regressions, one for each of the five models. We therefore dichotomised the initial Likert item scales into two values (0 = neutral, disagree or strongly disagree; 1 = agree or strongly agree). The independent variables are grouped into two large categories. First, the standard socio-demographic variables are included in our multivariate analysis: age, gender and level of education. We divided the latter into three categories (none or primary, secondary and higher education). We also integrated regions (Flanders and Wallonia, with a dummy variable) which in the context

of this book on the Belgian elections should let us determine whether there
are different political cultures in the north and south of the country.

Second, regarding the intermediate political attitudes, four variables should
be taken into account: political trust, political interest, internal political efficacy and external political efficacy. The level of political trust is measured
with the score of the only dimension emerging from a PCA of the responses
to the question, 'Can you on a scale from 0 to 10 assess your personal trust
in the following institutions: for political parties, politicians, the federal and
national government and the federal and regional government (Cronbach's
alpha = 0.917)?' Political interest is measured on a scale from 0 to 10 offered
to respondents with 10 meaning a very high political interest.

Internal political efficacy is measured by scoring in the first dimension of
the analysis of the main matches of the four scales related to the following
statements: 'I feel competent enough to participate in political life'; 'I think
I would do as good a job as most politicians we elect'; 'I think I'm better informed about politics and government than most other people' and 'I
think I understand the important issues facing our society well enough'. The
percentage of variance explained by the dimension is 50.820 (Cronbach's
alpha = 0.676). This allows us to determine whether the fact of considering
oneself competent to act in the political field, to understand the issues, influences the propensity to support a specific democratic model.

For the feeling of external political efficacy, we are using the score of the
first dimension of the analysis of main matches of the three scales related to
the following statements: 'An average citizen has a real influence on politics
and on the authorities' action'; 'Before elections, the parties promise a great
deal, but ultimately very few promises are carried out'; 'Going to vote is
meaningless, the parties do what they want anyway'. The percentage of variance explained by the dimension is 55.120 (Cronbach's alpha = 0.575). This
allows us to determine whether support for a democratic dimension is related
to the assessment of citizens of their influence in the representative political
system.

RESULTS

Who supports different types of democracy? The binomial logistic regression
analysis of which the results are presented in table 4.3 shows that there are
no real gender differences in the support of different models of democracy,
but that men do hold significantly more positive opinions about representative democracy. The age differences are also obvious. Generally, older generations are more supportive of elitist types of democracy in which power

Table 4.3. Binomial logistic regression predicting support for different models of democracy

	Direct democracy		Technocratic democracy		Deliberative democracy		Representative democracy		'Business' democracy	
	B (SE)	Sign.	B (SE)	Sign.	B (SE)	Sign.	B (SE)	Sign.	B (SE)	Sign.
Gender (ref.= woman)	-0.258 (0.140)	0.064	0.125 (0.098)	0.216	0.021 (0.121)	0.859	0.253 (0.101)	0.012	-0.067 (0.107)	0.531
Age	-0.012 (0.004)	0.004	0.015 (0.003)	0.000	0.002 (0.004)	0.524	0.026 (0.003)	0.000	0.015 (0.003)	0.000
Education (ref.= higher)										
Primary	0.865 (0.182)	0.000	-0.049 (0.135)	0.718	0.507 (0.160)	0.002	0.405 (0.135)	0.003	0.600 (0.145)	0.000
Secondary	0.712 (0.158)	0.000	-0.088 (0.121)	0.469	0.432 (0.139)	0.002	0.145 (0.122)	0.232	0.345 (0.135)	0.010
Region (ref.= Flanders)	0.199 (0.133)	0.136	-0.303 (0.098)	0.002	1.192 (0.122)	0.000	-0.517 (0.098)	0.000	-0.468 (0.104)	0.000
Political interest	-0.068 (0.032)	0.031	-0.044 (0.022)	0.043	0.015 (0.026)	0.570	0.036 (0.022)	0.098	-0.031 (0.022)	0.169
Political trust	-0.014 (0.006)	0.018	0.016 (0.004)	0.000	-0.005 (0.005)	0.280	0.016 (0.004)	0.000	0.002 (0.004)	0.566
Internal political efficacy	0.051 (0.040)	0.205	-0.015 (0.029)	0.600	-0.026 (0.035)	0.452	0.003 (0.029)	0.907	0.139 (0.031)	0.000
External political efficacy	-0.206 (0.036)	0.000	-0.079 (0.026)	0.003	-0.088 (0.031)	0.004	0.024 (0.026)	0.350	-0.141 (0.028)	0.000
Nagelkerke R^2	0.137		0.046		0.123		0.118		0.097	

is delegated to representatives, business owners and technocratic experts. Younger generations, however, who are generally assumed to hold more post-materialist value orientations (Inglehart 1997), are more supportive of directly involving citizens in politics. In addition, we do see strong regional differences in preferences for democratic models among the respondents. Flemings are much more in favour of indirect, elitist types of democracy, whereas recent innovations such as deliberative democracy are much more strongly supported by Walloons. This lends some support to the thesis that there exist different democratic cultures and preferences in the two regions (Abts, Swyngedouw and Jacobs 2012). Educational differences are also very clear from the results. Even though there are no educational differences in support for the technocratic model of democracy, we do find that the lower educated have a higher tendency to support all other types of democracy. The level of education seems here to be negatively correlated with support for direct, deliberative, representative and business types of democracy. These results refute the first hypothesis that support for more participatory types of democracy (direct and deliberative) will be higher among citizens with higher SES. Our findings indicate that the higher educated are generally more critical of all democratic models and are more aware of the limitations of different democratic processes, be they more participatory or more elitist.

Regarding the effects of political attitudes, the feeling of external political effectiveness is negatively correlated with support for almost every model. The more respondents argue that the current representative model gives citizens the opportunity to influence politics, the less they support alternatives to the representative model of democracy. Political trust also yields interesting results. Those respondents with higher levels of trust in the current political actors and institutions are generally more supportive of representative and technocratic models of democracy, whereas lower levels of political trust lead to a higher support of direct citizen involvement in politics. Those who are more distrustful of the current political elites are more in favour of direct democracy in which the decision-making powers of elites are bypassed in favour of more direct political engagement. Satisfaction thus breeds support, whereas dissatisfaction incentivises citizens to look for alternatives and roll up their sleeves. And finally, political interest has only a limited effect. Those who are more politically interested tend to be less supportive of technocratic and direct types of democracy.

Even though these are interesting results, we should be cautious when generalising the results. After all, the questionnaire assesses the support for different models of democracy, but this does not imply that these people, if faced with the actual opportunity to take part in a vote or discussion would actually get involved. We should thus be wary of overstretching the implications of our findings.

CONCLUSION

Our results lead to different conclusions. First, they suggest that it is useful not just to study democracy as a container concept but to also distinguish between different models of democracy. Such a multidimensional view allows us to more clearly study the social and attitudinal basis of the support for different democratic processes. Second, in terms of resources, one of the most important findings is that respondents with low levels of education attainment are generally more positive of all types of democracy than those who have completed higher education, even though the differences are not that great with regard to representative democracy. This might suggest two conclusions. On the one hand, the higher educated are generally more critical of the different democratic models than the lower educated. They might be more aware of the limitations of each model. On the other hand, the much stronger support for direct, deliberative and business democracy among the lower educated indicates that the most disadvantaged social categories tend to desire a change of democratic model, regardless of its form. This supports Webb's hypothesis (2013), according to which this type of question is more of a rejection – which he calls populist – of the current situation than the specific desire of another political model. Third, one of the interesting findings of our analysis is the existence of regional differences in democratic preferences. Flanders seems to favour more elitist types of democracy, whereas deliberative democracy finds strong support in Wallonia. Finally, in terms of political attitudes, external political efficacy, political trust and political interest are all strong indicators of citizens' preferences for democratic models. Those who trust the current political elites and institutions are likely to support them and are likely to have doubts about more participatory alternatives. And those who think the current political system allows them to make a difference are less likely to support alternatives to representative democracy.

REFERENCES

Abts, K., Swyngedouw, M. and Jacobs, D. (2012) 'Intérêt pour la politique et méfiance envers les institutions. La spirale de la méfiance enrayée', in L. Voyé, K. Dobbelaere and K. Abts (eds) *Autre temps, autres moeurs*, Bruxelles: Racine Campus, 173–214.

Arnstein, S. (1969) 'A Ladder of Citizen Participation', *Journal of the American Institute of Planners*, 35(4): 216–24.

Baiocchi, G. (2005) *Militants and Citizens: The Politics of Participatory Democracy in Porto Alegre*, Princeton, NJ: Princeton University Press.

Barber, B. (1984) *Strong Democracy: Participatory Politics for a New Age*, Berkeley: University of California Press.

Bengtsson, Å. and Mattila, M. (2009) 'Direct Democracy and Its Critics: Support for Direct Democracy and "Stealth" Democracy in Finland', *West European Politics*, 32(5): 1031–48.

Bornand, T., Biard, B., Baudewyns, P. and Reuchamps, M. (2017) 'Satisfaits de la démocratie? Une analyse du soutien démocratique à partir de la comparaison de deux méthodes de classification des citoyens', *Canadian Journal of Political Science*, 50(3): 795–822.

Caluwaerts, D. and Deschouwer, K. (2014) 'Building Bridges across Political Divides: Experiments on Deliberative Democracy in Deeply Divided Belgium', *European Political Science Review*, 6(3): 427–50.

Caluwaerts, D. and Reuchamps, M. (2014) 'Deliberative Stress in Deeply Divided Belgium', in J. E. Ugarriza and D. Caluwaerts (eds) *Democratic Deliberation in Deeply Divided Societies from Conflict to Common Ground*, Basingstoke: Palgrave, 35–52.

Caluwaerts, D. and Reuchamps, M. (2015) 'Strengthening Democracy through Bottom-Up Deliberation: An Assessment of the Internal Legitimacy of the G1000 Project', *Acta Politica*, 50(2): 151–70.

Chambers, S. (2003) 'Deliberative Democratic Theory', *Annual Review of Political Science*, 6(1): 307–26.

Coffé, H. and Michels, A. (2014) 'Education and Support for Representative, Direct and Stealth Democracy', *Electoral Studies*, 35: 1–11.

Cohen, J. (1989) 'Deliberation and Democratic Legitimacy', in A. Hamlin and P. Petit (eds) *The Good Polity*, Oxford: Blackwell, 17–34.

Dalton, R. J. (2004) *Democratic Challenges, Democratic Choices. The Erosion of Political Support in Advanced Industrial Democracies*, New York: Oxford University Press.

Dalton, R. J. (2005) 'The Social Transformation of Trust in Government', *International Review of Sociology*, 15(1): 133–54.

Donovan, T. and Jeffery, B. (2006) 'Popular Support for Direct Democracy', *Party Politics*, 12(5): 671–88.

Elster, J. (ed.) (1998) *Deliberative Democracy*, Cambridge: Cambridge University Press.

Fishkin, J. S. (2009) *When the People Speak. Deliberative Democracy & Public Consultation*, Oxford: Oxford University Press.

Font, J., Wojcieszak, M. and Navarro, C. J. (2015) 'Participation, Representation and Expertise: Citizen Preferences for Political Decision-Making Processes', *Political Studies*, 63(S1): 153–72.

Fung, A. (2006a) 'Democratizing the Policy Process', in M. Moran, M. Rein and R. E. Goodin (eds) *The Oxford Handbook of Public Policy*, Oxford: Oxford University Press, 669–85.

Fung, A. (2006b) 'Varieties of Participation in Complex Governance', *Public Administration Review*, 66(S1): 66–75.

Garbe, D. (1986) 'Planning Cell and Citizen Report: A Report on German experiences with New Participation Instruments', *European Journal of Political Research*, 14(1–2): 221–36.

Geissel, B. and Newton, K. (eds) (2012) *Evaluating Democratic Innovations: Curring the Democratic Malaise?* New York: Routledge.

Held, D. (2006) *Models of Democracy*, Stanford: Stanford University Press.

Herzberg, C., Röcke, A. and Sintomer, Y. (2005) *Participatory Budgets in a European Comparative Approach. Perspectives and Chances of the Cooperative State at the Municipal Level in Germany and Europe*, Berlin: Centre Marc Bloch/ Hans-Böckler-Stiftung/Humboldt-Universität.

Hibbing, J. R. and Theiss-Morse, E. (2002) *Stealth Democracy: Americans' Beliefs about How Government Should Work*, Cambridge: Cambridge University Press.

Inglehart, R. (1997) *Modernization and Postmodernization: Cultural, Economic, and Political Change in 43 Societies*, Cambridge: Cambridge University Press.

Inglehart, R. and Catterberg, G. (2002) 'Trends in Political Action: The Developmental Trend and the Post-Honeymoon Decline', *International Journal of Comparative Sociology*, 43(3–5): 300–316.

Jacquet, V. and Reuchamps, M. (2016) 'Who Wants to Pay for Deliberative Democracy? The Crowdfunders of the G1000 in Belgium', *European Political Science Review*, online first: https://doi.org/10.1017/S1755773916000163.

Janssen, D. and Kies, R. (2005) 'Online Forums and Deliberative Democracy', *Acta Politica*, 40(3): 317–35.

Joss, S. (1998) 'Danish Consensus Conferences as a Model of Participatory Technology Assessment: An Impact Study of Consensus Conferences on Danish Parliament and Danish Public Debate', *Science and Public Policy*, 25(1): 2–22.

Lijphart, A. (1968) 'Typologies of Democratic Systems', *Comparative Political Studies*, 1(1): 3–44.

Mair, P. and van Biezen, I. (2001) 'Party Membership in Twenty European Democracies, 1980–2000', *Party Politics*, 7(1): 5–21.

Manin, B. (1985) 'Volonté générale ou délibération? Esquisse d'une théorie de la délibération politique', *Le Débat*, 33(1): 72–94.

McHugh, D. (2006) 'Wanting to Be Heard But Not Wanting to Act? Addressing Political Disengagement', *Parliamentary Affairs*, 59(3): 546–52.

Mudde, C. (2007) *Populist Radical Right Parties in Europe*, Cambridge: Cambridge University Press.

Neblo, M. A., Esterling, K. M., Kennedy, R. P., Lazer, D. M. J. and Sokhey, A. E. (2010) 'Who Wants to Deliberate – and Why?' *American Political Science Review*, 104(03): 566–83.

Norris, P. (1999) 'Intoduction: The Growth of Critical Citizens', in P. Norris (ed.) *Critical Citizens: Global Support for Democratic Government*, Oxford: Oxford University Press, 1–27.

Pateman, C. (2012) 'Participatory Democracy Revisited', *Perspectives on Politics*, 10(1): 7–19.

Reuchamps, M. and Suiter, J. (eds) (2016), *Constitutional Deliberative Democracy in Europe*, Colchester: ECPR Press.

Rosanvallon, P. (2006) *La contre-démocratie. La politique à l'âge de la défiance*, Paris: Seuil.

Rowe, G. and Frewer, L. J. (2005) 'A Typology of Public Engagement Mechanisms', *Science, Technology & Human Values*, 30(2): 251–90.

Smith, G., John, P., Sturgis, P. and Nomura, H. (2009) 'Deliberation and Internet Engagement: Initial Findings from a Randomised Controlled Trial Evaluating the Impact of Facilitated Internet Forums', *5th ECPR General Conference*, Potsdam, Germany.

Verba, S., Schlozman, K. L. and Brady, H. E. (1995) *Voice and Equality: Civic Voluntarism in American Politics*, Cambridge, MA: Harvard University Press.

Wattenberg, M. P. (2000) 'The Decline of Party Mobilization', in M. P. Wattenberg and R. J. Dalton (eds) *Parties without Partisans: Political Change in Advanced Industrial Democracies*, Oxford: Oxford University Press, 64–78.

Webb, P. (2013) 'Who Is Willing to Participate? Dissatisfied Democrats, Stealth Democrats and Populists in the United Kingdom', *European Journal of Political Research*, 52(6): 747–72.

Chapter 5

Party families in a split party system

Kris Deschouwer, Jean-Benoit Pilet and Emilie van Haute

INTRODUCTION

One of the very peculiar characteristics of the Belgian political system is the absence of statewide parties. All parties that are represented in parliament – except for the small radical left Labour Party – limit their electoral mobilisation to one of Belgium's two main language groups. They field candidates in either the north or the south and only compete together in the Brussels constituency. There are therefore two sets of parties and two different party systems.

This absence of statewide parties is often evoked as causing problems for the quality of democratic governance (Pilet, De Waele and Jaumain 2009). First, such configuration is thought to prevent parties from contributing to national public opinion building, a traditional function of political parties (Sartori 2016). With separate electoral campaigns, separate media and separate debates, there is little room for a confrontation and presentation of alternative projects to the entire electorate. Parties tend to speak to only a part of the electorate, and thereby contribute to building distinct subnational public opinions. No one speaks for the centre (Deschouwer 2012). Second, the absence of national parties generates a lack of coordination across levels. For instance, Jans (2001) showed that the absence of national party actors in Belgium reduces the capacity of building compromises and agreements at the national level. Parties of the two main language groups are facing different public opinions and experience different pressures, which makes it difficult for them to agree on common policies. Representation and accountability are limited to each separate language group. Third, party organisations are agents of socialisation for their own political personnel. In the absence of national parties, the political personnel is socialised at the subnational level. Since the split of the party system, new generations of politicians can have a political career fully in their own community and in their own language without being socialised at the national level (Hooghe 2012). This awareness of a deficit in the democratic governance as a result of the absence of statewide parties is, for some, a good reason to defend a further or even final separation of the two communities. For others it has triggered a search for alternative devices that might create a minimal level of statewide representation and accountability, like the election of a number of federal MPs in a statewide district (Sinardet 2012; Deschouwer and Van Parijs 2013). Yet, for the time being, the country functions with a fully split party system.

The deficits in the democratic electoral representation in Belgium are actually not that different from those at the European level. Here too there are no political parties that appeal to the European public at large. Elections for the federal parliament in Belgium involve subnational parties that compete for seats in their community, like the elections for the European Parliament, which are basically national elections involving national parties that compete for national seats. At the European level an attempt was made in 2014 to 'Europeanise' the campaign with the introduction of *Spitzenkandidaten* by the major European parties, that is, their candidate for Commission president, albeit with limited effects (Hobolt 2014). National parties of the same family were still competing for the votes inside their own country only.

A crucial question is indeed to what extent political representation can work in a multinational and multilingual demos when the dialogue between parties and voters takes place at the national (in the EU) or subnational level (in Belgium). Mair and Thomassen (2010) argue that representation might function properly and better than assumed on the condition that the different national parties who subsequently collaborate in the same group in the European Parliament mobilise the same interests, identities and demands. The political representation might still function in an acceptable way and might produce sufficient congruence between voters and MPs if the national parties truly belong to the same party family. That is a question that is also quite relevant for Belgium. Do the Belgian parties of the two language groups really belong to the same party family?

ELECTORAL TRENDS

Looking at the way in which the partisan representation functions in Belgium, one can expect a negative answer to that question. Unlike the members of the European Parliament the members of the Belgian federal parliament do not form groups per party family. Only the two green parties form one single group, while there are two unilingual liberal, two socialist and two Christian democratic groups, each composed of the MPs of one party only. The two 'sister' or 'brother' parties in Belgium are furthermore not going through a process of coming together. On the contrary, they used to be one party and they fell apart because they deeply disagreed on the institutional future of the country. That institutional issue does remain salient in Belgian politics, which means that parties with the same ideological label do sometimes strongly oppose each other. The parties of the same family also face a different electorate, which means that their relations are far from symmetrical. Wallonia leans traditionally more to the left, with a strong socialist party. In Flanders the socialist party is fairly small, while Christian democrats have traditionally been strong. Internal tensions within the formerly national unitary parties were therefore not only institutional but also to some extent ideological (Delwit 2012).

Figure 5.1 displays the electoral evolution of the parties of the same family since 1978. These evolutions are quite similar in each of the families. Christian democrats have gradually lost voters in both language groups, while the liberals have gradually grown during the past few decades. The trend for the socialists is slightly downwards, but especially so in Flanders. And the greens have grown together, but then appear to start moving in different directions. The direction in which voters move per election is actually an interesting indicator of the common fate of the parties of a same family. Electoral politics

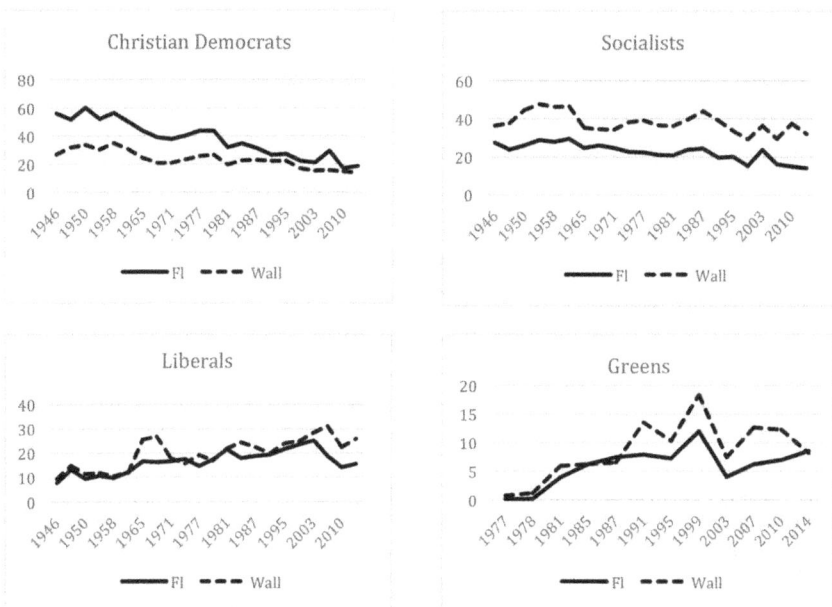

Figure 5.1. The electoral evolution (federal parliament) for four party families. Source: http://cevipol.ulb.be.

have in general become more nationalised (Caramani 2004), which means that voters all over the territory react to messages that come from one national centre. In the Belgian case, the voters of the same family regularly smove in different directions – that could be a confirmation of the fact that two different public opinions have developed, each responding in their own way to the message sent out by the parties.

The figures in table 5.1 show the electoral swings for each of the parties per family at the federal elections since 1981, that is comparing the result at one election with the result of the previous one. This produces an index that is larger than one in case of electoral progress and lower than one in case of losses. Overall, these swings are the same for the parties in the north and in the south: they move together up or down. And when there is a difference in the direction of the movement, the difference is rather small. Yet, when focussing on the most recent elections, it is very clear that this pattern has been changing. For each of the couples we see different movements in the elections of 2007, 2010 or 2014, and we also see larger gaps between the indices in the most recent elections. This phenomenon most probably reflects

Table 5.1. Electoral swings of parties of the same party family (1949–2014)

	Christian democrats			Socialists			Liberals			Greens		
	Fl	*Wall*	*Diff*	*Fl*	*Wall*	*Diff*	*Fl*	*Wall*	*Diff*	*Fl*	*Wall*	*Diff*
1949	0.92	1.18	0.26	0.86	1.04	0.18	1.70	1.58	0.12			
1950	1.16	1.06	0.10	1.10	1.18	0.08	0.72	0.78	0.06			
1954	0.86	0.90	0.04	1.11	1.07	0.04	1.14	1.03	0.11			
1958	1.09	1.15	0.06	0.97	0.97	0.00	0.92	0.89	0.03			
1961	0.89	0.88	0.01	1.06	1.00	0.06	1.23	1.13	0.10			
1965	0.87	0.80	0.07	0.83	0.76	0.07	1.37	2.15	0.78			
1968	0.89	0.85	0.04	1.06	0.98	0.08	0.98	1.05	0.08			
1971	0.97	1.00	0.03	0.95	1.00	0.05	1.02	0.66	0.36			
1974	1.07	1.11	0.04	0.92	1.11	0.19	1.06	0.88	0.18			
1977	1.08	1.10	0.01	0.99	1.02	0.03	0.83	1.22	0.40			
1978	1.00	1.05	0.05	0.94	0.94	0.00	1.19	0.88	0.31	2.00	1.71	0.29
1981	0.73	0.73	0.01	0.98	0.99	0.01	1.23	1.30	0.07	19.50	4.92	14.58
1985	1.08	1.15	0.07	1.15	1.09	0.06	0.83	1.11	0.28	1.59	1.05	0.54
1987	0.90	1.03	0.12	1.02	1.11	0.09	1.06	0.92	0.14	1.19	1.05	0.15
1991	0.86	0.97	0.11	0.80	0.89	0.09	1.03	0.89	0.13	1.07	2.08	1.01
1995	1.02	1.00	0.02	1.03	0.86	0.17	1.13	1.21	0.08	0.91	0.76	0.15
1999	0.82	0.75	0.07	0.75	0.87	0.11	1.08	1.03	0.05	1.67	1.78	0.11
2003	0.95	0.92	0.03	1.57	1.25	0.33	1.08	1.15	0.07	0.33	0.40	0.07
2007	1.40	1.02	0.38	0.68	0.81	0.13	0.75	1.10	0.35	1.55	1.72	0.17
2010	0.57	0.93	0.36	0.92	1.27	0.35	0.75	0.71	0.03	1.13	0.97	0.16
2014	1.09	0.95	0.14	0.94	0.85	0.09	1.11	1.16	0.06	1.23	0.67	0.56

Source: http://cevipol.ulb.be.

the fact that, since 2003, coalitions at the different levels of government have not been formed by the same parties and that the two parties of the same family did not always govern together after 2007. This does 'disturb' one of the elements that made the parties of the same family move together before that date: both parties were in each language group either a governing or an opposition party (Deschouwer 2009). The very fact that this symmetry at the federal level and the congruence between the national and regional levels has been broken is another indicator of the weakening ties between the members of the same party families. One might therefore wonder to what extent they do indeed (still) belong to the same family. The remainder of this chapter will offer a systematic answer to that question.

ON THE CONCEPT OF PARTY FAMILY

The concept of party family is quite central in the comparative analysis of political parties. It is used to classify parties belonging to different party systems into broader categories of parties that have a common programmatic and ideological profile. It is actually at the roots of party typologies and classifications (see, e.g., Seiler 1986; von Beyme 1985). Mair and Mudde (1998) have suggested the use of four criteria or approaches to define party families. Parties of the same family should in the first place have a *common name*. This self-declaration of parties as being 'liberal' or 'socialist' or 'conservative' is the most obvious and straightforward criterion. Next, one can also look at how national parties at the national level unite at the *transnational level*. When parties decide to be part of the same international party organisations or to sit in the same group in the European Parliament, they make a clear choice of belonging to one family rather than to another one. A third criterion is the *sharing of origins*. Parties of the same family have developed in the same way and are built on the same 'alignment of voters'. This refers to Lipset and Rokkan's (1967, 2008) classic theory of cleavage politics linking parties to the conflict in which they originated. Parties that originated on a specific structural conflict dividing society would then see this reflected in their sociological composition. Parties of the same family mainly organise the same specific segments of society. The fourth and final criterion is having a common ideology and *similar policy positions*. This refers to ideological congruence between parties and is closely linked to the third criterion that sees parties from the same family as sharing a common project, defending similar interests located on one specific side of societal conflicts.

The concept of party family is used to compare and group parties across countries, to classify parties that belong to different party systems. It can therefore also be used to compare the Flemish and francophone parties in

Belgium. They do not compete across the language border and belong therefore to two different party systems. Yet since they do compete for power in the same country, the question of whether there are in Belgium not only unilingual parties but also party families that represent similar demands in both parts of the country is quite relevant. In Belgian politics one uses terms like 'brother parties' (in French) and 'sister parties' (in Dutch) which does clearly suggest that there are family ties between them. For three of these pairs – the Christian democrats, the socialists and the liberals – there is a common history. When the statewide parties split, the two remaining parties were considered siblings, children of the same 'mother party'. Since the split of these three large parties in the late 1960s and 1970s, several new parties have seen the light. These include regionalist parties, radical right parties and green parties. They may belong to the same family but do not have a common history in the Belgian context, as in the case of the other three pairs. The regionalist parties of Flanders, Wallonia (now defunct) and Brussels have very different origins and obviously very different views on the territorial organisation of Belgium. They have always been each other's fierce critics. The radical right developed in Flanders first and combined that position with a plea for Flemish independence. The much weaker and more volatile radical right party in francophone Belgium has never seen itself as being a natural partner of its Flemish counterpart, among others because of its separatist stance. Only the two green parties, which developed more or less at the same time but independently from each other in their own party system, are among the new parties considering themselves as sisters and brothers. In the analysis that follows we will therefore focus on these four families of two parties (Christian democrats, socialists, liberals and greens). Following the criteria put forward by Mair and Mudde (1998), we will first look at the party names and at organisational ties within the families. Next we will look at the party positions and the rank-and-file profiles.

FAMILY NAME AND FAMILY TIES

The first type of organisational ties consists in sharing a common name. Before the three traditional parties fell apart, the unified party had one name that was translated into both languages. The Christian democrats were called 'Christian People's Party' or Christelijke Volkspartij (CVP) – Parti Social Chrétien (PSC). They kept the name, each in their own language only when they became two different parties in 1968. These names were, however, changed later on. When the Christian democrats were pushed out of power at the national level after forty years of constant presence in government in 1999, both parties went through a deep crisis and tried to redefine and reposition themselves. They did so independently from each other. The Flemish CVP renamed itself in 2001 into 'Christian Democratic and Flemish' or CD&V. It is quite interesting to note that the Flemish identity is now stressed in the name, together with Christian democracy. The francophone PSC renamed itself in 2002 into 'Democratic Humanist Centre' or cdH. In doing so, it abandoned the explicit reference to the Christian democratic heritage.

In 1972, the liberal 'Party of Liberty and Progress' or Parti de la Liberté et du Progrès (PLP) – Partij voor Vrijheid en Vooruitgang (PVV) split into two parties, each keeping their name in their own language (PLP and PVV). Yet that changed quite rapidly. On the francophone side the liberal party faced many splits and splinters and managed only in 1979 to regroup all components into one formation that was labelled 'Reformist Liberal Party' (Parti Réformateur Libéral). In 2002, the party was rebranded again into 'Reform Movement' (MR), thus dropping the reference to liberalism. Its Flemish 'sister' kept the name of PVV until a major organisational reform in 1993. It then chose the name 'Flemish Liberals and democrats' (VLD – Vlaamse Liberalen en Democraten). Here the reference to liberalism is kept and – like for the Flemish Christian Democrats – the explicit reference to Flanders is added. In 2007, the VLD became 'Open VLD', only to accommodate some important members who had left the Flemish regionalist party Volksunie which had been dissolved in 2001 (Delwit and van Haute 2002).

The socialist party was originally called 'Belgian Socialist Party' or Parti Socialiste Belge – Belgische Socialistische Partij. When the party split in 1978, both new parties dropped the reference to Belgium and became 'Socialist Party' (Socialistische Partij [SP] and Parti Socialiste [PS]). The Flemish SP has added 'different' (anders) to its name – now it is called SP.a – also to accommodate the arrival of people from the disintegrated Volksunie (Delwit, Pilet and van Haute 2011).

Finally, the greens never used the same name. In Flanders, the green party was originally called AGALEV, meaning 'A different way of living' (Anders Gaan Leven). It renamed itself into 'Green' (Groen) in 2003. The francophone greens have always used the name Ecolo.

Only Ecolo and PS have thus kept their name. While the name change of the Flemish greens was not an attempt to reposition themselves but rather to choose a more 'normal' name than the one that was – rather jokingly – chosen in 1979, the name changes in the Christian democratic and liberal families are revealing. The Flemish parties stress their Flemish identity and keep the ideological label, while the francophone parties do not stress their francophone identity but have chosen names that position them less explicitly into the ideological family. Today, reading party names does not allow someone unfamiliar with the Belgian party system to easily connect sister parties, except for the greens and the socialists.

The fact that party names have changed and that parties in Dutch-speaking and French-speaking Belgium did so independently from each other also reveals that the organisational ties between them have weakened and actually disappeared. In the early days after the split, they shared a same building, had a common study centre or some formal and informal organs for coordination, but all these ties have quite rapidly eroded. With new political generations being socialised in the unilingual parties, the personal ties that could provide some bridges between the parties have also by now disappeared.

The split of the three traditional parties was a hard one. They immediately became two different organisations and also considered themselves as being two different parties in the parliament. As soon as the central party organisation fell apart, the parliamentary groups followed suit. Party groups receive funding from the parliament and central party organisations receive funding from the Belgian state (Weekers, Maddens and Noppe 2009). For both channels of income, the split parties are treated as two separate entities. Nowhere in the organisation of the parliament or of the public subsidies for parties does the notion of party families play a role. Interestingly though, the parties of the same family still sit very close to each other in the hemicycle of the federal parliament. From left to right the seats are allocated to PS, SP.a, Groen and Ecolo, Open VLD, MR, CD&V and cdH (with the other parties in between or at the back). The logic of seat allocation is therefore based on ideological proximity (from left to right) rather than on language. As said earlier, the two green parties form one single group in parliament since 2007. The trigger to form a joint group was strategic in the first place: they would not have been able to form two separate groups given the small size of their respective parliamentary factions at the time. Yet they kept the common group when it was not needed anymore and presented it as proof of their ideological proximity and of their ability to find agreements between the two language groups on institutional matters.

Forming one single group in the federal parliament also means that both parties of the group must be either together in government or together in opposition. For the green parties that has since 2007 been the opposition (greens only governed at the federal level between 1999 and 2003). For the other three party families, the situation is different. One of the unwritten principles of coalition formation at the federal level in Belgium has been for a long time the 'symmetry' rule. It means that parties of the same party family govern together. All governments formed since the first party split in 1968 were formed according to that rule until it was for the first time broken in 2007. The federal government then contained the PS but not the SP.a. The 2014 government contains CD&V but not cdH. Today, only the two liberal parties have never been separated in government or in opposition, yet there is no reason to believe that it might not happen in the future. Non-symmetric federal governments are of course a context in which it is impossible to have one single group per party family in the parliament.

While the parties have formally split and sit in separate groups in the parliament, one might still expect that when MPs seek collaboration with colleagues for legislative or other initiatives, they think of colleagues of the same party family first. Yet even here the separation appears to have been fully consumed. In the *PartiRep MP survey* all respondents were asked to give up to three names of members of other party groups in their assembly with whom they had good contacts. Table 5.2 presents the answers given by the Belgian MPs at the federal level. It shows a clear preference for colleagues of the same language group. Only the liberal MPs have a stronger preference for family members and they also cross more easily the language border to colleagues of other parties. Overall, these figures show quite clearly how the split of the parties and the absence of common groups per party family has provided an institutional context in which language has become a very relevant and strong barrier.

One can also look beyond the Belgian context and see how parties build organisational family ties at the transnational – European or international – level. When the Belgian parties meet outside of Belgium, they do indeed cross the Belgian linguistic divide. Sister parties all belong to the same European political party: CD&V and cdH are members of the European People's Party; PS and SP.a belong to the Socialists and Democrats (S&D); Open VLD and MR belong to the Alliance of Liberals and Democrats for Europe (ALDE); and Ecolo and Groen are members of the European Green Party (EGP). At the international level, PS and SP.a are members of the Socialist International, MR and Open VLD are members of the Liberal International and Groen and Ecolo are members of the Global Greens. While CD&V belongs to the Centrist Democrat International, it is however not the case for the francophone cdH.

This overview of the formal organisational ties of the Belgian sister parties shows quite clearly that the ties are weakening. Except for the greens,

Table 5.2. Members of other party groups in the federal parliament with whom MPs have good contacts

	Sister party	Same language group only	At least one from other language group (not sister party)
CD&V and cdH	38.9	61.1	0.0
PS and SP.a	36.8	57.9	5.3
Open VLD and MR	58.8	29.4	11.8
Ecolo and Groen	16.7	83.3	0.0

Source: PartiRep MP survey.

the party names have diverged over time. Formal organisational ties at the Belgian level have disappeared, and the informal rule of symmetry in government formation has been relaxed. In Parliament, only the greens have formed a joint parliamentary group. The other parties physically sit alongside but do not form a joint group. It is only at European and transnational levels that formal ties persist, especially through the joint membership of European political parties. Yet at that level the functioning of party groups does not suppose and require the coherence that one can witness in party groups at the national level.

ORIGINS AND SOCIOLOGICAL BASIS

Next to organisational ties, Mair and Mudde propose to examine party families on the basis of their sociological basis and mobilisation. According to them, this approach aims 'to group together parties that mobilised in similar historical circumstances or with the intention of representing similar interests' (Mair and Mudde 1998: 215). The underlying idea is that parties from a same family are built upon the same cleavages and therefore represent social groups sharing common socio-demographic characteristics. The goal here is to determine whether this is the case for sister parties in Belgium.

There are *a priori* good reasons to believe that it could be the case. From a Rokkanian perspective, sister parties are born on the same side of the same cleavage (Deschouwer 2012; Delwit 2012). CD&V and cdH are the heirs of the Catholic Party that emerged on the Church side of the Church-State cleavage. It defended the interests of Catholics and of the Catholic pillar in the new independent state. The MR and Open VLD are the successors of the Liberal Party that initially emerged on the state side of the Church-State cleavage. In 1961, the Liberal Party transformed into PLP-PVV; its aggiornamento realigned the party primarily on the employers' side of the workers-employers cleavage, abandoning its anti-Catholic position and opening up to Catholics. The PS and SP.a are the children of the Belgian Workers' Party that emerged on the workers' side of the workers-employers cleavage. It defended the interests of the working class in urban and industrialised parts of Belgium. Finally, Ecolo and Groen were born in the 1980s from environmentalist movements, defending the same positions on issues related to the environment.

These common origins give ground to the idea that sister parties would be sociologically composed of the same groups of citizens. Catholics would remain over-represented among both CD&V and cdH. Liberal voters would be composed of both Catholics and non-Catholics but mostly belonging to the middle and upper classes. PS and SP.a would attract citizens in more industrialised and urban regions, and among citizens from the working class. Finally, Ecolo and Groen could be expected to remain mostly supported by middle class and highly educated citizens.

We use data from the *2014 PartiRep Voter Survey* to describe and compare the composition of the electorate of the different parties. Table 5.3 presents the results for religious affiliation. And these confirm that both Christian democratic parties CD&V and cdH still share a strong Catholic basis. Some 75 per cent of voters of the two parties self-report to be Catholic, as opposed to the broader category of 'Christian', non-believer or other religions. Catholics are however only a small majority in the electorate (54 per cent). Other parties are around that average, except for the greens which attracts a very low number of Catholic voters. The most important finding here is thus that CD&V and cdH remain strongly Catholic parties. The same (amplified) patterns were found for party members (*see* van Haute et al. 2013).

Table 5.4 presents the level of education of the voters of the parties, which we use as the proxy for social class. Here too the expectations are met. The

Table 5.3. Percentage of 'Catholic' voters per party (as opposed to Christian, non-believer or other) among voters and members

	Catholic, %
CD&V (134)	71.4
cdH (104)	77.1
SP.a (103)	45.1
PS (213)	51.9
Open VLD (110)	57.3
MR (136)	56.3
Groen (74)	27.0
Ecolo (57)	31.0
Total (N = 1,445)	54.0

Source: 2014 PartiRep Voter Survey.

Table 5.4. Education level of voters per party

	None/Primary	Secondary	Higher education
CD&V (134)	16.4	50.7	32.8
cdH (104)	14.4	47.1	38.5
SP.a (103)	21.4	51.5	27.2
PS (213)	24.9	55.9	19.2
Open VLD (110)	9.1	46.4	44.5
MR (136)	8.1	50.0	41.9
Groen (74)	9.5	45.9	44.6
Ecolo (57)	10.5	36.8	52.6
Total (N = 1,445)	15.4	52.3	32.4

Source: 2014 PartiRep Voter Survey.

two socialist parties clearly mobilise the lower classes. The francophone PS has, however, a sharper profile in this respect, with far less highly educated voters than the SP.a. Both liberal parties hardly attract lower educated voters but do mobilise the higher educated. They have a very similar profile. The Christian democrats are the parties of the middle. Their profile comes closest to the general population profile. Both green parties have voters who are mainly higher educated, even more so than the liberal parties. When we look at the origins and the sociological basis of the Belgian parties, we can clearly conclude that they belong to the same families. That is not a great surprise, since for three of the families there is a common origin and a long common history. The two green parties also appeared at the same time and are the product of the 'silent revolution' (Inglehart 1977).

IDEOLOGY AND POLICY POSITIONS

Expert judgements

According to Mair and Mudde, parties from a same party family should be congruent on their policies and ideological positions (Mair and Mudde 1998: 217). We test this for Belgian parties by looking at the self-placement of both voters and MPs on different issues. However, we first look at expert judgements. The 2015 Chapel Hill Expert Survey (Bakker et al. 2015) provides data on the general left-right position of a wide range of parties in all member states of the EU. This allows us not only to assess the positions and closeness of Belgian parties but also to place them in a larger context. We can thus at the same time answer the question of whether the parties of the same party family are perceived by the Belgian country experts as being ideologically close to each other, and check to what extent the distance between the Belgian parties is smaller or larger than the distance with parties of the same party family in other countries.

For the socialists and the liberals, we computed the average and the standard deviation of the scores of all the parties belonging to the European Parliament groups of, respectively, S&D and the ALDE, and for which there is a score in the Chapel Hill Expert Survey. For the Christian democrats, we used the membership of the Centrist Democrat International, and for the greens the membership of the EGP. The figures in table 5.5 tell us in the very first place that the Belgian parties are placed very close to each other. For liberals and greens, the average score of the experts for Belgium is identical, and for the socialists the difference is very small. Only for the two Christian democratic parties, there is a difference of 1 point, putting the francophone Christian democrats a bit more to the left. Yet while there is some distance between the

Table 5.5. Left-right position of the Belgian parties compared with the other members of their family in the EU

	All parties average	All parties standard deviation	Flanders	Wallonia
Christian democrats	6.75	0.75	5.4	4.4
Socialists	3.84	0.58	3.0	2.6
Liberals	5.85	1.26	7.0	7.0
Greens	3.45	1.11	2.2	2.2

Source: Chapel Hill Expert Survey 2014.

two parties, they both firmly belong to the more leftist Christian democrats in Europe. Actually, the Belgian cdH is by far the most leftist party of the family in Europe, followed by the Italian UDC (5.28) and then followed by the Flemish CD&V.

The Belgian socialists are seen by the experts as clearly on the left and on an almost identical position. Here also the Belgian parties are – together – on the left of their family. The Belgian PS is the most leftist party of the family, followed by the Polish SLD (2.76) and then followed by the Flemish SP.a. This leftist orientation is also present for the greens. Only the Green Party of the United Kingdom is placed a bit more to the left than Ecolo (1.86). Next are the Greek Green Party (2.25) and the Dutch GroenLinks (2.33), after which we arrive at the Flemish Groen that shares its position at 3 with the Austrian Greens. While Christian democrats, socialists and greens in Belgium are positioned on the leftist side of their family, the Belgian liberals are placed on the right. Their position is one standard deviation to the right of the average member of the ALDE, but the Belgian liberals are not the most extreme. They are, however, located on exactly the same position.

The voters

Experts might have of course a view that differs from the voters. Table 5.6 presents the self-placement of voters in electoral surveys conducted in Belgium between 1991 and 2014. Here also the distance between the voters of the sister parties is quite limited. It is remarkable to observe that decades after the splinter of the statewide parties, the gaps in the average left-right position of voters of sister parties range between 0.1 and 0.7 points on a scale from 0 to 10. The largest gap is in the socialist family, where the francophone PS is more to the left than the SP.a. In the liberal family, the MR is a bit more to the right than Open VLD. Green and Christian democratic voters in the north and in the south position themselves on average in an almost identical way.

Another way of measuring this closeness to the sister party is by asking the voters to give a score between 0 and 10 that indicates the degree in which

Table 5.6. Average left-right orientation of voters (scale 0–10)

	CD&V	cdH	PS	SP.a	Open VLD	MR	Groen	Ecolo
1991	6.2	5.8	3.6	4.3	5.9	6.0	4.6	4.5
1995	5.7	5.9	3.3	4.0	5.6	5.9	4.2	4.0
1999	5.7	6.0	3.3	4.2	5.5	5.9	3.9	4.0
2003	5.5	5.7	3.6	4.2	5.3	5.8	3.4	3.9
2007	5.5	5.5	3.5	4.1	5.6	6.2	3.8	4.3
2009	5.4	5.2	3.4	3.7	5.5	6.0	3.5	4.5
2010	5.3	5.3	3.5	4.0	5.7	6.1	3.8	4.1
2014	5.2	5.4	3.3	3.9	5.6	6.3	3.9	3.6
Average	5.7	5.6	3.4	4.1	5.6	6.0	3.9	4.1
Gap	0.1		0.7		0.4		0.3	

Sources: ISPO/PIOP Voter Surveys for 1991, 1995, 1999, 2003, 2007 and 2010. PartiRep Voter Surveys for 2009 and 2014.

Table 5.7. Agreement with the positions of the sister party (0–10)

	Sister party	Closest?
CD&V	4.2	N-VA: 4.6
cdH	4.5	yes
SP.a	5.6	yes
PS	4.5	cdH: 4.7
Open VLD	5.0	yes
MR	4.9	yes
Groen	6.8	yes
Ecolo	6.7	yes

Source: 2014 PartiRep Voter Survey.

they agree with the ideas of other parties. In the *2014 PartiRep Voter Survey* this question was asked to all voters, and for all the parties of the country. Voters in Wallonia could thus also give their opinion on Flemish parties and vice versa. The results of that are in table 5.7. Overall, the level of agreement with the positions of other parties is not very high. Only for the two green parties the agreement with the other one is quite high. Yet for the other party families the highest score is most of the time given to the sister party. That means that the positions of the sister party are seen as closer to one's own position than any of the other parties of the same language group. There are only two exceptions. The voters of CD&V appear to be a bit closer to N-VA than to cdH, but the difference is small and cdH comes third. The voters of the PS see the francophone cdH as a bit closer to them than the SP.a, yet here also SP.a is ranked third.

On these very broad measurements we do find strong family ties. We now also look at four more specific issues. Voters were asked in 2014 to position themselves – always with a 0–10 scale – on the choice between free market economy and state control of the economy and on the choice for the environment versus the choice for employment. They were also asked to give their opinion on two institutional questions. The first is the internal Belgian discussion on the degree to which the central state should have all the powers or whether, to the contrary, the substates should have a maximal autonomy. The second asks in a similar way whether European integration should be maximal or, to the contrary, the highest autonomy of the member states is preferred. Table 5.8 presents the results for these four issues.

On state control versus free enterprise, the distances within the families are minimal. We find the Christian democrats both perfectly in the middle, the liberals on the centre-right position (with MR slightly more on the right than Open VLD) and the socialists as well as the greens on the centre-left position. On the environment versus employment issue, we find the owners of the issue – the greens – at exactly the same position in Flanders and Wallonia. For the other parties, there are larger differences, all revealing a greater attention for employment in Wallonia than in Flanders. That does reflect the more difficult economic situation of Wallonia where unemployment is higher than in Flanders. And it illustrates nicely how the two party systems are located in a slightly different society, which leads to divergences within parties of the same family. These divergences actually existed before the split of the parties and were in part responsible for it (Delwit 2012).

The figures for the institutional issues are interesting because they are surprising. On the question of whether Belgium should move further in the direction of decentralisation or, to the contrary, keep more competences at the federal level, the parties north and south defend very different positions. When we look at the voters though, we do see this tension – the voters of the

Table 5.8. Average self-placement of voters on issues (0–10)

	State control–free enterprise (0–10)		Environment–employment (0–10)		Regional-federal (0–10)		Less–more EU integration (0–10)	
	Average	Gap	Average	Gap	Average	Gap	Average	Gap
CD&V	5.3	0.1	6.1	1.0	4.5	0.9	4.6	0.2
cdH	5.4		7.1		5.6		4.8	
SP.a	4.7	0.2	6.6	0.7	5.3	0.3	5.0	0.7
PS	4.9		7.3		5.6		4.3	
Open VLD	6.3	0.4	6.8	0.3	5.2	0.8	5.2	0.8
MR	5.9		7.1		6.0		4.4	
Groen	4.7	0.1	4.8	0.0	5.0	0.7	5.7	0.3
Ecolo	4.8		4.8		5.7		5.4	

Source: PartiRep Voter Survey.

Flemish parties are a bit more on the 'regional' side of the scale – but the gap is not extremely large. It does not go beyond 1 point on a scale from 0 to 10. The more radical regionalist positions that are present in Flanders, are among the voters of the regionalist N-VA and the radical right VB, and are therefore not displayed in table 5.8.

The positions on the future of the EU are also relatively coherent in each family. There are especially differences in the socialist and liberal parties, where in both cases the Flemish counterpart is more in favour of European integration. This does reflect a general tendency for a larger Euroscepticism in Wallonia than in Flanders. Yet here too the major gaps are not within party families. The strongest anti-European positions are found among the voters of the radical left PvdA/PTB and the radical right VB in Flanders and PP in Wallonia. The voters of N-VA are also less in favour of a deeper European integration.

The Members of Parliament

The results at the level of the voters show quite some degree of coherence. Voters of the sister parties are relatively close to each other, and quite often the sister parties are closer to each other than to a party in their own language group. For the MPs, we have similar measurements based on the Belgian sample of the PartiRep International MP survey (Deschouwer and Depauw 2014). Table 5.9 presents the left-right self-placement of MPs. For the Christian democrats and the greens, the gap inside the family is minimal. The position of the green MPs on the far left is however not reflecting the voter's positions (see table 5.8) that are much closer to the centre. For both socialist parties, the MPs position themselves further on the left than their voters. Yet they do reflect the slightly more leftist position of the Walloon socialists. Among the MPs of the liberal parties, we also see that the francophones – like their voters – are more on the right than their Flemish sister MPs.

For the MPs we also have three of the four issues that we looked at for the voters (the question on the choice between environment and employment was not asked to the MPs). They are displayed in table 5.10. On the question about state intervention in the economy (where a 1–5 scale was used), the findings are remarkable. The parties of the same family are very close to each other. The largest difference is for the socialists, where we find again the francophones more on the left than the Dutch speakers. Yet despite that difference, we find that in all cases the closest party is the sister party. It confirms the findings on the left-right cleavage and on the issues at the level of the voters. The parties of the same family are ideologically quite close. They could be the same party with some internal divergences.

Table 5.9. MPs' left-right self-placement (0–10)

	CD&V	cdH	PS	SP.a	Open VLD	MR	Groen	Ecolo
Average	5.6	5.3	1.6	2.1	5.2	6.3	1.8	1.9
Gap		0.3		0.5		1.1		0.1

Source: PartiRep MP survey.

Table 5.10. Average self-placement of MPs on issues

	Regional-federal (0–10)		Smaller–larger government intervention in economy (1–5)		Too much EU– federal EU (0–10)	
	Average	Gap	Average	Gap	Average	Gap
CD&V	2.7	0.2	2.0	2.5	7.3	0.4
cdH	2.5		4.5		6.9	
SP.a	2.0	0.4	3.3	0.0	7.0	0.8
PS	1.6		3.3		6.2	
Open VLD	3.2	0.1	2.5	2.7	7.2	0.2
MR	3.1		5.2		7.0	
Groen	1.4	0.1	4.3	0.4	9.0	2.1
Ecolo	1.3		4.7		6.9	

Source: PartiRep MP survey.

Next we look at the position of the MPs on a 0–10 decentralisation scale. As argued earlier, this issue has been the most controversial in Belgian politics since the 1960s. But for voters we have not observed a wide gap between sister parties. When it comes to MPs, we do find very contrasted results. The gaps between sister parties are quite significant for the liberal parties and the Christian democratic parties. MPs from the Flemish Christian democrats and liberals are clearly in favour of further transfers of powers to regions, while their francophone counterparts tend to preach the status quo. By contrast, we also observe that for the two other party families, gaps in MPs' average self-placement are almost non-existent. For Ecolo and Groen, the convergence is explained by the more moderate views of the Flemish green MPs that position them apart from other Flemish parliamentary party groups. For PS and SP.a, it is the more pro-decentralisation position of MPs from the PS that explains that they stand very close. Among francophone parties, the MPs from the PS are on average the closest to the mean position of Flemish parties. We thus find more divergences inside the party families, but also a gap between the voters, on the one hand – who are generally rather moderate – and the MPs, on the other hand, who take more extreme positions on this intra-Belgian debate.

The final indicator is the position on European integration. The average self-placement of MPs from all parties but Groen is around 6–7. It indicates a clear support for further EU integration. The outlying position of Groen is actually for even further integration with a mean score of 9. The more pro-European position of the Flemish parties, emphasised by the voters, is also visible at the level of the MPs. Yet even more important is – like for the intra-Belgian institutional debate – the difference between the positions of the voters and the position of the MPs. While the MPs (of the traditional parties and the greens) take a solid pro-integration position, the voters are much more reluctant and position themselves in the centre of the scale or slightly towards the strengthening of the national powers.

CONCLUSION

The Belgian party system is unique, simply because it does not exist. Except for a few smaller parties, of which only the radical left Labour Party is represented in the parliament, all parties limit their electoral mobilisation to either the Dutch-speaking north or the French-speaking south of the country. This split party system is one of the most important indicators of the gap between the north and the south. It is the consequence of deep disagreements within the former Belgian parties on the institutional future of the country. This split party system raises concerns about the democratic quality of political representation in Belgium, about the possibility of parties to be truly responsive to voters, and about the capacity of decision-making at the federal level. The functioning of parties and of party politics in Belgium is actually quite similar to that of the EU. In elections to the European Parliament, only national (and not Europe-wide) parties mobilise voters of their country. Reflecting on what that means for political representation at the European level, Mair and Thomassen (2010) have argued that it might still work properly if parties that subsequently sit in the same group in the European Parliament truly belong to the same party family and defend similar values, interests and identities in the different member states.

In this chapter, we have explored to what extent the split Belgian parties can be seen as belonging to the same party family. We have used the checklist suggested by Mair and Mudde (1998) to verify whether the two Christian democratic, the two socialist, the two liberal and the two green parties (still) have family ties. Our findings show that the parties are quite close to each other when one looks at party origin, cleavages, party ideology and sociological basis. There are some differences between north and south, but these are limited. We see that the francophone socialists are a bit more on the left than their Flemish sister party and that the francophone liberals are a bit more on the right. That picture is the same for the voters and the MPs of the parties.

Yet parties that to a large extent defend the same ideas and represent the same societal groups do themselves not act as family members. In the past few decades the parties have – exception made for the greens – removed all formal ties between them. They do not confer before making decisions on party labels and names, on party programmes and even on party strategy. They do not form – contrary to what happens at the European level – one single group in the federal parliament. Coalition formation at the federal level has so far seen twice a government that has split one family into one governing and one opposition party. While the ideological gaps inside the families are limited and remain small, the structural gaps are deepening. Each party looks at its own party system in the first place.

The Belgian parties have fallen apart because they could not (and still cannot) agree on the best institutional future for the country. During the past twenty years, the divide has clearly been between the Flemish parties wanting to move decentralisation further and francophone parties defending the status quo. That is also what we see when we look at the opinions and positions of the MPs. The party voters however are not reflecting this deep divide. They have a rather moderate position, at least if one looks at the three traditional party families and at the greens.

When looking at the positions on the future of the EU, we find yet another gap between MPs and voters. Here – as has been illustrated in research in other countries – the party elites are much more pro-European than their voters. There is in Belgium also some difference between north and south: in Flanders, the support for a deeper European integration is somewhat higher than in Wallonia. But the major difference is between the voters who position themselves in the centre and the party elites who position themselves firmly on the side of further European integration. The split Belgian parties are having great difficulties in acting like members of the same family. They might mobilise the same values, but they decide on their own about the way to do it and on the choice of entering or not a federal government. The language border has increasingly become a deep divide between them. Yet this gap between north and south is not the only one that characterises the Belgian parties. They are on institutional issues, both the Belgian and the European, not exactly in harmony with their voters.

REFERENCES

Bakker, R., Edwards, E., Hooghe, L., Jolly, S., Marks, G., Polk, J., Rovny, J., Steenbergen, M. and Vachudova, M. (2015) '2014 Chapel Hill Expert Survey', Version 2015.1. Available at chesdata.eu; Chapel Hill: University of North Carolina, Chapel Hill.

Caramani, D. (2004) *The Nationalization of Politics. The Formation of National Electorates and Party Systems in Western Europe*, Cambridge: Cambridge University Press.

Delwit, P. (2012) *La vie politique en Belgique de 1830 à nos jours*, Brussels: Editions de l'Université de Bruxelles, coll. UBLire, 2nd edition.

Delwit, P. and van Haute, E. (2002) 'L'implosion et la fin d'un parti: la Volksunie', *L'année sociale 2001. Revue de l'Institut de Sociologie*: 13–24.

Delwit, P., Pilet, J.-B. and van Haute, E. (2011) *Les partis politiques en Belgique*, Brussels: Editions de l'Université de Bruxelles.

Deschouwer, K. (2009) 'Coalition Formation and Congruence in Multi-layered Systems: Belgium 1995–2007', *Regional and Federal Studies*, 19(1): 13–35.

Deschouwer, K. (2012) *The Politics of Belgium. Governing a Divided Society*, Basingstoke: Palgrave, 2nd edition.

Deschouwer, K. and Depauw, S. (eds) (2014) *Representing the People*, Oxford: Oxford University Press.

Deschouwer, K. and Van Parijs, P. (2013) 'Electoral Engineering in a Stalled Federation. A State-Wide Electoral District for the Belgian Parliament', in B. O'Leary and J. McEvoy (eds) *Power-Sharing in Deeply Divided Places*, Philadelphia: University of Pennsylvania Press, 112–32.

Hobolt, S. B. (2014) 'A Vote for the President? The Role of Spitzenkandidaten in the 2014 European Parliament Elections', *Journal of European Public Policy*, 21(10): 1528–40.

Hooghe, M. (2012) 'The Political Crisis in Belgium (2007–2011): A Federal System without Federal Loyalty', *Representation*, 48(1): 131–38.

Inglehart, Ronald (1977) *The Silent Revolution. Changing Values and Political Systems Among the Western Publics*, New Haven: Princeton University Press.

Jans, Th.M. (2001) 'Leveled Domestic Politics. Comparing Institutional Reform and Ethnonational Conflicts in Canada and Belgium (1960–1989)', *Res Publica*, 43(1): 37–58.

Lipset, S. M. and Rokkan, S. (1967) *Party Systems and Voter Alignments: Cross-National Perspectives*, Toronto: The Free Press.

Lipset, S. M. and Rokkan, S. (2008) *Structures de clivages, systèmes de partis et alignement des électeurs: une introduction*, Brussels: Editions de l'Université de Bruxelles, coll. UBLire.

Mair, P. and Mudde, C. (1998) 'The Party Family and Its Study', *Annual Review of Political Science*, 1: 211–29.

Mair, P. and Thomassen, J. (2010) 'Political Representation and Government of the European Union', *Journal of European Public Policy*, 17(1): 20–35.

Pilet, J.-B., De Waele, J.-M. and Jaumain, S. (2009) *L'absence de partis nationaux: menace ou opportunité?* Brussels: Editions de l'Université de Bruxelles.

Sartori, G. (2016) *Parties and Party Systems*, London: ECPR Press.

Seiler, D.-L. (1986) *De la comparaison des partis politiques*, Paris: Economica.

Sinardet, D. (2012) 'Le projet de circonscription électorale fédérale', *Courrier hebdomadaire du CRISP*, 2142.

van Haute, E., Amjahad, A., Borriello, A., Close, C. and Sandri, G. (2013) 'Party Members in a Pillarised Partitocracy. An Empirical Overview of Party Membership Figures and Profiles in Belgium', *Acta Politica*, 48(1): 68–91.

von Beyme, K. (1985) *Political Parties in Western Democracies*, London: Ashgate Publishing.

Weekers, K., Maddens, B. and Noppe, J. (2009) 'Explaining the Evolution of the Party Finance Regime in Belgium', *Journal of Elections, Public Opinion and Parties*, 19(1): 25–48.

Chapter 6

Language identity and voting

Dave Sinardet, Lieven De Winter, Jérémy
Dodeigne and Min Reuchamps

IDENTITIES AND PREFERENCES ON DEVOLUTION
IN FEDERAL COUNTRIES

These past decennia, the social science literature on identities saw a consensus growing on the fact that identities are not a fixed, static, essentialist reality but have developed in specific historical and socio-economic contexts. They are, in other words, socially constructed (Gellner 1983; Hobsbawm 1990; Anderson 1983). Therefore, it is difficult to measure national identities as an empirical reality. What can be measured though is the extent to which people identify with such a social construct. It is not because they are socially constructed that (national) identities do not exist and even are in fact important for many people. However, when measuring these identifications, one has to take into account their fundamental complexity.

Particularly in federal, multilingual states, identity feelings can be very complex and ambiguous. Even if identities are often used in absolute and exclusive terms in the political debate, citizens often have multilayered identities. Some will be more activated in certain circumstances than in others. Abroad, people from Switzerland will present themselves as Swiss, while in their own country they can also emphasise the canton or the village in which they live.

In such multilingual states, sometimes also labelled as multinational, multilayered and mixed identities are generally not politically neutral. When such states are characterised by debates on the extent to which autonomy should be attributed to substate levels, feelings of regional or national identity easily acquire a political meaning and can be interpreted as political stands. This is in part because the strength of (sub)national identities is considered as one of the possible drivers and legitimisers of the demands for

113

the territorial reorganisation or breaking up of national states. Regionalist political entrepreneurs have crafted narratives in which specific regional economic strengths and cultural traditions are combined to mobilise for territorial autonomy (Keating 1996).

The causal relation can however also be inversed. Regional identifications can also be influenced by the political context. It can be expected that the increasing importance of regional authorities – be it in terms of competences or of a direct election of their parliament – will lead to stronger regional identities, as shown by past research in (quasi)-federal states like Spain, Canada and the United Kingdom (Guibernau 2006). Because they are often politically salient, identities and preferences on regional autonomy will also more easily tend to influence voting behaviour.

Territorial identities are complex as well as controversial, and therefore tend to be difficult to measure, especially in multilingual/multinational states. A neutral measurement of identity is not self-evident. Often, social science research will (unconsciously) be based on a normative vision on identity, which is projected onto the research subject. For instance, the way citizens are questioned in scientific surveys about their ethno-territorial identification contains unexpressed assumptions. If a respondent is asked whether he or she feels British or Scottish, one takes for granted that these two identities are mutually exclusive and/or in opposition to each other, while they can just as well be complementary. Survey research also encounters difficulties in capturing variation in time and context.

In this chapter, we will look into ethno-territorial identities in Belgium, using different measurements, and their relation with preferences on distribution of competences across policy levels as well as with voting behaviour. We will mostly use data drawn from the 2009 and 2014 PartiRep Surveys, as well as on some additional data from MEDW.

THE BELGIAN CASE: A COMPLEX WEB OF IDENTITIES AND STATE STRUCTURES

Since the 1960s the unitary Belgian state has been subject to a process of devolution that eventually transformed it into a self-declared federal state in 1993. This transformation produced a very complex institutional landscape. In contrast to other federations, two types of federated entities that partly overlap were created: three territorially based regions (the Flemish, Walloon and Brussels regions) and three language-based communities (the Flemish, French-speaking and German-speaking communities). The Flemish and French-speaking community overlap in the Brussels region, where they are both competent for matters such as education, culture and media. The borders of regions and communities have been based on those of the four language areas (Dutch-speaking, French-speaking, German-speaking and the bilingual Brussels area), through which language use is officially regulated: only the official language(s) can be used in administration, education and justice. Since 1963, the borders of these language areas have been legally frozen.

Notwithstanding the existence of three regions, three communities and four language areas, the federal political dynamics in Belgium is mostly based on the two main language communities: the Dutch speakers (approximatively 6.5 millions) and the French speakers (approximatively 4.5 millions). On the level of federal parliament and government, a number of consociational devices, institutionalising power-sharing between representatives of the two large language groups, were introduced in 1970. Since then all MPs have to belong to either the Dutch or the French language group, and a number of 'special majority laws' concerning institutional reform can only be passed by a majority in both language groups (and an overall majority of two-thirds). An 'alarm bell procedure' has been installed, permitting three-quarters of a language group to temporarily halt the parliamentary processing of a legislative initiative and send it to the Council of Ministers, which in turn is composed of an equal member of French- and Dutch-speaking ministers (parity) who traditionally decide in consensus (Deschouwer 2014; Sinardet 2010; Reuchamps 2007).

The consociational logic (see Lijphart 1981, 1999) is also reflected in the features of the Belgian party system. Indeed, consociationalism entails a far-reaching segmentation between groups and sees political elites as representatives of their own group who then have to build bridges to the elites of other groups. Hence, the party system is split on language basis and electoral districts are confined to the borders of the regions (Caluwaerts and Reuchamps 2015).

The role of political parties is very outspoken in the Belgian political system, which is often characterised as a partitocracy (De Winter 1998; Deschouwer 2009) – which in turn cannot be dissociated from its consociational nature (Deschouwer 2014; Sinardet 2010). The Belgian party system has changed dramatically between 1968 and 1978 due to the split along linguistic lines of the three traditional political parties: the Christian democrats in 1968, the liberals in 1971 and the social democrats in 1978. One of the reasons for this split was the rising competition from the 1960s onwards with substate nationalist or regionalist parties such as the Volksunie, the Rassemblement Wallon and the FDF. They successfully put linguistic and decentralisation issues on the agenda, forcing the mainstream parties to take a clear stand. Parties that were created later such as the greens followed the same organisational logic, although the greens do form a common political group in the federal parliament and most explicitly profile themselves as one single party family. The absence of statewide political parties, which is unique for a federal country (Swenden 2005; Deschouwer 2009; Sinardet 2010), has resulted in the existence of two separate party systems in one polity (De Winter, Swyngedouw and Dumont 2006).

The electoral system strongly contributes to this dynamics. While electoral districts for the federal House of Representatives are organised on a provincial basis since 2003, electoral reforms for other assemblies deliberately installed a language group logic, combined with a fixed distribution of seats. In 1979, Belgium was divided into two electoral colleges for the European Parliament elections: a Dutch-speaking and a French-speaking college, both electing their own representatives on the basis of a fixed distribution of seats. A similar system was introduced for the Parliament of the Brussels-Capital Region in 1989 and for the directly elected representatives in the federal Senate between 1995 and 2010. As from 2014, the Senate – which powers were strongly reduced – is mainly composed of indirectly elected representatives that already have a seat in the parliaments of the federated entities (Dandoy et al. 2015). For each of these elections, electoral districts do not cross the borders of the regions. In combination with the split party system, this causes voters – with the exception of those living in the Brussels region – to be able to vote only for representatives of their own language community.

The dynamics of the party and electoral system is also related to other aspects, such as media reporting on federal politics and the lack of a genuine countrywide public sphere (Sinardet 2010). The almost total absence of nationwide structured mass media is indeed another remarkable feature of the Belgian polity. This segregated media system is clearly interwoven with political dynamics since Dutch- and French-speaking federal ministers in Belgium have the tendency to communicate their decisions primarily through their 'own' media. The discourse of politicians also tends to vary, depending on whether they are interviewed by Dutch-speaking or French-speaking media. This is in line with how media frame political information according to the political consensus within their own community, particularly on linguistic matters.

The particular features of Belgium's political and federal systems are often viewed as (one of) the main reasons for its political instability. Indeed, most of the state reforms have occurred amidst a highly tense political atmosphere. At different times, quite long periods of polarisation and paralysis have preceded agreements on state reform. Between 1978 and 1981, Belgium had no less than seven short-lived governments. In 1988, Belgium broke its own record of government formation duration. That record was again broken in 2007 in attempts to negotiate a sixth state reform (194 days). The reform finally emerged during the government formation of 2010–2011 that required 541 days, the world record of government formation duration.

However, there are some important nuances to be made. While there may not be a genuine common public sphere at the political level, there are a number of common national cultural markers (Reuchamps et al. 2016). Sports are undoubtedly the best example of these with the statewide popularity of the Red Devils, the national football team. Combined with other international successes that boosted a form of national pride, such as those of Belgian singers like Stromae and the winning of the Nobel Prize for Physics by François Englert, it is sometimes argued there is the emergence of a new 'Belgitude'. Also, even if federal matters may often be reported in a biased way by the regionalised media, coverage of federal politics as such is still high, actually higher than coverage of regional politics. Nevertheless, with the structural segmentation of the political and media level over the past decades, the increasing federalisation of the country and growing importance of regional institutions, we expect that citizens' territorial identifications have been affected.

IDENTITIES AND THEIR EVOLUTION

Over the years, identities in Belgium have been measured in different ways (De Winter 1998; Reuchamps 2011; Reuchamps 2013a; Reuchamps, Kavadias and Deschouwer 2014; Deschouwer et al. 2015). The most often and consistently used measurement is the so-called hierarchical question, asking survey respondents to which territorial entity (such as Belgium, Wallonia, province, city/ commune out of a given list) they feel most closely related, in the first and in the second places (for an overview of the results based on this question between 1991 and 2009, see Deschouwer and Sinardet 2010). Another frequently used question is the internationally renowned Linz-Moreno question. As this has been used in most electoral surveys since 1995 and best allows comparison of Belgian data with those of other 'multi-national' countries, we will further focus on the results for this measurement (for a comparison of results between different identity measurements used in PartiRep, see Deschouwer et al. 2015). Also, the Linz-Moreno question presents the advantage that it allows respondents to give the same importance to their regional and national identities, while the hierarchical question forces to prioritise different levels.

However, the complexity of the institutional and identity landscape in Belgium, based on regional as well as community identities, is difficult to translate into the Linz-Moreno question that only allows for one type of regional identity to be measured. This difficulty mostly arises in the French-speaking part of Belgium. Indeed, while the Flemish identity covers relatively well the regional as well as the community component, on the other side of the language border there is an important difference between the Walloon and the francophone identities. This difference reveals itself in the institutional landscape (community and regional institutions not having been merged contrary to the Flemish side) and in political and intellectual debates among French speakers (where 'regionalists' and 'communitarians' have been some-times at odds). The problem also occurs for Dutch-speaking respondents in Brussels, most particularly in recent years where it is argued that a Brussels regional identity has developed. Hence, while a dual tension between substate and state does still more or less make sense for the 'Flanders versus Belgium' divide, it does not make sense for francophone Belgians who can be not only Belgian but also Walloon, francophone or 'Bruxellois'. Still we chose to use Belgian and Walloon identities for Walloon respondents, as this has also been the case in previous research.

Figures 6.1 and 6.2 show the evolution of Belgian versus regional identifi-cations between 1995 and 2014. This does not confirm our expectations of a rise of regional identities. The 'only Flemish' category, which most strongly

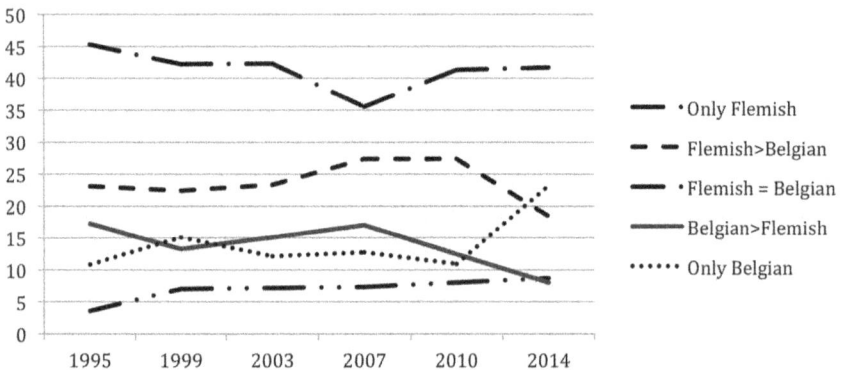

Figure 6.1.   Evolution of identities in Flanders (1995–2014) (in percentage). Source: ISPO-PIOP for data from 1995 to 2010 and PartiRep Voter Surveys for 2009 and 2014.

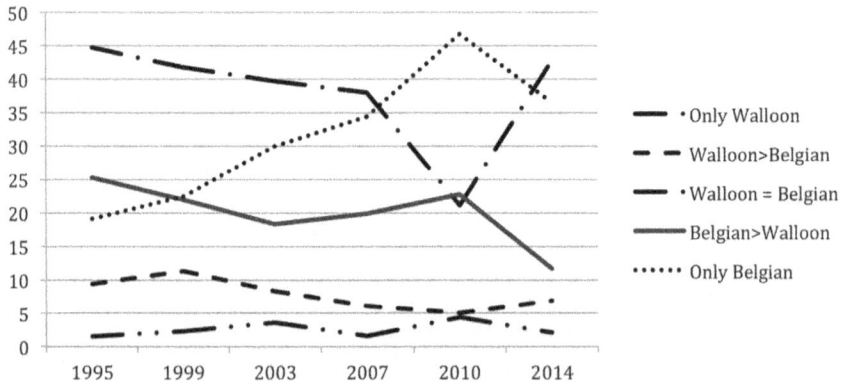

Figure 6.2.   Evolution of identities in Wallonia (1995–2014) (in percentage). Source: ISPO-PIOP for data from 1995 to 2010 and PartiRep Voter Surveys for 2009 and 2014.

expresses the Flemish identity, scores the lowest in figure 6.1. Between 2010 and 2014, it went from 8 per cent to 8.7 per cent, which is statistically not significant. That category is also the least chosen in the entire period (although precisely not in 2014). Clearly at the top, chosen by more than 40 per cent of Flemish respondents, is the category which puts Belgian and Flemish identities at equal strength. Also this did not change recently. We can notice an evolution for two response categories, though. The most remarkable is that in 2014 much more Flemish people felt only Belgian: at 23 per cent this is double the figure of 2010. Also, less Flemish people feel more Flemish than Belgian (from 27 per cent to 18 per cent).

The answers on the Linz-Moreno question point to an even stronger domination of the Belgian identity in Wallonia, but the trends are a little less linear (because of a change in 2010). In 2014, 37 per cent of the Walloons felt only Belgian and 12 per cent felt more Belgian than Walloon. Here also, the middle category always scores the highest (with the exception of 2010), while those that feel more Walloon than Belgian, or only Walloon form a very small minority (respectively 7 per cent and 2 per cent).

All in all, these analyses reveal quite stable patterns regarding the relative weight of the different identities that only very gradually evolve in time. And when they evolve, they do not in the expected direction of stronger subnational identities. This confirms previous research, regardless whether the Linz-Moreno question or the hierarchical question was used (De Winter 1998; Frognier and De Winter 1999; Deschouwer and Sinardet 2010). The results are therefore not simply the product of a volatile attitude, surfing on the waves of linguistic tensions in Belgium nor of the electoral success of language political entrepreneurs. In fact, when such parties lose votes (like the Volksunie in the 1990s or the Rassemblement Wallon before), or win votes (like VB after 1991 or the N-VA after 2009), this does not seem to be simply the result of fluctuations in identity feelings. These feelings appear to be more stable than voting behaviour. However, underneath there could be developments in the preferences of voters for the institutional future of Belgium, or in the importance they attach to the issue of the relations between Belgium's language communities.

As mentioned, the Linz-Moreno question has the important disadvantage that no distinction can be made between Walloon and francophone identity. The PartiRep survey also has an important limitation, as it does not contain any data for the Brussels' region. Not only does this exclude about 10 per cent of the Belgian population, in recent years the Brussels region has also become increasingly important in Belgium's debate on federalism. According to an increasing number of academics and other observers, a Brussels identity or even a Brussels community is developing, as the increasingly multicultural socio-demographic composition of the region can no longer simply reduce it to a mere meeting point for the two largest Belgian language communities. It

Table 6.1. Feelings of nationalism and identification with groups (scale 0–10)

	Feelings of nationalism	Identification				
		Flemish	Francophone	Belgian	Walloon	Brussels
Flanders (1,018)	5.09	6.92		7.07		
Wallonia (1,024)	4.64		7.59	8.53	6.41	
Brussels (738)	5.27	2.42	7.62	8.25		7.16
Dutch (71)	5.13	6.03	4.28	7.68		6.44
French (611)	5.25	2.03	8.07	8.41		7.27

Source: MEDW (2014).

is therefore interesting to see how identification with Brussels relates to the other forms of identification in Belgium.

To get some insight into this, we use data from MEDW (2014). This survey used a metric scale to measure identities, asking respondents to which extent different identities relate to them, by asking to position themselves on an 11-point scale, going from 0 (very weak) to 10 (very strong). Another question was also asked, relating specifically to 'regional nationalism'. The question asked was: 'In politics some talk about Brussels/Flemish/Walloon nationalism. Where do you place yourself on a scale from 0 to 10, where 0 means 'not a single feeling of nationalism' and 10 means 'a very strong feeling of nationalism'. The results are shown in table 6.1.

For the level of identification, the data confirm our results for the Linz-Moreno question, although to a lesser extent. Feeling of identification with the Belgian identity is also strongest here, but the difference with the Flemish identity is not that large. The difference with the Walloon identity is larger, but here we also see that Walloon respondents tend to have a stronger francophone than Walloon identity. The results in Brussels clearly show that the Belgian identity is also strongest in the capital region. We also see a strong Brussels identity emerging from these figures. Of the three regional identities, it is even the strongest. The Brussels identity also seems more developed among French-speaking inhabitants of the capital region than among their Dutch-speaking counterparts (but the number is probably too small for Dutch speakers in Brussels to be sure about this).

PREFERENCES ON DISTRIBUTION OF COMPETENCES

At different times in the past decades, Flemish and French-speaking party elites have clashed around the issue of state reform. This was particularly the case between 2007 and 2011, when the political system was in a permanent atmosphere of crisis, resulting in a world record-breaking 541 days before a new federal government was formed after the 2010 elections. Even though research has showed that at the level of the MPs polarisation was often less strong (Sinardet, Reuchamps and Dodeigne 2014), this is not the impression one got from party political and media discourse.

Again, one can wonder to what extent the elite-driven divides are reflected in the citizens' preferences regarding state reform. Do they want the regions and communities to get more competence or would they rather attribute more powers to the federal level? In the PartiRep Voter Surveys of 2009 and 2014 we asked respondents to position themselves on a scale going from 0 to 10, where 0 means 'all the competences to the regions/communities' and 10 'all the competences for the federal state' and 5 was explicitly defined as a choice for the status quo ('it's good as it is').

In table 6.2 we have reduced this 11-point scale to five categories. We have kept the two extreme positions (0 and 10), as well as the middle position (5). The category 'more competences to the regions/communities' is composed of points 1 to 4, while the category 'more competences for the federal state' is composed of points 6 to 9.

The figures in table 6.2 make clear that the polarisation between the party elites on this topic is not fully present between the voters. There are some minor differences between Flanders and Wallonia, the most important in the support for further decentralisation or for more federalisation: Flemish voters are more in favour of the first and Walloon voters of the second. But these differences are not large: about a quarter of Flemish voters also wants more competences for the federal state, while about as many Walloon voters want to see more of them going to the federated entities. The extreme positions are quite unpopular, although there is a little more support to attribute all competences to the federal state among Walloon voters. A surprising finding is that Flemish voters are more in favour of a status quo than their Walloon counterparts, while the status quo is typically a position associated with French-speaking politicians, who for years quite unanimously declared they did not want further devolution (Reuchamps 2013b).

Table 6.2. Preferences for the distribution of competences (in percentage)

	Flanders		Wallonia	
	2009	2014	2009	2014
All competences for regions and communities	4.9	4.0	5.5	1.1
More competences for regions and communities	47.0	34.5	33.5	24.7
It is good as it is	24.2	38.0	22.5	31.6
More competences for the federal state	20.3	19.6	29.6	31.8
All competences for the federal state	3.5	4.0	8.9	10.8

Source: PartiRep Voter Surveys for 2009 and 2014.

It is also interesting to compare the evolution of this variable between 2009 and 2014. The support for the status quo grew among all voters, which could be interpreted as the consequence of the agreement on the sixth state reform that was concluded in 2011. This interpretation can be based on two types of reasoning. The constitutional reform agreement could lead voters to leave aside the issue from the political agenda, at least for a while, or convince them that their previous preferences for more decentralisation have been satisfied. The latter seems to be confirmed when we compare the results between 2009 and 2014, as the other main difference we can see is that the support for further decentralisation diminished, in both regions. Thus, it seems likely that part of the voters who supported further devolution of competences have evolved towards a preference for an institutional status quo. Apart from this evolution from decentralisation to status quo, the figures remained quite stable between 2009 and 2014 in Flanders as well as in Wallonia.

IDENTITIES AND INSTITUTIONAL PREFERENCES

Earlier studies showed that identity and institutional preferences are strongly linked, although this relation is not systematic (Pattie et al. 1999; Bond 2009; Curtice and Heath 2009; McCrone and Bechhofer 2015). For Belgium, we can also expect such a link: those who identify more with Flanders or Wallonia can be expected to be more in favour of regional autonomy. Table 6.3 shows the mean score on the 11-point scale which measures competence distribution preferences for every answer on the Linz-Moreno question. Clearly, those who identify more with Flanders are also more in favour of Flemish autonomy. And those who rather identify with Belgium favour a status quo or a refederalisation of competences. More surprisingly, however, the expected relation cannot be found for Wallonia. For preferences for autonomy, the most regionalist are those who feel only Walloon (a very small group), with a preference for more regional competences that is, however, lower than the average for all Flemish voters. The figures shown in table 6.3 are for 2014, but a similar result also emerged from the figures of 2009 (Deschouwer and Sinardet 2010).

Table 6.3. **Preferences regarding distribution of competences and the identification with Belgium and Flanders/Wallonia (2014, average score on 11-point scale)**

	Flemish region	Walloon region
Only Flemish/Walloon	3.14	4.92
More Flemish/Walloon than Belgian	3.76	5.75
As much Flemish/Walloon as Belgian	4.47	5.22
More Belgian than Flemish/Walloon	5.68	6.26
Only Belgian	5.20	5.69

Source: 2014 PartiRep Voter Survey.

IDENTITIES, PREFERENCES AND VOTING BEHAVIOUR

As explained earlier, we can expect that identification with regional or national identities, as well as preferences regarding the distribution of competences, also translate in voting behaviour, particularly given the very different positions within Flanders and Wallonia on identities as well as on state reform. The expectation is of course that voters with a stronger regional identity and/or a preference for more regional autonomy will tend to vote for parties that advocate these positions.

For positions to have an effect on voting though, they need to be highly salient. Voters will not base their choice on all possible viewpoints they may have. So we asked respondents to which extent they considered state reform as an important issue to determine their vote. The results in table 6.4 show for 2014 a clear but very surprising difference between the two regions. Walloon voters seem to attach more importance to state reform: 56 per cent of them find the issue important or very important. Only 19 per cent says it is not important, a figure that is 10 per cent higher among Flemish voters. This is not only surprising because the demand for further state reform comes almost exclusively from the Flemish political elite, with francophone parties generally saying there are other priorities, but also because this is a change from previous research results, which showed that state reform was considered more important in Flanders than in Wallonia (Dodeigne et al. 2016; Reuchamps et al. 2016). The 2009 survey did already show that the difference between Flemish and Walloon respondents had become rather small (Deschouwer and Sinardet 2010) but in 2014 the situation has turned around – the issue is now more important for Walloon respondents. A possible explanation for this could be that the long institutional crisis had more effect on Walloon citizens, particularly those fearing a break-up of Belgium.

To further explore the question of salience, we need to compare the importance attached to state reform in relation to other issues. Voters may find many issues important but will also tend to prioritise policy domains when making up their mind. Therefore, we asked respondents to tell us which issue they found most important from a list, shown in table 6.5. Socio-economic themes clearly come first for many voters: economy and

Table 6.4. Importance attached to state reform in making an electoral choice (in percentage)

	Flanders	Wallonia
Very/rather important	42.5	56.5
Not important, not unimportant	28.4	25.0
Rather or very unimportant	29.1	18.6

Source: 2014 PartiRep Voter Survey.

Table 6.5. **Importance of different issue domains in making an electoral choice (in percentage)**

Issue domains	Flemish region	Walloon region
Employment	38.9	51.7
Economy	25.2	17.9
Fiscal issues	9.7	7.0
Environment	9.1	7.3
Crime	7.8	6.0
Immigration	6.2	6.9
State reform	3.1	2.6
Defence	0.0	0.6

Source: 2014 PartiRep Voter Survey.

employment together are regarded as more important by 64 per cent of Flemish voters and just under 70 per cent of Walloon voters. State reform is only considered most important by a particularly small proportion of voters: around 3 per cent in Flanders as well as in Wallonia. This extreme low saliency was also found in research in the previous two decades (Swyngedouw and Beerten 1996; Swyngedouw and Rink 2008; Frognier, De Winter and Baudewyns 2008; Deschouwer and Sinardet 2010). So while there are important differences concerning the views of voters on the institutional future of the country, for most voters these positions do not seem to determine their vote.

Finally, an important question raised in the literature is the link between national identity, constitutional preferences and vote choice (Bechhofer and McCrone 2009). In the Belgian case, it means that we need to check whether identities, institutional issues and their saliency actually matter for voting behaviour. Indeed, it is not because an issue is not salient that voters' identities and institutional preferences will not have any impact on their vote at all. They may still come into play in the complexity of voting behaviour, albeit not explicitly and consciously. The literature on substate nationalist and regionalist parties would make us expect that voters who identify more with their region will also tend to vote for regionalist parties, while voters with a more national or mixed identity will tend to choose other parties (Falkenhagen 2010; Gómez-Reino, De Winter and Lynch 2006; De Winter and Türsan 1998). Similarly, we also expect voters with regionalist institutional preferences to vote for regionalist parties.

However, it is not really possible to test this hypothesis for both regions in Belgium, as Walloon regionalist parties are not represented in parliament anymore since the *Rassemblement Wallon* disappeared in 1985. Still, some of the traditional francophone parties have a stronger regionalist tradition than others. This is particularly the case for the PS, which has often been considered as the main heir of the Walloon Movement. However, the regionalist leanings of the PS, which were strongest in the 1980s, gradually disappeared in the 1990s when it focused its discourse on the defence of the federal state (particularly regarding the defence of cross-regional social security solidarity).

An additional hypothesis is that when a strong regional identity is combined with a preference for regional autonomy or independence, the motivations to vote for a regionalist party are reinforced (Bechhofer and McCrone 2009). Similarly, voters with a strong Belgian identity and preference for more Belgian competences would be expected to vote for those parties best defending Belgian unity. As we saw earlier in this chapter, there is a relation between identities and institutional preferences in Flanders (but not one on one), while the relation could not be found at all for Wallonia. Therefore, it is necessary to measure the respective impact of both factors on voting behaviour and also to verify whether there is an effect of the combination of both variables.

This question is particularly relevant, given that in the 2014 election campaign, the N-VA did not so much advocate Flemish autonomy with classic nationalist arguments but rather with a focus on socio-economic policies, stating that more autonomy would give Flanders the right-wing policies it has been voting for since years but which were blocked by the strong socialist party in the south. One of the objectives of this type of discourse is obviously to attract voters with a more Belgian identity who could be convinced by these socio-economic arguments.

First, we look at the relation between identities and voting behaviour. Tables 6.6 and 6.7 show the answers to the Linz-Moreno question – recoded into three categories – for the electorate of each party in 2014. As the voting results are quite similar for the three assemblies that people could vote for (European Parliament, Regional Parliament and Federal House), we limit ourselves to the results for the latter.

Table 6.6. The relation between identification and voting behaviour in the Flemish region (2014)

	N-VA	CD&V	Open VLD	SP.a	Groen	VB	PvdA
Only or more Flemish than Belgian	45.5	21.8	13.8	16.3	9.7	52.6	19.0
As much Flemish as Belgian	40.2	48.1	45.9	38.5	48.6	21.1	38.1
Only or more Belgian than Flemish	13.3	30.1	40.4	45.2	41.7	26.3	42.9
Total, N	271	133	109	104	72	19	21

Source: 2014 PartiRep Voter Survey.

Table 6.7. The relation between identification and voting behaviour in the Walloon region (2014)

	PS	MR	cdH	Ecolo	PTB	PP
Only or more Walloon than Belgian	11.31	5.2	6.7	7.0	14.0	21.4
As much Walloon as Belgian	39.4	41.5	47.4	47.4	34.9	28.6
Only or more Belgian than Walloon	49.3	43.3	46.2	45.6	51.2	50.0
Total, N	213	135	104	57	43	28

Source: 2014 PartiRep Voter Survey.

Table 6.7 shows that within the Walloon electorate there are not many differences. The situation is different in the Flemish region though. Two groups can be distinguished. On the one hand, N-VA and VB (although the small number for the latter means we have to be cautious) have an electorate that clearly feels more Flemish than that of other parties. On the other hand, voters of the socialist, liberal, green and radical left parties tend more towards a stronger or exclusive Belgian identity. The Belgian feeling group is strongest among left-wing parties, SP.a and PVDA (although we again have to be cautious given the small numbers for the latter). In between, we find the electorate of the Christian democratic CD&V, with an electorate that is less Flemish than that of N-VA and VB, but also less Belgian than that of the other parties. This is not entirely surprising, as the Flemish Christian democrats have always had a more Belgian and a more Flemish wing (following the dichotomy between an autonomist tradition versus an 'entrist' tradition, that is bringing changes from within), although the latter clearly became stronger in the first decade of this century.

Another striking finding is that the mixed category is quite strong among all parties, with percentages all lying between 38 per cent and 48 per cent (except for VB and PTB). Feeling as strongly Belgian as Flemish/Walloon therefore does not seem to have a strong effect on party choice. This also means that more than half of the electorate of N-VA has a Belgian identity that is as strong as or even stronger than the Flemish one. This suggests that the party's attempts at broadening its electorate beyond the traditional Flemish nationalist public are a success, while the N-VA at the same time also manages to retain voters with a stronger Flemish identity.

Next, we examine the relation between institutional preferences and voting behaviour. Table 6.8 shows the average position regarding institutional preferences on the 11-point scale for the electorate of each party. First, compared to identities, regarding the distribution of competence differences between the voters of the parties are more limited. The different electorates find themselves between 3.7 and 6.6 on the scale from 0 to 10, or, in other words, between a very limited regionalisation and a very limited federalisation.

Table 6.8. Average preference on distribution of competences per party electorate

N-VA	3.7 (*N* = 271)	PS	5.5 (*N* = 213)
CD&V	4.5 (*N* = 133)	MR	6.0 (*N* = 135)
Open VLD	5.2 (*N* = 109)	cdH	6.6 (*N* = 104)
SP.a	5.3 (*N* = 104)	Ecolo	5.7 (*N* = 57)
Groen	5.0 (*N* = 72)	PTB	5.2 (*N* = 43)
VB	4.5 (*N* = 19)	PP	5.6 (*N* = 28)
PvdA	5.5 (*N* = 21)		
Flemish average	4.5	Walloon average	5.6

Source: 2014 PartiRep Voter Survey.

Still, for the Flemish region, we find a similar pattern as in the previous tables on identities, although it is less strong. Parties whose voters tend to favour (to a small extent) more competences for Belgium again choose Open VLD, SP.a and PvdA. Voters of CD&V again hold a middle position. This is quite congruent with the average positions of the MPs of these parties on the same 11-point scale (Sinardet, Reuchamps and Dodeigne 2016). On the other side of the status quo, we find N-VA voters who clearly favour increased regionalisation, even though they are still very far away from their party's official separatist position. Figure 6.3 details the distribution of N-VA voters in terms of their institutional preferences. The N-VA average of 3.7 is not the result of a combination of outspoken pro-Flanders voters and outspoken pro-Belgium voters. Rather, it is mostly the result of voters being in the area around the average. This is also reflected in the lack of congruence with the MPs of N-VA who have a mean score of 0.6, hence more than 3 points below their voters' score (Sinardet, Reuchamps and Dodeigne 2016).

These results, even more than the previous ones, suggest that N-VA has been able to convince an important number of voters who do not agree with its quite radical reform plans. However, they can also be simply related to the fact that N-VA has become a large party and that voters of other parties do not take a radical position in the Belgian direction: in this context it is difficult for the N-VA electorate to differ strongly from the other parties (Baudewyns, Dandoy and Reuchamps 2015; Dandoy, Baudewyns and Reuchamps 2015). The comparison with 2009 supports both explanations. At that time, when N-VA did not yet focus as strongly on socio-economic issues and had not yet moved strongly to the right on these issues, the average position of its voters on the scale was 3.1 (the Flemish average then being 4.3). Even though already in 2009 this position was not really congruent with the party's programme, between 2009 and 2014 the N-VA attracted more voters with moderate preferences on state reform. This being said, the difference between the average voter of SP.a (5.3) and that of N-VA (3.7) is significant, making N-VA the only party with an electorate that has a (moderately) more Flemish profile, mostly not only concerning identities but also concerning

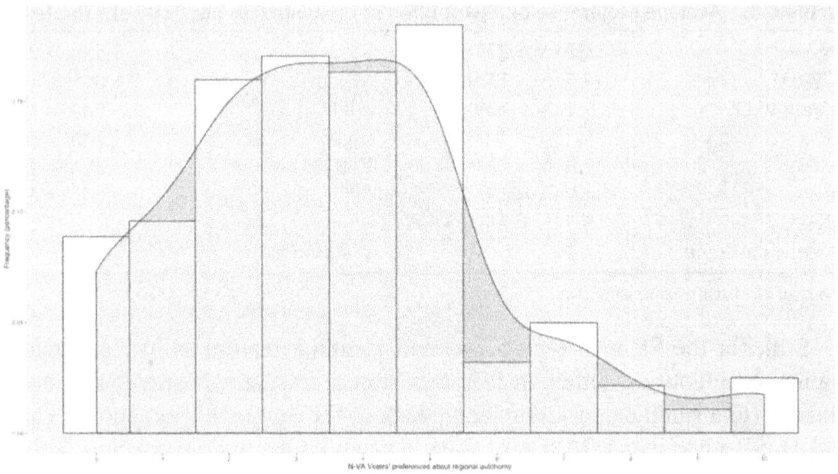

Figure 6.3. Distribution of N-VA voters in terms of their institutional preferences (2014). Source: 2014 PartiRep Voter Survey.

competence distribution. Whether this also goes for separatist VB is difficult to say. Contrary to the identities table, the VB electorate is surprisingly also in the middle here, but as was previously said, the small number invites us to be very cautious with the results for this party. However, past research showed that its voters differentiated themselves more by their positions on migration and crime than on identity and state reform (Swyngedouw and Abts 2011). Differences between the electorates of the French-speaking parties are again less strong but a bit more pronounced than in the previous tables on identities. The cdH voters favour mostly more competences for Belgium, which is more or less in tune with the party's quite pro-Belgian discourse. However, electorates of other parties are within 1 point distance of the cdH and thus compete for voters in favour of Belgian unity. In any case, no francophone party explicitly defends increased regionalisation of the country.

CONCLUSION

In multilingual, multinational and multilevel Belgium, we can observe a remarkable stability of identities and state reform preferences over time, certainly given the rapidly increasing decentralisation and all the political turmoil on identities and state reform in this country. Surprisingly, we find a rather limited division of public opinion on identity and state reform questions, despite the much-divided structure of Belgium's party and media systems. Successive waves of surveys demonstrate the strength of mixed identities, and even an increasing importance of Belgian identity, in line with a limited demand for far-reaching autonomy in contrast with political elite and media discourse.

It could be argued that research focusing solely on the ethno-territorial form of identity feelings can create the impression that this is the most important or even only relevant form of identification, while it is plausible that respondents identify much more strongly with their professional identity, social class and religion than with their city, region or country. Research in Belgium (Doutrelepont, Billiet and Vandekeere 2000) showed that when respondents were asked to determine which is the most important entity they belong to, only about 5 per cent spontaneously named a territorial community. Nonetheless, we notice links among identities, preferences and voting behaviour. In fact, most differences are to be found within language groups, especially in Flanders. We also find these differences in voting behaviour and how it relates to feelings of identities and preferences: three groups of parties could be distinguished, partially overlapping with a left-right division. Differences between the electorates of the French-speaking parties are less strong, with also congruence between voters and parties.

However questions remain both in terms of the way we measure these complex realities that are identities and preferences on devolution and in terms of the political consequences. Further research is needed to reflect on different ways to grasp these concepts empirically and also on how they impact the voters-parties relationship and more largely the political dynamics in Belgium. Our findings call for further investigation into how complex identities and preferences influence the organisation of a complex political system.

REFERENCES

Anderson, B. (1983) *Imagined Communities: Reflections on the Origin and Spread of Nationalism*, London: Verso.

Baudewyns, P., Dandoy, R. and Reuchamps, M. (2015) 'The Success of the Regionalist Parties in the 2014 Elections in Belgium', *Regional and Federal Studies* 25(1): 91–102.

Bechhofer, F., & McCrone, D. (Eds.). (2009). *National Identity, Nationalism and Constitutional Change*. Houndmills: Palgrave Macmillan.

Bond, R. (2009) 'Political Attitudes and National Identities in Scotland and England', in Bechhofer, F. and McCrone, D. (eds) *National Identity, Nationalism and Constitutional Change*, Houndmills: Palgrave Macmillan, 95–121.

Caluwaerts, D. and Reuchamps, M. (2015) 'Combining Federalism with Consociationalism: Is Belgian Consociational Federalism Digging its Own Grave?' *Ethnopolitics* 14(3), 277–95.

Curtice, J. and Heath, A. (2009) 'England Awakes? Trends in National Identity in England', in Bechhofer, F. and McCrone, D. (eds) *National Identity, Nationalism and Constitutional Change*, Houndmills: Palgrave Macmillan, 41–63.

Dandoy, R., Baudewyns, P. and Reuchamps, M. (2015) 'The 2014 Federal and European Elections in Belgium', *Electoral Studies* 39: 164–68.

Dandoy, R., Dodeigne, J., Reuchamps, M. and Vandeleene, A. (2015) 'The New Belgian Senate. A (Dis)continued Evolution of Federalism in Belgium?' *Representation* 51(3): 327–39.

Deschouwer, K. (2009) 'The Rise and Fall of the Belgian Regionalist Parties', *Regional & Federal Studies* 19(4): 559–77.

Deschouwer, K. (2014) 'Federalisme tussen oplossing en probleem', in Devos, C. (ed.) *België#2014. Een politieke geschiedenis van morgen*, Gent: Borgerhoff & Lamberigts, 299–320.

Deschouwer, K. and Sinardet, D. (2010) 'Identiteiten, communautaire standpunten en stemgedrag', in Deschouwer, K., Delwit, P., Hooghe, M. and Walgrave, S. (eds) *De stemmen van het volk. Een analyse van het stemgedrag in Vlaanderen en Wallonië op 7 juni 2009*, Brussel: VUB Press, 75–98.

Deschouwer K., De Winter, L., Reuchamps, M., Sinardet, D. and Dodeigne, J. (2015) 'Les attitudes communautaires et le vote', in Deschouwer, K., Delwit, P., Hooghe, M., Baudewyns, P. and Walgrave, S. (eds) *Décrypter l'électeur : Le comportement électoral et les motivations de vote*, Leuven: Lannoo Campus, 156–73.

De Winter, L. (1998) 'Ethnoterritoriale identiteiten in Vlaanderen: verkenningen in een politiek en methodologisch mijnenveld', in Swyngedouw, M., Billiet, J., Carton, A. and Beerten, R. (eds) *De (on)redelijke kiezer. Onderzoek naar de politieke opvattingen van Vlamingen. Verkiezingen van 21 mei 1995*, Leuven: Acco, 159–80.

De Winter, L. and Frognier, A.-P. (1999) 'Les identités politiques territoriales: explorations dans un champ de mines politique et méthodologique', in Frognier, A.-P. and Aish, A.-M. (eds) *Des Elections en Trompe-l'œil. Enquête sur le comportement électoral des Wallons et des Francophones*, Bruxelles: De Boeck, 67–96.

De Winter, L. and Türsan, H. (1998) *Regionalist Parties in Western Europe*, London: Routledge.

De Winter, L., Swyngedouw, M. and Dumont, P. (2006) 'Party System(s) and Electoral Behaviour in Belgium: From Stability to Balkanisation', *West European Politics* 29(5): 933–56.

Dodeigne, J., Gramme, P., Reuchamps, M. and Sinardet, D. (2016) 'Beyond Linguistic and Party Homogeneity: Determinants of Belgian MPs' Preferences on Federalism and State Reform', *Party Politics* 22(4): 427–39.

Doutrelepont, R., Billiet, J. and Vandekeere, M. (2001) 'Profils identitaires en Belgique', in Bawin-Legros, B., Voyé, L., Dobbelaere, K. and Elchardus, M. (eds) *Belge toujours. Fidélité, stabilité, tolérance. Les valeurs des Belges en l'an 2000*, Bruxelles: De Boeck, 213–56.

Erk, J. and Anderson, L. (2009) 'The Paradox of Federalism: Does Self-Rule Accommodate or Exacerbate Ethnic Divisions?' *Regional and Federal Studies* 19(2): 191–202.

Falkenhagen, Frédérique (2010) *Les électorats ethno-regionalistes en Europe occidentale. Etude comparée en Bavière, Ecosse, Flandre et au Pays de Galles*, Doctorat de Science Politique, Paris: Cevipof.

Frognier, A.-P., and Aish, A.-M. (eds). (1999). *Des élections en trompe-l'oeil. Enquête sur le comportement électoral des Wallons et des Francophones.* Bruxelles: De Boeck.

Frognier, A., De Winter, L. and Baudewyns, P. (2008) 'Les Wallons et la réforme de l'Etat. Une analyse sur la base de l'enquête post-électorale de 2007', Louvain-la-Neuve: Pôle Interuniversitaire sur l'Opinion publique et la Politique (PIOP).

Gellner, Ernest (1983) *Nations and Nationalism*, Oxford: Blackwell.

Gómez-Reino, M., De Winter, L. and Lynch, P. (2006) 'Conclusion: The Future Study of Autonomist and Regionalist Parties', in Gómez-Reino, M., De Winter, L. and Lynch, P. (eds) *Autonomist Parties in Europe: Identity Politics and the Revival of the Territorial Cleavage*, Barcelona: ICPS, 247–70.

Guibernau, M. (2006) 'National Identity, Devolution and Secession in Canada, Britain and Spain', *Nations and Nationalism* 12(1): 51–76.

Hobsbawm, E. J. (1990) *Nations and Nationalism since 1780. Programme, Myth, Reality*, Cambridge: Cambridge University Press.

Keating, M. (1996) *Nations against the State. The New Politics of Nationalism in Quebec, Catalonia and Scotland*, London: Macmillan Press.

Lijphart, A. (ed) (1981). *Conflict and coexistence in Belgium: the dynamics of a culturally divided society.* Berkeley: Institute of International Studies, University of California.

Lijphart, A. (1999). *Patterns of Democracy: Government Forms and Performance in Thirty-Six Countries.* New Haven: Yale University Press.

McCrone, D. and Bechhofer, F. (2015) *Understanding National Identity*, Cambridge: Cambridge University Press.

Moreno, L. (2007) 'Identités duales et nations sans État (la Question Moreno)', *Revue internationale de politique comparée* 14(4): 497–513.

Pattie, C., Denver, D., Mitchell, J. and Bochel, H. (1999) 'Partisanship, National Identity and Constitutional Preferences: An Exploration of Voting in the Scottish Devolution Referendum of 1997', *Electoral Studies* 18(3): 305–22.

Reuchamps, M. (2007) 'La parité linguistique au sein du conseil des ministres', *Res Publica* 49(4): 602–27.

Reuchamps, M. (2011) *L'avenir du fédéralisme en Belgique et au Canada: Quand les citoyens en parlent*, Brussels: P. I. E. Peter Lang.

Reuchamps, M. (2013a) 'The Future of Belgian Federalism through the Eyes of the Citizens', *Regional & Federal Studies* 23(3): 353–68.

Reuchamps, M. (2013b) 'The Current Challenges on Belgian Federalism and the 6th Reform of the State', in Lopez Basaguren, A. and Escajedo San-Epifanio, L. (eds) *The Ways of Federalism in Western Countries and the Horizons of Territorial Autonomy in Spain*, vol. 1, Berlin and Heidelberg: Springer, 375–92.

Reuchamps, M., Kavadias, D. and Deschouwer, K. (2014) 'Drawing Belgium: Using Mental Maps to Measure Territorial Conflict', *Territory, Politics, Governance* 2(1): 30–51.

Reuchamps, M., Meulewaeter, C., Baudewyns, P. and De Winter, L. (2016) 'Les facteurs d'unité en Belgique: Diables rouges, attitudes politiques et sentiments identitaires', in Caron, J.-F. (ed.) *Les conditions de l'unité politique et de la sécession dans les sociétés multinationales: Catalogne, Écosse, Flandre, Québec*, Québec: Presses de l'Université Laval, 99–126.

Reuchamps, M., Sinardet, D., Dodeigne, J. and Caluwaerts, D. (2016) 'Reforming Belgium's Federalism: Comparing the Views of MPs and Voters', *Government and Opposition: an International Journal of Comparative Politics*, online first: https://doi.org/10.1017/gov.2015.29.

Sinardet D. (2010) 'From Consociational Consciousness to Majoritarian Myth. Consociational Democracy, Multi-Level Politics and the Belgian Case of Brussels-Halle-Vilvoorde', *Acta Politica. International Journal of Political Science* 45(3): 346–69.

Sinardet D. (2013) 'How Linguistically Divided Media Represent Linguistically Divisive Issues. Belgian Political TV-Debates on Brussels-Halle-Vilvoorde', *Regional and Federal Studies* 23(3): 311–30.

Sinardet, D., Reuchamps, M. and Dodeigne, J. (2014) 'De communautaire breuklijn in België: kloof of spleetje', in Devos, C. (ed.) *België#2014. Een politieke geschiedenis van morgen*, Gent: Borgerhoff & Lamberigts, 273–97.

Sinardet, D., Reuchamps, M. and Dodeigne, J. (2016) 'Een Belgiëbocht? Parlementsleden over de bevoegdheidsverdeling', *Samenleving en Politiek* 23(2): 74–86.

Swenden, W. (2005). What – "if anything" – can the European Union learn from Belgian federalism and vice versa? *Regional & Federal Studies*, 15(2): 187–205.

Swyngedouw, M. and Abts, K. (2011) 'Les électeurs de la N-VA aux élections fédérales du 13 juin 2010', *Courrier hebdomadaire du CRISP* (2125).

Swyngedouw, M. and Beerten, R. (1996) 'Cognitieve en affectieve motieven van partijkeuze. De nationale verkiezingen van 21 mei 1995', *Res Publica* 36(4): 555–74.

Swyngedouw, M. and Rink, N. (2008) *Hoe Vlaams-Belgischgezind zijn de Vlamingen? Een analyse op basis van het postelectorale verkiezingsonderzoek 2007*, Leuven: Centrum voor Sociologisch Onderzoek, Instituut voor Sociaal en Politiek Opinieonderzoek (ISPO).

Chapter 7

A three-level game: Citizens' attitudes about the division of competences in a multilevel context

Soetkin Verhaegen, Louise Hoon, Camille
Kelbel and Virginie Van Ingelgom

EU INTEGRATION AND REGIONALISATION:
A THREE-LEVEL GAME

Until 1993, Belgium was officially a unitary state, although processes of decentralisation had started in the 1960s. From 1970 onwards, six consecutive state reforms contributed to the development of Belgium into the current federation (1970, 1980, 1988–1989, 1993, 2001 and 2013). An increasing amount of competences was moved to the regions and communities. Meanwhile, as in all member states of the EC/EU, other competences have been moved from the state to the EU level. Such bidirectional movements of competences are not unique to Belgium. In twenty-nine out of forty-two Organisation for Economic Co-operation and Development (OECD) countries, regional authority has increased between 1950 and 2006 (Hooghe, Marks & Schakel 2010). In Belgium, however, the pace and scope of the phenomenon is remarkable. From a relatively centralised state, it has transformed into one of the most federalised and Europeanised countries in the EU (Hooghe & Marks 2001). Having experienced continuous and fundamental shifts of competences, and being governed by three fully developed, overlapping and interacting levels, Belgians are an excellent example of multilevel governed citizens.

Given this general movement of authority and competences, away from centralised states, a question that almost naturally comes to mind is how competences should be divided among various governance levels. This chapter posits that it is of key importance that citizens perceive this division of competences as legitimate and thus agree with it. As such, we aim to explain Belgian citizens' preferences about the division of competences between the regional, the federal and the EU levels. Our assumption that citizens' perceptions matter clearly challenges the majority of previous studies on regionalisation, for which questions of competence (re-)distribution are apprehended and legitimised from the perspective of political elites, based on the assumption that they are the ones who ultimately take decisions on federalisation issues (Deschouwer 2013). By contrast, there has been a vivid public and academic debate about the role of citizens in the European integration process. Indeed, much of the critique addressed to European integration precisely concerns the allegedly elite-driven nature of the process and its endemic democratic deficit. As a result, individual-level attitudes are often taken into consideration in studies of EU integration.

Despite this flourishing debate on citizens' attitudes towards EU integration, we still lack an integrated approach that takes into account the different governance levels. Until today, empirical studies almost invariably consider shifts of competences and their rationale either to the sub- or to the supranational level and often fail to account for the division of competences as a trade-off between levels in a multilevel governance system (but see, e.g., De Winter, Swyngedouw & Goeminne 2008; Dupuy & Van Ingelgom 2014b, 2017). The literatures on attitudes towards EU integration and regionalisation have developed separately, each studying attitudes about one specific level. Such perspectives should be combined, as in isolation they fail to reflect a situation where competences move between multiple levels. Of course, since they mostly use the national level as a reference point, these literatures do not deny the existence of other levels. Most famously, the second-order model (Reif & Schmitt 1980) has stressed how attitudes about the national government play a role in voting in both EU and regional elections. Hence, if attitudes towards different levels are related in a two-by-two manner, this urges us to look at the whole picture. This chapter aims to do so by comparing (competing) explanations of citizens' attitudes towards the regional, the national and the EU levels.

In this context, the well-anchored concept of 'multi-level governance' highlights the necessity to align explanatory perspectives in a multilevel game perspective. What is often referred to as 'type I' multilevel governance, in particular, pictures a distribution of competences between a rather limited number of stable governance levels, each comprising a particular territory and fulfilling a wide range of tasks such as policymaking in a broad range of areas, having a court system and having a representational function (Marks & Hooghe 2004). The regionalisation of Belgium – defined as the decentralisation of governance authority to the regions and communities – and European integration are hence generally considered forms of type I multilevel governance. It particularly insists on the concomitance of shifts towards various sub- and supra-national levels. Not only does Belgium fit well the definition of a multilevel governance system, which consists of rather stable governance levels each of which fulfil a wide range of tasks (Marks & Hooghe 2004;

Börzel & Hosli 2003), but it also applies to individual states – including Belgium – within the EU.

Above all, this multilevel setting has a profound impact on legitimation dynamics (Scharpf 2007). In a context of multilevel governance, legitimacy can no longer be considered isolated at one level or as a trade-off between the national and only one other level. If governance is considered as a three-level game, where the regional, national and the European levels of government compete and interact, then so should be legitimacy. Hence, we should study citizens' evaluations of the legitimacy of governance in a multilevel governance system by taking into account their views on all three levels. Building on these considerations, we argue in this chapter that citizens' views of competence division deserve specific attention. After all, the legitimacy of a system strongly depends on public agreement with 'the "rules of the game", including the division of labour between different levels of governance' (De Winter & Swyngedouw 1999: 66). Citizens' agreement with 'who does what' is a prerequisite for 'output legitimacy' – that is, popular legitimacy of public action and policies (Scharpf 1999). Hence, there is a need to account for preferences towards multilevel governance at large.

This chapter therefore aims to explain which attitudes drive citizens' preferences about competence distribution. The guiding question is: What are the sources of citizens' preferences towards different governance levels? More precisely, we look at why citizens are willing to attribute a broader set of competences to one level over another. Citizens' preferences about each level may be driven by different or similar considerations. Insight into these mechanisms is the key to our understanding of citizens' evaluation of multilevel governance and of the legitimacy of governance in EU member states.

The Belgian case and the individual-level data of the 2014 PartiRep Voter Survey provide us with an excellent opportunity to look at citizens' attitudes towards competence division in a way that does justice to the reality of multilevel governance. We study citizens' preferences on competence division as a three-level game, between the regional, federal and EU levels of governance. We start this chapter by discussing how economic utilitarian motivations, identity and attitudes about political institutions could structure citizens' preferences about competence division. In a second section, we put forward a unique operationalisation of such measure(s). In the third part, we present the results, before concluding remarks are drawn.

CITIZENS' PREFERENCES ON THE DIVISION OF COMPETENCES

To explain the movement of competences to sub- or supra-national levels, two main approaches can be distinguished in the literatures on multilevel

governance and federalism: functionality, economic efficiency and utilitarian rationality, on the one hand, and identity, on the other (Schakel 2009).
However, as we focus on the perspective of citizens, we add a third type of
consideration: citizens' perceptions of the political institutions that would be
in charge of the competences attributed to each level. Accordingly, we group
our hypotheses around three sets of potential sources of citizens' preferences
about the division of competences: economic utilitarian motivations, identity-
based mechanisms and attitudes about political institutions.

Economic utilitarian motivations

The principle of subsidiarity, which is mobilised in elite discourse on Belgian decentralisation, as well as in the EU treaties (Sinnott 1995; De Winter,
Swyngedouw & Goeminne 2008), relies on efficiency and effectiveness. It
contends that a given competence should be located as closely to the citizen
as possible. Only when it is more efficient and effective to organise a policy
area for a larger group of citizens, this competence should move to a higher
level (Article 5 Treaty on European Union; see also Føllesdal 1998). Similarly, Oates's Theorem of Decentralisation states that 'the provision of public
services should be located at the lowest level of government encompassing
the relevant benefits and costs' (Oates 1999: 1122). For a number of policy
areas, the advantage of economies of scale and the need for cross-border
solutions has legitimised the upward movement of competences (Börzel &
Hosli 2003). The same principle may serve as an argument for regionalisation. Since the birth of the Belgian state, Flemish and Walloon economies
have been distinctive. In the nineteenth century and well into the twentieth century, Wallonia profited from early industrialisation while Flanders
remained a poorer, agricultural region. With the collapse of the coal industry
after World War II, Flanders outgrew Wallonia economically, resulting in a
new imbalance (Hooghe 2004; Deschouwer 2006). Flemish separatist elites
now often argue that Flanders would enjoy economic and efficiency benefits
from independence. From their perspective, wealthy Flanders is subsidising
poor Wallonia through a centralised security system (Swenden & Jans 2006;
Béland & Lecours 2005). The devolutionary agenda of the largest party in
Belgium relies on this functional argument to defend a separatist agenda;
the N-VA is 'a textbook case of modern, economic nationalism' (Boonen &
Hooghe 2014: 63).

    If these arguments indeed legitimise the upward and downward move-
ments of competences, we should expect efficiency, functionality and rationality to be reflected in citizens' legitimacy beliefs. We focus on *economic*
utilitarian motivations, that is, judgements that are based on the rational outweighing of economic benefits over costs. Van Keersbergen (2000) describes

such a relationship between the ruler and the ruled with the term 'allegiance'. A direct exchange of security and prosperity for public support characterises this relationship between the citizen and the state (rather than trust, loyalty or obedience). Economic utilitarian motivations can be either sociotropic or egocentric. These motivations can also be either perceived or objective (Verhaegen, Hooghe & Quintelier 2014). In this study, we only focus on objective egocentric economic utilitarian motivations. Sociotropic utilitarian motivations concern one's group (a country or a region), whereas egocentric utilitarian motivations concern one's individual situation.

The literature has demonstrated that sociotropic economic utilitarian motivations are at play both for EU integration and regionalisation. Whereas EU integration is, in essence, homogenising the economies of its member states, it has also led to diversification and new inequalities (Magone 2011), a dynamic that plays between the indebted and the bailout countries in the wake of the financial and monetary crisis, as well as between the Western versus the East and Central member states. Support for the EU varies according to national economic and social performance, both over time and cross-nationally (Anderson & Kaltenthaler 1996; Gabel 1998).

In a similar way, sociotropic economic utilitarian motivations have been brought forward to legitimise Belgian regionalisation. As explained earlier, Flemish citizens may feel that they are 'subsidising' Wallonia through the federal social security. More competences at the regional level would mean less transfers and could be perceived as economically beneficial for Flemish citizens. Such links between fiscal and economic imbalances between regions and regional nationalism have been observed by Béland and Lecours (2005) in the cases of Belgium, Canada and the United Kingdom and by Guibernau (2014) in Catalonia. However, as the goal of this study is not to compare different EU member states or Flanders and Wallonia on the aggregate level, sociotropic motivations cannot be tested with regard to EU integration.

Egocentric economic utilitarian motivations (Hooghe & Marks 2005; Verhaegen, Hooghe & Quintelier 2014) concern the costs or benefits that different individuals within a country or region may experience. Globalisation and, with that, supra-national integration and economies of scale are generally more advantageous to those who are better educated and have higher a income and occupational status. For the higher educated, cosmopolitan elite, the EU has offered great opportunities to travel and work abroad (Ingehart 1970). The integration of markets and disappearing borders have also benefited export and production at lower costs, because labour-intensive production can be moved to lower-wage countries, and companies in higher-wage countries can benefit from cheap labour and competition between member states. However, those whose income depends on lower-skilled jobs, and who compete with immigrants on the housing market, may experience EU integration as a costlier experience. Kriesi et al. (2006) have argued that this conflict between winners and losers of globalisation takes the shape of a fundamental new cleavage, which may redraw the outlines of party competition (Van der Eijk & Franklin 2004; Hooghe, Marks & Wilson 2002). We can then expect that those who are more educated and have a higher occupational status are more likely to favour the movement of competences, whereas those in a more sensitive socio-economic position should be against it.

Simultaneously, egocentric utilitarian motivations can be at play when citizens consider movements of competences from the federal to the regional levels. As for the European level, we may expect that education and occupational status increase one's benefits of economies of scale. Whereas we have no knowledge of studies that have looked at this relationship directly, there are indirect indications in the literature. Béland and Lecours (2005) argue that the regionalisation of social policy has been a key instrument of strengthening Flemish nationalism. From other cases, scholars have concluded that the best strategy to avoid separatist tendencies is economic development and the encouragement of cohesion while simultaneously tolerating cultural diversity (Hesli 1995). Also, regionalist parties (i.e. parties favouring devolution or even independence) are generally seen to receive more support from less-educated and less-affluent voters. Deschouwer (2013) shows this is the case for the extreme-right separatist VB, but less so for the N-VA. However, the same analysis demonstrates that state reform is not a pre-eminent issue for Belgians when voting (see also chapter 6), which reinforces the need to look at preferences on competence distribution, rather than support for regionalist parties. Furthermore, Cole and Loughlin (2003: 266) show that UK citizens adopt an 'instrumental or pragmatic stance towards extending the domain of regional policy intervention'. Building on the concept of 'ethno-centrism', De Winter, Swyngedouw and Goeminne (2008) identify 'regio-centrism' and show that citizens who think that foreigners or 'outsiders' will take advantage of the country's economy are also more likely to favour the regional over the federal level. Following this logic of egocentric economic utilitarianism, we expect that:

Hypothesis 1: Respondents who are more likely to economically benefit from the attribution of competences to a higher governance level are expected to prefer to attribute more competences to a higher level.

Identity-based mechanisms

The second approach, embedded in social constructivism, stresses that citizens also expect political institutions to embody them in a more emotional, personal way. When citizens identify as part of a community, they tend to aspire self-governance and the representation of this community's interests in political decision-making (Anderson 1991; Billig 1996; Gellner 2006/1983). If citizens want to see competences move to the level they feel most closely attached to, identity is an important mechanism in legitimising the competence of one level or the other (Beetham & Lord 1998). In a context of moving competences, citizens are expected to shift or divide their loyalties, expectations and political activities towards new centres (Risse 2005).

In the initial stages of EU integration, identity was seen as a secondary and natural consequence of gradual functional and economic integration (Haas 1958). However, the absence of a strong and widespread collective European identity and community has become central to a debate about the EU's democratic deficit (Habermas 2011). The perceived inputs (participation) and outputs (policy implementation) of EU democracy have been shown to rely upon a feeling of being part of an EU community (Beetham & Lord 1998; Verhaegen 2016). Whereas EU institutions have made several attempts to build a 'people's Europe' and to foster a European identity (through the creation of EU citizenship, symbols [Bruter 2009; Cram 2012] and subsidising European cultural and educational exchange [Sigalas 2010]), the success of such efforts has been questioned. For instance, exchange programmes are shown to preach to the converted as they attract students that already identify more strongly as European (Kuhn 2012). Participation in EU elections remains low, and anti-European, nationalist discourse has become more prominent in most member states. Linking the EU to immigration and diversity as a cultural threat, these actors propose an inherent conflict between European identity and national identity (Laffan 1996; Luedtke 2005). It is thus often assumed that the strongest territorial identities are national (thus, neglecting links between European or national and regional or local identities), and that national identity constrains preferences for European integration (Marks & Hooghe 2004; Kriesi & Lachat 2004). Research into the relationship between national and European identities, however, provides compelling evidence that for many citizens both identifications peacefully coexist (Duchesne & Frognier 2008; Kostakopoulou 2001), and that a large part of the European population currently identifies partly as European, even if the strength of this identity is often weaker than their national identity (Bruter 2012; Risse 2014).

European identity, independent of national identity, can thus be expected to influence one's preferences towards moving competences to the EU level, while national identity, independent of European identity, is expected to be linked to preferring to attribute more competences to the national level.

Similarly, identity may structure preferences for more regionalisation. The appeasement of tensions between the Flemish and Walloon regions is another argument advanced for further regionalisation. The division of competences between the federal level and the regional and community levels is at the heart of proposed solutions to appease tensions between mainly the Flemish and Walloon regions in Belgium. Flanders and Wallonia have developed separate cultural and media landscapes and have separate party systems (Billiet, Maddens & Frognier 2006). Consequently, it is often argued that Belgian politics are dysfunctional because of irreconcilable attitudes and preferences on both sides of the language border. In Belgium, competences were initially (primarily) moved to pacify ideological and socio-economic conflict (Billiet, Maddens & Frognier 2006). Until the late 1950s, Belgian society was above all marked by deep cleavages between Catholics, socialists and liberals. Ideological divides were more salient than linguistic differences and also cross-cut the latter (Deschouwer 2006). Various consociational mechanisms appeased these conflicts in the late 1960s, opening up space for mobilisation along the linguistic divide, strongly linked to media, education and culture and above all to regional identity (Huyse 1971; Swenden & Jans 2006; Hooghe 2004). The legislative confirmation of official Dutch, French, German and bilingual language zones in the 1960s was – and remains – contentious, especially around Brussels – a 'mainly French-speaking urban agglomeration surrounded by Dutch-speaking territory' (Swenden & Jans 2006: 879). Territorial conflict between the Flemish and the Walloon regions thus essentially has linguistic roots (Hooghe 2004).

Deschouwer et al. (2014) show that regional identity is significantly related to people's views on granting power to the subnational level. Whereas overall support for regionalisation has decreased between 2009 and 2014 (which the authors interpret as an argument for the status quo eschewed from the Sixth State Reform), the study finds a link between Flemish identity and demands to move competences to the regions and communities. Those who identify more with Belgium, in turn, prefer to see competences moved to the federal level. However, no such relationship is found in Wallonia, possibly because of the weaker regionalist discourse that would politically mobilise Walloon identity (Deschouwer & Sinardet 2010). However, it remains unclear how this relationship between identity and competence distribution compares to other considerations and to other levels. To guide our test of identity-based mechanisms, the literature proposes that:

Hypothesis 2: The stronger one's identification with a political or territorial community, the more competences one would like to attribute to the corresponding governance level.

Attitudes about political institutions

In a recent review, Hobolt and de Vries (2016) detail three main approaches to explain variation in support of European integration: utilitarian, identity and benchmarking approaches. These three approaches are complementary and have been the subject of dozens of political science articles dealing with the legitimacy of European governance (see already Hooghe & Marks 2005). The first approaches have been addressed in the previous sections. Based on the EU studies literature, we include a third set of explanations for citizens' preferences about the division of competences, which are at the heart of the benchmarking approach: attitudes about political institutions.

In this context, the Eastonian framework has been mobilised in EU studies (Van Ingelgom 2014). From an Eastonian perspective, legitimacy is defined as the interplay between specific and diffuse support (Easton 1965, 1975). The concept of diffuse support refers 'to evaluations of what an object is or represents – to the general meaning it has for a person – not of what it does' (Easton 1975: 444), whereas specific support is related to the satisfaction with the perceived outputs and performance of political authorities among the members of the system (Easton 1975: 437). Legitimacy or 'consent' with a governance level is thus facilitated by both specific and diffuse support with decision-making bodies. Hence, when determining which level is most fit to govern, citizens are expected to take the general image of institutional functioning and performance of these levels into account. In empirical studies, diffuse support is typically translated into trust in institutions, and specific support can be looked at by studying citizens' satisfaction with the performance of these institutions.

Relying on this, in EU studies, a positive relationship between trust in EU institutions and support for EU integration in specific policy areas has been observed (Hooghe & Verhaegen 2017). However, trust in other political institutions, especially national institutions, is shown to determine support for the EU as well (Franklin, Marsh & McLaren 1994; Harteveld, van der Meer & de Vries 2013). Scholars have come to divergent conclusions about the relationship between trust in national institutions and attitudes about the EU. Some argue that citizens take cues from the national level when forming opinions about the EU (Anderson 1998; Hobolt 2012); others argue that there is a negative relationship between evaluations of institutions at the two levels, one level being an exit from the other (Sánchez-Cuenca 2000; Rohrschneider 2002). Arnold, Sapir and Zapryanova (2012), in turn, argue that the level of corruption in their country moderates this relationship.

The core argument underlying these approaches is that European integration is too remote from most citizens' daily life for them to have sufficient interest, awareness or emotional attachment to base their attitudes on an evaluation of the implications of the integration process (Anderson 1998; Hobolt & de Vries 2016). In this context, citizens are supposed to use proxies – such as trust in national institutions – when supporting (or not) the EU.

In our study, where we aim to explain respondents' preferences about attributing competences to the regional, federal or EU level, relative to attributing them to one of the other levels, we can expect a more direct relationship.

We expect that trust in regional, federal or EU institutions will translate into preferences to attribute competences to these levels, independent of one's level of trust in other political institutions. A parallel relationship is expected for satisfaction with policymaking. Finally, to address the issue of the remoteness from one's daily life, perceptions of the impact of a governance level on one's life are taken into account.

Hypothesis 3a: The more trust one has in the institutions of a governance level, the more competences one would like to attribute to that level.

Hypothesis 3b: The more satisfied one is with policymaking at one level, the more competences one would like to attribute to that level.

Hypothesis 3c: The more citizens perceive a governance level to be able to impact their lives, the more competences they would like to attribute to that level.

MEASURES

Preference about attributing competences to a level

Citizens' preferences about the appropriate level of governance (regional, national or EU) are crucial for the legitimacy of multilevel governance. The amount of competences that citizens want to allocate to a specific level reflects their perception of the legitimacy of this governance level. As De Winter and Swyngedouw (1999: 66) put it, 'International governance, like national or regional government, can only gain legitimacy when the public agrees with the rules of the game, including the division of labour between different levels of governance'. As we are interested in citizens' preferred allocation of competences in the three-level game setting, we look at the number of competences citizens prefer to attribute to a particular governance level *relative* to other levels. In the 2014 PartiRep Voter Survey, respondents were asked for eight policy areas to indicate which governance level (regional, federal or EU) they find the most appropriate to deal with each of them. This operationalisation reflects the 'three-level' game where competences are divided between different levels. Therefore, it is much more in line with the reality of multilevel governance than more often used survey questions that measure respondents' support for EU integration or regionalisation without asking respondents to make a trade-off between different governance levels. The policy areas are employment, environment, criminal justice, immigration, economics, state reform, defence and taxes. Using this survey question, we can examine how many competences each respondent would like to attribute to each governance level.

However, respondents attribute varying levels of importance to these policy areas. Consequently, it is more telling when respondents attribute a policy area which they find very important to a particular policy level than one that is seen as unimportant. To take this into account, for each respondent the sum of competences attributed to each governance level has been weighted by the importance the respondent attaches to each competence. To construct this weight, we use a question that asked respondents how important they find each of the eight policy areas for making up their mind about which party to vote for. They could rate the importance of each policy area on a scale from 1 to 5, ranging from 'very unimportant' to 'very important' (the responses were rescaled to range from 1 to 2, while keeping the distribution). Hence, we combine two survey questions to compute the weighted preferred competence attribution to each of the three governance levels (regional, federal and EU). For each respondent, the number of policy areas that they would like to attribute to a particular level (first survey question) was multiplied (weighted) by their own rating of importance of these particular policy areas (second survey question).

Finally, we use these weighted variables for the number of policy areas that each respondent would like to attribute to each governance level to operationalise the trade-off between governance levels. We compute three dependent variables: one displaying the weighted amount of competences a respondent would like to attribute to the regional level, relative to the federal level; one for the preferred attribution of competences to the EU level relative to the federal level and one variable showing the amount of competences a respondent would like to attribute to the EU level relative to the regional level. To compute the first dependent variable, for instance, we subtracted the weighted amount of competences one would like to attribute to the federal level from the weighted amount of competences one would like to attribute to the regional level. In the next section, we describe the data used for the dependent variables.

The first part of the information for our dependent variables is the governance level to which respondents would like to attribute the eight different policy areas. As we want to inquire differences and similarities in sources of citizens' preferred division of competences between the Flemish and Walloon regions in Belgium, we display the preferred governance levels per policy area for each region separately in figure 7.1. Overall, respondents prefer to attribute most competences to the national level, and they would attribute least competences to the regional level. Only environment, which clearly has a cross-border character, is attributed to the EU level by a majority of the respondents in both regions. In the Walloon sample, there is also a majority of respondents that would prefer the EU to be in charge of immigration. These observations are similar to the study of De Winter and Swyngedouw (1999)

Wallonia

■Regional   ▪Federal   ■EU

Flanders

■Regional   ▪Federal   ■EU

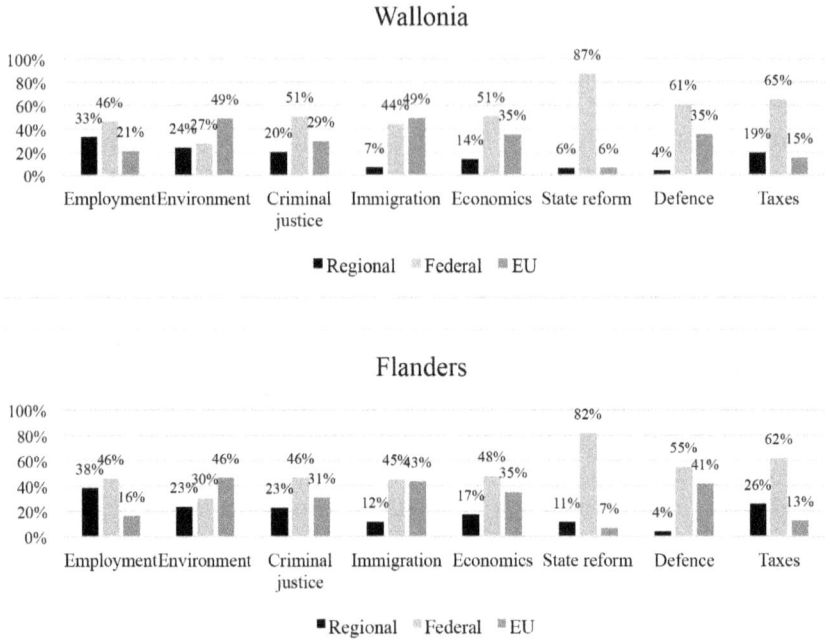

Figure 7.1.   Preferred governance level per policy area. Source: 2014 PartiRep Voter Survey.

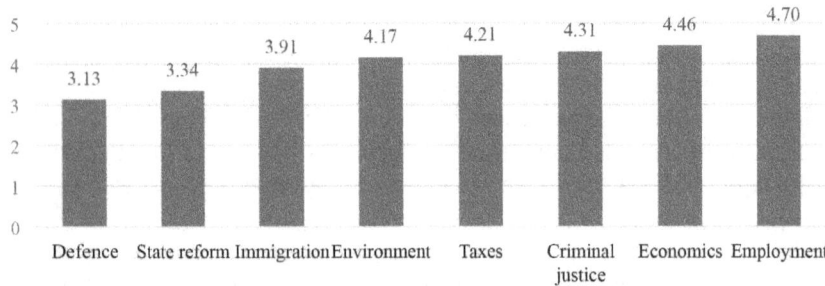

Figure 7.2.   Mean importance attributed to each policy level. Source: 2014 PartiRep Voter Survey.

who studied to which policy level respondents of twelve EU member states would attribute the areas that they find most important. Furthermore, we observe that the regional level is slightly less popular in the Walloon sample than in the Flemish sample, although most patterns are very similar.

The second source of information is the importance that respondents attach to each of the policy areas in the survey. Figure 7.2 shows that, on average, defence was seen as the least important issue area and employment as the most important issue area. The same order from least to most importance is observed in the Walloon and Flemish subsamples.

Based on this information, the dependent variables that indicate the relative preferences of competence attribution to the three governance levels in this study (regional, federal and EU) are computed. The distribution of these variables is presented in figure 7.3. A positive score on the first dependent variable, regional level relative to federal level, for instance, indicates that a respondent wants to attribute more competences to the regional level than to the federal level, taking into account the importance attributed to the various policy areas. For example, a respondent might want to attribute three policy areas that the respondent regards as very important to the regional level, and three policy areas to which the respondent attributes little importance to the federal level. As a result of weighing the results by the importance one attaches to each policy area, these respondents will score higher on how many competences they would like to attribute to the regional level than to the federal level.

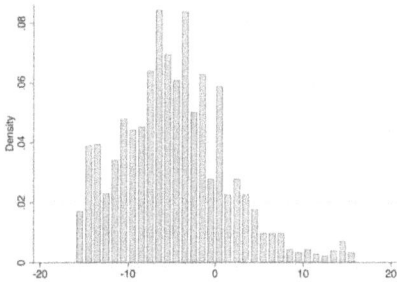

Regional level relative to federal level   EU level relative to federal level

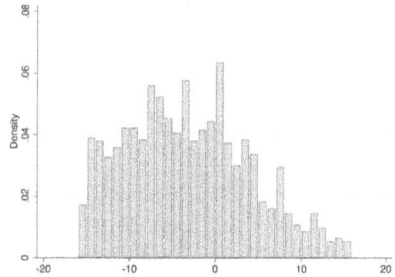

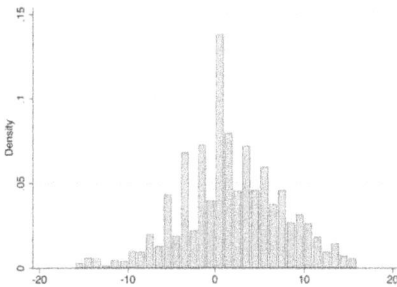

EU level relative to regional level

Figure 7.3.   Distribution of the dependent variables: relative preferences of competence attribution. Source: 2014 PartiRep Voter Survey.

Figure 7.3 shows that, on average, respondents prefer to attribute more competences to the federal level than to the regional or EU level, and more to the EU level than to the regional level.

Explanatory variables

In order to test the three groups of hypotheses that have been presented earlier in this chapter, three (groups of) measurements are included in the analyses. First, egocentric economic utilitarian explanations are tested by using occupation and education level as objective egocentric measures (Gabel & Whitten 1997; Hooghe & Marks 2005; Verhaegen, Hooghe & Quintelier 2014).

Second, identification with the regional, federal and European levels is measured by three separate questions. Respondents were asked to indicate how strongly they identify as Flemish/Walloon, Belgian and European. Scores on this question range from 0 (not at all) to 10 (very strongly).

Third, we measure three types of attitudes towards the political institutions active at the regional, federal and EU levels. Political trust is measured for all levels on a scale from 0 (no trust at all) to 10 (full trust). At the regional level, trust in the regional government and parliament is measured (a sum scale is made with these two items and has been rescaled to range from 0 to 10), on the national level, trust in the federal government and parliament is measured (sum scale rescaled to 0–10) and on the EU level, one survey question asked about respondents' trust in the EU. Policy satisfaction was measured in the same way for all three levels. Respondents were asked how satisfied they are with the policymaking of the regional government, the federal government and the EU on a scale from 1 (very unsatisfied) to 5 (very satisfied). Finally, respondents were asked how much influence they think that the institutions on the regional, federal and EU level have on their life. Responses ranged from 1 (very much influence) to 5 (no influence) and are reversely coded for the analyses.

Control variables

The control variables included are a number of potential mediating factors and socio-demographics: gender (1 = female, 0 = male), age (recoded so that score 0 is 18 years old) and political knowledge. One factual knowledge question was asked to the respondents about each of the three policy levels in our study. In line with the literature on using knowledge measures in political science studies, do-not-know answers are coded as incorrect answers (e.g. Jennings 1996).

ANALYSES

The results of the multivariate regression analyses are displayed in tables 7.1, 7.2 and 7.3. Regression coefficients are displayed for each trade-off between two governance levels. The tables show whether and to what extent egocentric economic utilitarian motivations, identity and attitudes about political institutions explain respondents' preferences about which governance level should be in charge of a broader set of competences. First, the results for these three types of potential sources for respondents' preferences to attribute more competences to one level than to another are discussed. Then, a comparison is made between the three sets of results.

Overall, egocentric economic utilitarian motivations hardly explain respondents' preferences to attribute more competences to one governance level than to another. No significant relationship is observed between education or occupation and the trade-off between attributing competences to the regional or the federal level (table 7.1). Moreover, the observations that Flemish non-active respondents are more in favour than clerks of moving competences to the EU level compared to the federal level (table 7.2), and that Flemish students prefer more competences to the regional level compared to the EU level (table 7.3) run against hypothesis 1. We expected that respondents, who are – from an egocentric point of view – more likely to benefit from attributing competence to a higher level, would prefer to do so. Rather, for the trade-off between the regional level and the federal level, additional analyses show a distinction between both regions on the aggregate level. On average, Flemish respondents are in favour of moving a significantly larger share of competences to the regional level, compared to the federal level, than Walloon respondents are. The mean score on the dependent variable is -4.358 (SE 0.204) in the Flemish sample and -5.351 (SE 0.189) in the Walloon sample. Hence, the rational utilitarian approach does not explain different preferences for competence attribution between individual citizens. Nevertheless, it may explain the difference in mean scores for Flanders and Wallonia as a whole. What we cannot test, however, is whether this aggregate-level difference is driven by sociotropic economic utilitarian motivations, as mobilised by Flemish nationalist discourse that argues that Flemish independence would result in economic benefits for Flanders as a whole, or by other factors (Boonen & Hooghe 2014; Béland & Lecours 2005).

One exception is the observation among Walloon respondents that self-employed respondents are more in favour of attributing competences to the EU level, compared to the federal level (table 7.2). This observation is in line with the theoretical expectation that people who are more likely to benefit from scaling-up to the EU level will prefer to attribute more competences to that level. With just this small exception in mind, however, we are to conclude that while egocentric economic utilitarian motivations have consistently been observed to explain support for EU integration in the past (although in more general measures of attitudes towards the EU that do not take into account a trade-off with other governance levels), our analyses suggest that such motivations are less important when citizens need to choose between governance levels (Gabel & Whitten 1997; Hooghe & Marks 2004; van Klingeren, Boomgaarden & de Vreese 2013).

The second hypothesis proposed that the more citizens identify with a particular political or territorial community, the more competences they prefer to attribute to the corresponding governance level. This hypothesis is confirmed for all trade-offs in the Flemish sample, but not in the Walloon sample. Just as Flemish respondents, Walloons are more likely to prefer to attribute more competences to the EU level when they have a stronger European identity (tables 7.2 and 7.3). However, the strength of their regional identity is not significantly related to preferring more competences at the regional level compared to the federal or EU level (tables 7.1 and 7.3). This observation echoes the findings of Sinardet et al. in chapter 6 of this book. Chapter 6 used slightly different measures for regional identity and for attitudes about the division of competences in a bivariate analysis; our analyses show the robustness of their observation. Finally, Walloon respondents' Belgian identity is only significantly related to preferring to attribute more competences to the federal level compared to the EU level (and not to the federal level compared to the regional level; see table 7.1).

In sum, hypothesis 2 is confirmed for both regions in the trade-off between the EU and the federal level (table 7.2), and it is confirmed for the Flemish sample in the other trade-offs (tables 7.1 and 7.3). Hypothesis 2 is rejected for the Walloon sample in the trade-off between the regional and federal level (table 7.1), and for the Walloon sample in the trade-off between the EU and regional level, the hypothesis is confirmed for European identity and rejected for regional identity (table 7.3).

Finally, we find support for the idea that some types of attitudes towards political institutions (but not all) explain preferences about competence attribution. First, hypothesis 3a, in which we expected that respondents with more trust in the institutions of a governance level prefer to attribute more competences to that level, is confirmed in the Flemish sample for all three trade-offs. The significant negative coefficient of trust in the federal institutions in table 7.1, for instance, indicates that respondents who have more trust in the federal institutions are less likely to prefer attributing competences to the regional level, compared to the federal level.

For the Walloon sample, however, political trust provides a weaker explanation for preferences about competence attribution. Only trust in federal institutions significantly corresponds to preferring more competences on that level compared to the regional or EU level (tables 7.1 and 7.2). In sum, institutional trust affects citizens' preferences about competence distribution, but more so in the Flemish sample than in the Walloon sample.

Second, it was expected that satisfaction with policymaking at a particular governance level would be positively related to preferring to attribute competences to that level (hypothesis 3b). However, this hypothesis is rejected in all tests, as a significant relationship was observed in only one case, and this observation is in the opposed direction of what hypothesis 3b proposed. Flemish respondents (but not Walloons) who are more satisfied with policymaking at the federal level are more supportive of allocating competences at the EU level, compared to the federal level (table 7.2).

Third, the perceived impact of the institutions of a governance level on one's life is significantly related to the competences this person would like to attribute to that level, independently of how satisfied he or she is with policymaking at that level. Hence, hypothesis 3c is clearly confirmed for preferring the EU level and the federal level. In both Flanders and Wallonia, respondents who perceive that the EU has a stronger impact on their life are more in favour of attributing competences to the EU level compared to the federal or regional level. With one exception, the same is observed for the perception that federal institutions affect one's life (the exception being the Flemish sample in table 7.1). The results for the perceived impact of regional level institutions, however, are highly mixed (tables 7.1 and 7.3).

If we then look at the general picture, some variation can be observed in the sources of preferences about competence attribution to each level. For the regional level, trust in the regional institutions and regional identity provides a significant explanation in the Flemish sample, but not in the Walloon sample. The perceived impact of regional institutions significantly explains Walloon respondents' preferences about competence attribution to the regional level compared to the federal level (table 7.1) and Flemish respondents' preferences about competence attribution to the EU level, compared to the regional level (table 7.3).

For the federal level, trust in the federal institutions is a clear source for attitudes about competence attribution to this level, compared to the others. Also Belgian identity is an important source for respondents' preferences about competence attribution to the federal level, except when we look at the trade-off between the regional and the federal level in the Walloon sample. Similarly, respondents who have the impression that federal institutions affect their daily life are more in favour of attributing more competences to the federal level, but the trade-off between the regional and federal level among Flemish respondents is an exception.

Finally, for the EU level, both European identity and the perception that EU institutions affect one's life are significant sources for respondents' preference to attribute more competences to the EU level. Trust in EU institutions is only significantly related to these preferences in the Flemish sample. Hence, the most consistent patterns are observed for the EU level.

Table 7.1. Regression analyses explaining competence attribution to the regional level, compared to the federal level

	Flanders		Wallonia	
	Coefficient	*SE*	*Coefficient*	*SE*
Utilitarian				
Occupation (reference: clerk)				
Self-employed	0.531	0.758	1.234	0.780
Blue-collar worker	0.256	0.801	0.227	0.795
Pensioner	−0.397	0.851	0.534	0.782
Student	0.309	0.713	−0.213	0.798
Unemployed	1.352	1.165	0.783	0.899
Other non-active	0.764	0.806	1.008	0.865
Education (reference: low education)				
Middle education	−1.171	0.619	−0.470	0.520
High education	−0.640	0.626	−0.350	0.558
Identity				
Belgian identity	−0.470***	0.106	−0.279	0.152
Regional identity	0.232*	0.111	−0.154	0.133
Attitudes towards political institutions				
Federal satisfaction	−0.188	0.316	0.079	0.309
Regional satisfaction	0.049	0.363	0.437	0.330
Federal level affects life	−0.521	0.274	−0.985**	0.302
Regional level affects life	0.562	0.353	1.054**	0.363
Federal trust	−0.787***	0.217	−0.579*	0.260
Regional trust	0.494*	0.232	0.310	0.264
Control variables				
Female	−0.180	0.461	0.357	0.435
Age	0.030	0.020	−0.008	0.021
Federal knowledge	−0.008	0.457	−1.180*	0.520
Regional knowledge	−0.675	0.475	0.473	0.460
Intercept	−0.948	1.462	−1.603	1.517
R^2	11.09%		8.22%	
N	904		931	

Source: 2014 PartiRep Voter Survey.

Note: *$p < 0.05$; **$p < 0.01$; ***$p < 0.001$.

Table 7.2. Regression analyses explaining competence attribution to the EU level, compared to the federal level

	Flanders		Wallonia	
	Coefficient	SE	Coefficient	SE
Utilitarian				
Occupation (reference: clerk)				
Self-employed	0.182	0.889	2.749*	1.279
Blue-collar worker	−0.212	0.862	0.879	0.969
Pensioner	0.093	0.944	0.294	0.964
Student	−1.362	0.858	−1.528	0.946
Unemployed	2.103	1.369	0.292	1.064
Other non-active	2.607*	1.046	1.802	1.008
Education (reference: low education)				
Middle education	−0.324	0.653	−1.092	0.653
High education	−0.870	0.725	−0.405	0.731
Identity				
Belgian identity	−0.598***	0.119	−0.588***	0.141
European identity	0.440***	0.120	0.770***	0.127
Attitudes towards political institutions				
Federal satisfaction	0.725*	0.357	0.105	0.362
EU satisfaction	−0.687	0.375	0.337	0.381
Federal level affects life	−0.935**	0.334	−0.999**	0.379
EU level affects life	1.412***	0.342	2.119***	0.379
Federal trust	−0.772***	0.214	−0.586*	0.233
EU trust	0.453*	0.195	−0.100	0.197
Control variables				
Female	−0.314	0.493	−0.384	0.515
Age	−0.009	0.023	0.010	0.025
Federal knowledge	0.208	0.484	−1.881**	0.568
EU knowledge	−0.249	0.519	−0.536	0.499
Intercept	−0.249	0.519	−2.027	1.895
R^2	10.31%		15.73%	
N	900		930	

Source: 2014 PartiRep Voter Survey.

Note: *$p < 0.05$; **$p < 0.01$; ***$p < 0.001$.

Table 7.3. Regression analyses explaining competence attribution to the EU level, compared to the regional level

	Flanders		Wallonia	
	Coefficient	SE	Coefficient	SE
Utilitarian				
Occupation (reference: clerk)				
Self-employed	−0.611	0.677	1.669	0.933
Blue-collar worker	−0.581	0.744	0.913	0.701

(Continued)

Table 7.3.   (Continued)

	Flanders		Wallonia	
	Coefficient	SE	Coefficient	SE
Pensioner	0.231	0.780	−0.369	0.771
Student	−1.862**	0.698	−0.673	0.762
Unemployed	0.533	1.100	−0.034	0.857
Other non-active	1.494	0.849	1.133	0.847
Education (reference: low education)				
Middle education	1.064	0.581	−0.400	0.537
High education	0.055	0.602	0.202	0.577
Identity				
Regional identity	−0.267*	0.105	−0.094	0.124
European identity	0.422**	0.098	0.523***	0.108
Attitudes towards political institutions				
Regional satisfaction	−0.123	0.342	−0.398	0.306
EU satisfaction	−0.055	0.293	0.379	0.310
Regional level affects life	−0.788*	0.313	−0.275	0.304
EU level affects life	0.823**	0.272	1.001***	0.267
Regional trust	−0.497**	0.175	−0.011	0.217
EU trust	0.454**	0.146	−0.220	0.213
Control variables				
Female	−0.492	0.419	−0.576	0.417
Age	−0.029	0.020	0.008	0.019
Regional knowledge	−0.143	0.399	0.407	0.418
EU knowledge	0.123	0.409	−0.202	0.391
Intercept	2.439	1.421	−1.084	1.496
R^2	12.27%		9.61%	
N	902		930	

Source: 2014 PartiRep Voter Survey.

Note: $^*p < 0.05$; $^{**}p < 0.01$; $^{***}p < 0.001$.

CONCLUSION

The aim of this chapter was to explain citizens' views on the division of competences in the context of multilevel governance in Belgium. While objective or normative inferences could be used to decide upon the economically and functionally most efficient level to govern in particular policy areas, the popular legitimacy of the attribution of competences to various governance levels depends on citizens' preferences.

One subfield in political science has specialised in studying support for EU integration, which involves moving competences to the EU level, and another subfield developed around questions of regionalisation. Our aim was to study attitudes about the division of competences between different governance levels at the same time. After decades of experience with the movement of competences between the regional, federal and EU levels, Belgian public opinion presents a perfect case to investigate these preferences.

By taking multilevel governance as a starting point, the chapter showed how EU integration and regionalisation are connected. Also, we discussed how economic utilitarian motivations, identity and attitudes about political institutions can potentially explain citizens' preferences about the attribution of more competences to a particular governance level, compared to the other levels. By using the same explanatory framework to study attitudes about the attribution of competences to three different governance levels, we are able to identify similarities and differences in sources for citizens' attitudes about attributing competences to the regional level, the federal level and the EU level. Our analyses show that attitudes about regionalisation and European integration follow partly similar and partly different logics in the minds of Belgian citizens. And among Belgian citizens, we observe a divide between citizens in both regions, most distinctly when it comes to moving competences to the regional level.

In the normative and system-level literature on multilevel governance, and in empirical studies on sources for support for EU integration, economic utilitarian evaluations take the overhand, or are at least placed on equal footing with identity factors (e.g. van Klingeren, Boomgaarden & de Vreese 2013). However, egocentric economic utilitarian motivations are shown to provide a very weak explanation for citizens' preferences about competence attribution when they are presented with a trade-off between governance levels. Also, the expectation that citizens would prefer to attribute more competences to the governance level about which they think it provides best policymaking is rejected. As the underlying mechanism of this link is also built on rationality, this observation strengthens our conclusion that rational explanations are less fit to explain Belgian citizens' preferences about the division of competences between the regional, federal and EU levels. When we study citizens' preferred attribution of competences to various governance levels, emotional sources play a more important role. We observed that identity and trust in political institutions explain Belgian citizens' preferences about the division of competences between the regional, federal and EU levels, and this is most consistently the case for the Flemish respondents.

The gap between Flanders and Wallonia that is central to this book is also reflected in this study of attitudes in the context of multilevel governance. In explaining preferences about the division of competences between the regional and the federal levels, there is a gap in sources to explain these preferences between both communities. For Flemish respondents, identifying more strongly as Belgian makes them more reluctant to attribute competences to the regional level, while identifying more strongly as Flemish makes them more likely to demand the attribution of competences to the regional level. In Wallonia, in contrast, identity-based sources are not observed for such preferences. These findings are in line with the weaker politicisation and mobilisation of Walloon identity compared to Flemish identity in debates about state reform in Belgium.

A similar pattern is found, for the importance of European identity, and the role of Belgian and European identity in the trade-off between the corresponding two governance levels. In both regions in Belgium, the extent to which citizens identify as Belgian creates some reluctance to attribute competences to the EU level, while the strength of their European identity is a source for support for moving competences to the EU level. Taking into account that national and European identities are combined in most citizens' minds, this might result in preferring the attribution of some competences to each level.

A gap between Flanders and Wallonia is also observed with regard to the importance of political trust as a source for preferences about the division of competences. Trust in federal institutions is for both Flemish and Walloon respondents linked to preferring more competences at the federal level, compared to the EU or regional level. A distinction is observed though, for the other two governance levels. No significant relationships are observed for Walloons' trust in the EU or in regional institutions, while this is observed in the Flemish sample. Hence, political trust is a significant explanation in all trade-offs for all levels in the Flemish sample, while it is a much weaker explanation in the Walloon sample.

In sum, we see that even though EU integration and regionalisation in Belgium are the same types of multilevel governance, the sources for support or contestation among citizens for EU integration and regionalisation, compared to governance on the federal level, differ. In addition to this 'gap' between governance levels, we also observe that on questions of multilevel governance, the largest gap between Walloon and Flemish citizens is situated exactly at the division of competences towards both regions. The regional differences reinforce this argument and the Belgian case opens very stimulating avenues for further researches to this regard that could certainly feed comparative research on the legitimation at the regional level.

Linking these findings to a reflection on legitimacy has several implications. First, identifying similarities and differences in sources for citizens' attitudes about attributing competences to the regional, federal and EU levels supports the idea that citizens have specific attitudes about the governance levels within a multilevel environment, rather than a less-sophisticated general opinion. Citizens do express preferences when attributing different competences to different levels. On the normative level, this means that we identified a number of legitimation and delegitimation mechanisms for multilevel governance, some of which are shared by all three levels, some of them are different.

Regarding the similarities in explanations, another important implication for legitimacy is found in the fact that the perception that a level affects respondent's daily life is a crucial explanation for citizens' preferred division of competences. The underlying mechanism is the necessity for any level of authority to develop a certain visibility of its public policies. When citizens experience that a given governance level affects their daily lives, they are more inclined to be willing to transfer competences to this level. This result is observed to hold independent from the evaluation of the decisions taken. It is even observed that one's satisfaction with policymaking of a governance level is not significantly related to one's preferences about the division of competences. Consequently, our analyses suggest that output legitimacy lies more in experiences than in evaluation. A second vital theoretical result is the importance of identity-based and trust mechanisms, even if they play different roles depending on the level and the region studied. This also implies that input legitimacy is part of the equation and should therefore be analysed in a multilevel governance setting. These results are in line with Easton's theoretical expectation that legitimacy typically arises from two sources: socialisation and direct experience (Easton 1975: 446). To this regard, our results call for further empirical and theoretical investigations. Looking at how new policies create new politics appears as a fruitful avenue (Dupuy & Van Ingelgom 2014a).

REFERENCES

Anderson, B. (1991) *Imagined Communities*, revised edition. London/New York: Verso.

Anderson, C. J. (1998) 'When in Doubt, Use Proxies: Attitudes toward Domestic Politics and Support for European Integration', *Comparative Political Studies*, 31(5), 569–601.

Anderson, C. J. and Kaltenthaler, K. (1996) 'The Dynamics of Public Opinion toward European Integration, 1973–1993', *The Journal of International Relations*, 2(2), 175–99.

Arnold, C., Sapir, E. V. and Zapryanova, G. (2012) 'Trust in the Institutions of the European Union: A Cross-Country Examination', *European Integration Online Papers*, 16(2).

Beetham, D. and Lord, C. (1998) *Legitimacy and the European Union*. London: Longman, 1–39.

Béland, D. and Lecours, A. (2005) 'Nationalism, Public Policy, and Institutional Development: Social Security in Belgium', *Journal of Public Policy*, 25(2), 265–85.

Billiet, J., Maddens, B. and Frognier, A. P. (2006) 'Does Belgium (still) Exist? Differences in Political Culture between Flemings and Walloons', *West European Politics*, 29(5), 912–32.

Billig, M. (1996) 'Nationalism as an International Ideology: Imagining the Nation, Others and the World of Nations', in G. Breakwell and E. Lyons (eds) *Changing European Identities: Social Psychological Analyses of Social Change* (181–94). Oxford: Butterworth-Heinemann.

Boonen, J. and Hooghe, M. (2014) 'Do Nationalist Parties Shape or Follow Sub-National Identities? A Panel Analysis on the Rise of the Nationalist Party in the Flemish Region of Belgium, 2006–11', *Nations and Nationalism*, 20(1), 56–79.

Börzel, T. A. and Hosli, M. O. (2003) 'Brussels between Bern and Berlin: Comparative Federalism Meets the European Union', *Governance*, 16(2), 179–202.

Bruter, M. (2009) 'Time Bomb? The Dynamic Effects of News and Symbols on the Political Identity of European Citizens', *Comparative Political Studies*, 42(12), 1498–536.

Bruter, M. (2012) 'The Difficult Emergence of a European People', in J. Hayward and R. K. Wurzel (eds) *European Disunion: Between Sovereignty and Solidarity* (17–31). London: Palgrave Macmillan.

Cole, A. and Loughlin, J. (2003) 'Beyond the Unitary State? Public Opinion, Political Institutions and Public Policy in Brittany', *Regional Studies*, 37(3), 265–76.

Cram, L. (2012) 'Does the EU Need a Navel? Implicit and Explicit Identification with the European Union', *Journal of Common Market Studies*, 50(1), 71–86.

De Winter, L. and Swyngedouw, M. (1999) 'The Scope of EU Government', in H. Schmitt and J. Thomassen (eds) *Political Representation and Legitimacy in the European Union* (47–73). Oxford: Oxford University Press.

De Winter, L., Swyngedouw, M. and Goeminne, B. (2008) 'The Level of Decision Making: The Preferences of the Citizens after Enlargement', in J. Thomassen (ed) *The Legitimacy of the European Union after Enlargement* (117–40). Oxford: Oxford University Press.

Deschouwer, K. (2006) 'And the Peace Goes On? Consociational Democracy and Belgian Politics in the Twenty-First Century', *West European Politics*, 29(5), 895–911.

———. (2013) 'Party Strategies, Voter Demands and Territorial Reform in Belgium', *West European Politics*, 36(2), 338–58.

Deschouwer, K. and Sinardet, D. (2010) 'Identiteiten, Communautaire Standpunten en Stemgedrag', in K. Deschouwer, P. Delwit, M. Hooghe and S. Walgrave (eds) *De Stemmen van het Volk. Een Analyse van Kiesgedrag in Vlaanderen en Wallonië op 7 Juni 2009* (75–98). Brussel: Vrije Universiteit Brussel University Press.

Deschouwer, K., De Winter, L., Reuchamps, M., Sinardet, D. and Dodeigne, J. (2014) 'Communautaire Overtuigingen en Stemgedrag', in K. Deschouwer, P. Delwit, M. Hooghe, P. Baudewyns and S. Walgrave (eds) *De Kiezer Ontcijferd* (151–67). Leuven: Lannoo.

Duchesne, S. and Frognier, A. P. (2008) 'National and European Identifications: A Dual Relationship', *Comparative European Politics*, 6, 143–68.

Dupuy, C. and Van Ingelgom, V. (2014a) 'Social Policy, Legitimation, and Diverging Regional Paths in Belgium', in Kumlin, S. and Stadelmann-Steffen, I. (eds) *How Welfare States Shape the Democratic Public. Policy Feedbacks, Participation, Voting, and Attitudes* (198–222). Cheltenham: Edward Elgar.

————. (2014b) 'Les politiques publiques et la légitimation : un jeu d'échelles ? Le cas de la Belgique', *Gouvernement et action publique*, 4(1), 27–59.

————. (2017) 'Comment l'Union européenne fabrique (ou pas) sa propre légitimité. Les politiques européennes et leurs effets-retours sur les citoyens', *Politique européenne*, 54, 152–87.

Easton, D. (1965) *A Systems Analysis of Political Life*. Chicago: The University of Chicago Press.

————. (1975) 'A Re-Assessment of the Concept of Political Support', *British Journal of Political Science*, 5(4), 435–57.

Føllesdal, A. (1998) 'Survey Article: Subsidiarity', *The Journal of Political Philosophy*, 6(2), 190–218.

Franklin, M., Marsh, M. and McLaren, L. (1994) 'Uncorking the Bottle: Popular Opposition to European Unification in the Wake of Maastricht', *Journal of Common Market Studies*, 32(4), 455–72.

Gabel, M. (1998) 'Public Support for European Integration: An Empirical Test of Five Theories', *The Journal of Politics, 60*(2), 333–54.

Gabel, M. and Whitten, G. (1997) 'Economic Conditions, Economic Perceptions, and Public Support for European Integration', *Political Behaviour, 19*(1), 81–96.

Gellner, E. (2006/1983) *Nations and Nationalism: Second Edition*. Oxford: Blackwell Publishing.

Guibernau, M. (2014) 'Prospects for an Independent Catalonia', *International Journal of Politics, Culture, and Society*, 27(1), 5–23.

Haas, E. B. (1958) *The Uniting of Europe. Political, Social and Economic Forces, 1950–1957*. California: Stanford University Press.

Habermas, J. (2011) *Zur Verfassung Europas. Ein Essay*. Berlin: Suhrkamp.

Harteveld, E., van der Meer, T. and de Vries, C. E. (2013) 'In Europe We Trust? Exploring Three Logics of Trust in the European Union', *European Union Politics*, 14(4), 542–65.

Hesli, V. L. (1995) 'Public Support for the Devolution of Power in Ukraine: Regional Patterns', *Europe-Asia Studies*, 47(1), 91–121.

Hobolt, S. (2012) 'Citizen Satisfaction with Democracy in the European Union', *Journal of Common Market Studies*, 50(S1), 88–105.

Hobolt, S. and de Vries, C. (2016) 'Public Support for European Integration', *Annual Review of Political Science*, 19, 413–32.

Hooghe, L. (2004) 'Belgium: Hollowing the Center', in Amoretti, U.M. and Bermeo, N. (eds) *Federalism and Territorial Cleavages*, 55–92. Baltimore: John Hopkins University Press.

Hooghe, L. and Marks, G. (2001) 'Types of Multi-Level Governance', *European Integration online Papers*, 5(11), 1–24.

————. (2004) 'Does Identity or Economic Rationality Drive Public Opinion on European Integration?' *PS: Political Science and Politics*, 37(3): 415–20.

————. (2005) 'Calculation, Community and Cues Public Opinion on European Integration', *European Union Politics*, 6(4), 419–43.

Hooghe, M. and Verhaegen, S. (2017) 'The Democratic Legitimacy of European Institutions and Support for Social Policy in Europe', in F. Vandenbroucke, C. Barnard and G. De Baere (eds) *A European Social Union after the Crisis* (120–140). Cambridge: Cambridge University Press.

Hooghe, L., Marks, G. and Schakel, A. H. (2010) *The Rise of Regional Authority: A Comparative Study of 42 Democracies*. London: Routledge.

Hooghe, L., Marks, G. and Wilson, C. J. (2002) 'Does Left/Right Structure Party Positions on European Integration?' *Comparative Political Studies*, 35(8), 965–89.

Huyse, L. (1971) *Passiviteit, Pacificatie en Verzuildheid in de Belgische Politiek*. Antwerpen: Standaard Wetenschappelijke Uitgeverij.

Inglehart, R. (1970) 'Cognitive Mobilization and European Identity', *Comparative Politics*, 3(1), 45–70.

Jennings, M. K. (1996) 'Political knowledge over time and across generations', *Public Opinion Quarterly*, 60(2), 228–52.

Kostakopoulou, T. (2001) *Citizenship, Identity, and Immigration in the European Union: Between Past and Future*. Manchester: Manchester University Press.

Kriesi, H. and Lachat, R. (2004) 'Globalization and the Transformation of the National Political Space: Switzerland and France Compared', *CIS Working Paper 1*, available at SSRN: https://ssrn.com/abstract=1514444 or http://dx.doi.org/10.2139/ssrn.1514444. Last accessed: 5/10/2017.

Kriesi, H., Grande, E., Lachat, R., Dolezal, M., Bornschier, S. and Frey, T. (2006) 'Globalization and the Transformation of the National Political Space: Six European Countries Compared', *European Journal of Political Research*, 45(6), 921–56.

Kuhn, T. (2012) 'Why Educational Exchange Programmes Miss Their Mark: Cross-Border Mobility, Education and European Identity', *Journal of Common Market Studies*, 50(6), 994–1010.

Laffan, B. (1996) 'The Politics of Identity and Political Order in Europe', *Journal of Common Market Studies*, 34(1), 81–102.

Luedtke, A. (2005) 'European Integration, Public Opinion and Immigration Policy: Testing the Impact of National Identity', *European Union Politics*, 6(1), 83–112.

Magone, J. M. (2011) 'Centre-Periphery Conflict in the European Union? Europe 2020, the Southern European Model and the Euro-Crisis', in A. Ágh (ed.) *European Union at the Crossroads: European Perspectives*. Budapest: Budapest College of Communication, Business and Arts, 2011, 71–122.

Marks, G. and Hooghe, L. (2004) 'Contrasting Visions of Multi-Level Governance', in I. Bache and M. Flinders (eds) *Multi-Level Governance* (17–30). Oxford: Oxford University Press.

Oates, W. E. (1999) 'An Essay on Fiscal Federalism', *Journal of Economic Literature*, 37(3), 1120–49.

Reif, K. and Schmitt, H. (1980) 'Nine Second-Order National Elections: A Conceptual Framework for the Analysis of European Election Results', *European Journal of Political Research*, 8(1), 3–44.

Risse, T. (2005) 'Neofunctionalism, European Identity, and the Puzzles of European Integration', *Journal of European Public Policy*, 12(2), 291–309.

———. (2014) 'No Demos? Identities and Public Spheres in the Euro Crisis', *Journal of Common Market Studies*, 52(6), 1207–15.

Rohrschneider, R. (2002) 'The Democracy Deficit and Mass Support for an EU-Wide Government', *American Journal of Political Science*, 46(2), 463–75.

Sánchez-Cuenca, I. (2000) 'The Political Basis of Support for European Integration', *European Union Politics*, 1(2), 147–71.

Schakel, A. H. (2009) 'Explaining Policy Allocation over Governmental Tiers by Identity and Functionality', *Acta Politica*, 44(4), 385–409.

Scharpf, F. W. (1999) *Governing in Europe: Effective and Democratic?* Oxford: Oxford University Press.

———. (2007) 'Reflections on Multilevel Legitimacy', *MPIfG Working Paper*, 7(3), Max Planck Institute for the Study of Societies, 1–21.

Sigalas, E. (2010) 'Cross-Border Mobility and European Identity: The Effectiveness of Intergroup Contact during the ERASMUS Year Abroad', *European Union Politics*, 11(2), 241–65.

Sinnott, R. (1995). 'Policy, subsidiarity, and legitimacy', in O. Niedermayer and R. Sinnott (eds) *Public Opinion and Internationalized Governance. Beliefs in Government 2*. Oxford: Oxford University Press, 246–76.

Swenden, W. and Jans, M. T. (2006) 'Will It Stay or Will It Go?' Federalism and the Sustainability of Belgium', *West European Politics*, 29(5), 877–94.

Van der Eijk, C. and Franklin, M. N. (2004) 'Potential for Contestation on European Matters at National Elections in Europe', in Marks, G. and Steenbergen, M. R. (eds) *European Integration and Political Conflict*, 32–50. Cambridge: Cambridge University Press.

Van Ingelgom, V. (2014) *Integrating Indifference. A Comparative, Qualitative and Quantitative Approach to the Legitimacy of European Integration*. Colchester: ECPR Press.

Van Keersbergen, K. (2000) 'Political Allegiance and European Integration', *European Journal of Political Research*, 37(1), 1–17.

van Klingeren, M., Boomgaarden, H. G. and de Vreese, C. H. (2013) 'Going Soft or Staying Soft: Have Identity Factors Become More Important than Economic Rationale When Explaining Euroscepticism?' *Journal of European Integration*, 35(6), 689–704.

Verhaegen, S. (2016) *European Identity and the Perceived Importance of EP Elections in Belgium*. Politicologenetmaal, 2–3 June 2016, Brussels.

Verhaegen, S., Hooghe, M. and Quintelier, E. (2014) 'European Identity and Support for European Integration: A Matter of Perceived Economic Benefits?' *Kyklos*, 67(2), 317–36.

Chapter 8

Economic voting in a federal country: Overcoming the limited clarity of responsibility[1]

Ruth Dassonneville, Marc Hooghe
and Marc Debus

INTRODUCTION

In electoral democracies, voters are expected to use their vote to hold incumbents accountable. By rewarding and punishing incumbents according to how these perform while in office, voters can effectively incentivise those who govern to act in the best interest of the citizens (Przeworski et al. 1999). A large number of studies have brought forth evidence that electorates are fulfilling this basic requirement, and are using their vote to hold incumbents accountable. Most of this literature does so by focusing on economic performance, and it shows that incumbents are receiving a larger share of the vote under good economic conditions than what holds when the economy is deteriorating (Lewis-Beck 1988; Duch and Stevenson 2008; Van der Brug et al. 2007). In their comparative study on the impact of the economy on electoral results in European democracies, for example, Dassonneville and Lewis-Beck (2014: 382) find that 'a 1 percentage increase in GDP growth yields about a 0.7 percentage point increase in incumbent support'.

While the literature on economic voting generally offers evidence of mechanisms of accountability, the comparative work on this topic has also pointed out substantial cross-national variation to the extent to which citizens vote economically. According to a dominant perspective in this literature, institutional contexts strongly affect the extent to which economic voting occurs. More specifically, for voters to reward and punish the incumbents according to the state of the economy, it should be clear for them as to who is responsible for the economy (Powell and Whitten 1993; Hobolt et al. 2013). As a result, in low-clarity contexts, where this condition is not met, the economic vote is reduced or even absent. Given the complex nature of federalism in Belgium, the country offers an ideal setting to investigate the occurrence and the strength of this mechanism. The Belgian federal system is often accused of being 'too complex' for most citizens, and the prevalence of economic voting therefore could serve as a litmus test to ascertain whether this really is the case.

The absence of economic voting, and of mechanisms of accountability in voting more generally, could be considered a major challenge for democracy. If in some contexts incumbents are not punished by voters, this basically implies incumbents – once elected into office – do not have to care all that strongly about the interests or preferences of the citizens nor would they feel bound to fulfil their electoral promises. For the well-functioning of representative democracy, it is thus important that accountability considerations drive the electorate's choices to some extent.

In light of the general importance of mechanisms of accountability in representative democracies, in this chapter we examine patterns of economic voting in Belgium. The Belgian context is generally characterised as a low-clarity setting, where multiple parties, the presence of governing coalitions, the federal structure as well as the presence of two different party systems can all be thought to lower the clarity of who governs, who is responsible and who is to be held accountable (Deschouwer 2012). We seek to investigate whether voting behaviour in Belgium is influenced to some extent by the economy. Given the low-clarity institutional context, we do not expect to find strong economic effects, but we aim to investigate which voters in particular succeed in overcoming clarity barriers and manage voting economically.

ECONOMIC VOTING AND CLARITY OF RESPONSIBILITY

Economic conditions affect how incumbents fare on Election Day. In democracies across the globe, scholars find incumbents to be rewarded for prosperous economic conditions, while the probability of incumbents losing office increases as the economy deteriorates (Lewis-Beck and Stegmaier 2000). This basic correlation between economic conditions and incumbents' electoral performance is considered an indication that electorates are voting retrospectively and are holding incumbents into account. Democratic theorists consider such retrospective evaluations affecting the vote choice a key mechanism for realising democratic representation. If incumbents feel voters will hold them accountable, they are incentivised to deliver, fulfil their promises and govern in the best interest of their voters (Healy and Malhotra 2013; Przeworski et al. 1999).

Research on economic voting was originally focused on a limited number of countries only, but by now, the presence of economic voting has been shown in a vast and varied set of democracies worldwide (Lewis-Beck and Stegmaier 2013). This work includes several studies that rely on data from multiple countries, either at an aggregate level or at an individual level, to show the impact of the economy on election results and on voting behaviour (Dassonneville and Lewis-Beck 2014; Duch and Stevenson 2008; Nadeau et al. 2013; Van der Brug et al. 2007). Next to showing indications of economic voting in a large number of countries, this work also highlights that there is substantial variation in the strength of the economic vote. This variation, it is argued, can be partly explained by the institutional context within which voters have to decide whom to vote for. More specifically, it is claimed that the institutional clarity of responsibility mitigates economic voting. When it is not clear who is governing, and who is responsible for the policies pursued and decisions taken, the economic vote is weakened (Powell and Whitten 1993; Nadeau et al. 2002). The question, therefore, is whether the complexity of the Belgian federal system indeed inhibits the mechanism of economic voting.

The institutional factors that are argued to have an effect on the clarity of responsibility in the literature are manifold and diverse. These measures include structural features of particular systems. The clarity of responsibility is claimed to be reduced in systems with strong parliamentary committees as well as in bicameral systems (Powell and Whitten 1993). Furthermore, a federal state structure as well is argued to weaken the clarity of responsibility (Cutler 2004; León and Orriols 2016). In addition, more dynamic elements of power-sharing have a strong impact on how clear it is about who is being held responsible for the economy. Minority governments, coalition governments, how dominant is the main governing party in a coalition, as well as how many viable options voters can choose between are all thought to affect the extent to which voters can attribute responsibility for the economy (Anderson 2000; Hobolt et al. 2013). Regardless of what specific indicators are used to determine the clarity of responsibility, the Belgian context could arguably be considered a low-clarity context. The high number of parties that are split along linguistic lines and the fact that governments are consistently (large) coalitions of multiple parties can blur responsibility. In addition, the federal structure of the country results in multiple levels of government, and each level has its own competencies and government (Deschouwer 2012). At different levels, furthermore, it is not necessarily the same parties that are forming the government. In summary, the Belgian institutional and political context can be expected to significantly diminish clarity of responsibility, potentially reducing the economic vote.

For elections to serve as an effective mechanism for realising democratic representation, however, the presence of accountability in voting is considered as important. While Belgium is without any doubt a hard case for finding indications of economic voting, in a large number of different settings, it has been shown that voters manage holding incumbents into account, despite the presence of barriers to accountability. Research on the French case, for example, has indicated that under cohabitation – when different parties hold the offices of president and prime minister – voters effectively reward and punish the prime minister, who is mainly in charge of economic policy (Lewis-Beck 1997). Furthermore, previous research on economic voting in multiparty systems such as Germany or the Scandinavian democracies suggests that when government coalitions are in office, the electorate mainly holds the party of the prime minister accountable for the state of the economy (Debus et al. 2014; Larsen 2016). These studies indicate that one should not look only at the impact of the economic evaluations on the coalition government as a whole. To express it differently, when not differentiating between parties that control key cabinet posts like the prime minister or the minister of finance, the conclusion would be that a perception of economic improvement by the voters either has no effect or has a negative effect on support for the government (Debus et al. 2014: 63–64).

Previous research has shown that even though limited clarity of responsibility reduces the strength of the economic vote, the economic vote is pervasive – and is correlated in some ways to election results even in low-clarity contexts. For the Belgian case, more specifically, a limited number of studies have already suggested the presence of a link between economic indicators and electoral behaviour (Anderson 2009; Dassonneville and Hooghe 2012; Hooghe and Dassonneville 2014). Given all these considerations, it seems reasonable to expect a weak link between economic conditions and electoral results in Belgium. In line with previous studies on economic voting under coalition governments, we furthermore expect the relation between the economy and electoral results to be stronger when focusing on the party of the prime minister.

HETEROGENEITY IN ECONOMIC VOTING

Previous research has shown that the economic vote not only varies between contexts but that there is substantial heterogeneity in economic voting within electorates as well. More specifically, it has been argued that economic considerations are most important in guiding the vote choices of politically sophisticated voters (De Vries and Giger 2014; Gomez and Wilson 2001) and of those voters who consider the economy an important issue when deciding whom to vote for (De Vries and Giger 2014; Singer 2011).

First, a number of studies have focused on the relation between political sophistication and economic voting. Originally, economic voting was thought of as less cognitively demanding compared to voting according to one's ideological preferences or issue positions. This holds in particular when thinking of the economic voting in terms of retrospective evaluations (Fiorina 1981). Empirical work, however, indicates exactly the opposite: economic considerations are particularly important in guiding the vote choices of citizens with higher levels of political sophistication (De Vries and Giger 2014). There is some debate around the question of whether this holds for pocketbook evaluations (Gomez and Wilson 2001; Godbout and Bélanger 2007). Nevertheless, it is quite clear that the impact of sociotropic evaluations, that is, evaluations about the state of the national economy, are having a stronger impact among the high political sophisticates than what holds for citizens with lower levels of political sophistication (De Vries and Giger 2014; Godbout and Bélanger 2007). Even though evaluating the past performance of the incumbent and voting accordingly is arguably less cognitively demanding than comparing party platforms and issue positions of all parties or candidates, it hence seems that economic voting as well is strengthened with higher levels of political sophistication. The reason is that economic voting requires citizens to monitor the state of the economy and to subsequently attribute responsibility for these economic conditions to who is in office (De Vries and Giger 2014). In particular, in a low-clarity political context such as the Belgian one, we expect the impact of economic evaluations on the vote choice to strengthen as a citizen's level of political sophistication increases.

Second, scholars have drawn attention to the fact that the strength of the economic vote is dependent on the weight that is accorded to economic considerations on Election Day. This work, which is closely connected to studies on issue salience (Bélanger and Meguid 2008), expects, for example, that in times of economic downturn – when there is more attention for economic conditions – the economic vote will be stronger (Singer 2011). This reasoning applies to the individual level as well, as it is expected that the economic vote will be stronger among citizens who care more strongly about economic conditions. The economy is one of the most important issues guiding the vote choice overall (Wlezien 2005). Clearly, however, some voters give more weight to other issues, such as crime, migration or the environment, when casting a vote. De Vries and Giger (2014), for example, in their comparative study on mechanisms of accountability show that the economy was the most important issue for one in four voters. As a result, there is considerable variation in the extent to which voters effectively base their decision on an evaluation of the state of the economy (Singer 2011). The expectation, therefore, is that the effect of economic considerations will be strengthened among voters who consider the economy as an important issue.

DATA AND METHODS

For examining economic voting in Belgium, we make use of two different approaches. In a first step, we investigate whether we observe a correlation between objective economic indicators and incumbent vote shares in Belgium. Next, we examine more in depth which voters are holding incumbents into account. We make use of the data from the 2014 PartiRep Election Study to assess whether political sophistication and the importance attached to the economy strengthen the economic vote.

For assessing at an aggregate level whether the state of the economy is correlated to how the incumbent fares in a Belgian context, we make use of two different datasets. First, we estimate the correlation between economic indicators and how incumbent parties perform on Election Day. We present correlations for the performance of the party of the prime minister only as well as for the combined performance of all parties in the incumbent coalition, which allows us to verify whether the link is indeed stronger when focusing on the head of government alone. Given that Belgium can be considered a country with two separate party systems (Brack and Pilet 2010), we present separate analyses for the Flemish and francophone parties.

To complement these small number analyses, we also make use of polling data to assess whether the popularity of incumbent parties, in general, and the party of the prime minister, specifically, correlates with the state of the economy. To avoid any polling house effects, we only make use of the vote intention polls conducted by the newspaper *La Libre Belgique*. As this broadsheet newspaper has been conducting election polls since 1984, it offers the longest time series of vote intention polls in Belgium.

For examining whether the incumbent popularity correlates with the state of the national economy, we consider gross domestic product (GDP) growth and unemployment rates. These two economic indicators have regularly been found to be related to the incumbent performance on Election Day as well as incumbent popularity. In a large number of studies, incumbents are found to be rewarded for high GDP growth and for low unemployment rates, leading Lewis-Beck and Stegmaier (2013: 376) to refer to GDP growth and unemployment as the 'big two' indicators that voters take into account when evaluating the state of the economy. We use quarterly information for both GDP growth (growth compared to the same quarter in the previous year) and unemployment rates, which we retrieve from the OECD database. The incumbent vote share or share of the vote intentions is dependent on the initial size of parties and on the number of parties in the governing coalition. For reasons of comparability, we do not assess the correlation between economic indicators and incumbents' vote share or share of the vote intention, but instead the correlation between economic indicators and how the incumbent performs compared to the previous election. That is, we use a ratio of the incumbent vote (intention) share divided by the vote share obtained in the previous election. A ratio higher than 1 implies the incumbent wins votes, a ratio lower than 1 implies the incumbent is losing votes compared to the previous election.

While the aggregate-level analyses will give us insights into the extent to which economic conditions affect electoral results and incumbent popularity in the Belgian context, assessing who holds incumbents into account for the state of the economy requires an analysis of individual-level data. Therefore, in a second step we make use of the data from the 2014 PartiRep Election Study and investigate economic voting at an individual level. Given that objective macro-economic conditions do not vary between individuals in a single election year, we make use of respondents' evaluation of the state of the national economy. The questionnaire included a traditional sociotropic retrospective evaluation measure of the economy, asking respondents to indicate how they thought the national economy had evolved over the past twelve months. Answering options to this question were as follows: worsened a lot, worsened somewhat, remained the same, improved somewhat or improved a lot. While we thus make use of information from a single question item, it is important to point out that a sociotropic and retrospective measure of economic conditions is generally found to have the strongest effects on voting behaviour (Lewis-Beck and Stegmaier 2013). A reliance on subjective economic evaluations for examining economic voting has previously been criticised. Van der Brug et al. (2007: 26) argue that economic evaluations are influenced by other political attitudes, such as partisanship or ideological orientations and therefore 'subject to severe endogeneity problems'. While not denying that economic evaluations are subject to partisan reasoning, however, Stevenson and Duch (2013) claim that subjective evaluations are still theoretically relevant indicators, because economic voting theories do not make predictions about the 'true' economy but instead about the impact of how citizens observe the state of the economy. In addition, it is reassuring to note that on average, subjective economic evaluations do correlate with objective indicators of the economy. Furthermore, previous work that relies on subjective economic evaluations to examine economic voting, on the one hand, and work that focuses on the impact of objective indicators of the state of the economy, on the other, find largely similar indications of incumbents being held accountable by voters (Stevenson and Duch 2013). We hence can be confident that both our aggregate-level analyses of the impact of objective economic indicators and our individual-level analyses based on subjective evaluations provide important insights into the same basic mechanism of accountability.

We examine the effect of economic evaluations on the probability of voting for a party in the outgoing federal government and present separate analyses for respondents in Flanders and Wallonia. In addition, as the incumbent prime minister in 2014 was a member of a francophone party (the socialist party PS), we also examine the impact of economic evaluations on Walloon respondents' probability of voting for the party of the prime minister (within the Belgian electoral system, Flemish voters cannot vote for francophone parties, and vice versa). The dependent variable for these analyses is dichotomous, that is, a respondent either voted for an incumbent party/the party of the prime minister (= 1) or he or she did not (= 0). Therefore, we present the results of a series of logistic regression analyses. We are interested in the impact of economic evaluations on voting for the incumbent, but control for a number of socio-demographic characteristics that are regularly found to affect voting behaviour in Belgium. We control for respondents' gender, age, social class and their level of education. In addition, we add a control for respondents' self-placement on a left-right scale. While the data do not allow controlling of respondents' partisanship, including the left-right position should partially account for some of the endogeneity in citizens' assessment of economic conditions.

Examining whether some citizens are more likely to vote economically, we are interested in knowing whether the impact of economic evaluations on the vote choice is stronger for the high politically sophisticated and for those who consider the economy a more important issue. As an indicator of political sophistication, we make use of a sum scale of respondents' correct answers on five political knowledge questions. On average, respondents responded correctly to 2.11 of these five knowledge questions, while the standard deviation was 1.38. We thus make use of a single proxy indicator of political sophistication, though it is important to point out that political knowledge is argued to be the best single indicator of political sophistication (Lachat 2007). As a measure of how salient respondents' considered the economy, we make use of a question asking respondents how important the economy would be as an issue affecting their vote choice. Answering options on this question were as follows: not important at all, rather unimportant, neither important nor unimportant, rather important or very important. The average response on this 1 to 5 scale was 4.69, and the standard deviation was 0.69. Belgian voters thus considered the economy a highly salient issue when deciding whom to vote for in 2014.

AGGREGATE-LEVEL ANALYSES: IS ANYONE HELD ACCOUNTABLE?

As a first step, we assess whether the performance of incumbent parties on Election Day is related to the state of the economy. We make use of two indicators of national economic conditions: GDP growth and unemployment rates. We incorporate a lag time and opt for a lag of two-quarters. As such, we take into account that voters assess the economy retrospectively (Dassonneville and Lewis-Beck 2014). The economic voting paradigm leads us to expect that GDP growth will be positively correlated with the incumbent's performance, while unemployment rates are expected to correlate negatively to how the incumbent performs on Election Day. As indicated before, for reasons of comparability we use as an indicator of the incumbent's performance a ratio of the incumbent's performance in the current election divided by the vote share in the previous election.

In table 8.1, we present the results of a series of simple bivariate correlation analyses. We report the Pearson's correlation coefficients and indicate the significance levels. As evident from the results in table 8.1, GDP growth correlates positively with how incumbent parties perform on Election Day, as we expected. This correlation, however, is only significant on the 10 per cent level, that is at $p < 0.10$, when we focus on the performance of the prime minister's party. For unemployment rates, by contrast, correlations do not reach a conventional level of statistical significance. This holds regardless of whether we look at the performance of the incumbent coalition in the two language groups or when we focus on the party of the prime minister alone. As a result, these bivariate tests offer only weak evidence of economic voting in Belgium. This is in line with our expectations, as low levels of clarity of responsibility mark the Belgian political context.

The only indications of a significant correlation between incumbent performance and economic conditions can be found when looking at how GDP growth correlates with the performance of the prime minister's party. This correlation is graphically presented in figure 8.1 and clarifies that as the economy grows more strongly, the probability of the party of the prime minister being rewarded (a ratio higher than 1) increases. The finding that we only observe a significant correlation when focusing on the party of the prime minister is in line with the expectation we derived from the literature review: in a context of coalition governments, the attribution of responsibility is directed mostly to the party that leads the government and not to all coalition parties.

Table 8.1. Incumbent performance and economic indicators – correlations

	Prime Minister's party	*Coalition (Dutch language)*	*Coalition (French language)*
GDP growth	0.558[+]	0.319	0.153
Unemployment	0.437	0.433	0.268
N	11	11	11

Note: Pearson's correlation coefficients between incumbent performance and economic indicators are shown. Significance level: [+] $p < 0.10$.

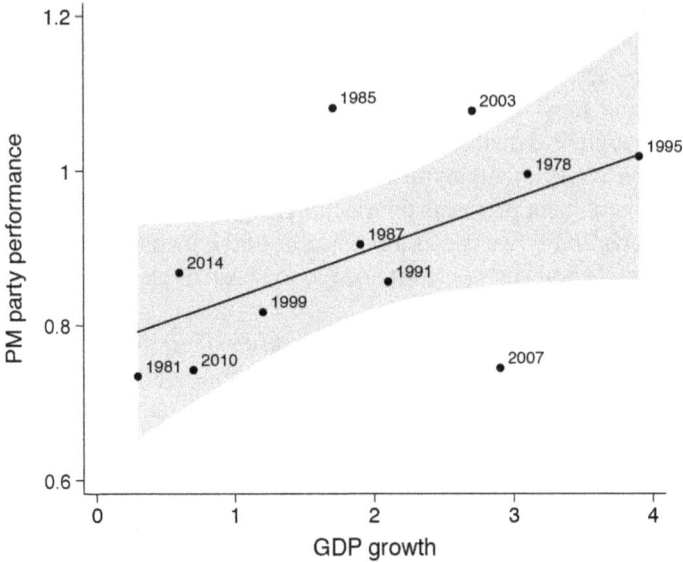

Figure 8.1. Prime minister's party performance and GDP growth

While insightful, our examination of the correlation between economic indicators and incumbents' performance on Election Day suffers from data limitations. With a total number of only eleven elections, the correlation analyses are sensitive to the impact of outliers, and the 1985 and 2007 elections could be ones. As an additional test, we therefore also examine the correlation between objective economic indicators and incumbents' popularity, as captured by vote intention polls. We proceed in the same way as we did for the correlation tests based on electoral results, and correlate economic indicators with a popularity ratio (dividing the share of vote intentions obtained by incumbent parties by their vote share in the previous election). We expect the GDP growth to be positively and unemployment rates to be negatively correlated with the incumbent popularity ratio.

The time series of vote intention polls covers the time period between 1984 and 2016 and allows analysing vote intentions in both language groups. We examine the correlation between the economic indicators and summed share of the vote intentions obtained by all incumbent parties in a language group as well as the share of vote intentions obtained by the party of the prime minister in his language group. From the start of the time series until 2010, the prime minister was a member of a Flemish party. Since 2010, incumbent prime ministers have been members of francophone parties (Elio Di Rupo from the francophone socialist party PS and Charles Michel from the francophone liberal party MR). The results of these correlation tests are reported in table 8.2.

Table 8.2. Incumbent popularity and economic indicators – correlations

	Prime Minister's party (Dutch language)	Coalition (Dutch language)	Prime Minister's party (French language)	Coalition (French language)
GDP growth	0.119	0.167[+]	0.749**	0.162[+]
Unemployment	−0.049	0.068	0.277	−0.333***
N	129	148	16	120

Note: Pearson's correlation coefficients between incumbent performance and economic indicators are shown. Significance level: [+] $p < 0.10$; * $p < 0.05$; ** $p < 0.01$; *** $p < 0.001$.

In line with what could be observed when focusing on electoral results (see table 8.1 and figure 8.1), we find most evidence for mechanisms of economic voting when considering GDP growth as an indicator of the state of the national economy. It should be observed, however, that we also find a strong negative correlation between unemployment rates and the vote share obtained by francophone governing parties in vote intention polls. Furthermore, it can be noted that correlations are not particularly pronounced either, when focusing only on the party of the prime minister.

In summary, a look at the correlation between objective economic indicators, on the one hand, and election results or the share of vote intentions, on the other, offers only weak evidence of mechanisms of economic voting in Belgium. We found some indications that larger GDP growth rates are associated with incumbents receiving a larger share of the vote, but this association is rather weak and unstable. This observation, however, fits theoretical expectations. The federal and multiparty political structure of Belgium, where large coalitions of parties form the government, makes for a low-clarity context, where it can be considered particularly difficult for voters to hold incumbents accountable for the state of the economy. In a next step we, therefore, examine more in depth which voters are able to overcome the barriers of a low-clarity context and hold their incumbents into account.

INDIVIDUAL-LEVEL ANALYSES: WHO HOLDS THE GOVERNMENT ACCOUNTABLE?

For investigating sources of individual-level heterogeneity in economic voting, we make use of the data from the 2014 PartiRep Election Study. We present a series of logistic regression models explaining voting for an incumbent party in both regions and voting for the party of the prime minister among voters in Wallonia. Our focus is on the impact of subjective evaluations of the state of the economy on the vote choice.

In table 8.3, we present the main models, including the main effect of respondents' evaluation of the state of the economy and all of our control variables. In Models 1 and 2, we explain voting for one of the incumbent parties at the Flemish or Walloon side of the party spectrum, respectively. For both of these models, it can be observed that socio-demographic characteristics are not strongly related to choosing an incumbent party over one of the parties in opposition. This is not surprising, as for both language groups the coalition was a fairly heterogeneous set of different parties. More importantly, it can be observed that in both Flanders and Wallonia, respondents who evaluated the state of the national economy more positively were more likely to vote for an incumbent party. The size of the effect, furthermore, is roughly similar. Calculating the marginal effect of economic evaluations, while holding all other covariates at the mean value, indicates that a one-unit increase on the economic evaluation scale increases the probability of voting for an incumbent party by 5.9 per cent in Flanders and by 4.8 per cent in Wallonia. This is a substantively important effect and indicates that despite the low-clarity context, voters in Belgium are punishing and rewarding incumbents according to how they evaluate the economy. It has to be noted, however, that even though we control for ideological positions, endogeneity problems could imply that this effect is somewhat inflated. The results of Model 3 in table 8.3 indicate that when focusing on the party of the prime minister only, economic evaluations appear to be significantly related to the vote choice as well. In contrast to what we hypothesised, however, this effect is not more pronounced than what holds when considering the vote for any of the parties in the governing coalition. In this regard, it is important to point out that the party of the outgoing prime minister in 2014 was the socialist party PS. It is hence reasonable to assume that the punishment this party receives from voters who evaluate the economy negatively is to some extent counter-balanced by a pattern of policy voting. Previous research has argued that leftist parties generally benefit from worsening economic conditions, as some voters are policy-oriented and choose the party closest to their own economic policy position (Dassonneville and Lewis-Beck 2013). In line with the study mentioned earlier, Adams et al. (2009) argue and show that parties of the left are stronger policy-seeking organisations than centrist or right-wing parties in order to shape public opinion rather than to be shaped by it. Left-wing parties are traditionally considered to defend the interests of those who are economically less well-off and attract votes among this group. Such an association, then, might have protected the PS from losing a larger amount of votes among those who evaluated the economy negatively, diluting the reward-and-punishment mechanism. This explanation does, however, need a more detailed test, which could be performed in future research.

Table 8.3. Explaining voting for the incumbent – main effects

	Model 1	Model 2	Model 3
	Coalition (Flanders)	Coalition (Wallonia)	Prime Minister's party (Wallonia)
	b (s.e.)	*b* (s.e.)	*b* (s.e.)
Female	0.027	0.023	0.370
	(0.168)	(0.216)	(0.219)
Age	0.005	0.023***	0.016*
	(0.005)	(0.007)	(0.006)
Middle educated (ref.: low)	−0.363	0.140	−0.394
	(0.236)	(0.291)	(0.262)
Higher educated (ref.: low)	−0.207	−0.158	−1.162***
	(0.257)	(0.301)	(0.276)
Blue collar (ref.: non-active)	0.126	−0.203	−0.059
	(0.273)	(0.352)	(0.341)
White collar (ref.: non-active)	0.299	−0.295	−0.442
	(0.207)	(0.242)	(0.236)
Self-employed (ref.: non-active)	0.030	0.370	−0.367
	(0.334)	(0.501)	(0.423)
Left-right placement	−0.146***	0.105*	−0.241***
	(0.042)	(0.045)	(0.050)
Economic evaluation	0.237*	0.258*	0.234*
	(0.095)	(0.107)	(0.107)
Political knowledge	−0.083	−0.140	−0.189*
	(0.070)	(0.072)	(0.076)
Economy important	0.261*	0.452**	0.493**
	(0.123)	(0.173)	(0.179)
Constant	−0.562	−2.031*	−1.415
	(0.613)	(0.877)	(0.879)
N	737	595	595
Pseudo-R^2	0.035	0.066	0.136

Note: Unstandardised coefficients are reported and standard errors (s.e.) are presented within parentheses. Significance levels: * $p < 0.05$; ** $p < 0.01$; *** $p < 0.001$.

Overall, it appears that citizens' assessment of the state of the economy influences their probability of voting for an incumbent party. While the value of subjective economic evaluations is somewhat disputed in the literature, because they are considered to suffer from an endogeneity problem (Duch and Stevenson 2013; Hansford and Gomez 2015; Van der Brug et al. 2007), an individual-level approach has the advantage of allowing investigating sources of heterogeneity in who holds incumbents accountable for the state of the economy. We hypothesised that both the higher politically sophisticated and citizens who consider the economy an important issue would show stronger patterns of economic voting.

In table 8.4, we examine the effect of the interaction between respondents' evaluation of the state of the national economy and their level of political knowledge – which is our indicator of how politically sophisticated they are. In line with how we proceeded for the main effects, we present three models: a model explaining voting for an incumbent party in the Flemish region, a model explaining voting for an incumbent party in Wallonia and a model explaining voting for the party of the prime minister.

The results listed in table 8.4 offer no indications of the impact of economic evaluations being strengthened significantly as voters are more politically sophisticated. For interpreting the conditioning effect of political knowledge on economic evaluations, however, we should assess the marginal effect of economic evaluations for the full range of values on the political knowledge scale (Brambor et al. 2005). Figure 8.2 presents these marginal effects for each of the three models estimated in table 8.4. This graphical presentation of the conditioning impact of political knowledge confirms that economic evaluations do not significantly affect the probability of a low knowledgeable voter choosing an incumbent party. For each of the three dependent variables we look at, we can observe that the effect of economic evaluations is not significant at the lower end of the knowledge scale. While economic evaluations appear to significantly affect the vote choice of voters with a middle level of political knowledge, interestingly, the impact of economic evaluations falls short of statistical significance among respondents with the highest levels of knowledge about politics. The same holds if we limit the analyses to examining the moderating impact of knowledge about the governing coalitions only (the regional and federal coalitions). Here as well, we observe a significant impact of economic evaluations among the middle knowledgeable (who answered correctly to one of both questions) but not among the high knowledgeable (who answered correctly to both coalition-related questions). These results suggest that it does require some level of political knowledge to see clearly whom to hold accountable for the state of the economy. For the most knowledgeable voters, however, evaluations no longer affect the electoral choices made. The absence of a significant effect among this group of voters might be a result of the fact that even though high knowledgeable voters can identify who is responsible for the economy as well as what is the state of the economy, they have already made up their mind, are perhaps close to one particular party and hence are not open to changing opinions (Zaller 1992).

Table 8.4. **Explaining voting for the incumbent – the moderating effect of political sophistication**

	Model 1	Model 2	Model 3
	Coalition (Flanders	Coalition (Wallonia)	Prime Minister's party (Wallonia)
	b (s.e.)	b (s.e.)	b (s.e.)
Female	0.026 (0.168)	0.022 (0.216)	0.377 (0.220)
Age	0.005 (0.005)	0.023*** (0.007)	0.016* (0.006)
Middle educated (ref: low)	−0.367 (0.236)	0.147 (0.292)	−0.405 (0.263)
Higher educated (ref: low)	−0.206 (0.258)	−0.142 (0.303)	−1.179*** (0.276)
Blue collar (ref: non-active)	0.121 (0.274)	−0.216 (0.352)	−0.046 (0.346)
White collar (ref: non-active)	0.299 (0.207)	−0.287 (0.243)	−0.456 (0.236)
Self-employed (ref: non-active)	0.040 (0.334)	0.380 (0.503)	−0.386 (0.424)
Left-right placement	−0.145*** (0.042)	0.107* (0.045)	−0.243*** (0.049)
Economy important	0.261* (0.122)	0.463** (0.175)	0.486** (0.180)
Economic evaluation	0.166 (0.181)	0.393 (0.209)	0.094 (0.206)
Political knowledge	−0.087 (0.070)	−0.160* (0.077)	−0.173* (0.077)
Political knowledge × ec. evaluation	0.037 (0.076)	−0.056 (0.072)	0.062 (0.075)
Constant	−0.563 (0.611)	−2.038* (0.884)	−1.401 (0.879)
N	737	595	595
Pseudo-R^2	0.035	0.067	0.137

Note: Unstandardised coefficients are reported and standard errors (s.e.) are presented within parentheses.
  Significance levels: * $p < 0.05$; ** $p < 0.01$; *** $p < 0.001$.

Our results suggest that having a certain level of political knowledge helps voters to hold incumbents accountable for the state of the economy. It can be observed that for voters with a middle level of political knowledge, economic evaluations significantly affect their probability of voting for an incumbent party. This is clear from the fact that for middle knowledgeable voters, both

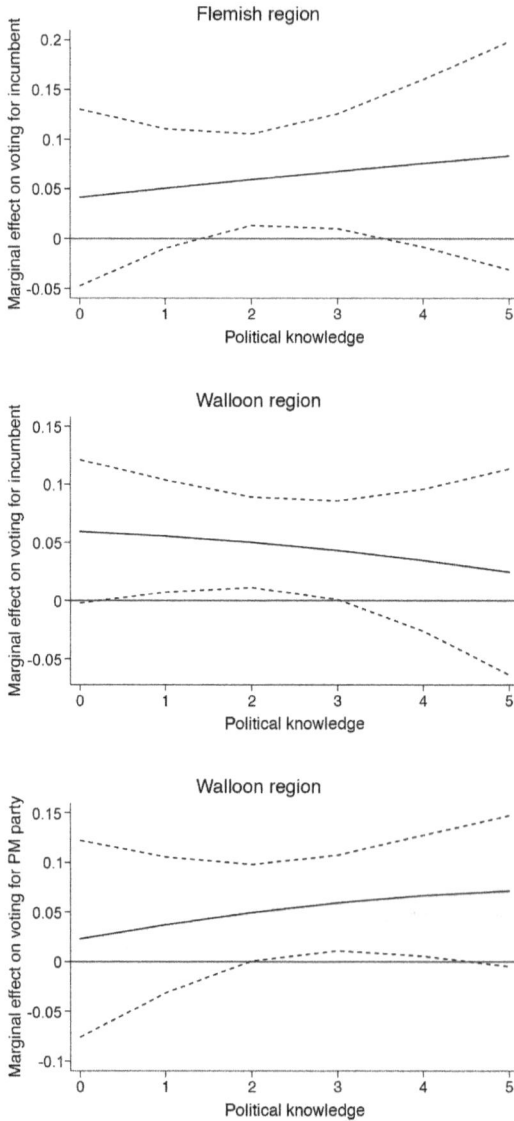

Figure 8.2. Marginal effect of economic evaluation by level of political knowledge

Note: Marginal effect and 95 per cent confidence intervals of one unit change in economic evaluations, at varying levels of political knowledge are shown. All other variables are set at the sample mean. Marginal effects are based on estimates from Models 1 to 3 in table 8.4.

the lower and upper bound of the confidence interval is higher than 0. However, we find no significant effects of economic evaluations on the choices made by high knowledgeable voters.

A second factor, of which we hypothesised that it would serve as a facilitator of economic voting, is how important a voter considers the issue of the economy. In particular, in a multiparty context like Belgium, where multiple policy dimensions characterise politics, the economy is not necessarily the most important theme on which elections are fought. For voters who do consider the economy highly important when deciding whom to vote for, however, we would expect clear indications of economic voting.

To test this hypothesis, we present a series of models in table 8.5 where we add to the main effects an interaction between the salience of the economy for

Table 8.5. **Explaining voting for the incumbent – the moderating effect of salience**

	Model 1	Model 2	Model 3
	Coalition (Flanders)	Coalition (Wallonia)	Prime Minister's party (Wallonia)
	b (s.e.)	b (s.e.)	b (s.e.)
Female	0.028 (0.168)	0.026 (0.216)	0.371 (0.219)
Age	0.005 (0.005)	0.023*** (0.007)	0.016* (0.006)
Middle educated (ref: low)	−0.364 (0.236)	0.143 (0.290)	−0.391 (0.262)
Higher educated (ref: low)	−0.211 (0.258)	−0.148 (0.301)	−1.157*** (0.276)
Blue collar (ref: non-active)	0.123 (0.273)	−0.214 (0.354)	−0.067 (0.342)
White collar (ref: non-active)	0.302 (0.207)	−0.294 (0.242)	−0.439 (0.237)
Self-employed (ref: non-active)	0.031 (0.335)	0.380 (0.500)	−0.364 (0.424)
Left-right placement	−0.147*** (0.042)	0.105* (0.045)	−0.240*** (0.050)
Economic evaluation	0.030 (0.565)	−0.083 (0.823)	−0.043 (0.893)
Political knowledge	−0.083 (0.070)	−0.143* (0.073)	−0.191* (0.077)
Economy important	0.260* (0.121)	0.478** (0.180)	0.512** (0.183)
Economy important × ec. evaluation	0.046 (0.124)	0.076 (0.181)	0.060 (0.194)
Constant	−0.549 (0.609)	−2.143* (0.897)	−1.504 (0.898)
N	737	595	595
Pseudo-R^2	0.035	0.067	0.136

Note: Unstandardised coefficients are reported and standard errors (s.e.) are presented within parentheses. Data are weighted by socio-demographic characteristics. Significance levels: * $p < 0.05$; ** $p < 0.01$; *** $p < 0.001$.

a voter and his or her evaluation of the state of the economy. In line with our hypothesis, we expect to find that the effect of economic evaluations is stronger among voters who consider the economy an important issue when deciding which party to vote for. The interaction terms in table 8.5 are positive,

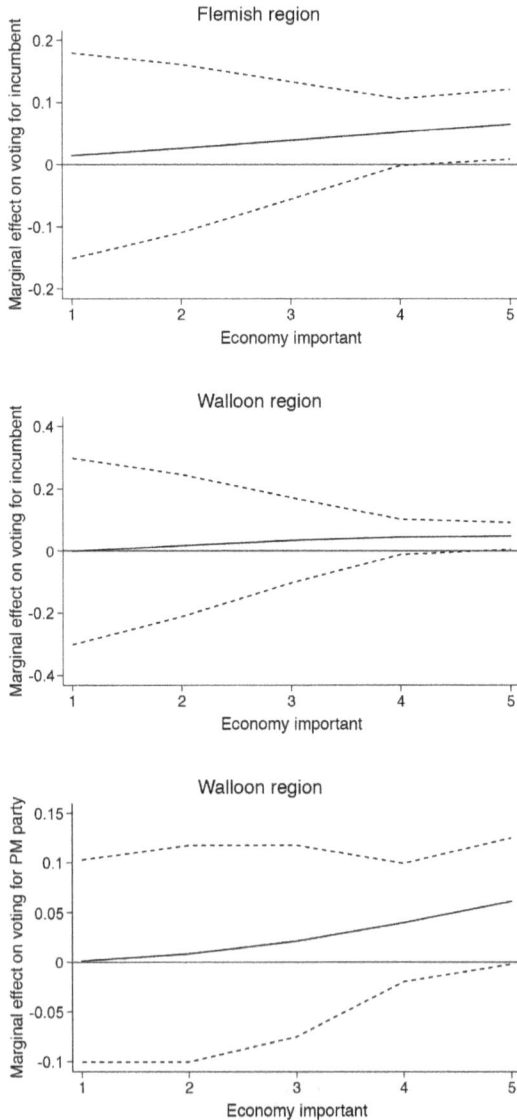

Figure 8.3.   Marginal effect of economic evaluation by level of salience of the economy

Note: Marginal effect and 95 per cent confidence intervals of one unit change in economic evaluations, at varying levels of political knowledge are shown. All other variables are set at the sample mean. Marginal effects are based on estimates from Models 1 to 3 in table 8.5.

though the coefficients do not reach a conventional level of statistical significance. In line with how we proceeded for examining the conditioning impact of political knowledge, however, we present some marginal effects for the full range of values on the economic salience variable. As such, we can get a better grasp of how important voters should consider the economy for their economic evaluations to affect their vote choice.

The results of these marginal effect calculations are plotted in figure 8.3. These plots clarify that the marginal effect of a one unit increase in the respondents' evaluation of the state of the economy does increase as the respondents think the economy is a more important issue. The upper and middle panels clearly show that economic evaluations only significantly affect the probability of choosing an incumbent party among those who think the economy is either fairly or very important (values 4 and 5 on the salience of the economy measure). We observe a similar trend when focusing on voting for the party of the prime minister only, though at a lower level of significance (the marginal effect of economic evaluations at an economic importance value of 5 is significant at $p < 0.10$).

CONCLUSION

The Belgian political context is generally considered a low-clarity setting for voters. In their seminal study on how clarity of responsibility conditions economic voting, Powell and Whitten (1993) classified Belgium in the low-clarity group. Other elements, not part of the original Powell and Whitten index of clarity of responsibility – such as federalism – can be thought to further blur how clear it is who is responsible for the national economy in a Belgian context. Despite this low-clarity setting, our results suggest that the state of the economy and economic considerations are affecting voting behaviour in Belgium.

Furthermore, our individual-level analyses suggest that the mechanism of economic voting is fairly general. We find that casting a vote according to one's evaluation of the state of the economy does require a certain level of political knowledge, but economic voting clearly is not restricted to the most politically sophisticated. In addition, while we only find indications of a significant impact of economic evaluations on the vote choice among voters who think the economy is an important issue, it has to be noted that a large majority of over 90 per cent of voters thought the economy was a fairly or very important issue. At least in the context of the 2014 elections, where the financial crisis and the Eurozone crisis were major issues, it can be observed that Belgian voters consider the economy a very important issue, and voters take this issue into account when deciding whom to vote for.

Previous studies examining economic voting in a context of coalition governments find that the attribution of responsibility is not directed to all parties in government equally. Instead, parties that hold portfolios that are relevant for managing the economy, and in particular the party that holds the office of the prime minister are held accountable more strongly (Debus et al. 2014; Larsen 2016). Our aggregate-level analyses suggested somewhat stronger correlations between economic indicators and the vote share of the party of the prime minister than what was found for the coalition as a whole. Somewhat surprisingly, however, our individual-level analyses did not show stronger effects when examining the impact of economic evaluations on the probability of voting for the party of the prime minister only. Potentially, this is due to the fact that at the time of the 2014 general elections, the incumbent prime minister was a member of the socialist party PS. As previous research showed, leftist parties benefit somewhat from worsening economic conditions, as policy-oriented voters who think the economy is not doing well prefer a party that will provide welfare in times of crisis (Dassonneville and Lewis-Beck 2013). Consequently, these considerations somewhat moderate the reward-and-punishment mechanism of economic voting. More research, however, is needed to reveal whether this is indeed the reason why we do not find the lead party to be held accountable more than the coalition in general. The next general elections will be interesting in this regard, as the current prime minister is a member of the liberal party MR.

Overall, however, we find indications of economic voting in Belgium. The fact that we do observe such effects in the Belgian context is quite relevant. Within political rhetoric, the Belgian political system is often being portrayed as being 'too complex to understand'. Some politicians have even argued that Belgium should be considered as two distinct democracies as there is not a single public opinion in the country. Despite these allegations, the current results suggest that the basic mechanism of electoral accountability with regard to the functioning of the economy, which can be observed in most liberal democracies, is present in Belgium as well. Despite the obvious complexity of the Belgian federal system, apparently the Belgian voters still manage to see the forest for the trees, which is a positive finding in terms of democratic responsiveness in complex institutional political systems.

NOTE

1. We thank Benny Geys for generously sharing his dataset of vote intention polls in Belgium. We also thank Christophe Davis for research assistance in updating this dataset.

REFERENCES

Adams, J., Haupt, A. B. and Stoll, H. (2009) 'What moves parties? The role of public opinion and global economic conditions in Western Europe', *Comparative Political Studies*, 42(5): 611–39.

Anderson, C. D. (2009) 'Institutional change, economic conditions and confidence in government. Evidence from Belgium', *Acta Politica*, 44(1): 28–49.

Anderson, C. J. (2000) 'Economic voting and political context: A comparative perspective', *Electoral Studies*, 19(2/3): 151–70.

Bélanger, É. and Meguid, B. M. (2008) 'Issue salience, issue ownership, and issue-based vote choice', *Electoral Studies*, 27(3): 477–91.

Brack, N. and Pilet, J.-B. (2010) 'One country, two party systems? The 2009 Belgian regional elections', *Regional and Federal Studies*, 20(4/5): 549–59.

Brambor, T., Clark, W. R. and Golder, M. (2005) 'Understanding interaction models: Improving empirical analyses', *Political Analysis*, 14(1): 63–82.

Cutler, F. (2004) 'Government responsibility and electoral accountability in federations', *Publius: The Journal of Federalism*, 34(2): 19–38.

Dassonneville, R. and Hooghe, M. (2012) 'Election forecasting under opaque conditions: A model for Francophone Belgium, 1981–2010', *International Journal of Forecasting*, 28(4): 777–88.

Dassonneville, R. and Lewis-Beck, M. S. (2013) 'Economic policy voting and incumbency: Unemployment in Western Europe', *Political Science Research and Methods*, 1(1): 53–66.

Dassonneville, R. and Lewis-Beck, M. S. (2014) 'Macroeconomics, economic crisis and electoral outcomes: a national European pool', *Acta Politica*, 49(4): 372–94.

De Vries, C. E. and Giger, N. (2014) 'Holding governments accountable? Individual heterogeneity in performance voting', *European Journal of Political Research*, 53(2): 345–62.

Debus, M., Stegmaier, M. and Tosun, J. (2014) 'Economic voting under coalition governments: Evidence from Germany', *Political Science Research and Methods*, 2(1): 49–67.

Deschouwer, K. (2012) *The Politics of Belgium: Governing a Divided Society*, Houndmills, Basingstoke: Palgrave Macmillan.

Duch, R. M. and Stevenson, R. T. (2008) *The Economic Vote: How Political and Economic Institutions Condition Election Results*, Cambridge: Cambridge University Press.

Duch, R. M. and Stevenson, R. T. (2013) 'Voter perceptions of agenda power and attribution of responsibility for economic performance', *Electoral Studies*, 32(3): 512–16.

Fiorina, M. (1981) *Retrospective Voting in American National Elections*, New Haven, CT: Yale University Press.

Godbout, J.-F. and Bélanger, É. (2007) 'Economic voting and political sophistication in the United States. A reassessment', *Political Research Quarterly*, 60(3): 541–54.

Gomez, B. T. and Wilson, M. (2001) 'Political sophistication and economic voting in the American electorate: A theory of heterogeneous attribution', *American Journal of Political Science*, 45(4): 899–914.

Hansford, T. G. and Gomez, B. T. (2015) 'Reevaluating the sociotropic economic voting hypothesis', *Electoral Studies*, 39(1): 15–25.

Healy, A. and Malhotra, N. (2013) 'Retrospective voting reconsidered', *Annual Review of Political Science*, 16(1): 285–306.

Hobolt, S., Tilley, J. and Banducci, S. (2013) 'Clarity of responsibility: How government cohesion conditions performance voting', *European Journal of Political Research*, 52(2): 164–87.

Hooghe, M. and Dassonneville, R. (2014) 'Party members as an electoral linking mechanism. An election forecasting model for political parties in Belgium, 1981–2010', *Party Politics*, 20(3): 368–80.

Lachat, R. (2007) *A Heterogeneous Electorate: Political Sophistication, Predisposition Strength, and the Voting Decision Process*, Baden-Baden: Nomos.

Larsen, M. V. (2016) 'Economic conditions affect support for Prime Minister parties in Scandinavia', *Scandinavian Political Studies*, 39(3): 226–41.

León, S. and Orriols, L. (2016) 'Asymmetric federalism and economic voting', *European Journal of Political Research*, 55(4): 847–65.

Lewis-Beck, M. S. (1988) *Economics and Elections. The Major Western Democracies*, Ann Arbor: University of Michigan Press.

Lewis-Beck, M. S. (1997) 'Who's the chef? Economic voting under a dual executive', *European Journal of Political Research*, 31(3): 315–25.

Lewis-Beck, M. S. and Stegmaier, M. (2000) 'Economic determinants of electoral outcomes', *Annual Review of Political Science*, 3(1): 183–219.

Lewis-Beck, M. S. and Stegmaier, M. (2013) 'The VP-function revisited: A survey of the literature on vote and popularity functions after over 40 years', *Public Choice*, 157(3–4): 367–85.

Nadeau, R., Lewis-Beck, M. S. and Bélanger, É. (2013) 'Economics and elections revisited', *Comparative Political Studies*, 46(5): 551–73.

Nadeau, R., Niemi, R. G. and Yoshinaka, A. (2002) 'A cross-national analysis of economic voting: Taking account of the political context across time and nations', *Electoral Studies*, 21(3): 403–23.

Powell, G. B., Jr. and Whitten, G. D. (1993) 'A cross-national analysis of economic voting: Taking account of the political context', *American Journal of Political Science*, 37(2): 391–414.

Przeworski, A., Stokes, S. C. and Manin, B. (1999) *Democracy, Accountability, and Representation*, Cambridge: Cambridge University Press.

Singer, M. (2011) 'Who says "it's the economy"? Cross-national and cross-individual variation in the salience of economic performance', *Comparative Political Studies*, 44(3): 284–312.

Stevenson, R. T. and Duch, R. (2013) 'The meaning and use of subjective perceptions in studies of economic voting', *Electoral Studies*, 32(2): 305–20.

Van der Brug, W. Van der Eijk, C. and Franklin, M. (2007) *The Economy and the Vote: Economic Conditions and Elections in Fifteen Countries*, Cambridge: Cambridge University Press.

Wlezien, C. (2005) 'On the salience of political issues: The problem with "most important problem"', *Electoral Studies*, 24(4): 555–79.

Zaller, J. (1992) *The Nature and Origins of Mass Opinion*, Cambridge: Cambridge University Press.

Chapter 9

Policy and ideology volatility during the campaign

Stefaan Walgrave and Christophe Lesschaeve

INTRODUCTION

Electoral campaigns have effects on voters. A host of work has showed that campaigns have (some) influence on diverse phenomena such as voter turnout, the actual party/candidate people vote for, the issues voters take into account when voting (priming), voter evaluation of party/candidate traits and voter knowledge. The found effects are often small (Lazarsfeld, Berelson & Gaudet 1945) and mixed but, by and large, we know that campaigns make some difference (Brady, Johnston & Sides 2006). However, the vast work on the effects of campaigns on voters has not focused that much on another and quite straightforward effect campaigns may have on voters: the influence of campaigns on the *ideological* and the *policy positions* people hold (for exceptions, see Bartels 2006; Sciarini 2003). In fact, a lot of the information people get during campaigns is precisely information about issues, policies and ideologies. This is what parties and candidates predominantly talk about during campaigns, at least when they are not busy trying to discredit the competing party/candidate for being crooked, corrupt or incompetent. In many campaigns, voters are confronted with a flood of policy-related and substantive information. Does this information inspire people to update their ideological and policy positions during the campaign? Do parties/candidates manage to actually influence the policy-related beliefs of voters; are they able to persuade voters that their solution to policy issues is better than those of their competitors? We do not really know a lot about that.

The Belgian campaign of 2014 was an excellent case to tackle this void in the literature. First, although we do not have longitudinal evidence to definitely prove it, the 2014 campaign in Belgium was remarkably policy-focused. The actual financial cost and budget implications of parties' policy proposals were calculated by experts and discussed at length in the major news media; the news media organised their election coverage around a number of policies and extensively highlighted parties' diverging positions, and voting advice applications (VAAs) informing voters about the precise policy positions of parties were more popular than ever: the main VAA, *Stemtest/Test Electoral*, generated 2.7 million voting advices. Second, thanks to the 2014 PartiRep Voter Survey, we have unique data including evidence of voters' policy preferences measured before and right after the campaign and we also have ideological left-right self-placement before and after the campaign. This places us in a good position to scrutinise, in the context of two campaigns, the Flemish and the Walloon, how, and especially why, voter policy positions and ideological self-definition change through a campaign.

IDEOLOGY AND POLICY PERSUASION

Under the header 'campaign persuasion' there is a quite substantial body of work addressing how campaigns manage to change people's party or candidate preference (Bartels 2006), but this is a different matter from what we want to study in this chapter. Campaigns can affect voters' substantive opinions, both policies and ideology, without affecting their actual vote, and campaigns can change how people vote without influencing how they think about policies and their own ideology. The work specifically dealing with ideology and policy persuasion during electoral campaigns is limited (see also Sciarini 2003). We do not really know a lot about whether people actually change opinion during campaigns at all, nor do we know who the voters are who change opinion and why they do so. And, as far as we know, there is simply no previous work on whether, and how, changes in people's policy positions in a campaign are related to changes in people's ideological placement (for a longitudinal account of how policy positions are related with ideological left-right placement, see de Vries, Hakhverdian & Lancee 2013).

The older campaign 'activation' literature suggests that, rather than changing peoples' attitudes or positions, campaigns make people's existing but latent predispositions salient and accessible which then, in a next step, makes them vote for a party matching these preferences (Lazarsfeld, Berelson & Gaudet 1945). Because there is plenty of policy (and other) information available during a campaign, voters are likely to learn about their own preferences during a campaign (Alvarez 1998). Recent work by Lenz (2009) offers an alternative account by suggesting that a good deal of people's policy updating during campaigns, their shifts in policy positions, is done as a consequence of voters following their preferred party. Instead of a priming effect that does not imply opinion change as suggested by the activation scholars, people do effectively change their policy opinions in order to match their preferred party, he says. In sum, in contrast to the older studies, the current literature suggests that some people do change their beliefs during a campaign. But, who are the people who change their policy opinions more often and why do they change?

Answering the first question, classic work in the United States has suggested that the policy opinions of the lower educated, and thus the low politically aware, are more volatile compared to those of the higher educated (Zaller 1992; Kriesi 2002). Lower educated voters' policy positions are more likely to change, simply because they are less likely to have a firm position to begin with, reflecting the randomness accompanying what Converse (1964) labelled 'non-attitudes'. Also, they do not so clearly perceive the potential contradiction between their existing predispositions and the newly incoming information. And, their policy opinions are not so strongly embedded in their attitudinal structure as those of the highly educated so that, as a consequence, they are less resistant to opinion change (Sciarini 2003). Because of all these reasons, the lower educated are more easily swayed.

People can change opinion for many reasons. One is that they try to bring their policy preferences in line with the positions held by the party they prefer. Earlier, citing Lenz (2009), we already referred to the mechanism of people getting informed about their and other parties' position and their consecutive adjustment of their policy position. This is a well-known mechanism leading to opinion change (Abramowitz 1978; Zaller 1994). Our concrete expectation is straightforward: the larger the policy mismatch between a voter and the party that he or she is currently preferring, the larger is the chance that this voter will change his or her policy position (in the direction of the preferred party).

The two expectations formulated earlier – that, during a campaign, the lower educated would change policy position more and that people would update their position as to maximise the policy congruence with their party – do relate to the policy positions people have. We are not aware of work discussing the volatility of people's *ideological* placement. But, we think that there are reasons to expect that education and congruence factors also hold for explaining people's potential ideology updating. In fact, policy positions are related to ideology and, if one knows how people define their own ideology, one can make mostly good predictions of where they stand on concrete policies as well and vice versa (de Vries, Hakhverdian & Lancee 2013). This would suggest that if voters, during a campaign, updated their policy positions, they would also update how they define their ideological position. Still, ideological self-definition is a much more abstract and symbolic exercise than determining one's position on concrete policy issues. So, it is likely that both elements are correlated but they might evolve differently and there could be partly other factors driving policy and ideology change over time. For example, if during a campaign the debate revolves around ideology, it may be the case that there is more ideology than actual policy position change, while campaign information about concrete policy positions without connecting those positions to the wider ideology may lead to policy position change without ideology updating.

DATA AND METHODS

To study changes in the policy and ideological positions of voters, we use the twenty-three concrete policy statements (see the appendix) and the left-right self-placement scale that were presented to the respondents in both waves of the PartiRep survey. The answers of voters to the policy statements were measured on a 4-point scale, ranging from strongly agree to strongly disagree with two moderate options in the middle (agree and disagree). All twenty-three policy statements deal with national competences. For the left-right positions, the classic 11-point scale was used. We compare the positions of voters between the two waves to measure the extent to which they change their stances during the campaign. The 2014 campaign in Belgium involved the election of candidates to three political levels: the regional, national and European Parliament. This led to a dense campaign, focused on substantive policy information. Several VAAs were developed highlighting parties' policy positions. The media made detailed calculations as to the exact costs and benefits of the respective party manifestos. The often technical intricacies of the party programmes were discussed at length in the newspapers. As this campaign was focused on policies, it is a good case to examine whether policy information actually affects voters' policy and ideological positions.

Note that, in this chapter, we will speak of a 'campaign effect' when we find a difference in policy or ideological position between two waves, one before and one right after the campaign. But we cannot be sure whether it actually is the campaign that made people change their mind; we only know that they changed *during* the campaign. It could be that the people we found to update their preferences during the campaign itself would have done so without the campaign. Still, due to the enormous increase in policy information available to citizens during the campaign, we think it is likely that that information contributed to the changes we record.

The two dependent variables in our analyses are policy and ideological switching. For 'policy switching', we first calculated, for every statement, the absolute distance between the positions in wave one and the position in wave two. Then, we took the average across the twenty-three statements and divide the mean by 3 (the maximum possible score) to have the resulting variable range from 0 to 1. 'Ideological switching' was calculated in a similar way. First, the absolute distance between the left-right positions in waves one and two was calculated. Then the outcome was divided by 10, the maximum possible difference between the two waves. The result is a measure of ideological switching ranging from 0 to 1, similar to policy switching.

The main independent variables are education and policy and ideological congruence mismatch. For the first, voters are divided into three education categories. Lower educated voters have no or only an elementary school degree. Middle educated voters comprise those who finished their secondary education. Higher educated voters are voters who graduated from graduate school or have a university degree. Our three education categories thus indicate increasing years of formal education and allow us to test whether higher educated voters change their policy and ideological preferences more than their lower educated counterparts.

We also expect that the potential gains in congruence affect whether voters switch policy or ideological preferences or not. We measure these potential gains through two congruence mismatch variables. Considering that voters can change their party preference during the campaign; it grasps the incongruence or mismatch, between the policy or the ideological positions in wave one and those of their party preference in wave two. In other words, the variable grasps the leap forward in policy congruence with their actual party preference a voter can maximally make by changing their policy/ideological preferences. We make two versions of this variable, one for policy positions (policy congruence mismatch) and one for the ideological positions (ideological congruence mismatch). The first is the percentage agreement between the positions of a voter and the positions of that voter's preferred party. This simply entailed dividing the numbers of statements on which a voter and his or her party preference agree by the number of statements (twenty-three) and taking the inverse of the result. The second is calculated by taking the absolute difference between a voter's left-right position in wave one and the left-right position of his party preference in wave two. A party's left-right position is the average placement of the party on the left-right scale by the party's candidates. For this we used the data of the Belgian Comparative Candidate Survey.

While a panel design is clearly the preferred approach for this study, as it allows us to come closer to identifying causal effects, it is not without its downsides. The first disadvantage is the so-called instrument effect; the mere asking of a policy question in wave one can affect exposure to information about that policy in between the waves and thus affect the wave two answers to the same policy question. We cannot rule out this possibility here. One of the possible remedies is to make sure that the distance between the waves is not too short (Wlezien & Erikson 2001). The average fifty-two days, with a

Table 9.1. Descriptives of variables (*n* = 976)

	Mean	S.D.	Min.	Max.
Policy switching	0.19	0.09	0.03	0.56
Ideology switching	0.14	0.16	0	0.91
Education (low [1] – high [3])	2.05	0.80	1	3
Policy congruence mismatch	0.44	0.12	0.04	0.81
Ideology congruence mismatch	1.68	1.27	0.03	8.13
Gender (male [0] – female [1])	1.47	0.50	1	2
Age (years)	49.26	16.80	18	84
Income (lowest decile [1] – highest decile [10])	5.62	2.50	1	10
Region (Flanders [0] – Wallonia [1])	1.41	0.49	1	2
Party switch	0.23	0.42	0	1
VAA user	0.39	0.49	0	1
Political Interest (low [0] – high [10])	5.28	2.68	0	10
Time between waves (days)	51.78	17.20	9	98

Note: S.D.: Standard deviation.

minimum of nine and a maximum of ninety-eight days, between the waves in this study at least partially alleviates the possible instrument effect here. Furthermore, we are unaware of studies establishing that the instrument effect would be unequally distributed across education groups. In addition, we control for the time lag between interviews in the following models ('time between waves' in the models). The second problem is that of panel attrition. As the survey's main topic was about politics, it is likely that politically interested voters are over-represented among the respondents, a bias which is likely to be greater in the second wave. To compensate for this, we control for political interest in all our analyses. In addition, we also control for a voter's age, gender, income, region, participation in the online VAA where the party positions where shown and whether a voter changed party choice during the campaign. Finally, the data in the analyses are weighted as to accurately reflect the eligible voting population in Belgium in terms of region, gender, age and education. Table 9.1 presents the descriptives of all variables.

One final note on the Belgian case is in order. Belgium is a small consociational democracy consisting of two main regions: Flanders and Wallonia, with a separate party and media landscape (Deschouwer 2012). Our voter sample also consists of Flemish and Walloon voters. This presents us with a unique opportunity to test the validity of our results. Therefore, each analysis will be repeated for each region separately to check the robustness of our conclusions.

RESULTS

Our measures of policy position and ideological change in the 2014 campaign in Belgium suggest there to be quite a bit of substantive volatility during the campaign. Figures 9.1a and 9.1b present the evidence. Looking at policy switching first (figure 9.1a), we see that none of our respondents held the same position on all twenty-three policies presented to him or her. A small fraction of the electorate changes position on more than half of the policy statements. The modal category is the 20 per cent bin. On average, a respondent changes position on about one-fifth of all statements (19 per cent). We can conclude that there is quite some short-term volatility during the campaign.

Regarding ideology switching, the results are similar. Although one may have expected that ideological self-placement would be more robust, figure 9.1b seems to oppose that expectation. The modal categories are those who do not switch at all (34 per cent) and those who do switch only one step on the 0–10 self-placement scale (33 per cent) – this small step may simply be measurement error due to wrong recall. Yet also with regard to ideology switching do we witness a good deal of people who considerably change their self-placement during the campaign. For instance, 9 per cent of the voters change their self-placement on the left-right scale with no less than four steps. On average, a Belgian voter shifted 1.4 steps on the left-right scale. Comparing both measures of substantive campaign volatility, we can say that there is significantly more policy switching than ideology switching ($t = 9.01$; df(975); $p < 0.001$).

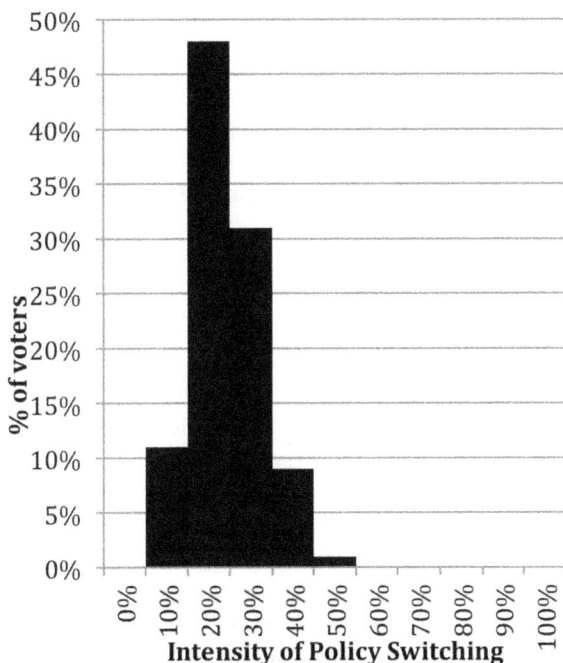

Figure 9.1a. Policy switching ($n = 976$ voters)

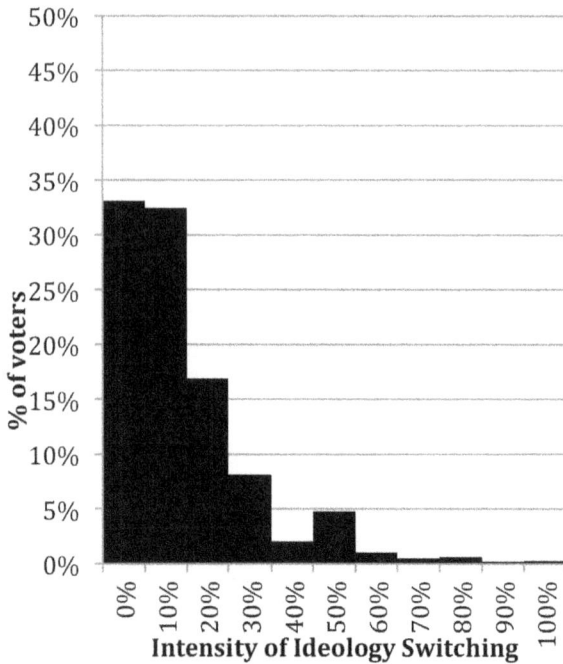

Figure 9.1b. Ideology switching (*n* = 976 voters)

There is volatility, but in what direction did voters switch position? Were it the right-wing or the left-wing parties that have been more successful in pulling voters in their direction in the 2014 campaign in Belgium? Not all twenty-three statements we confronted our respondents with are related to typical left-right policies, though. Therefore, we just look at those twenty-one statements that we consider connected to the left-right divide (e.g. 'Large capitals should be taxed more' and 'Wages should be frozen if they rise faster than in neighbouring countries'). In what direction did the Belgian voters move? The answer is simple: in no particular direction. Taking all voter/left-right statement combinations into account (*n* = 20,496), in 77 per cent of the cases there is no change, in 12 per cent of the cases the move is to the right, while in 11 per cent of the cases the change is towards the left; the difference is not significant. Thus, we can say that, with regard to policy positioning, there was no clear winner of the policy contest: voters were not systematically swayed in a left- or right-wing direction. We split up the dataset distinguishing the Flemish from the Walloon voters – remember that we are talking here about completely separated electoral arenas with separate parties and different media – and the results are basically the same in the separate regions: there is no left-right pattern in how voters shifted during the campaign.

The story considering ideology switching is very different, though. Here we do see a clear pattern in the data: voters in both regions of the country predominantly placed themselves more at the right side of the left-right scale at the end of the campaign compared to at the beginning of the campaign. So, in terms of the symbolic ideological struggle, the right parties clearly won the 2014 campaign both in Flanders and in Wallonia. Table 9.2 presents the evidence for the country as a whole.

The data show that 34 per cent of the voters do not move at all but, of those who move, a significantly larger part moves to the right (40 per cent) than to the left (27 per cent). Moreover, not only do *more* people move to the right than to the left, they also take on average a larger step on the left-right scale. So, the move to the right is on average *larger* than the move to the left: in terms of the steps on the 0–10 left-right scale, the average move to the right is 2.24, while the average move to the left is only 1.96.

Again, although the Flemish and Walloon campaigns were almost entirely disconnected and with different parties, a different electorate and different media coverage, we do observe that the left-right shifts are remarkably similar on both sides of the language border. On both sides the culture war about ideology was won by the right-wing parties. This could explain why it were primarily right-wing parties (e.g. MR in Wallonia and N-VA in Flanders) that won additional parliamentary seats in the 2014 elections or, alternatively, the ideological move to the right could also be the consequence of people's preceding vote preference change. Table 9.3 presents the evidence.

There is more ideology change in Wallonia compared to Flanders (29.8 versus 35.4 stable voters); the share of movers to the right is somewhat larger in Wallonia compared to Flanders (41.4 versus 37.6) and, most remarkably,

Table 9.2. Ideology switching on the left-right (LR) self-placement scale (n = 977)

# steps on LR scale	0	1	2	3	4	5	6	7	8	9	10	Total
No change, %	33.7											33.7
To the left, %		13.9	6.1	2.9	0.9	2.1	0.4	0.1	0.3	0.0	0.0	26.5
To the right, %		17.1	11.2	5.3	1.7	2.8	0.6	0.6	0.2	0.1	0.2	39.8

Table 9.3. Ideology switching on the left-right self-placement scale in Flanders (n = 573) and Wallonia (n = 403)

Ideology switch	Flanders		Wallonia	
	Changes, %	Mean step	Changes, %	Mean step
Same placement	35.4	–	29.8	–
To the right	37.6	2.01	41.4	2.53
To the left	27.0	2.00	28.8	1.91

the steps to the right are larger in Wallonia than in Flanders (2.53 versus 2.01). In sum, on both sides of the language border the right-wing parties were more successful in making voters adopt their general ideological stance but the Walloon right-wing parties (mostly MR) were more successful than the Flemish right-wing parties (Open VLD and N-VA).

Our analysis so far only provided descriptive evidence; we now turn to the explanatory analysis. Table 9.4 shows the results from an OLS regression taking policy position and ideology stance switching as the dependent variable.

Our results show clear support for the three expectations we had, namely that low education would increase policy and ideology switching, that voters are aligning their positions and ideological placement with those of the party they vote for and that policy and ideology switching are correlated.

First, education matters and this applies to both policy switching (Model 1) and ideology switching (Model 2). Compared to the lower educated, the middle and the higher educated switch considerably less. The more one is educated, the more one sticks to one's policy preference and ideological placement.

Table 9.4.   **Explaining policy and ideology switching (OLS regressions)**

	Model 1: Policy switching				Model 2: Ideology switching			
	B	Beta	S.E.	Sig.	B	Beta	S.E.	Sig.
Middle education (ref. cat: lower education)	−0.02	−0.13	0.01	0.004	−0.04	−0.12	0.02	0.010
Higher education (ref. cat: lower education)	−0.03	−0.18	0.01	0.000	−0.06	−0.18	0.01	0.000
Policy congruence mismatch	0.06	0.08	0.02	0.005	0.12	0.09	0.05	0.008
Ideology congruence mismatch	0.00	−0.04	0.00	0.201	0.03	0.22	0.00	0.000
Ideology switching	0.12	0.21	0.03	0.000				
Policy switching					0.43	0.23	0.10	0.000
Female (ref. cat: male)	0.00	0.00	0.01	0.924	0.02	0.07	0.01	0.055
Age	0.00	0.09	0.00	0.006	0.00	0.00	0.00	0.986
Income	−0.01	−0.15	0.00	0.000	0.00	−0.04	0.00	0.285
Wallonia (ref. cat: Flanders)	0.04	0.22	0.01	0.000	0.02	0.07	0.01	0.043
Party switch	0.00	0.00	0.01	0.983	−0.01	−0.01	0.01	0.660
VAA user	0.00	−0.03	0.01	0.414	0.01	0.03	0.01	0.257
Political interest	0.00	0.06	0.00	0.182	0.00	−0.07	0.00	0.127
Time between survey waves	0.00	0.08	0.00	0.012	0.00	0.03	0.00	0.338
Constant	0.10		0.02	0.000	−0.06		0.05	0.229
N	976				976			
R²	27.03%				21.67%			

Second, the larger the mismatch between a voter's policy and ideology position (measured before the campaign) and the party he or she eventually votes for (measured after the campaign), the larger is the chance that that voter will change his or her policy positions and his or her ideological placement. Both in the policy switching and in the ideology switching models the relevant variable is a significant predictor. This strongly suggests that during the campaign voters brought their policy and ideology opinions in line with their ultimately preferred party. Since we do not have three panel waves but only two we cannot be sure that opinions were brought in line with the vote instead of the vote being brought in line with opinions – although our controlling for party switching in the model suggests the former to be the case. Either way, the results suggest that part of the opinion change during campaigns is linked to party alignment.

Third, policy opinion change and ideology placement change are connected. Voters who switch policy position more often also self-place themselves more differently over time on the ideology scale, and the opposite is true as well. This suggests that when voters, during a campaign, come to realise that they have updated their ideological position, they then also update their policy opinions. Conversely, voters strongly changing policy positions draw the (correct) conclusion that they also have changed their broader ideological stance. These three findings suggest that policy and ideology updating is not a random process. It is at least partly driven by real information and there clearly is some rationality to the process.

The effects of the control variables in the models are not consistent and vary across both models. Female voters are more volatile on their ideology but not on their policy positions. Older voters, in contrast, switch policy positions more often but do not update their ideological placement so frequently. Higher income leads to less policy switching but is unrelated to ideology switching. Policy switching happened more in Wallonia than in Flanders, but ideology switching occurred at similar levels in the two regions. And, the longer the time span between the two survey waves, the higher is the chance a respondent has changed policy positions but not ideological self-placement. As a robustness check, we repeated the analyses with versions of the dependent variables that discount small changes in policy positions (changes between agree and strongly agree and between disagree and strongly disagree) and ideological positions (changes of one position on left-right scale between wave one and wave two), but found similar results.

Do these findings apply to the 2014 campaigns in Flanders and Wallonia separately as well? In other words, are these results robust across two political systems? We ran identical models for the two regions, the results of which are presented in table 9.5.

Table 9.5. Explaining policy and ideology switching; Flanders and Wallonia separately (OLS regressions)

| | Flanders | | | | | | | | Wallonia | | | | | | | |
| | Model 1: Policy switching | | | | Model 2: Ideology switching | | | | Model 3: Policy switching | | | | Model 4: Ideology switching | | | |
	B	Beta	S.E.	Sig.	B	Beta	S.E.	Sig.	B	Beta	S.E.	Sig.	B	Beta	S.E.	Sig.
Middle education (ref. cat: lower educ.)	-0.01	-0.09	0.01	0.144	-0.01	-0.03	0.02	0.675	-0.03	-0.14	0.01	0.031	-0.08	-0.18	0.03	0.004
Higher education (ref. cat: lower educ.)	-0.03	-0.14	0.01	0.013	-0.04	-0.13	0.02	0.025	-0.03	-0.15	0.01	0.029	-0.08	-0.18	0.02	0.000
Policy congruence mismatch	0.06	0.08	0.03	0.073	0.04	0.03	0.06	0.564	0.05	0.07	0.03	0.140	0.20	0.13	0.08	0.018
Ideological congruence mismatch	0.00	-0.05	0.00	0.352	0.02	0.20	0.01	0.000	0.00	-0.02	0.00	0.669	0.04	0.24	0.01	0.000
Ideology switching	0.09	0.17	0.03	0.002					0.15	0.34	0.06	0.006				
Policy switching					0.32	0.17	0.10	0.001					0.64	0.29	0.22	0.003
Female (ref. cat. male)	0.00	-0.01	0.01	0.814	0.01	0.05	0.01	0.353	0.00	0.00	0.01	0.936	0.04	0.09	0.02	0.072
Age	0.00	0.11	0.00	0.027	0.00	-0.01	0.00	0.901	0.00	0.10	0.00	0.039	0.00	0.03	0.00	0.559
Income	0.00	-0.16	0.00	0.001	0.00	-0.05	0.00	0.339	-0.01	-0.15	0.00	0.010	0.00	-0.05	0.00	0.408
Party switch	0.00	-0.02	0.01	0.705	0.03	0.10	0.02	0.075	0.00	0.00	0.01	0.974	-0.07	-0.13	0.02	0.003
VAA user	0.00	-0.02	0.01	0.714	0.00	0.00	0.01	0.926	-0.01	-0.03	0.01	0.487	0.03	0.06	0.02	0.102
Political interest	0.00	0.03	0.00	0.698	0.00	-0.05	0.00	0.354	0.00	0.13	0.00	0.076	-0.01	-0.12	0.01	0.123
Time between waves	0.00	0.14	0.00	0.003	0.00	0.05	0.00	0.293	0.00	0.03	0.00	0.699	0.00	0.04	0.00	0.580
Constant	0.13		0.03	0.000	0.01		0.06	0.880	0.17		0.03	0.000	-0.10		0.10	0.289
N	573				573				403				403			
R²	17.43%				14.58%				29.35%				39.14%			

Largely the same patterns emerge in the two regions although our results are a less strong. This is most likely because the separate sample sizes are smaller. In both regions and in all models, the higher educated switch policy opinions and ideology placements less than the lower educated; the results of the middle educated go in the right direction but do not reach statistical significance in both Flemish models. The mismatch variables grasping the effect of the party preference on opinion change are not all significant in all models, but when they do they go in the right direction: the larger the mismatch between a party's and a voter's opinions, the higher is the chance that the voter will adapt his or her opinion and bring it in line with that of his or her party. Further, the separate models strongly support the notion that voters' policy and ideology updating are correlated to a considerable extent. In both regions, the relevant coefficients are statistically significant. So, overall, our results are fairly robust. They do apply not only to the pooled Belgian voters but also to the Flemish and Walloon voters separately. It is, however, important to note that the amount of explained variance (adjusted R^2) of our models is lower in Flanders than in Wallonia. This might be the result of the fact that the panel attrition between wave one and wave two was different in both regions. In Flanders, 83 per cent of the voters in wave one participated in wave two, while this was only 69 per cent in Wallonia. This could have affected, for instance, the type of lower, middle and higher educated voters in each regional sample, and subsequently, for instance, the relation between level of education and position switching in each region.

CONCLUSION

Campaigns not only matter because they affect people's actual vote choice, mobilise voters, inform them and change the criteria voters use to evaluate the parties and candidates – this is what the campaign literature basically talks about – but they can also make the people change their policy preferences and even their ideological self-perception. Drawing on unique Belgian panel data including twenty-three different policies and classic left-right self-placement data, we found that opinions effectively evolve during a campaign. Voter opinion change is not random. The opinions of the lower educated voters are less robust and are more easily swayed by campaign information, or at least by information acquired during the campaign. This fits a recurring finding of public opinion scholarship that the less politically aware are most easily influenced and update their beliefs more frequently. Moreover, people tend to bring their policy beliefs and ideological placement in line with that of the party they prefer; we find a quite strong tendency of party opinion alignment. The most relevant contribution of this chapter probably is our finding a strong link between position and ideology change. When people update their concrete policy positions, they adjust their broader ideological self-placement accordingly, or vice versa. This is good news for studies relying on ideological self-placement data. The measure taps into real policy preferences and it is dynamic in the sense that it interacts with people's actual policy preferences.

Our data come from one country and one campaign only, so we cannot claim that what we found can simply be generalised to other countries and/ or campaigns. The 2014 election campaign in Belgium was extraordinarily information-dense, we believe, with a lot of information about policies being available and with a decisively ideologically strong debate. So, it may be the case that this has led to higher levels of policy and ideology change than we would expect to find in other campaigns. Still, we think that the mechanisms we propose to explain policy and ideology change during campaigns may apply to other countries and other campaigns.

Finally, is the fact that people update their policy opinions and ideological placement good news for democracy? We think it is (see also Brady, John-ston & Sides 2006). Campaigns are exceptional periods with an abundance of policy-related (and unfortunately also a lot of non-policy-related) informa-tion. Imagine that this flood of policy and ideology information would not affect voters at all. This would mean that voters are basically not responsive to policy information provided during campaigns. It would be a waste of time and resources and it would imply that campaigns could as well be void of any policy information at all. The fact that voters do react and do update their beliefs suggests that campaigns are really informative and teach people about the things that should matter when they elicit their vote.

REFERENCES

Abramowitz, A. I. (1978) 'The Impact of a Presidential Debate on Voter Rationality', *American Journal of Political Science*, 22(3), 680.

Alvarez, R. M. (1998) *Information and elections* (Rev. to include the 1996 presiden-tial election), Ann Arbor: University of Michigan Press.

Bartels, L. (2006) 'Priming and Persuasion in Presidential Campaigns', in Henry E. Brady and Richard Johnston (eds) *Capturing Campaign Effects* (78–112), Ann Arbor: University of Michigan Press.

Brady, H. E., Johnston, R. & Sides, J. (2006) 'The Study of Political Campaigns', in Henry E. Brady and Richard Johnston (eds) *Capturing Campaign Effects* (1–26), Ann Arbor: University of Michigan Press.

Converse, P. E. (1964) 'The Nature of Belief Systems in Mass Publics', in D. Apter (ed.) *Ideology and Discontent* (206–61), London: Macmillan.

de Vries, C. E., Hakhverdian, A. & Lancee, B. (2013) 'The Dynamics of Voters' Left/ Right Identification: The Role of Economic and Cultural Attitudes', *Political Science Research and Methods*, 1(2), 223–38.

Deschouwer, K. (2012) *The Politics of Belgium: Governing a Divided Society*, London: Palgrave Macmillan.

Kriesi, H. (2002) 'Individual Opinion Formation in a Direct Democratic Campaign', *British Journal of Political Science*, 32(1), 171–85.

Lazarsfeld, P., Berelson, B. & Gaudet, H. (1945) *The People's Choice*, New York: Duell Sloan and Pearce.

Lenz, G. S. (2009) 'Learning and Opinion Change, Not Priming: Reconsidering the Priming Hypothesis', *American Journal of Political Science*, 53(4), 821–37.

Sciarini, P. (2003) 'Opinion Stability and Change during an Electoral Campaign: Results from the 1999 Swiss Election Panel Study', *International Journal of Public Opinion Research*, 15(4), 431–53.

Wlezien, C. & Erikson, R. S. (2001) 'Campaign Effects in Theory and Practice', *American Politics Research*, 29(5), 419–36.

Zaller, J. (1992) *The Nature and Origins of Mass Opinion*, Cambridge: Cambridge University Press.

Zaller, J. (1994) 'Elite Leadership of Mass Opinion. New Evidence from the Gulf War', in L. Bennet & D. Paletz (eds) *Taken by Storm* (186–209), Chicago: University of Chicago Press.

Appendix

The used policy statements, the recorded change during the campaign and their left-right coding

Table 9.6. The VAA statements and their left-right orientation

Statement	Statement's direction
All nuclear weapons stored on Belgian territory should be removed	Leftist
All prisoners should serve their sentences in full	Rightist
If the railways are on strike, there should be minimum service	Rightist
Company vehicles must be taxed more heavily	Leftist
Belgium should allow migrants from outside the EU to cope with labour shortages	Rightist
The federal government should sell its shares in Belgacom	Rightist
Wages should be frozen if they are rising faster than in neighbouring countries	Rightist
The speed limit on the Brussels ring road should be reduced to 100 kilometre per hour	Leftist
The minimum age for local administrative fines should be higher than the current age of 14	Leftist
The government should more fiscally encourage retirement savings	Leftist
The expenditures of the federal government should not increase in the coming years	Rightist
The president of the European Commission should be directly elected by the European voters	Leftist
An asylum seeker who arrived as a minor cannot be sent back	Leftist
A mother must be able to anonymously give up her child for adoption	Neutral
We should keep using nuclear power plants	Rightist
Large capitals should be taxed more	Leftist
The Belgian army must invest in a successor to the F-16 fighter	Rightist
It should be legally prohibited for parents to spank their children	Leftist
Illegal downloading is to be treated more harshly	Rightist
The voting age should be lowered to 16 years old	Leftist

Statement	Statement's direction
Living wage beneficiaries should be required to perform community work	Rightist
People who invest their money instead of saving it must be fiscally rewarded	Rightist
Flanders should become an independent state	Neutral

Chapter 10

The time of the vote choice: Causes and consequences of late-deciding

Ruth Dassonneville, Pierre Baudewyns, Marc Debus and Rüdiger Schmitt-Beck[1]

Over the past decades, mass electoral behaviour in advanced democracies has been fundamentally affected by a process of weakening links between voters and parties. Different explanations for this trend have been introduced in the literature. Scholars have pointed out a decreasing explanatory power of socio-structural characteristics for citizens' party orientations (Dalton et al. 2000; Franklin et al. 2009). In addition, it has been argued that factors more closely tied to the specific circumstances of particular elections, such as candidates, issues or the economy, are all becoming increasingly important in determining vote choice (Rose and McAllister 1986; Van der Brug 2010; Walczak et al. 2012). As a consequence, electoral behaviour appears to be changing fundamentally. Indeed, scholars have noted an increase in levels of electoral volatility (Dalton et al. 2000; Dassonneville and Hooghe 2016; Drummond 2006; Pedersen 1979). At an individual level, furthermore, it is evident that voters increasingly change preferences during an election campaign and that they tend to take their decisions about which party or candidate to choose later and during the campaign (Dalton et al. 2000; Lachat 2007).

Research on campaign dynamics already dates to the first studies of voting behaviour. Both the Columbia and Michigan school scholars analysed what factors affect the timing of the vote decision. In their work, they distinguish two types of voters: those who decide a long time before the election – the 'early deciders' – and those who decide during the election campaign or on Election Day – the 'late deciders'. According to the Columbia school, it is, in particular, those voters who feel cross-pressured by different socio-demo-graphic characteristics who tend to delay their vote choice in comparison to the early deciders (Berelson et al. 1954; Lazarsfeld et al. 1968). According to the Michigan school perspective, what characterises late-deciding voters is their weak partisan attachments (Campbell et al. 1980).

Revising these original insights by means of an analysis of the 1976 presidential elections in the United States, Chaffee and Choe (1980) suggest that campaign attentiveness is another important predictor of when voters take their decisions. According to their research, early deciders are choosing a long time before because they have a strong party identification while they are also moderately attentive to the campaign. Chaffee and Choe also suggest that the late deciders can be split into two subgroups: those who make up their minds early in campaigns, on the one hand, and those who decide only close to the election or even on the day of the election itself, on the other. The observation that partisanship and campaign attentiveness are important predictors of the timing of the vote choice is highly important, as it helps us understand how the secular process of partisan dealignment, and the increasing importance of campaign factors, is associated with a trend towards voters deciding ever-later which party or candidate to vote for (Dalton et al. 2000).

While the phenomenon of late-deciding has thus attracted quite some scholarly attention, it has not yet been thoroughly studied in the case of Belgium. The aim of this chapter is to explore the timing of the voting decision among Belgian voters. Belgium is a particularly interesting case for investigating this issue. While voting behaviour in Belgium was not traditionally conceived of as driven by partisan attachments, the importance of attachments to particular social groups in society implied that voting behaviour was fairly stable for several decades. Over time, however, the structuring impact of socio-demographics in politics and society at large has waned – a process referred to as 'depillarisation' (Deschouwer 2012). As a result, in Belgium as well campaign factors are assumed to become increasingly important. So far, however, no one has systematically assessed whether there is indeed a trend towards late-deciding and what the implications of this behaviour are for how Belgian voters choose a party. Moreover, without testing them, it cannot be taken for granted that the same regularities that in other countries have been found to determine when voters cast their votes also hold in Belgium.

In addition, certain institutional attributes make the Belgian case particularly interesting. The country's electoral system allows citizens to cast preferential votes for the candidates of their party they would like to see elected. Such a system gives voters more control over the outcome of an election, but it is cognitively quite demanding. As a result, Belgian voters can be thought to require more time to decide whom to vote for than in systems where only a party vote or only a candidate vote can be cast. While this idea can only be investigated in an internationally comparative perspective, what our study can test is whether voters who take advantage of the opportunity for more differentiated vote choices take longer to arrive at their decisions than those who do not and simply vote for party lists.

In a first step, drawing on time series from PIOP/ISPO data we describe the overtime trend in the time of voting decisions for federal elections since 1991, and particularly the link between the time of the voting decision and campaign volatility. Subsequently, we use the 2014 PartiRep Voter Survey to test a number of hypotheses about the reasons why voters decide late and what characterises late deciders. In a final section, we apply a heterogeneity perspective to explore whether and how early and late deciders differ with regard to what factors affect their vote choice. In particular, it will be explored how well the choices of voters who decided before, during and at the end of the campaign can be explained by standard voting models, and whether and how these voters differed with regard to the considerations they took into account when choosing (socio-demographics, ideology and partisanship as long-term factors and candidates and/or issues as short-term factors).

OVERTIME TRENDS IN THE TIMING OF
THE VOTE DECISION

In a number of countries, scholars have observed a clear trend of vote choices being made increasingly late (Dalton et al. 2000; Lewis-Beck et al. 2008; McAllister et al. 2002; Schmitt-Beck and Partheymüller 2012). Do we observe a similar pattern among the Belgian electorate? Unfortunately, while in some other countries time series reach back as far as the 1960s, data that allow us to address this question for Belgium have only been collected over a rather short span of time. Since 1991, Belgian election studies include a question asking respondents to report when they decided which party to vote for. The answering options for this question allow us to distinguish between three groups of voters: the early deciders – those who have decided before the campaign – and two groups of late deciders: those who made up their minds early in the campaign, that is, during the last weeks before the election, and those who decided late in the campaign, that is, on the day of the election. In this chapter, we refer to the latter two groups – subcategories of the late deciders – as campaign deciders and Election Day deciders, respectively.

In table 10.1 we list the proportion of respondents in each of the three time-categories and how these proportions have changed over time. We do so for voters in the two main regions of Belgium (Flanders and Wallonia) separately. A look at table 10.1 clarifies that despite the comparably short period of observation in long-term perspective for both regions we can observe a decrease of the number of early deciders. This trend appears to be somewhat more pronounced in Flanders than in Wallonia. The real change, however, can be observed among campaign deciders. In Flanders, the share

Table 10.1. Distribution of time of voting decision, 1991–2014 (row percentages)

Region	Election	Early deciders	Campaign deciders	Election Day deciders	N
Flanders	1991	53.69	28.20	13.34	2,522
	1995	56.04	30.28	13.68	2,037
	1999	50.81	37.85	11.34	2,137
	2003	45.91	41.34	12.75	1,169
	2007	–	–	–	–
	2010	–	–	–	–
	2014	44.22	37.21	18.57	763
Wallonia	1991	50.85	38.29	10.86	1,307
	1995	56.21	32.58	11.20	1,134
	1999	57.95	37.36	4.69	1,358
	2003	44.15	45.44	14.48	713
	2007	47.06	44.10	8.85	696
	2010	31.45	51.87	16.67	372
	2014	44.17	40.62	15.21	612

Note: The data are weighted by age, gender, education and vote. Information on voters in Brussels is not reported. Data: PIOP/ISPO for 1991–2010 and 2014 PartiRep Voter Survey. In the PIOP/ISPO surveys, the question is formulated as: 'When did you decide to vote for a particular party for the House of Representatives? (1) The day of the elections; (2) The last few days before the elections; (3) The last few weeks before the election day; (4) The start of the election campaign; (5) Longer ago than that'. Categories 2, 3 and 4 collapsed. For 2014, only three categories have been used: '(1) On the day of the elections; (2) During the campaign; (3) Before the beginning of the campaign'. Those three categories were reversed and labelled in table: 'Early deciders', 'Early campaign deciders' and 'Late campaign deciders'.

of campaign deciders grew from 28 per cent in 1991 to 37 per cent in 2014. In Wallonia, the same trend can be observed but in a lower amplitude. The trend in the proportion of Election Day deciders is, however, somewhat different in both regions. In Flanders, we note stability until 2003 but a notable increase in the number of Election Day deciders in the 2014 elections. In Wallonia (where the time series is complete while it has gaps in Flanders) the overall trend is increasing, but the 1999 and 2007 elections appear to show exceptionally low numbers of Election Day deciders. The trend is thus not fully linear, although nonetheless quite clear on the long run. The increase of late-deciding voters (i.e. campaign deciders as well as Election Day deciders) observed in Belgium may at first sight appear somewhat less pronounced than what can be observed in other countries (based on varying definitions of 'late' and 'early' deciding, due to country-specific measurement standards). In Norway and Sweden, for instance, the share of late deciders has increased from 20 per cent in the 1960s to 60 per cent in 2010. In Denmark, it has increased from 20 per cent in 1971 to 40 per cent in 2011, and in Finland from 35 per cent in 1983 to 50 per cent in 2003 (Bengtsson et al. 2014). In Germany, at the most recent elections about four out of ten voters decided when the campaign was under way while the share had been only 5 per cent in the 1960s (Schmitt-Beck and Partheymüller 2012).

Late deciders are more responsive to election campaigns (Fournier et al. 2004). The increase in their numbers thus constitutes a real challenge for candidates, parties and political marketers because late-deciding voters are introducing a considerable amount of uncertainty and unpredictability in how the campaign evolves (Joslyn 1984; Dalton et al. 2000; Schmitt-Beck and Partheymüller 2012).

WHY SOME VOTERS DECIDE LATER THAN OTHERS

Hypotheses

As we have seen, many voters know early on which party they will vote for, whereas others – in increasing numbers – take longer to make up their minds. Indeed, in more than just a few cases voters seem to decide virtually on the doorstep of the polling station. Why is this the case? Why do some voters take longer than others to arrive at their final voting decisions?

The classic hypothesis, already stated by Lazarsfeld and his colleagues in their seminal study of decision-making at the 1940 US Presidential Election (Lazarsfeld et al. 1968), sees the key to early choices in voters' political involvement. This research found early deciders much more concerned about politics than their fellow citizens that took longer to arrive at their final verdicts. They displayed strong partisan loyalties and were highly interested in politics. In contrast, those who made up their minds only when the campaign was already under way appeared generally detached from politics and led a more or less apolitical life. They were not particularly interested in elections and did not care much about their outcomes. More recent studies, also from European democracies, confirm this finding (Schmitt-Beck and Partheymüller 2012).

Voters who cannot rely on clear-cut political predispositions as guidance for judging candidates and parties may have a hard time making up their minds at elections, especially if they are also not particularly interested in politics and thus unlikely to know much about this domain of life. As a result, they probably find it quite challenging to choose, and therefore delay their decisions until shortly before polling day, when they can no longer be postponed. We thus expect that weak or inexistent partisan affect and interest in politics are related to late choices. Assuming that ideological extremity also goes along with more intense political feelings, we likewise assume that centrist voters also tend to choose rather late.

The same line of reasoning also leads us to expect voters' attention to sources of political information to be negatively related to the tendency to choose later rather than earlier. However, in recent years this view has come under challenge (Reinemann et al. 2013). Sometimes it is argued that the ease with which voters in modern media societies can get access to political information is one of the factors that contributed to the increase in late-deciding. According to this view, voters who attend strongly to the mass media and the parties' campaign communications seek to base their vote choices on a broad reservoir of topical information and therefore wait as long as possible before they decide. Although ultimately unable to ever match the ideal of full information (Downs 1957), they aim to incorporate as much information as possible into their decision-making process in order to avoid making mistakes and choosing the wrong party (Lau and Redlawsk 2006). In stark contrast to the 'floating voter' hypothesis, this leads to the expectation that voters who are highly attentive to the coverage of mass media and the parties' campaign communication vote later rather than earlier.

Another strand of hypothesising that also dates back to the groundbreaking work of Lazarsfeld and his colleagues (1968) builds on the notion of cross-pressure. According to this line of thought, vote choices are easy if voters' attitudes converge on a particular party, which then on all accounts appears more attractive than its competitors. If, on the other hand, voters' views are more mixed and speak for one party on some accounts and for one or more of its rivals on others, choosing becomes difficult. Rephrasing this idea in terms of modern political psychology, a study by Mutz (2002) presented strong evidence that attitudinal ambivalence has a delaying effect on vote choices at American Presidential Elections. A German study presented similar evidence for elections under the conditions of a European multiparty system (Schmitt-Beck and Partheymüller 2012). Finding several competing parties similarly attractive, ambivalent voters are drawn in different directions at the same time. As a consequence, they have a hard time making up their minds and therefore can be expected to decide late rather than early.

Besides ambivalence, indifference, the cousin with which it is often confused, can also affect the timing of electoral choices. While ambivalence indicates strong but contradictory preferences, indifference denotes a lack of preference, since no party appears especially attractive (Davis 2015). Indifferent citizens feel that the existing electoral alternatives do not have much to offer in terms of their comparative advantages over one another. To indifferent voters, nothing of importance stands out when they compare the options they can choose between at an election. Rather, all available alternatives leave them cold. Hence, we expect that indifferent voters also tend to cast their votes relatively late.

Besides personal attributes, features of institutional contexts may also play a significant role for the timing of voters' choices. In the Belgian case one aspect of the institutional architecture of electoral politics appears especially important. Belgian voters can opt for party lists like their colleagues in countries with closed list systems. But they also have the option of gaining more control over the outcome of the election by casting preference votes.

Arguably, preferential voting is more demanding than just picking a party list. Simple heuristics may be sufficient to do the latter. But preferential voting presupposes a stock of rather detailed information about current politics and considerable cognitive effort to process it in order to rank the candidates. Hence, we expect that voters who make use of preferential voting take longer to arrive at their decisions than their colleagues who choose party lists.

Determinants of late-deciding

Our dependent variable distinguishes between voters who decided before the campaign (coded 0) and two groups of late deciders: those who decided during the campaign (coded 1) and those who decided on Election Day itself (coded 2). To test our expectations, we estimate a sequence of ordered logistic regression models. With few exceptions, our predictors are taken from the pre-election wave of the 2014 PartiRep election panel survey. They thus are not contemporaneously measured which does not eliminate but diminishes the problem of potential endogeneity in our data. To measure partisanship we refer to a question on respondents' closeness to a party (5-point scale from 'not close to any party' to 'very close'). Interest in politics is measured by the standard self-report question and registered on an 11-point scale (from 'not interested at all' to 'very interested'). To determine respondents' ideological extremity, we calculate for each respondent the absolute distance between his or her self-placement on an 11-point left-right scale and the scale midpoint.

To test for the relationship between the timing of respondents' electoral choices and their attentiveness to political information, we refer to a broad range of both traditional and online sources of electoral information (included in the post-election wave): traditional mass media (newspapers, television and/or radio, with usage being registered on a 4-point scale from 'never' to 'daily'), online news sources (count index based on items registering usage or non-usage of websites or blogs providing campaign information and political online videos, ranging from 'none' to 'both'), online vote-advice applications (dummy variable), party meetings (dummy variable), party leaflets and the like (4-point scale from 'never' to 'daily') as well as online communications of parties and candidates (count index based on items registering usage or non-usage of websites or Facebook profiles and subscription to twitter feeds or electronic newsletters, ranging from 'none' to 'both').

To register respondents' ambivalence about the parties, we use an adaptation of the Griffin ambivalence index used by Mutz (2002, cf. Thompson et al. 1995; Schmitt-Beck and Partheymüller 2012). It is based on the 11-point feeling thermometers for the parties and takes into account both the dissimilarity and the intensity of attitudes in a multiparty setting. It assumes high values, indicating strong ambivalence, if more than one party is evaluated very positively, and its minimum value, indicating the complete absence of ambivalence, if one single party is evaluated extremely positively and all other parties are evaluated very negatively.

We rely on two instruments to determine respondents' indifference about the parties. The first is a direct question, registering whether voters perceive the parties as offering 'clear and distinct programs' (5-point Likert scale). The second is an indirect measure referring to valence issues. For eight policy areas (employment, the environment, crime, immigration, the economy, state reform, defence and taxes), the pre-election wave of the survey registered voters' assessments of the parties' problem-solving competence (Bellucci 2006). We consider respondents indifferent if they responded that either 'no party' or 'all parties' were in their view capable of dealing with an issue, and construct a count index of such responses across all eight issues.

Whether voters made use of the option to cast preference votes was determined by a direct question in the post-election wave. In addition to these predictors, our models include a set of socio-demographic control variables (gender, age, education and region). We begin our analysis with a sequence of partial models that include only one hypothetically relevant subset of predictors each as well as the control variables and conclude with a full model encompassing all predictors. The results of these analyses are presented in table 10.2.

According to Model 1, which tests the 'floating voter' hypothesis, both partisanship and political interest are important predictors of the time of decision-making. Obviously, weak partisanship and a lack of interest in politics make later choices more likely. This finding is in line with extant research and suggests a universal regularity. This is underlined by the fact that in terms of its explanatory power this model clearly surpasses all other partial models. When analysed separately, ideological extremism is related to the time of decision-making in the expected way. But this effect is apparently mediated by partisanship and political interest, so that it is no longer significant in Model 1.

Concerning the relationship between voters' attentiveness to political communications and the time of decision-making, contradictory expectations exist in the literature. Model 2 registers such effects only for two sources of political information, and both are in line with the more general 'floating voter' hypothesis. Our findings suggest that using traditional news media and attending parties' campaign meetings makes a difference for the timing of electors' choices. In each case the signs of the effects are negative which indicates that attending to these sources of electoral information was related to early rather than late choices. Online sources of non-partisan information as well as both traditional and computerised forms of mediated party contact seem unrelated to when voters make their choices.

Table 10.2. Determinants of the time of decision-making

	Model 1	Model 2	Model 3	Model 4	Model 5	Model 6
Partisanship	-0.25***					-0.22***
	(0.04)					(0.04)
Political interest	-0.12***					-0.09**
	(0.02)					(0.03)
Ideological extremity	-0.06					-0.05
	(0.05)					(0.05)
Traditional news media		-0.22**				-0.11
		(0.08)				(0.08)
Online media		-0.01				0.07
		(0.09)				(0.09)
VAA		0.06				-0.00
		(0.13)				(0.13)
Party meetings		-1.07***				-0.75**
		(0.25)				(0.26)
Party leaflets		-0.06				-0.03
		(0.06)				(0.07)
Parties' online communications		-0.11				-0.06
		(0.12)				(0.12)
Ambivalence			0.12***			0.06+
			(0.03)			(0.03)
Indifference valence issues				0.08*		0.04
				(0.03)		(0.03)
Indifference party platforms				0.16**		0.16**
				(0.05)		(0.06)
Preference vote					-0.26*	-0.12
					(0.11)	(0.12)

(Continued)

Table 10.2. (Continued)

	Model 1	Model 2	Model 3	Model 4	Model 5	Model 6
Female	0.16	0.27*	0.33**	0.33**	0.35**	0.14
	(0.12)	(0.12)	(0.11)	(0.11)	(0.11)	(0.12)
Age	-0.02***	-0.02***	-0.02***	-0.02***	-0.02***	-0.02***
	(0.00)	(0.00)	(0.00)	(0.00)	(0.00)	(0.00)
Education	0.01	-0.02	-0.03	-0.03	-0.02	-0.01
	(0.02)	(0.02)	(0.02)	(0.02)	(0.02)	(0.03)
Region: Wallonia	-0.13	-0.06	-0.11	-0.21+	-0.12	-0.14
	(0.12)	(0.12)	(0.11)	(0.11)	(0.11)	(0.12)
_cut1	-2.32***	-2.00***	-1.35***	-1.03***	-1.52***	-1.91***
	(0.29)	(0.31)	(0.26)	(0.29)	(0.26)	(0.37)
_cut2	-0.24	0.00	0.64*	0.95**	0.45+	0.22
	(0.28)	(0.31)	(0.26)	(0.29)	(0.26)	(0.37)
N	1,311	1,311	1,311	1,311	1,311	1,311
Pseudo-R^2	0.066	0.043	0.033	0.033	0.028	0.079
Akaike's information criterion	2450.95	2516.38	2532.88	2534.39	2545.21	2437.87

Source: 2014 PartiRep Voter Survey.

Notes: Estimates from ordered logit models are shown; standard errors are presented in parentheses. $^+ p < 0.10$; $^* p < 0.05$; $^{**} p < 0.01$; $^{**} p < 0.001$.

Whether voters decide earlier or later is also a function of their ambivalence about the parties (Model 3). This suggests that if they like several parties similarly well, they have a hard time deciding and therefore tend to delay their choices. Moreover, both measures of indifference are likewise related to the time of decision-making (Model 4). As it seems, late-deciding has both a valence component pertaining to issue competence and a more general component that concerns the perceptional distinctiveness of parties' electoral platforms overall. These findings are again in line with previous research (Mutz 2002; Schmitt-Beck and Partheymüller 2012).

Moreover, according to Model 5, it also makes a difference whether voters make use of the option to cast a preference vote instead of simply accepting the list order suggested by the parties. However, the effect is opposite to the one expected. Although opting for preferential voting places greater cognitive demand on voters, it does not lead to longer processes of decision-making. In fact, it is quite strongly related to early rather than late choices.

While these findings offer tentative support for most of our hypotheses, the ultimate proof is of course the forced contestation between them all. Not all relationships observed in the partial models survive this more demanding test. In Model 6 exposure to traditional news media appears no longer relevant. Presumably, this is due to its strong relationship to political interest. The effect of indifference derived from issue-competence perceptions also evaporates in this model, as does the institutional effect of preferential voting. All other effects are sustained, although mostly diminished and at least in one case (ambivalence) only marginally significant.

Finally, it deserves mention that we also see interesting patterns in the control variables. Late-deciding appears related to age and gender. In all models, that is independently of all other predictors included in our analysis, younger voters decide later than older voters. This echoes findings from a German study by Schmitt-Beck and Partheymüller (2012). The pattern for gender is less clear-cut. In their German study, Schmitt-Beck and Partheymüller (2012) registered a stronger tendency to decide late among female voters at the 2009, but not the 2005 Federal Election. At the 2014 Belgian election likewise female voters more often decided late, but in this case this seems to reflect differences in male and female voters' political involvement, as this otherwise quite strong effect does not appear in Models 1 and 6.

In sum, with the exception of the institutional hypothesis pertaining to the cognitive demand placed on voters by preferential voting, all hypotheses obtain at least partial support by these analyses. Clearly, the 'floating voter' hypothesis is the one most strongly supported. This echoes results of several other studies. This finding also offers an explanation for the observation of a long-term trend towards increasing late-deciding. If, in particular, voters with weak or inexistent partisan loyalties take longer to make up their minds at elections, the weakening of party loyalties through the secular process of partisan dealignment necessarily on the long run leads to growing numbers of late deciders (Dalton et al. 2000). But to some extent later choices are also the product of ambivalence and indifference. If party-related ambivalence is not merely a product of voters' minds but also reflects parties' increasing programmatic similarity, late-deciding may also be on the rise as a result of the parties' policy convergence.

THE VOTE CHOICES OF EARLY AND LATE DECIDERS

Hypotheses

The previous section of this chapter indicated in what ways campaign and Election Day deciders are different from voters who decide long before which party to vote for. As we have observed important differences between groups of voters, this raises the question of whether these voters make different vote choices as well, and whether different factors determine the vote choices of these different groups of voters. This question is particularly relevant as we found partisanship to strongly determine the timing of the vote decision. If late deciders are more likely to be non-partisan, the implication is that their vote choice is probably based on other factors than a strong attachment to one particular party.

From the literature, we can distil a number of theoretical expectations with regard to the vote choices and the vote choice process of early and late-deciding voters. First, we would expect a vote choice model to explain less well the choices of late deciders than what holds for early deciders. Previous research has indicated that late deciders find choosing a party or candidate difficult (Schmitt-Beck and Partheymüller 2012), and in this chapter as well we have shown that late deciders are less interested and more indifferent towards the party offer. Consequently, an element of randomness is likely to enter the vote choice calculus of those voters who are somewhat indifferent but still choose a party to vote for, decreasing the explanatory power of theoretically relevant vote choice determinants.

Second, a large number of studies have indicated the presence of substantial heterogeneity in voting behaviour. In brief, this work shows that voters are not all making their vote choices in the same way, but that there are important differences in terms of the vote calculus and the criteria that voters use to decide whom to vote for (Bartle 2005; Blumenstiel and Plischke 2015). With regard to early and late decision makers as well, it is natural to expect these voters to use different criteria when deciding on their vote choice. More specifically, we can expect long-term factors to have more weight in the decision of early deciders and short-term factors to be of more importance for late deciders' decision.

What is meant by long- and short-term factors? Since the publication of *The American Voter* (Campbell et al. 1980), the concept of a funnel of causality has become a dominant theoretical construct for explaining voting behaviour. This funnel can be thought to enclose a large number of factors that are affecting the vote choice, while these factors are interconnected as well. One important distinction between factors within the funnel is the contrast between long-term and short-term factors. The nature of this distinction was summarised by Lewis-Beck et al. (2008: 26): 'Social demographic factors such as gender, race, and social class are long term. Two important predispositions are also considered long term: party identification and political ideology. By contrast, the candidates competing in a campaign and the issues raised in it are considered short-term factors'.

In this section, we investigate whether both of these expectations are confirmed for early and late-deciding voters in Belgium. While we have previously distinguished among early deciders, campaign deciders and Election Day deciders, in this section we limit the contrast to early and late deciders (i.e. voters who decided either during the campaign or on Election Day). The reason therefore is the more limited number of observations included in our analyses, as we are estimating different models for explaining the vote choice in the two main regions of Belgium: Flanders and Wallonia. In what follows we first examine differences in the outcome of the vote choice process, the party choice, for both groups of voters. We then assess reported vote choice motivations before estimating multivariate vote choice models explaining the choices made by early and late deciders, respectively.

The choices made

Before analysing the vote choice process and what factors affect the vote choices of early and late deciders, it is instructive to look at differences in the choices that are made by both groups of voters. For doing so, we present the proportion of early and late deciders, respectively, who reported having voted for each of the main parties in the two main regions of Belgium.

Figure 10.1 presents these vote shares, as well as 95 per cent confidence intervals, for respondents in the Flemish region. We include vote choices for the federal elections, as reported in the post-electoral wave of the 2014 PartiRep Election Study. Importantly, while we did take into account voting for smaller parties as well as casting blank and invalid votes for the calculation of the vote shares for both groups, the proportions for these fairly limited groups are not included in figure 10.1. We can thus assess whether each of the main parties was supported to a similar degree by early and late deciders or whether they did particularly well or, on the contrary, poorly among late-deciding voters.

From the results in figure 10.1, we can observe some minor differences in the success of Flemish parties between both groups of voters. Interestingly, the Flemish nationalist party N-VA, the party that is generally considered to have won the 2014 federal elections (Dandoy et al. 2015), appears to have done somewhat less well among late deciders than they did among early deciders. Overall, however, for none of the main parties we observe significant differences in the vote share among early deciders, on the one hand, and late deciders, on the other.

In figure 10.2, we look at voting behaviour in the Walloon region and present the vote shares the main parties obtained among early and late deciders, respectively. For the Walloon region, we observe some significant differences: it can be noted that the socialist (PS) and liberal party (MR) performed less well among late deciders than they did among early deciders. As none of the other main parties performed significantly better among late deciders, it is suggested that late deciders were more likely to vote for some of the smaller parties or to cast blank or invalid votes. Early deciders, thus, appear to be

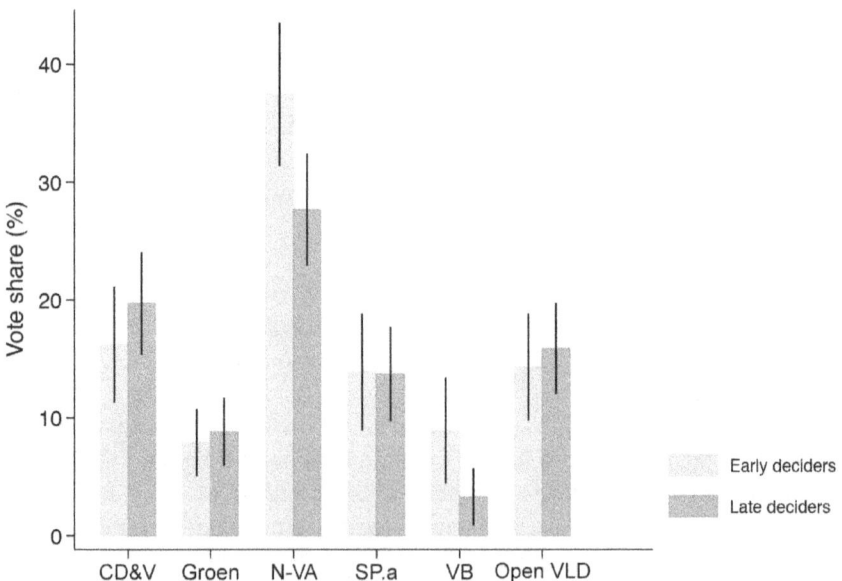

Figure 10.1.   Comparison of the reported vote choice of early and late decision makers, 2014 federal elections – Flemish region. Source: 2014 PartiRep Voter Survey.

Note: Means and 95 per cent confidence intervals reporting proportion of voters choosing a particular party are shown.

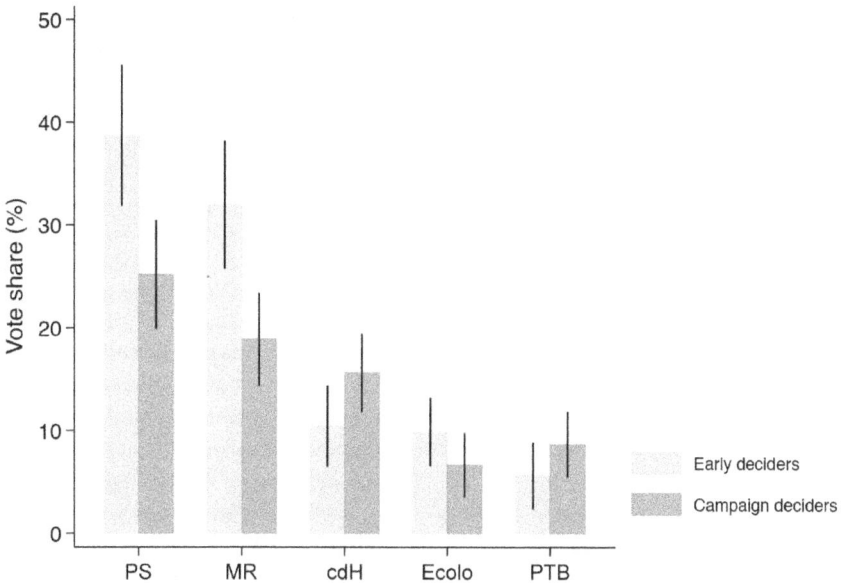

Figure 10.2. Comparison of the reported vote choice of early and late decision makers, 2014 federal elections – Walloon region. Source: 2014 PartiRep Voter Survey.

Note: Means and 95 per cent confidence intervals reporting proportion of voters choosing a particular party are shown.

somewhat more likely to vote for the traditional parties. An explanation for this observation could be found in the strong links of these traditional parties with particular social groups and organisations, which has for decades been a key element of Belgian politics (Deschouwer 2012).

Motivating the vote choice

We observe some – albeit fairly small – differences in the party choices made by early deciders, on the one hand, and late deciders, on the other. These differences, furthermore, as they indicate that early deciders in the Walloon region are somewhat more likely to support traditional parties than late deciders, would suggest differences in terms of what motivates the vote choice as well. The reason therefore is that traditional parties are historically connected more strongly to particular groups and organisations in society. As a consequence, one could assume that being a member of such organisations or belonging to a particular social group has more of an impact on the vote choices made by early deciders than what holds for late deciders.

As the first approach to investigating whether what drives the vote choice of both groups of voters differs, we assess how respondents motivated their choice for a particular party in the post-electoral survey of the PartiRep Election Study. Immediately following the vote choice question, motivations for this choice were gauged by means of an open-ended question. The main advantage of this relying on open-ended questions lies in the fact that respondents are not restrained to motivating their choice by means of a limited number of pre-imposed categories that researchers think of as important (for a critical review of the advantages and disadvantages of such questions, see Lefevere 2011; Van Aelst and Lefevere 2012). The answers to these open-ended questions were subsequently coded by means of a detailed coding scheme that allowed distinguishing between different vote choice heuristics (Lefevere 2011; Rosema 2004). In this chapter, we present the results for the nine main categories distinguished. These include (1) references to individual politicians; (2) references to following the vote choice advice of other people, which we label endorsements; (3) references to who should be in power or the need to remove a party from power, which is labelled the 'government and opposition' heuristic; (4) references to group interests, which could be particular social, ethnic or even geographical groups; (5) a habitual choice for a particular party; (6) motivations related to the size of a party, which could, for example, be linked to the fact that a party risks not passing the electoral threshold; (7) ideology and values, such as left and right; (8) issues and (9) a party heuristic, which could be an expression of an attachment to a particular party, a reference to the party image (Lefevere 2011).

Table 10.3 presents the proportion of voters in the early and late-deciding categories, respectively, motivating their vote choice by means of a reference to a particular vote choice heuristic. Note that the percentages within a single column do not add up to 100 per cent, as coders could use as many as three different categories for coding respondents' vote choice motivations. Examining the extent to which voters refer to particular vote choice heuristics for motivating their party choice, and the contrast between early and late deciders, respectively, a number of differences are significant. As can be read from table 10.3, late deciders are significantly more likely to motivate their vote choice by referring to individual politicians, the size of a party and issues. At least in terms of how they motivate their vote choice, late deciders appear to make use more of typical short-term factors such as politicians and issues, while strategic considerations lead them to refer to the size of a party as a reason for their vote choice. Furthermore, late deciders are significantly less likely to refer to groups, habits and ideology and values when motivating their choice for a particular party. Late-deciding voters, thus, significantly less often refer to heuristics that are typically related to long-term factors.

Table 10.3. Comparison of the extent to which particular vote choice heuristics are referred to by early and late-deciding voters

Motivation	Early deciders, %	Late deciders, %	Significance
Politicians	16.12	22.48	**
Endorsements	15.52	17.05	ns
Government and opposition	14.74	15.27	ns
Groups	21.37	11.59	***
Habit	19.25	6.31	***
Size	0.74	2.92	**
Ideology and values	21.98	16.76	*
Issues	23.33	29.89	*
Party	17.91	14.84	ns

Source: 2014 PartiRep Voter Survey.

Note: Difference between both groups tested by means of an adjusted Wald test is shown. Significance levels: ns: not significant; * $p < 0.05$; ** $p < 0.01$; *** $p < 0.001$.

Vote choice determinants

Even though insightful, an analysis of how voters motivate their choice for a particular party also comes with some disadvantages. Importantly, respondents limit their answers to one or a limited number of different heuristics only, even though we know that the making a vote choice is a complex and varied process in which a large number of more or less distant factors have an influence. Our analysis of vote choice heuristics among early and late deciders clarifies that late deciders are more likely to *motivate* their vote choice by referring to short-term factors. This indicates that these are the elements they think of as important for making their vote choices, but this does not preclude other factors to have an impact on their party choices as well. To ascertain whether short-term factors are indeed more important for late deciders, in terms of their weight in the vote choice process and importance for determining the vote choice, it is imperative to estimate their impact by means of a full vote choice model as well. Additionally, doing so gives insights into the extent to which traditional theories of voting behaviour succeed in explaining the choices made by early and late-deciding voters, respectively.

For analysing the determinants of the vote in a multiparty system, we follow the recommendation of Alvarez and Nagler (1998) and present the results of a McFadden conditional logit model. This methodological approach allows investigating the impact of individual-specific characteristics, such as respondents' gender or age, as well as choice-specific elements, such as the ideological distance to a particular party. We present the estimates from four separate models: a model explaining the vote choice of early deciders in the Flemish region, a model explaining the vote choice of late deciders in the Flemish region, a model explaining choices of early deciders in Wallonia and a model doing so for late deciders in the Walloon region.

For both regions, we focus on the main parties only and specify a vote for the centrist Christian democratic party as the reference category. Due to data limitations, we are somewhat restricted in what variables we can include to explain the vote choice, though we aim to develop a Michigan-style vote choice model, which includes long-term as well as short-term factors.

We include three different choice-specific variables in the vote choice models. First, we add a measure of the left-right ideological distance between a voter and a party, using the absolute difference between a voter's self-place-ment on a 0-to-10 left-right axis and the mean left-right placement accorded to a party by all respondents to the survey. As such, we take into account spatial theories of voting that expect voters to choose a party that is ideologi-cally close by (Downs 1957; Joesten and Stone 2014). Second, we include a measure of issue competence, measured as the number of times a voter refers to a particular party as the most competent party for dealing with the eight issue areas already referred to in the previous section. Third, we include as a measure of the closeness of a voter to a political party (5-point scale from 'not close to any party' to 'very close'). As an alternative, we assume that if a voter indicates his or her feeling of closeness to a particular party, the party he or she has in mind is the party he or she likes the most (as measured by means of like/dislike scales for all parties).

Furthermore, we include a number of individual-specific variables, which are unique to an individual and of which the values do not vary for different choice options. We include a traditional retrospective sociotropic measure of respondents' economic evaluations, with a scale from 1 (the economic situ-ation deteriorated a lot) to 5 (improved a lot). Furthermore, we control the impact of a number of socio-demographic characteristics; we include respon-dents' gender, age, their level of education (distinguishing lower, middle and higher educated), social class (distinguishing blue collar, white collar and self-employed, while the non-active are the reference group), as well as an indicator of religious practice.

The results of these analyses are presented graphically in figure 10.3 (vot-ers in the Flemish region) and figure 10.4 (voters in the Walloon region). First, it is important to point out that the explanatory power of the models explaining the vote choice of early deciders is indeed substantially higher than what holds for late deciders. More specifically the pseudo-R^2 statistics for early deciders are 0.63 and 0.59 in Flanders and in Wallonia, respectively.

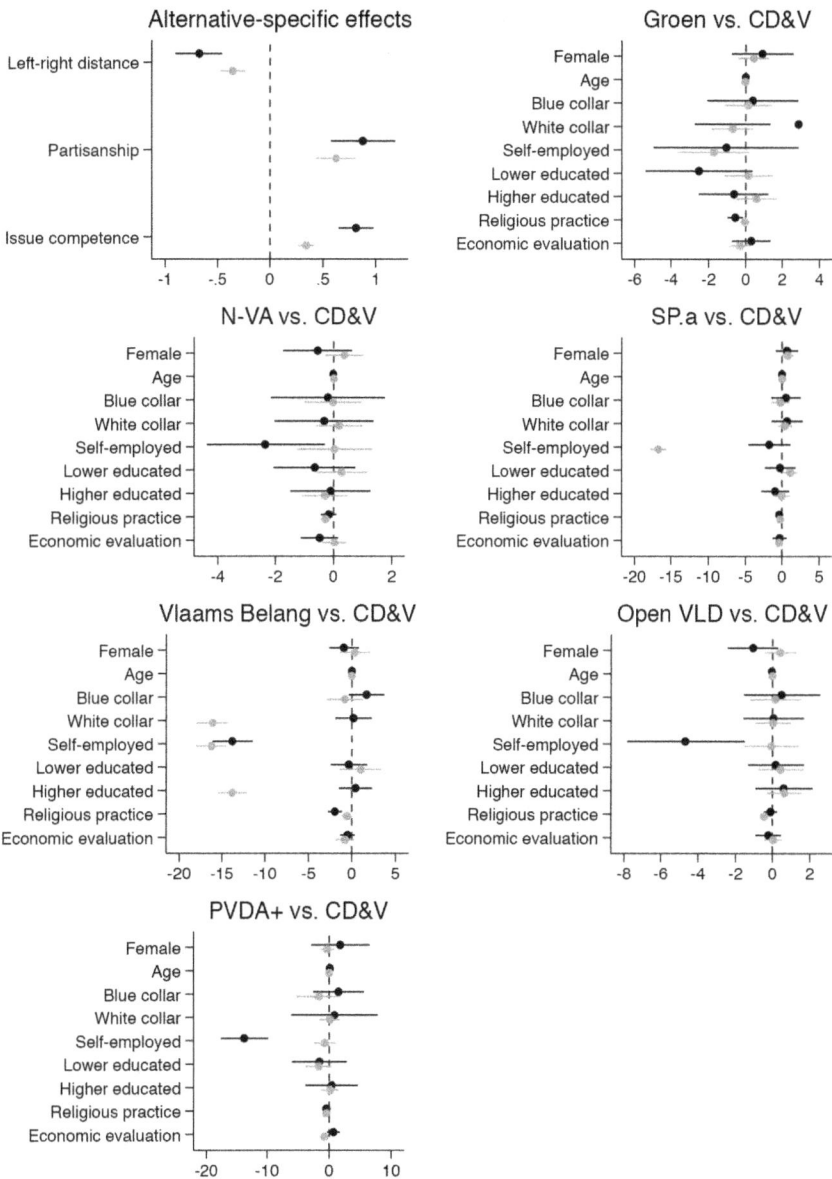

Figure 10.3. Comparison of conditional logit coefficients of early (black) and late decision makers (grey), explaining the vote in the 2014 federal elections – Flemish region. Source: 2014 PartiRep Voter Survey.

Note: Logit coefficients and 95 per cent confidence intervals are plotted. Estimates of two different vote choice models are estimated through a McFadden conditional logit model. Estimates of the early deciders are presented in black, whereas estimates of late deciders are presented in grey. Model fit statistics of the early deciders model: Log pseudolikelihood = –180.41. Wald χ^2 = 1885.59 (p < 0.000). N = 312. Model fit of the late deciders model: Log pseudolikelihood = –496.31. Wald χ^2 = 4931.35 (p < 0.000). n = 402.

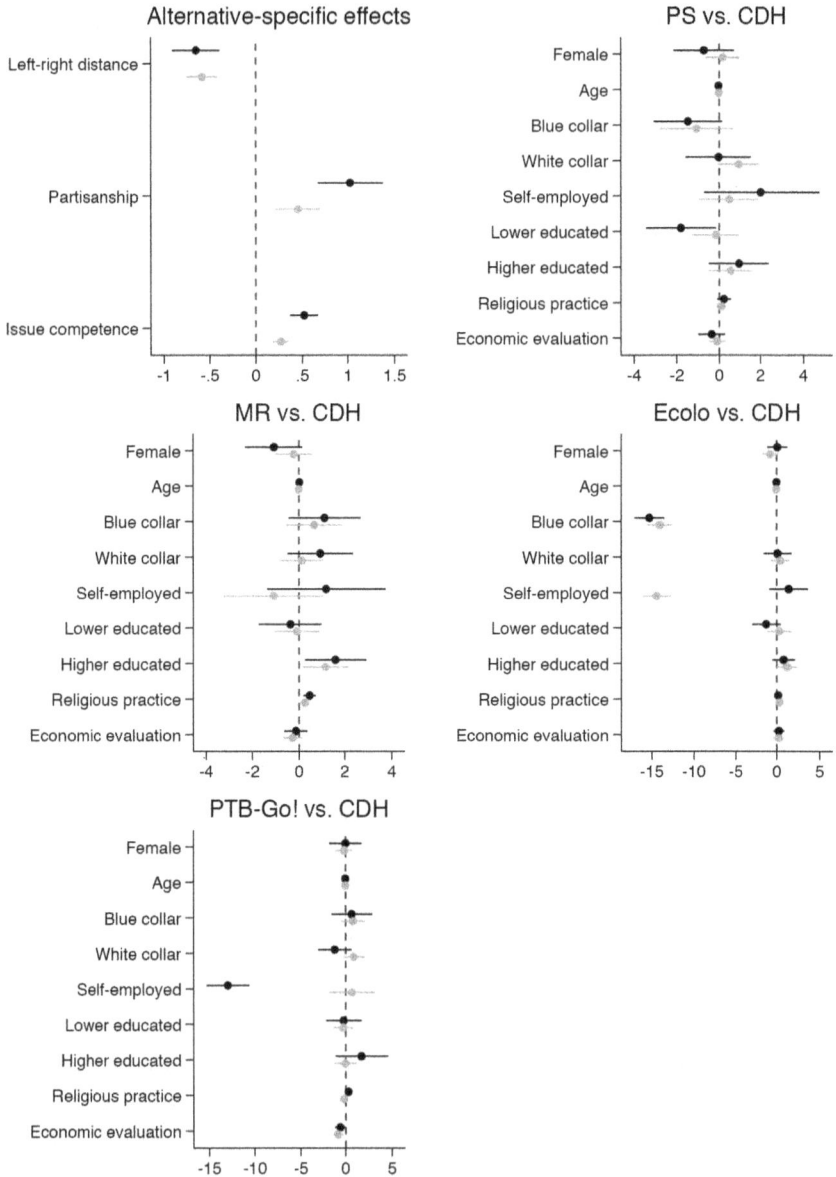

Figure 10.4. Comparison of conditional logit coefficients of early (black) and late decision makers (grey), explaining the vote in the 2014 federal elections – Walloon region. Source: 2014 PartiRep Voter Survey.

Note: Logit coefficients and 95 per cent confidence intervals are plotted. Estimates of two different vote choice models are estimated through a McFadden conditional logit model. Estimates of the early deciders are presented in black, whereas estimates of late deciders are presented in grey. Model fit statistics of the early deciders model: Log pseudolikelihood = –135.41. Wald χ^2 = 1811.28 (p < 0.000). N = 248. Model fit of the late deciders model: Log pseudolikelihood = –308.90. Wald χ^2 = 1391.82 (p < 0.000). N = 289.

For late deciders, by contrast, these statistics only amount to 0.27 in both Flanders and Walloon regions.

Looking at the impact of alternative-specific variables, the analyses for both regions indicate that partisanship has a somewhat stronger impact on the vote choice of early deciders in the Walloon region than what holds for late deciders. Furthermore, for both regions we do not find ideology (left-right distance) to have a different impact for early deciders, on the one hand, and late deciders, on the other. Finally, we observe that assessing a party as competent on multiple issues has a stronger impact on the vote choices of early deciders than what holds for late deciders, though this difference is most pronounced for voters in the Flemish region.

For the impact of individual-specific variables, we look at socio-demographics first. For both regions there are only few indicators for which we find the impact to differ between early deciders, on the one hand, and late deciders, on the other. Furthermore, when we observe differences, these do not consistently point out a stronger impact of these long-term factors among the early deciders than what holds for late deciders. For economic evaluations, finally, in a total of ten tests, there is not a single one for which we observe its impact to differ clearly between early and late deciders.

Overall, our analyses offer only weak evidence of differences in what determines the vote choice of early deciders, on the one hand, and late deciders, on the other. We find partisanship to be more important in determining the choices of early deciders than for those deciding late. But this holds only for voters in the Walloon region. As a result, our expectation that long-term factors have somewhat more weight in the vote choice process of early deciders receives only mixed support. The same goes for socio-demographic characteristics, which seem to have more or less a similar impact among both groups of voters.

For short-term factors, our results do not offer strong evidence of these determinants being of more weight among late deciders. The data allowed considering the impact of two types of short-term factors: economic evaluations and issue competence. For none of both determinants do we find clear indications of differences between early and late deciders. When we do observe differences, as for example with regard to issues in the Flemish region, effects are contrary to our expectations and indicate a somewhat stronger impact among early deciders.

DISCUSSION

In a large number of advanced democracies, voters are found to decide increasingly late as to which party to vote for. This trend not only indicates that electoral behaviour is changing fundamentally but also implies a challenge for parties, as their electoral prospects depend increasingly on what happens during the election campaign.

Our results show that in line with what can be observed in other countries, Belgian voters increasingly postpone their voting decision. In particular, the group of early deciders appears to be decreasing in both Flanders and Wallonia. When searching to characterise these voters, furthermore, we find that theories that hold in other democracies explain late-deciding in Belgium as well. By far the most important theoretical framework to explain why voters decide late is that of the 'floating voters'. More specifically, we observe that those who postpone their voting choice are less attached to political parties and also less interested in politics. This is in line with the literature that considers late-deciding an indicator of a broader process of dealignment in advanced democracies. Importantly, however, we also find that parties affect the extent to which voters decide late. This is evident from the fact that voters who are ambivalent about or indifferent towards the parties are more likely to decide late. The party offer thus matters as well.

Our expectation that institutional aspects of the electoral system, in particular the opportunity to cast preferential votes, also plays a role, for the time of decision-making was not substantiated by our findings. When not tested against the predictors of the time of decision-making those casting preferential votes appeared to be more numerous among the early deciders. But this relationship evaporated in the full model. Presumably preferential voting is a domain of more involved voters and therefore has no independent effect of its own.

Given that late deciders are less partisan, we expected to find important differences in how late and early deciders make a voting decision. Our results, however, are somewhat mixed. On the one hand, in terms of how voters motivate their own vote choice, late deciders are more likely to mention typical short-term vote choice motives, such as issues and politicians. When it comes to the actual vote choices, however, we observe only minor differences in terms of what parties late and early deciders choose. In addition, we find hardly any difference in what factors affect the choices made by late and early deciders. As a result, it is not surprising that the explanatory power of vote choice models explaining the party choice of late deciders is substantially lower than what holds for early deciders. The conclusion seems to be that traditional vote choice theories simply do not explain well how late deciders choose a party.

Late-deciding is on the rise in Belgium, a trend that is observed in many advanced democracies. The Belgian context hence does not seem to be particular in any way, and we find that the presence of preference voting is not leading to more late-deciding. Instead, the trend towards voters postponing their voting decisions fits a general pattern of dealignment in industrialised societies, which is a fundamental challenge for representative democracies. This challenge lies in the fact that late deciders are not very interested in politics and do not feel attached to a particular party. Parties, however, do have some leverage over the extent to which voters postpone their decisions. By offering a clear set of options that are sufficiently ideologically diverse, voters will be less ambivalent and indifferent, enabling them to make up their minds early on. If not, it seems like campaigns will increasingly determine how parties fare on Election Day, and who eventually governs. Somewhat disquietingly, furthermore, we do not know what it is they are waiting for. In any case it does not seem to be more information on the current election. Traditional theories of voting behaviour do not seem to explain well how late deciders choose which party to vote for and neither is there strong evidence of issues or economic evaluations affecting the choices of late deciders to a stronger extent.

NOTE

1. Rüdiger Schmitt-Beck gratefully acknowledges the hospitality of the Peter Wall Institute for Advanced Studies of the University of British Columbia, which enabled him to work on this chapter during a visiting scholarship.

REFERENCES

Alvarez, R.M. and Nagler, J. (1998) 'When Politics and Models Collide: Estimating Models of Multiparty Elections', *American Journal of Political Science*, 42(1): 55–96.

Bartle, J. (2005) 'Homogeneous Models and Heterogeneous Voters', *Political Studies*, 53(4): 653–75.

Bellucci, P. (2006) 'Tracing the Cognitive and Affective Roots of "Party Competence": Italy and Britain, 2001', *Electoral Studies*, 25(3): 548–69.

Bengtsson, A. Hansen, K., Hardarson, O., Narud, H. and Oscarsson, H. (2014) *The Nordic Voter. Myths of Exceptionalism*, Colchester: ECPR Press.

Berelson, B., Lazarsfeld, P.F. and McPhee, W.N. (1954) *Voting: A Study of Opinion Formation in a Presidential Campaign*, Chicago: University of Chicago Press.

Blumenstiel, J.E. and Plischke, T. (2015) 'Changing Motivations, Time of the Voting Decision, and Short-Term Volatility – the Dynamics of Voter Heterogeneity', *Electoral Studies*, 37: 28–40.

Campbell, A., Converse, P.E., Miller, W.E. and Stokes, D.E. (1980) *The American Voter. Unabridged Edition*, Chicago: University of Chicago Press.

Chaffee, S.H. and Choe, S.Y. (1980) 'Time of Decision and Media Use during the Ford-Carter Campaign', *Public Opinion Quarterly*, 44(1): 53–69.

Dalton, R.J., McAllister, I. and Wattenberg, M.P. (2000) 'The Consequences of Partisan Dealignment', in R.J. Dalton and M. Wattenberg (eds) *Parties without Partisans: Political Change in Advanced Democracies*, Oxford: Oxford University Press, 37–63.

Dandoy, R., Reuchamps, M. and Baudewyns, P. (2015) 'The 2014 Federal and European Elections in Belgium', *Electoral Studies*, 39: 153–77.

Dassonneville, R. and Hooghe, M. (2016) 'Economic Indicators and Electoral Volatility: Economic Effects on Electoral Volatility in Western Europe, 1950–2013', *Comparative European Politics*, first published online in 2015. doi:10.1057/cep.2015.3.

Davis, N. (2015) 'The Role of Indifference in Split-Ticket Voting', *Political Behaviour*, 37: 67–86.

Deschouwer, K. (2012) *The Politics of Belgium: Governing a Divided Society* (2nd edition), Basingstoke: Palgrave Macmillan.

Downs, A. (1957) *An Economic Theory of Democracy*, New York: Harper and Row.

Drummond, A. (2006) 'Electoral Volatility and Party Decline in Western Democracies: 1970–1995', *Political Studies*, 54(3): 628–47.

Fournier, P., Nadeau, R., Blais, A., Gidengil, E. and Nevitte, N. (2004) 'Time-of-Voting Decision and Susceptibility to Campaign Effects', *Electoral Studies*, 23: 661–81.

Franklin, M.N., Mackie, T.T. and Valen, H. (2009) *Electoral Change: Responses to Evolving Social and Attitudinal Structures in Western Countries*, Colchester: ECPR Press.

Joesten, D. and Stone, W.J. (2014) 'Reassessing Proximity Voting: Expertise, Party, and Choice in Congressional Elections', *Journal of Politics*, 76(3): 740–53.

Joslyn, R. (1984) *Mass Media and Elections*, Reading, MA: Addison-Wesley.

Lachat, R. (2007) *A Heterogeneous Electorate: Political Sophistication, Predisposition Strength, and the Voting Decision Process*, Baden-Baden: Nomos.

Lau, R.R. and Redlawsk, D.P. (2006) *How Voters Decide: Information Processing in Election Campaigns*, Cambridge: Cambridge University Press.

Lazarsfeld, P.F., Berelson, B. and Gaudet, H. (1968) *The People's Choice: How the Voter Makes Up His Mind in a Presidential Campaign*, New York: Columbia University Press.

Lefevere, J. (2011) *Campaign Effects on Voter Decision Making*, PhD Dissertation, Antwerp, University of Antwerp.

Lewis-Beck, M.S., Jacoby, W.G., Norpoth, H. and Weisberg, H.E. (2008) *The American Voter Revisited*, Ann Arbor: University of Michigan Press.

McAllister, I. (2002) 'Calculating or Capricious? The New Politics of Late Deciding Voters', in D. Farrell and R. Schmitt-Beck (eds) *Do Political Campaigns Matter?* London: Routledge, 22–40.

Mutz, D.C. (2002) 'The Consequences of Cross-Cutting Networks for Political Participation', *American Journal of Political Science*, 46(4): 838–55.

Pedersen, M.N. (1979) 'The Dynamics of European Party Systems: Changing Patterns of Electoral Volatility', *European Journal of Political Research*, 7(1): 1–26.

Reinemann, C., Maurer, M., Zerback, T. and Jandura, O. (2013) *Die Spätentscheider. Medieneinflüsse auf kurzfristige Wahlentscheidungen*, Wiesbaden: Springer VS.

Rose, R. and McAllister, I. (1986) *Voters Begin to Choose: From Closed Class to Open Elections in Britain*, London: Sage.

Rosema, M. (2004) *The Sincere Voter. A Psychological Study of Voting*, Enschede: Febodruk.

Schmitt-Beck, R. and Partheymüller, J. (2012) 'Why Voters Decide Late: A Simultaneous Test of Old and New Hypotheses at the 2005 and 2009 German Federal Elections', *German Politics*, 21(3): 299–316.

Thompson, M. M., Zanna, M. P. and Griffin, D. W. (1995) 'Let's Not Be Indifferent about (Attitudinal) Ambivalence', in R. E. Petty and J. A. Krosnick (eds) *Attitude Strength: Antecedents and Consequences*, Mahwah, NJ: Lawrence Erlbaum Associates, 369–71.

Van Aelst, P. and Lefevere, J. (2012) 'Has Europe Got Anything to Do with the European Elections? A Study on Split-Ticket Voting in the Belgian Regional and European Elections of 2009', *European Union Politics*, 13(1): 3–25.

Van der Brug, W. (2010) 'Structural and Ideological Voting in Age Cohorts', *West European Politics*, 33(3): 586–607.

Walczak, A., Van der Brug, W. and de Vries, C.E. (2012) 'Long- and Short-Term Determinants of Party Preferences: Inter-Generational Differences in Western and East Central Europe', *Electoral Studies*, 31(2): 273–28.

Chapter 11

Gender-based voting

Silvia Erzeel, Sjifra de Leeuw, Sofie Marien
and Benoît Rihoux

INTRODUCTION

Since the early 1990s, the political under-representation of women has been a central concern for many scholars in Europe. Although women's under-representation features many dimensions, the descriptive under-representation of women – that is their numerical under-representation in elected assemblies compared to men – remains one of the most visible and problematised forms in both research and policy (Childs & Lovenduski 2013). To redress persisting gender inequalities in politics, governments and parties have made efforts to improve the conditions for women's electoral success. In many cases these efforts took the form of gender quotas designed to remove structural barriers for female politicians. Other measures included gender awareness campaigns to encourage voters to cast votes for women. The rationale behind this is that it is often not enough to motivate parties to select female candidates – as gender quotas do – but that voters also need encouragements to elect more women to parliament.

While many studies have examined the effects of gender quotas (Dahlerup 2006; Krook & Zetterberg 2014), we know less about the role voters' choices play in the current under-representation of women. Do female candidates, for instance, attract less-preferential votes? Moreover, is there such a thing as 'gender-based voting', that is do voters prefer candidates of their own gender? Do women in politics draw disproportionately from the support of female voters? To date, few studies have considered the influence of voters' choices for male or female candidates in the election of female candidates (Giger et al. 2014; Holli & Wass 2010). A reason for this scarcity of studies is the absence of actual opportunities for gender-based voting in many electoral systems (e.g. only one candidate per political party or a closed list).

The Belgian flexible list system offers extensive opportunities for voters to advance or harm gender equality in the election of representatives. Hence, this offers a particularly interesting case to study how voters use these opportunities.

The existing research draws primarily on cases with majoritarian electoral systems, in particular the United States (Sanbonmatsu 2002; Dolan 2004, 2008). This literature shows that, all other things remaining equal, voters tend to display a 'baseline gender preference' (Sanbonmatsu 2002), that is a basic propensity to support candidates of one gender over candidates of the other gender. However, whether this basic inclination transforms itself into an actual vote for candidates of their preferred gender depends strongly on the context. Research on voters' candidate choice outside the United States remains limited, particularly in PR systems. Most PR systems are closed list systems where voters, by design, do not have the possibility to cast a (preferential) vote for an individual candidate but must choose between party lists on which candidates are already ranked. Recently, a small number of studies have focused on gender-based voting in Finland and Ireland. Together, these studies find that vote choice is to some extent socially stratified, but the prevalence of gender-based voting varies substantially between and within countries (Giger et al. 2014; Holli & Wass 2010; McElroy & Marsh 2010).

In this chapter, we further contribute to this debate by uncovering the magnitude, nature and determinants of gender-based voting in Belgium. In particular, we will analyse (1) whether and to what extent gender-based voting exists in Belgium and (2) which individual voter and institutional factors account for the observed variation in gender-based voting. The Belgian case is in theory a likely case for gender-based voting because of its institutional context. First, due to strict quota regulations, all political parties are obliged to select an equal number of candidates from both sexes (Meier 2012). Voters thus have the option to vote for a candidate of their preferred gender without having to change political parties. Second, the Belgian electoral system applies multiple preferential voting, which gives voters the opportunity to express their support for one or more candidates, and to do so for different reasons. Finally, given Belgium's long history of accommodating differences in society, gender-based claims for group representation are well established and might influence voters' considerations too.

To study gender-based voting, we analyse data from the 2014 PartiRep Voter Survey. These data were collected using an innovative 'mock-ballot' technique, where respondents were asked to copy the selection made on their voting ballot onto a copy of that ballot. The advantage of this approach is that it provides us with detailed information on preference voting behaviour and allows us to link the information of the voters to information about the candidates they voted for. In what follows, we first discuss the literature on gender-based voting and formulate a number of hypotheses on correlates of gender-based in Belgium. This is followed by a description of the Belgian case and data in a methods section. Finally, we present and discuss the findings themselves.

WHAT IS GENDER-BASED VOTING?

Although studies generally assume that PR systems with party lists are more inclusive towards women than other electoral systems, they often remain inconclusive as to whether closed lists or open lists are more conducive to women's political representation (Kunovich 2012). If anything, open lists or flexible lists make women's political presence less predictable (Ballmer-Cao & Tremblay 2008; Wauters, Weekers & Maddens 2010), because women's chances depend not only on parties' strategic choices but also on voters' behaviour. The voter side has always been the least understood part of the story, and recently studies have begun to fill this gap by studying voters' preferences for male or female candidates.

In her seminal work on gender and candidate choice in the United States, Sanbonmatsu (2002: 20) finds that 55 per cent of the voters have a 'baseline gender preference', or a basic inclination to prefer candidates of one gender over candidates of the other gender. This baseline gender preference is partially influenced by voters' own gender, as voters are somewhat more likely to prefer candidates of their own gender, if all other factors are held constant. Although Sanbonmatsu's baseline gender preference is not the same as gender-based voting – after all, a baseline gender preference is measured at the attitudinal level and not at the behavioural level – it does tell us something about voters' propensity to support either male or female candidates and how this is linked to voters' own gender.

The concept of gender-based voting itself was first coined by Holli and Wass (2010) in the Finnish context. Contrary to Sanbonmatsu (2002), Holli and Wass (2010) focus on the actual act of preferential voting and define gender-based voting as a situation in which voters 'cast their vote for a candidate of their own gender' (Holli & Wass 2010: 601). Hence, a synonym for gender-based voting is same-gender voting. The opposite of gender-based voting is cross-gender voting, which refers to a situation in which voters cast a vote for candidates of the opposite gender. Reasons for gender-based voting can be multiple, but important is that voters have an affinity for the candidates they vote for that is based on a shared gender (Dolan 2008). Women (men) will only vote for women (men) if they identify with members of their own group, feel connected to them and believe they share some common faith with them.

Overall, however, insights on gender-based voting remain limited. The impact of voters' own gender on their candidate choice varies strongly across settings. Some studies show that voters are indeed pulled towards candidates of the same gender, and that gender-based voting even transcends party differences between voters (Plutzer & Zipp 1996). Other studies, however, do not detect a similar gender effect. Gender-based voting patterns either disappear after controlling for third variables (Paolino 1995; McElroy & Marsh 2010) or are found to be conditional upon individual voter characteristics or institutional context factors (Dolan 2004, 2008; Giger et al. 2014). In order to move beyond these contradicting results, we need to know more about the specific determinants of gender-based voting.

DETERMINANTS OF GENDER-BASED VOTING: HYPOTHESES

Although we state that the Belgian case is a likely setting for gender-based voting, we do not expect that gender-based voting will be equally strong for all groups of voters or that it will appear under all circumstances. In the following subsections, we formulate some hypotheses on how individual voter characteristics and institutional factors might influence patterns of gender-based voting behaviour.

Individual-level determinants

First, we hypothesise that patterns of gender-based voting behaviour will be different for male and female voters, and hence that gender will steer gender-based voting. Gender-based voting presupposes the existence of a (strong) identity link between candidates and voters. This identity link will arguably be stronger when a group is dissatisfied with the current state of affairs. A state of relative deprivation, in which a group feels deprived of certain resources and opportunities compared to another, fosters group affinity and feelings of group solidarity (Walker & Pettigrew 1984). When applied to men and women, it can be theorised that women, because they occupy a disadvantaged socio-economic and political position, will develop stronger feelings of group affinity and solidarity than men. If so, the inclination to cast a same-gender vote would be stronger for women – a hypothesis that has been corroborated in studies focusing on the United States (Dolan 2004, 2008). Holli and Wass (2010), in contrast, find that gender-based voting is more prevalent among men than among women in Finland. They explain this by the fact that the overall high level of gender equality has made young men more aware of their own gender. Gender equality in Belgium, however, has not yet reached the Finnish level, and the first hypothesis is therefore as follows:

Hypothesis 1: The propensity to cast a gender-based vote is higher for female voters than for male voters.

Gender-based voting is also likely to be influenced by voters' age, but this has led to the formulation of contradicting hypotheses. On the one hand, some have hypothesised that gender-based voting will depend on voting habits, which develop during socialisation processes of individuals and remain relatively stable afterwards (Franklin 2004; Holli & Wass 2010). Older generations of voters have developed their voting habits in a time when men were over-represented on candidate lists, while younger voters might be more accustomed to a more equal presence of men and women in politics. Due to these differences, we may hypothesise that both older men and older women are more likely to vote for men, while younger generation of women are more likely to have developed a habit of voting for women (see also Holli & Wass 2010). Tied back to gender-based voting this means that:

Hypothesis 2a: The propensity to cast a gender-based vote increases with age for men and decreases with age for women.

On the other hand, we can also hypothesise that if gender-based voting is linked to feelings of identity and group solidarity, the likelihood of gender-based voting will increase when voters have been explicitly confronted with their deprived status in society. As older women are more likely to have experience in being discriminated against than younger women, the gender link between voters and candidates might be particularly strong for older women (Duncan & Loretto 2004):

Hypothesis 2b: The propensity to cast a gender-based vote increases with age for women.

Gender-based voting might furthermore be influenced by levels of political sophistication. Here too, conflicting hypotheses have been formulated in the literature. Voters sometimes use candidate's sex as a heuristic voting cue, that is, they take sex as an informational shortcut to make assessments about candidates' beliefs and policy positions (Sanbonmatsu 2002). This informational shortcut is more often used by voters with low levels of political sophistication because they lack the cognitive skills or motivation to collect and process political information. Voters with higher levels of political sophistication will be less likely to rely on descriptive characteristics of candidates, including candidates' sex, to make voting decisions:

Hypothesis 3a: The propensity to cast a gender-based vote decreases with political sophistication.

The opposite hypothesis assumes that preferential voting is a more sophisticated form of voting behaviour. Making a distinction between various

Chapter 11

candidates, learning about them and comparing their qualities are quite demanding on the part of voters (Shugart, Valdini & Suominen 2005). It can be argued that voting for women is an activity that requires even higher levels of political sophistication than voting for men or casting a list vote. Female candidates, due to party or media biases, might have fewer chances of demonstrating their personal qualities and characteristics during election campaigns (Wauters, Weekers & Maddens 2010). Hence the cognitive investment of voters required to assess women's qualities is larger, and only (female) voters who display higher levels of political interest and political knowledge will vote for women.

Hypothesis 3b: The propensity to cast a gender-based vote increases with political sophistication but only for women.

Institutional-level determinants

Gender-based voting will also depend on contextual factors. The electorate can rely on many different pieces of information to make a voting decision. Prior studies theorise that if these pieces of information are not salient or readily available, voters will compensate for this lack of information by taking the sex of the candidate as an informational shortcut (Sanbonmatsu 2002). If this assumption holds, then the propensity to cast a gender-based vote should be higher in electoral contexts for which little information is available, often labelled 'second-order' elections. As opposed to so-called first-order elections, second-order elections are generally deemed less important by voters, the media and political parties themselves (Reif & Schmitt 1980). In Belgium, the European elections are considered a textbook case of second-order elections. Due to its system of compulsory voting, the lack of information caused by the second-order character of these elections does not result in a lower turnout, and voters are strongly encouraged to make a voting decision regardless of their amount of information. Thus, we hypothesise that:

Hypothesis 4: The propensity to cast a gender-based vote is higher in European elections than in federal elections.

Finally, the magnitude of the district in which elections are held is important for gender-based voting. High district magnitude tends to foster a more balanced political representation of gender groups because political parties are more likely to diversify their lists (and their top list positions) when more seats can be won (Matland 1993). In smaller districts parties are more reluctant to select women out of a fear that they would be less successful than men in securing the few seats available. In addition, competition for the 'winning seats' within the party is fiercer in such districts, and male candidates frequently exert more influence than their female counterparts in the intra-party candidate selection procedures (Caul 1999; Vandeleene 2016). Further, voters might follow parties' cues by voting strategically for candidates who they feel are more likely to win. If male candidates have an advantage in small districts, the opportunities for women increase in larger districts. This might have an effect on gender-based voting: women might cast more preferential votes for women candidates in larger districts (Giger et al. 2014).

Hypothesis 5: The propensity to cast a gender-based vote increases with district magnitude for women.

RESEARCH DESIGN

Belgium: A case in point

Belgium constitutes a particularly interesting case because it combines a flexible list PR system with multiple preferential voting, compulsory voting and legally binding gender quotas. Preferential voting is optional, as voters can also opt to cast a vote for the party list. Belgian voters can cast as many preference votes as they want, but voting for (candidates on) different party lists is not allowed. The allocation of seats to candidates is influenced by the order in which candidates appear on the list and by the number of preferential votes candidates receive. Candidates who receive enough preference votes to pass the election threshold are automatically elected, regardless of their position on the list. For candidates not reaching this threshold, the list order defines their electoral chances. Although it is not uncommon for candidates on lower list positions to gain enough preference votes to breach the list order (especially in recent years), the candidates at the top of the list have a clear advantage and stand a (much) higher chance of getting elected. This has proven to be a disadvantage for women because parties were (and are) less likely to select them as top list candidates (Marien, Schouteden & Wauters 2017; Vandeleene 2016).

Overall, the presence of women in Belgian politics has significantly increased since 1995, mostly because the Belgian government has progressively adopted gender quota laws. The current gender parity law, adopted in 2002, stipulates that the proportion of female and male candidates on all electoral lists for all levels of government must be balanced and that the two top positions on each list must be occupied by individuals of different sexes (Meier 2012). While the quota laws have not led to complete gender parity in the Belgian federal and regional parliaments or in the Belgian representation in the European Parliament, the situation has improved significantly. In 2014, 38 per cent of the representatives of the Belgian House of Representatives and 28 per cent of the Belgian members of the European parliament were women (www.ipu.org, 2017).

Model specification

Dependent variable

Previous studies have defined gender-based voting as a situation in which voters 'cast their vote for a candidate of their own gender' (Holli & Wass 2010: 601). This definition is straightforward in situations in which voters are only allowed to cast one preferential vote: voters either vote for a candidate of their own gender or for a candidate of the opposite gender. Belgian voters, however, have the possibility to cast multiple preferential votes and this makes measuring gender-based voting more complex. For measuring gender-based voting, we therefore decided to make a distinction between three types of voting: (1) same-gender voting, which refers to a situation in which voters vote exclusively for candidates of their own gender; (2) cross-gender voting, referring to a situation in which voters vote exclusively for candidates of the opposite gender and (3) mixed voting, where voters vote for both male and female candidates.

The 2014 PartiRep Survey measured preference voting behaviour across three electoral contexts, namely the regional, federal and European elections. In this chapter, we focus on the first-order federal elections and the second-order European elections. In the initial data structure (table 11.1), voting behaviour in these elections was captured by two separate variables (voting behaviour in the federal elections and voting behaviour in the European elections). To facilitate a comparison across the two electoral contexts, we generated a stacked data matrix, nesting voting behaviour into individual respondents (table 11.2). This transformation resulted in a data matrix in which each respondent's voting behaviour was measured twice across the two different electoral contexts, for which an additional independent variable was generated. Not taking the nested structure into account would subsequently

Table 11.1. Initial data matrix

Id	Voting behaviour – federal elections	Voting behaviour – European elections	Gender	Age	. . .
1	Same gender	Cross-gender	Man	41	. . .
2	Cross-gender	Same gender	Woman	23	. . .
3	Mixed	Mixed	Woman	21	. . .
. . .	. . .	. . .	. . .	. . .	. . .

Table 11.2.   Stacked data matrix

Id	Election	Voting behaviour	Gender	Age	...
1	Federal	Same gender	Man	41	...
1	European	Cross-gender	Man	41	...
2	Federal	Cross-gender	Woman	23	...
2	European	Same gender	Woman	23	...
3	Federal	Mixed	Woman	21	...
3	European	Mixed	Woman	21	...
...	...	...	...	...	...

result in an underestimation of the standard error, thereby increasing the likelihood of finding significant effects when they are absent. To correct this underestimation, we applied a cluster-robust correction to the standard error.

Independent variables

To test the hypotheses, five independent variables are studied: sex, age, political sophistication, election context and district magnitude. Summary statistics can be found in the appendix. Respondents' sex is coded as a dummy variable (man = 0, woman = 1). Age is measured as a categorical variable with four age cohorts (18–31, 32–42, 43–59 and 60 and older). This categorisation is in line with different periods of gender quota laws. While the youngest age cohort has been socialised in a period in which the current strict quota laws were enforced, this is not the case for the older age cohorts. Political sophistication is generally operationalised by two components: cognitive and motivational components (Luskin 1990). We measure the cognitive component as the political knowledge of the respondent, using a five-item Guttman scale. Each of the items contained a multiple choice question gauging a respondent's political knowledge. This resulted in a variable that referred to the number of correct answers (ranging from 0, 'no questions answered correctly', to 5, 'all questions answered correctly'). The motivational component is operationalised as political interest, measured on a scale from 0 ('no interest at all') to 10 ('a lot of interest').

The election context is operationalised as a dummy variable, distinguishing between European and federal elections. Finally, district magnitude is measured as the number of legislative seats to be distributed within an electoral district.

Control variables

We also include four control variables. First, we control for the ideological self-placement of the respondents. Erzeel and Caluwaerts (2015), as well as Marien, Wauters and Schouteden (2017), argue that left-wing voters show greater support for female candidates than right-wing voters. Therefore, the analysis also controls for differences in voters' ideological self-placement, measured on an 11-point scale with a value 0 indicating a left-wing ideology and a value 10 indicating a right-wing ideology. Second, to make sure that the findings were not solely defined in function of the composition of the lists, we also controlled for whether respondents voted for the top candidate on the list in one or both elections. Third, we controlled for the total number of preference votes cast. Finally, we also included educational attainment as a control variable. This variable included four categories: (1) none or primary education, (2) completed lower secondary education, (3) completed higher secondary education and (4) completed tertiary higher education.

EMPIRICAL RESULTS

The presentation of the results consists of two parts. First, we present the descriptive analyses in which we discuss the extent of gender-based voting in Belgium. Second, we test the hypotheses formulated earlier by investigating which individual and institutional factors play a role. The subsequent analyses were conducted using only the data collected among respondents who cast one or multiple preference votes in the federal elections, the European elections or both. Out of the 1,532 respondents who participated in the second wave of the survey, 628 (41 per cent) cast one or multiple preference votes in the federal elections, compared to 571 (37.3 per cent) in the European elections.

Descriptive results

Table 11.3 depicts preferential voting behaviour for men and women. The results show that, in general, voters appear to have a preference for candidates of the same sex. *Post-hoc* analyses reveal that with 40.7 per cent of the voters casting a same-gender vote in Flanders and 40.5 per cent in Wallonia, same-gender voting is a significantly more popular choice than mixed or cross-gender voting.

To investigate whether this finding applies for both male and female voters, we disaggregated the (relative) frequencies according to voters' sex. Same-gender voting appears to be especially popular among male voters, with over half of the male voters (53.7 per cent in Flanders and 56.6 per cent in Wallonia) casting a vote for candidates of their own sex. The analyses reveal that female voters also have a clear preference for male candidates. Indeed, in Flanders and Wallonia, respectively, 49 per cent and 57.3 per cent of the women voted for male candidates only.

Table 11.3. Preferential voting by sex

		Preferential vote			
		Same gender, % (N)	Mixed, % (N)	Cross-gender, % (N)	Total, %
Men	Flanders	53.7 (183)	30.2 (103)	16.1 (55)	100 (341)
	Wallonia	56.6 (146)	24.8 (64)	18.6 (48)	100 (258)
Women	Flanders	28.0 (97)	23.0 (80)	49.0 (170)	100 (347)
	Wallonia	24.1 (61)	18.6 (47)	57.3 (145)	100 (253)
Total	Flanders	40.7 (280)	26.6 (183)	32.7 (225)	100 (688)
	Wallonia	40.5 (207)	21.7 (111)	37.8 (193)	100 (511)

Flanders: $\chi^2 = 88.037$; df $= 2$; Cramer's $V = 0.358$; $p < 0.001$
Wallonia: $\chi^2 = 86.218$; df $= 2$; Cramer's $V = 0.411$; $p < 0.001$

Source: 2014 PartiRep Voter Survey.

Note: Frequencies refer to the pooled data of voting behaviour in the European and federal elections; see table 11.2.

These findings suggest that both men and women have a baseline gender preference for male candidates, with men, in particular, being very likely to cast a gender-based vote. Nevertheless, the data presented in table 11.3 may be slightly misleading. Scholarship on baseline gender preferences assumes that all other factors are held constant. In this respect, women may be hampered in their willingness to express support for a candidate of the same sex by the mere fact that female candidates are often placed on less-attractive positions on the list (Vandeleene 2016). Even in Belgium, where quota legislation dictates that the supply of male and female candidates on every list must be equal, parties still have a large degree of freedom in deciding upon the gender balance for the most visible and more secure seats on their lists. One of the most important factors explaining the number of preference votes of a candidate is whether the candidate occupies the top position on the list. In both Flanders and Wallonia, these positions are more frequently occupied by men than women (Vandeleene 2016). In effect, for most female voters, the inclination to vote for a candidate based on their sex must compete with a much more salient cue – the position of a candidate on the list.

For gaining more insight into the influence of ballot composition, we take a closer look at the propensity for men and women to cast a vote for a top candidate of the same sex (table 11.4). Overall, an overwhelming majority of the voters (72.7 per cent) cast a vote for a male top candidate, which is not surprising, given that most top candidates are male. Consequently, both men and women are more likely to vote for a male candidate than for a female candidate. However, contrary to the findings in table 11.3, we observe that when a party has a female top candidate, women are significantly more likely to vote for this candidate (38.0 per cent in Flanders; 26.2 per cent in Wallonia) than their male counterparts (21.1 per cent in Flanders; 23.2 per cent in Wallonia). This

Table 11.4. Voted for top candidate

	Voted for top candidate		
	Male candidate, % (N)	*Female candidate, % (N)*	*Total, % (N)*
Flanders	71.1 (374)	28.9 (152)	100 (526)
Male voters	78.9 (224)	21.1 (60)	100 (284)
Female voters	62.0 (150)	38.0 (92)	100 (242)
Wallonia	75.5 (222)	24.5 (72)	100 (294)
Male voters	76.8 (126)	23.2 (38)	100 (164)
Female voters	73.9 (96)	26.2 (34)	100 (130)
Total	72.7 (596)	27.3 (224)	100 (820)
Male voters	78.1 (350)	21.9 (98)	100 (448)
Female voters	66.1 (246)	33.9 (126)	100 (372)

$\chi^2 = 1.845$; df $= 2$; Cramer's $V = -0.05$; $p = 0.17$.

Source: 2014 PartiRep Voter Survey.

Note: Frequencies refer to the pooled data of voting behaviour in the European and federal elections.

suggests that not taking the ballot composition into account would not provide a comprehensive picture of the nature of gender-based voting behaviour.

Explanatory results

In this section, we further investigate the effect of two sets of determinants on the propensity to cast a gender-based vote, namely individual-level voter characteristics (sex, age and political sophistication) and institutional characteristics (election type and district magnitude).

Individual-level determinants

Building on the assertion that women still occupy a disadvantaged status in society, we hypothesised that the likelihood of casting a gender-based vote would be higher for women than for men in Belgium (hypothesis 1). We tested this hypothesis in two steps. First, we estimated a model with the respondent's sex as the only predictor. In line with the descriptive analyses, we find that the probability to cast a same-gender vote is almost twice as high for men as that of women ($\beta = -0.42$, SE $= 0.19$, $p = 0.02$). Inversely, we find that women are approximately three times more likely to cast a cross-sex vote as compared to their male counterparts ($\beta = 1.45$, SE $= 0.19$, $p = 0.00$). This effect, however, vanishes when we control for whether the respondent voted for the top candidate on the list or not, the results of which are displayed in table 11.5. Model 1 shows that there is no significant difference between men and women in the overall likelihood to cast a gender-based

Table 11.5. Explaining gender-based voting using individual-level characteristics (sex, age)

	Model 1		Model 2	
	Same	Cross	Same	Cross
Sex: female	-0.34 (0.23)	1.42 (0.24)***	-1.11 (0.59)†	1.31 (0.64)*
Age (ref. 18–31) in years				
32–42	-0.78 (0.40)†	-0.30 (0.42)	-1.32 (0.50)**	-0.27 (0.59)
43–59	0.01 (0.30)	0.29 (0.41)	-0.29 (0.45)	0.40 (0.50)
60>	-0.70 (0.35)*	0.22 (0.38)	-1.09 (0.44)*	0.08 (0.52)
Sex * Age, years				
Female 32–42			1.22 (0.78)	0.14 (0.81)
Female 43–59			0.64 (0.81)	-0.11 (0.80)
Female 60>			0.86 (0.72)	0.35 (0.75)
Control variables				
Education				
Lower secondary	-0.66 (0.89)	-0.39 (0.82)	-0.71 (0.87)	-0.44 (0.82)
Upper secondary	-0.84 (0.90)	-0.51 (0.83)	-0.82 (0.87)	-0.56 (0.84)
Higher	-0.76 (0.91)	-0.50 (0.84)	-0.75 (0.89)	-0.54 (0.84)
Ideology	-0.09 (0.05)†	-0.11 (0.05)*	-0.09 (0.05)†	-0.11 (0.05)*
Vote top candidate				
One election	-0.25 (0.42)	-0.20 (0.43)	-0.24 (0.43)	-0.17 (0.43)
Both elections	-0.79 (0.33)*	-0.41 (0.36)	-0.78 (0.34)*	-0.43 (0.36)
No. of votes	-0.26 (0.09)**	-0.72 (0.09)***	-0.25 (0.09)**	-0.73 (0.09)***
Constant	3.94 (0.91)***	3.19 (0.85)***	4.30 (0.88)***	3.29 (0.92)***
Log-pseudo likelihood	-632.671		-630.381	
Pseudo-R^2	0.2571		0.2598	

Source: 2014 PartiRep Voter Survey.

Notes: ***$p < 0.001$; **$p < 0.01$; *$p < 0.05$; †$p < 0.10$. $N = 844$ (422 clusters, average cluster size = 2). Entries are the result of a cluster robust multinomial logistic regression analysis. All parameters were calculated in function of the reference category 'mixed vote'. In the federal elections, 250 respondents cast a same-sex vote, 160 cast a mixed vote and 216 cast a cross-sex vote. In the European elections, 234 respondents cast a same-sex vote, 133 cast a mixed vote and 198 cast a cross-sex vote.

vote, whereas women remain significantly more likely to cast a cross-gender vote. In sum, we find no empirical evidence to support the claim that women are more likely to cast a gender-based vote and we cannot confirm hypothesis 1. Instead, we find that men are systematically more likely to cast a vote for a candidate of the same sex, but that this gender gap can be largely explained by the composition of the ballot.

In addition, we investigated to what extent voters' age influences their voting behaviour. Age is important, because voters' experiences and voting habits are greatly determined by the environment in which they were raised. First, we hypothesised that, because voters are unlikely to change their voting habits, older men and younger women would be more likely to cast a gender-based vote (hypothesis 2a). Second, as older women are more likely to have some experience in being discriminated against, we hypothesised that this experience of convergence between individual and collective deprivation would encourage them to vote for a candidate of the same sex (hypothesis 2b). These expectations were tested by including an interaction term between sex and age (table 11.5, Model 2). No significant effect, however, could be detected. The propensity to cast a gender-based vote is not influenced by voters' age, and this holds for both men and women. To have an accurate interpretation of each interaction effect, we also plotted the marginal effects which supported the findings in Model 2 and offered no support for hypothesis 2a or hypothesis 2b (figure 11.1).

Moreover, we hypothesised that the sex of a candidate could serve as an informational cue for voters with low levels of political sophistication. On the one hand, we expected that gender-based voting would decrease with political sophistication (hypothesis 3a). On the other hand, we expected that for highly sophisticated women, the opposite might also be the case: highly sophisticated women could intentionally vote women into parliament to improve their descriptive representation (hypothesis 3b). These hypotheses

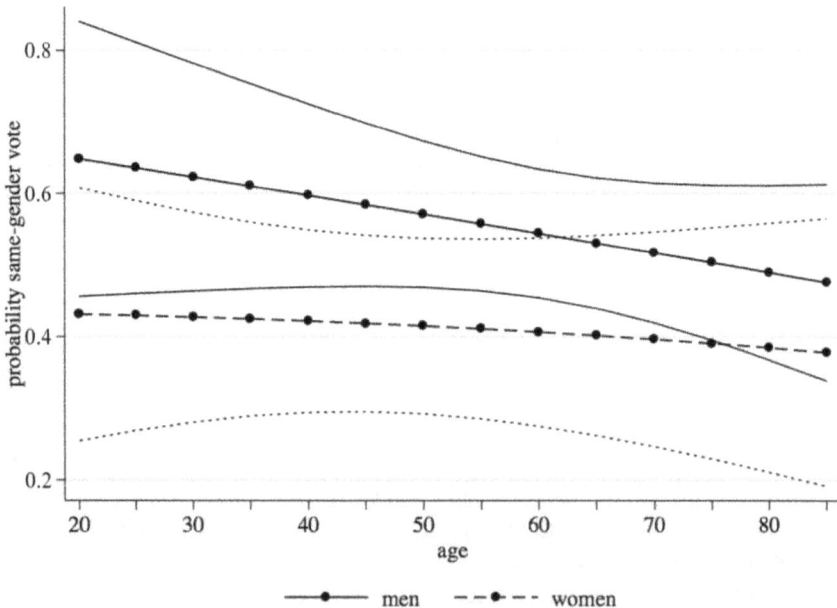

Figure 11.1.   Marginal probabilities of same-gender voting according to respondents' age.
Source: 2014 PartiRep Voter Survey.

Table 11.6. Explaining gender-based voting using individual-level characteristics (political sophistication)

	Model 3		Model 4	
	Same	Cross	Same	Cross
Political interest	-0.12 (0.06)*	-0.08 (0.05)	-0.07 (0.07)	-0.10 (0.07)
Political knowledge	-0.15 (0.10)	-0.04 (0.09)	-0.14 (0.10)	-0.03 (0.09)
Sex*Political interest			-0.10 (0.10)	0.01 (0.10)
Control variables				
Sex: female	-0.56 (0.23)*	1.31 (0.24)***	-0.03 (0.67)	1.31 (0.65)*
Age (ref. 18–31), in years				
32–42	-0.65 (0.42)	-0.25 (0.43)	-0.67 (0.42)	-0.26 (0.43)
43–59	0.18 (0.41)	0.37 (0.42)	0.17 (0.41)	0.35 (0.42)
>60	-0.48 (0.36)	0.33 (0.39)	-0.50 (0.36)	0.32 (0.39)
Education				
Lower secondary	-0.57 (0.77)	-0.25 (0.79)	-0.51 (0.76)	-0.36 (0.72)
Upper secondary	-0.74 (0.77)	-0.34 (0.80)	-0.70 (0.75)	0.45 (0.73)
Higher	-0.49 (0.75)	-0.25 (0.79)	-0.46 (0.73)	0.36 (0.72)
Ideology	-0.09 (0.05)†	-0.10 (0.05)*	-0.09 (0.05)†	-0.11 (0.05)*
Vote top candidate				
One election	-0.23 (0.41)	0.17 (0.43)	-0.23 (0.41)	0.19 (0.42)
Both elections	-0.73 (0.35)*	-0.44 (0.37)	-0.73 (0.35)*	-0.41 (0.37)
No. of votes	-0.24 (0.08)**	-0.71 (0.09)***	-0.24 (0.08)**	-0.73 (0.09)***
Constant	4.74 (0.91)***	3.06 (1.02)**	4.45 (0.92)***	3.79 (0.94)***
Log-pseudo likelihood	-626.223		-625.111	
Pseudo-R^2	0.2647		0.2660	

Source: 2014 PartiRep Voter Survey.

Notes: ***$p < 0.001$; **$p < 0.01$; *$p < 0.05$; †$p < 0.10$. $N = 844$ (422 clusters, average cluster size = 2). Entries are the result of a cluster robust multinomial logistic regression analysis. All parameters were calculated in function of the reference category 'mixed vote'.

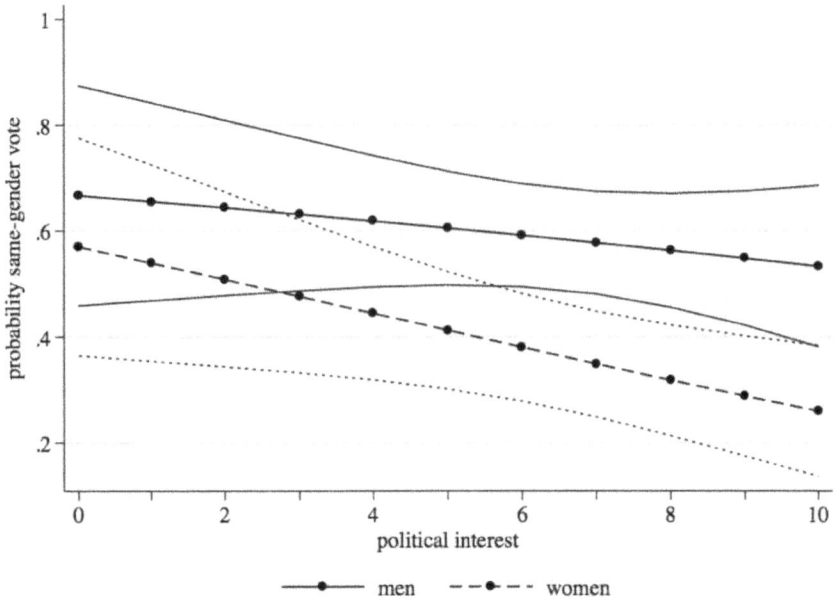

Figure 11.2. Marginal probabilities of same-gender vote according to political interest. Source: 2014 PartiRep Voter Survey.

were tested in table 11.6. Model 3 first evaluates the effect of political sophis-tication. The results indicate that there is indeed a significant negative effect on the motivational component of political sophistication, that is political interest, but that no discernible effect could be detected for the cognitive component, that is political knowledge. Hence the support for hypothesis 3a is mixed.

In order to evaluate hypothesis 3b, we included an interaction term between political interest and sex (displayed in Model 4 in table 11.6). Analogously to the interpretation of the interaction effect in table 11.5, we rely on the marginal effects analyses for the interpretation (see figure 11.2). Although the marginal effect does not display a significant value, the clear negative pattern for both male and female voters displayed in figure 11.2 does suggest that gender-based voting is the result of the application of an informational shortcut, rather than the result of a clear intention of highly sophisticated women to improve women's descriptive representation. Hypothesis 3b does not receive support.

Institutional determinants

In a last step, we investigate the influence of the institutional context. We theorised that other than the limited ability of low sophisticated voters to collect relevant information, the limited availability of information within the context of the second-order European elections would also increase the likelihood of casting a gender-based vote (hypothesis 4). The analysis displayed in Model 5 of table 11.7, however, provides little support for the assertion, as the likelihood of casting a same-gender vote in the European elections is not significantly different from that in the federal elections, that is hypothesis 4 does not receive any support. The habitual voting argument might offer an

Table 11.7. **Explaining gender-based voting using institutional factors**

	Model 5		Model 6	
	Same	*Cross*	*Same*	*Cross*
Sex: female	−0.34 (0.24)	1.42 (0.24)***	0.63 (0.54)	2.09 (0.63)***
Election: European	0.13 (0.27)	0.08 (0.26)	0.13 (0.24)	0.00 (0.26)
District magnitude	−0.00 (0.03)	−0.02 (0.03)	0.03 (0.03)	0.00 (0.04)
DM * Sex			−0.07 (0.04)†	−0.05 (0.05)
Control variables				
Age (ref. 18–31) in years				
32–42	− 0.78 (0.40)†	− 0.31 (0.42)	0.78 (0.40)†	− 0.30 (0.42)
43–59	0.01 (0.39)	0.39 (0.41)	− 0.00 (0.39)	0.28 (0.41)
60>	− 0.70 (0.35)*	0.20 (0.38)	− 0.71 (0.35)*	0.20 (0.39)
Ideology	−0.09 (0.05)†	−0.11 (0.05)*	−0.09 (0.05)†	−0.10 (0.05)*
Vote top candidate				
One election	− 0.25 (0.42)	0.21 (0.42)	− 0.26 (0.41)	0.20 (0.42)
Both elections	− 0.77 (0.34)*	− 0.38 (0.36)	− 0.77 (0.33)*	− 0.39 (0.36)
No. of votes	−0.26 (0.09)**	−0.73 (0.09)***	−0.26 (0.10)*	−0.73 (0.09)***
Education				
Lower secondary	− 0.66 (0.90)	− 0.38 (0.83)	− 0.66 (0.91)	− 0.38 (0.83)
Upper secondary	− 0.84 (0.91)	− 0.50 (0.84)	− 0.84 (0.91)	− 0.50 (0.84)
Higher	− 0.75 (0.91)	− 0.50 (0.84)	− 0.75 (0.92)	− 0.50 (0.85)
Constant	3.90 (0.92)***	3.40 (0.94)**	3.50 (0.92)**	3.12 (1.01)*
Log-pseudo likelihood	−632.019		−630.542	
Pseudo-R^2	0.2579		0.2596	

Source: 2014 PartiRep Voter Survey.

Notes: ***$p < 0.001$; **$p < 0.01$; *$p < 0.05$; †$p < 0.10$. N = 844 (422 clusters) Entries are the result of a cluster robust multinomial logistic regression analysis. All parameters were calculated in function of the reference category 'mixed vote'.

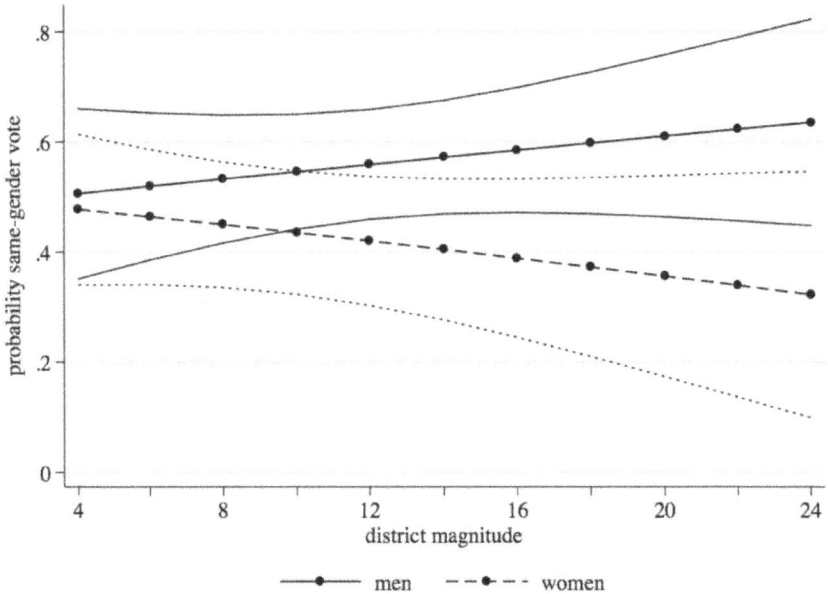

Figure 11.3.   Marginal probabilities of same-gender voting according to district magnitude. Source: 2014 PartiRep Voter Survey.

explanation here. Voters might display the same voting habits for the two elections, which could explain why we observe similar gendered voting patterns across levels despite the different information environments.

Finally, we investigate whether a larger district magnitude acts more favourably upon the election of women by women by including an interaction term between district magnitude and sex. While Model 6 shows that this interaction is indeed significant, the marginal effects analysis in figure 11.3 displays no significant results. Similarly, there appears to be no indication suggesting that larger district magnitude increases the probability for women to cast a same-gender vote. Instead, the opposite appears to be the case: for men, the probability slightly increases (non-significantly) with district magnitude, whereas for women the probability slightly decreases (non-significantly). This leads us to reject hypothesis 5.

CONCLUSION

This chapter examined whether there is such a thing as 'gender-based voting' in Belgium. Are voters more likely to cast preference votes for candidates of their own gender? Because of the high supply of women on candidate lists, the system of multiple preferential voting and the history of accommodating social difference in society, we expected Belgium to be a 'likely case' for gender-based voting. However, evidence is mixed. Patterns of gender-based voting identified in the 2014 federal and European elections in Belgium were not that strong, and men proved far more likely to cast a gender-based vote than women. Additional variation in gender-based voting is furthermore not easily explained. Voters' age and levels of political sophistication did not affect patterns of gender-based voting, and neither did the type of elections and district magnitude.

The bottom line of most of our findings is that gender-based vote from the part of female voters (i.e. women opting to vote for women) is still limited as a phenomenon, and certainly much more limited than the phenomenon of voters – both male and female – casting a vote for male candidates. This means that the introduction of gender parity quotas in the Belgian context has not yet led citizens to deeply change some quite traditional patterns in their voting behaviour. On the one hand, the political elites, and party selectorates in particular, have indeed complied with the quotas. In this regard, the quotas have had a very strong impact, even if their implementation is frequently tweaked in favour of male candidates. The more frequent presence of male candidates in the top-of-the-list position is, for instance, one of the indications of this. On the other hand, the voters – and female voters in particular – have not seized the new situation and have not strongly engaged in strategic voting in the favour of female candidates. This is, of course, a rather strong limitation in terms of the effect of the gender quotas, that is in terms of the actual proportion of female politicians being elected.

There are multiple potential explanations for this state of affairs. Here we just discuss a few, for which further research, through both surveys and more qualitative approaches, would be necessary. To start with, one question that remains to be empirically assessed is the extent to which Belgian women actually perceive that they have a deprived status (compared to men) in society, the extent to which this has made them gender-conscious and, more importantly (for this chapter), to what extent this gender-consciousness is strong enough to clearly shape their voting behaviour more in favour of female candidates.

Further, another hypothesis we could formulate is that voting in favour of female candidates is a form of 'strategic voting'. If that is the case, it means that the potential public that is likely to engage in such a voting behaviour needs to meet two characteristics: (1) having a high cultural capital and a high level of political information and sophistication and (2) being 'culturally liberal' and, in particular, gender-conscious. However, this public only constitutes a small proportion of the whole electorate, at least in the current Belgian society (Rihoux, Meulewaeter & Baudewyns 2014), and therefore the overarching picture of the median Belgian voter is still that of a not-so-strategic voter and not-so-gender-conscious.

Next, turning to the party-political and institutional context: the fact that the party lists are so numerous given the multiparty nature of the Belgian political system, and the fact that the lists of candidates are frequently quite long (at least in the larger constituencies) encourages voters to cast a list vote, and not a 'strategic' vote in favour of female candidates. The particular context of the 2014 elections could also have played a role: as these were simultaneous regional, federal and European elections, this could have produced a sort of 'fatigue' of the voters, also leading them to cast a list vote – except for the smaller proportion of more politicised or more strategic voters, as discussed earlier.

These Belgian findings speak well to the emerging literature on gender-based voting such as the recent study of gender-based voting in Finland, where, in a similar vein, stronger same-gender voting patterns among men have been identified (Holli & Wass 2010; Giger et al. 2014). This study echoes their findings that institutional factors might go a long way in explaining gender-based voting among men, particularly the crucial role of ballot composition. This study, furthermore, adds to this in that it shows that exploratory frameworks such as habitual voting and strategic voting need to be taken into consideration in future studies trying to explain gender-based voting.

REFERENCES

Ballmer-Cao, T. H. and Tremblay, M. (2008) 'Modes de scrutin, partis politiques et élection des femmes: une introduction', *Swiss Political Science Review*, 14(4): 609–33.

Caul, M. (1999) 'Representation in Parliament: The Role of Political Parties', *Party Politics*, 5(1): 79–99.

Childs, S. and Lovenduski, J. (2013) 'Political Representation', in G. Waylen, K. Celis, J. Kantola and L. Weldon (eds) *The Oxford Handbook of Gender and Politics*, Oxford: Oxford University Press, 489–513.

Dahlerup, D. (ed.) (2006) *Women, Quotas and Politics*, Abingdon: Routledge.

Dolan, K. (2004) 'The Impact of Candidate Sex on Evaluations of Candidates for the US House of Representatives', *Social Science Quarterly*, 85(1): 206–17.

Dolan, K. (2008) 'Is there a "Gender Affinity Effect" in American Politics? Information, Affect and Candidate Sex in U.S. House Election', *Political Research Quarterly*, 61(1): 79–89.

Duncan, C. and Loretto, W. (2004) 'Never the Right Age? Gender and Age-Based Discrimination in Employment', *Gender, Work & Organization*, 11(1): 95–115.

Erzeel, S. and Caluwaerts, D. (2015) 'Is It Gender, Ideology or Resources? Individual-Level Determinants of Preferential Voting for Male and Female Candidates', *Journal of Elections, Public Opinion & Parties*, 25(3): 265–83.

Franklin, M. (2004) *Voter Turnout and the Dynamics of Electoral Competition in Established Democracies Since 1945*, Cambridge: Cambridge University Press.

Giger, N., Holli, A. M., Lefkofridi, Z. and Wass, H. (2014) 'The Gender Gap in Same-Gender Voting: The Role of Context', *Electoral Studies*, 35: 303–14.

Holli, A. M. and Wass, H. (2010) 'Gender-Based Voting in the Parliamentary Elections of 2007 in Finland', *European Journal of Political Research*, 49(5): 598–630.

Krook, M. L. and Zetterberg, P. (2014) 'Electoral Quotas and Political Representation: Comparative Perspectives', *International Political Science Review*, 35(1): 3–11.

Kunovich, S. (2012) 'Unexpected Winners: The Significance of an Open-List System on Women's Representation in Poland', *Politics & Gender*, 8(2): 153–77.

Luskin, R. C. (1990) 'Explaining Political Sophistication', *Political Behavior*, 12(4): 331–61.

Marien, S., Wauters, B. and Schouteden, A. (2017) 'Voting for Women in Belgium's Flexible List System', *Politics & Gender*, 13(2): 305–35.

Matland, R. (1993) 'Institutional Variables Affecting Female Representation in National Legislatures: The Case of Norway', *The Journal of Politics*, 55(3): 737–55.

McElroy, G. and Marsh, M. (2010) 'Candidate Gender and Voter Choice: Analysis from a Multimember Preferential Voting System', *Political Research Quarterly*, 63(4): 822–33.

Meier, P. (2012) 'From Laggard to Leader: Explaining the Belgian Gender Quotas and Parity Clause', *West European Politics*, 35(2): 362–79.

Paolino, P. (1995) 'Group-Salient Issues and Group Representation: Support for Women Candidates in the 1992 Senate Elections', *American Journal of Political Science*, 39(2): 294–313.

Plutzer, E. and Zipp, J. F. (1996) 'Identity Politics, Partisanship, and Voting for Women Candidates', *Public Opinion Quarterly*, 60(1): 30–57.

Reif, K. and Schmitt, H. (1980) 'Nine Second-Order National Elections – a Conceptual Framework for the Analysis of European Election Results', *European Journal of Political Research*, 8(1): 3–44.

Rihoux, B., Meulewaeter, C. and Baudewyns, P. (2014) 'L'électorat wallon, au-delà des enjeux socio-économiques: le libéralisme/conservatisme culturel compte-t-il?' in P. Baudewyns (ed.) *Etre électeur en Wallonie. Le comportement électoral des Wallons lors des élections législatives de 2007 et 2010*, Louvain-la-Neuve: Presses Universitaires de Louvain, 121–44.

Sanbonmatsu, K. (2002) 'Gender Stereotypes and Vote Choice', *American Journal of Political Science*, 46(1): 20–34.

Shugart, M., Valdini, M. E. and Suominen, K. (2005) 'Looking for Locals: Voter Information Demands and Personal Vote-Earning Attributes of Legislators under Proportional Representation', *American Journal of Political Science*, 49(2): 437–49.

Vandeleene, A. (2016) *Does Candidate Selection Matter? A Comparative Analysis of Belgian Political Parties' Selection Procedures and Their Relation to the*

Candidates' Profile, Université catholique de Louvain, Louvain-La-Neuve. [PhD dissertation].

Walker I. and Pettigrew T. (1984) 'Relative Deprivation Theory: An Overview and Conceptual Critique', *British Journal of Social Psychology*, 23(4): 301–10.

Wauters, B., Weekers, K. and Maddens, B. (2010) 'Explaining the Number of Preferential Votes for Women in an open-list PR system: An Investigation of the 2003 Federal Elections in Flanders (Belgium)', *Acta Politica*, 45(4): 468–90.

Appendix

Table 11.8. Summary statistics

Variable	N	Mean	Std Dev.	Min	Max
Elections: European	4,038	.5	.50	0	1
District magnitude	2,940	12.96	5.11	1	24
Age: 32–42 years	786	0.19		0	1
Age: 43–59 years	1,316	0.32		0	1
Age: >60 years	1,068	0.26		0	1
Left-right self-placement	3,942	4.94	2.09	0	10
Gender: female	4,038	.50	.50	0	1
Region: Wallonia	2940	.46	.50	0	1
Vote top candidate: one election	854	.31	.56	0	1
Vote top candidate: both	854	.54	.50	0	1
No. of preferential votes	4,038	1.50	4.70	0	56
Political interest	4,034	4.79	2.77	0	10
Political knowledge	4,038	2.19	1.46	0	5
Education: lower secondary	4,038	.22	.41	0	1
Education: higher secondary	4,038	.36	.48	0	1
Education: higher education	4,038	.34	.47	0	1

Chapter 12

The nature of preference voting: Disentangling the party and personal components of candidate choice

Audrey André, Sam Depauw
and Jean-Benoit Pilet

INTRODUCTION

Is it candidates or parties that people vote for? In modern democracies, the two are almost always closely intertwined and hard to disentangle. Ultimately, it is candidates that voters elect to the parliament. Yet, in most electoral systems, voters are not asked to make distinct choices for the party and the candidate they support (see Shugart 2005). Even in systems that do, most notably in preferential list systems, most of these candidates run on a party platform and in this sense a preference vote is always also a vote for the party (van Holsteyn and Andeweg 2010). Once elected, most act following a strict party discipline. Is it then the candidate or alternatively the party that matters most in the voter's mind? Put differently, is a preference vote really a *personal* vote? This latter concept specifically denotes 'the part of a candidate's vote share that is unique to him or her' (Coates 1995: 277; see also Cain, Ferejohn and Fiorina 1987). Conceptually, the critical question is whether the person or the candidate is capable of inducing the voter to cross party lines. Or could it possibly be that voters first decide on the party and only then settle on an individual candidate running under the party label (van Holsteyn and Andeweg 2012)?

The question directly links with one of the most important evolutions in electoral studies over the past twenty years. Whereas most of scholarly attention has focused on party choice, the growing debate on the personalisation of politics has put forward a shift from political parties towards the empowerment of individual politicians. Rooted in the global trend towards partisan dealignment and the advent of television, it is argued, the study of individual candidate traits in elections has gained more salience. One of the key indications in the debate is whether citizens cast a preference vote for individual

251

candidates more than in the past. Though the comparative evidence of per-sonalisation is mixed, Belgium stands out as a most affirmative case in this regard (Karvonen 2010). Yet, logically, prior to concluding on the growing salience of candidates on this basis is the puzzle of whether preference voting is nested within to voters' party choice (see Marsh 2007).

Using the data from the 2014 PartiRep Voter Survey, we contribute to the scholarly endeavour to conceptually disentangle the personal and party com-ponents of the preference vote. Not only is Belgium something of a case in point in the personalisation literature, as we explained, but the peculiarities of the Belgian electoral system also present a more straightforward case for our argument, compared to systems such as Finland, Poland or the Netherlands where voters can only mark a preference for a candidate. In Belgium, voters can either vote for the entire party list or alternatively mark a preference vote for one or more candidates within a party list. After setting out in more detail the rules and practices of preference voting in Belgium, the second section will critically build on the existent literature to develop clear expectations about the determinants of the personal vote, as distinct from preference voting in general. The third section presents the data, our measures, and – perhaps most interestingly – a first indication of the extent of the personal vote in Bel-gium. The fourth section introduces our key results, before discussing their implications in the conclusion.

PREFERENCE VOTING IN BELGIUM: RULES AND PRACTICE

The Belgian electoral system could be qualified as a semi-open (or flexible) list PR system with optional preference voting. For the election of the federal House of Representatives, 150 MPs are elected in eleven districts of varying district magnitudes (ranging from three to twenty-four). Within each district, seats are allocated to lists applying PR D'Hondt, and then to candidates within lists. The allocation of seats within lists is determined on the basis of both list and preference votes.

Belgian voters have the option to cast a vote for the entire party list with-out marking any candidate preference, or to cast preference votes for one or several candidates. The ballot paper presents one column for each party list[1] at the top a small box. Voters ticking that box cast a list vote and choose to support a party without intervening in the choice of candidates within the list. Their decision can be understood as an implicit approval of the party's rank-ing of candidates or as a disinterest for who will be sent to parliament. Voters who do want to have a say in who gets elected can try to change the party's predetermined order of candidates by ticking the box next to the name(s) of the candidate(s) they want to support. Voters can cast as many preference votes as there as seats to be filled in the district and can support both effective and substitute candidates. The latter candidates cannot be elected directly but their preference votes contribute to determining the ranking that applies in case one of the candidates elected on their party list resigns before the end of the legislative term.

The preference votes cast have no impact on the allocation of seats between parties. They only affect who is elected within a party list. After determining the number of seats each list has obtained, a Droop quota is calculated equalling the number of votes the party won in the district divided by its number of seats plus one. Candidates whose preference vote tally exceeds this eligibility threshold are directly elected. To allocate the remaining seats, list votes are transferred to the candidate occupying the first position on the list until he or she reaches the eligibility threshold. The remaining list votes are then transferred to the second candidate on the list and so on. When half of the list votes have been redistributed and more seats are to be allocated, the remaining candidates are elected in the order of the preference votes they polled irrespective of their position on the party list.

One important mechanical consequence of the previously mentioned rules is that the system clearly works to the advantage of those candidates occupying the top positions on the lists. Between 1945 and 1991, only 23 of the 3,382 members of the House of Representatives would not have been elected if not for their preference votes (Dewachter 2003). In 2000, the weight of preference votes in the allocation of seats increased significantly by stipulating that not all but only half of the list votes cast would be redistributed to the first-listed candidates. In the 2003 general election alone, for instance, no less than eighteen elected candidates leapfrogged past higher-ranked co-partisans (André et al. 2017). These figures suggest however that the semi-open list system used in Belgium is still more akin to a closed than an open list system.

Nevertheless, previous studies have shown that the personal nature of elections in Belgium is very important. Despite its relatively limited impact on who gains a seat in parliament, the majority of Belgian voters do express a candidate preference. The use of preference votes has steadily increased over time in Belgium as could be seen in figure 12.1 (see Wauters, Weekers and Pilet, 2004; Wauters and Weekers, 2008). After World War I less than a fifth of the electorate opted for a preference vote. In the late 1970s and early 1980s this number already reached 50 per cent. In recent elections around two-thirds of the electorate decided to mark an intra-party candidate choice. This is a particularly large share when compared to other European countries using semi-open list systems: 22 per cent in Sweden (2006), 27 per cent in Austria (2013) and 44 per cent in the Czech Republic (2010) (André and Depauw 2016).

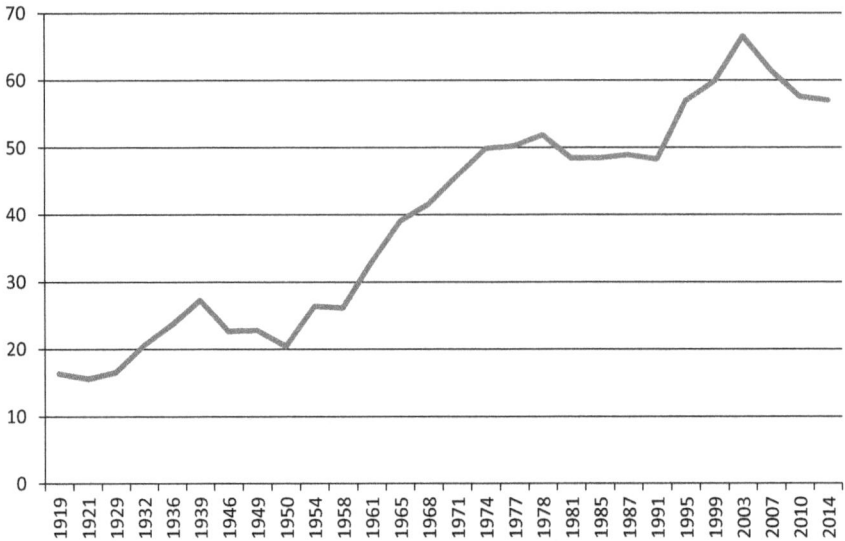

Figure 12.1. The use of preference voting in Belgian elections

Note. st. dev.: Standard deviation.

Candidates on their part invest a lot of resources in campaigning to attract preference votes. About 44 per cent of the candidates, De Winter and Baudewyns (2015) estimated, ran a mainly personalised campaign in the 2007 general elections, 56 per cent contributing only to the party campaign. Three-quarters of the candidates, moreover, had personal posters, personal ads in the local press, personal flyers and/or their own website. The scope of their efforts, studies indicate, is determined mainly by their electoral incentives in the short and in the long term. The bills parliamentarians in Belgium initiate (Bräuninger, Brunner and Däubler 2012), and the time they spend in the constituency (André, Depauw and Martin 2015), as well as their efforts promoting local projects and meeting with local interest groups (André and Depauw 2013), can all be explained by the incentive to court preference votes. Candidates who obtain more preference votes are further rewarded by political parties with higher positions on the party list in the next election (André et al. 2017).

All these elements point towards a very personalised nature of Belgian elections. However, we still do not know much about the actual magnitude of personal voting. Are Belgian voters really motivated by candidates and their personal characteristics? Alternatively, does the candidate remain a second-order factor that comes only after the choice of the party? One recent study (Däubler, Bräuninger and Brunner 2016) finds that Belgian voters reward assiduous legislative activity. Yet, as to whether legislators' efforts really succeed in chasing non-aligned voters and convincing them to cross party lines, or alternatively whether they only mobilise the party faithful to vote for one of the party's candidates, we continue to be in the dark.

HYPOTHESES

To answer this important question, we need to conceptually separate the personal and party components of preference voting. By bridging two literatures that thus far have developed in isolation, we can deduce a number of theoretical expectations about the factors that determine a voter's propensity to cast not a preference but a personal vote – that is, the likelihood that the candidate outweighs the party in his or her voting calculus. One strand of literature has inquired into the personalisation of voting behaviour; the other has focused on the personal vote-seeking efforts on the part of politicians. Combining the two, we argue that personal voting can be explained by the voter's partisanship, the timing of the decision and the nature of campaigning in a particular setting.

The first factor to examine in that respect is party identification. The very notion of a personal vote suggests that it is independent from the party. While some voters decide on the basis of their partisan affiliation, the government's performance or the state of the economy, others decide on the basis of their evaluation of a candidate's individual qualifications, qualities or behaviour (Cain, Ferejohn and Fiorina 1987: 9). It can therefore be reasoned that, if captured correctly, the personal vote should be related to that growing part of the electorate who lack a firm party identification (see also André, Depauw and Beyens 2015). A major component of the personal vote, Cain, Ferejohn and Fiorina (1987) noted, is the incumbent's constituency service – a reputation for accessibility that is especially important to independents and partisans of other parties. Kam (2009) similarly observed that voters with weak partisan attachments respond far more positively to MPs breaking ranks with the party than voters with strong partisan attachments. These various elements led to the formulation of the following hypothesis:

Hypothesis 1: The propensity to cast a personal vote increases as voters' party attachment weakens.

Waning party identifications have also led a growing number of voters in recent decades to delay their decision until the later stages of the campaign (Dalton and Wattenberg 2000; Fournier et al. 2004; Norris et al. 1999). The timing of a voter's decision is fundamentally related to his or her vote (Blumenstiel and Plischke 2015). Previous studies indicate that late deciders have weaker partisan attachments than those who decide long before the campaign starts and who rely more on long-term, partisan cues. Beyond differences in partisanship, however, scholars disagree on any enduring demographic, attitudinal or behavioural differences between the two. The reason is the heterogeneity found among late deciders: some with little or no interest in politics put off making a decision until Election Day forces them to do so, while others delay their decision until all the evidence concerning the campaign, the candidates and their positions is in (see also Gopoian and Hadjiharalambous 1994; Kogen and Gottfried 2011). We therefore expect the impact of the time of decision to be mediated by voters' political sophistication: especially among political sophisticates, late deciders should be more candidate-centred. Among non-sophisticates, there is probably not much of a relationship between the time of the decision and the decision itself.

Hypothesis 2: The propensity to cast a personal vote is higher among the late deciders than among the early deciders, but only for those with high levels of political sophistication.

In addition, the cues that the voters rely on largely depend on the information made available to them. That is certainly the conclusion offered by experimental studies (Canache, Mondak and Cabrera 2000): if given personal information about candidates, voters will respond to it. We may expect the nature of the campaign, most notably differences in personalised campaign efforts, to have an impact. From previous studies, we know that candidates of right-wing parties, candidates of mainstream parties and candidates in rural areas tend to run more personalised campaigns. We may therefore expect these factors also to be reflected among candidate-centred voters.

First, the literature has also strongly emphasised that personalised campaigns are a strategic response on the part of candidates to the electoral system and whether attracting a personal vote would improve their probability of (re)election (André, Depauw and Martin 2016; Carey and Shugart 1995; Giebler and Wessels 2013). Personalised campaign norms also translate into the issues covered by the campaign, the campaign organisation and campaign spending (see Zittel 2015). In addition, there are important differences between political parties. Campaign norms across fifteen countries, André, Depauw and Martin (2016) found, gravitate more towards attracting attention for the candidate's person in the parties of the right than in the parties of the left. Giebler and Wessels (2013) similarly noted that leftist parties tend to have more of a tradition of the mass party and a strong collectivist discipline (see also Lisi and Santana-Pereira 2014). Given that candidates of right-wing parties run more personalised campaigns, it can be argued that party ideology should impact the personal vote. That is, a right-wing voter's propensity to decide on the basis of the candidate should be greater than a left-wing voter's.

Hypothesis 3: The propensity to cast a personal vote is higher for voters of right-wing parties than for those of left-wing parties.

Mainstream parties, moreover, run more personalised campaigns than niche parties (see Cross and Young 2015; Eder, Jenny and Müller 2015; Papp and Zorigt 2016; Zittel and Gschwend 2008). The difference may be one of size and organisational strength (Zittel and Gschwend 2008): candidates in smaller, niche parties have fewer resources and therefore fall back on the party campaign. The difference can also be related to niche parties being more ideology-driven (see D'Alimonte 1999; Kitschelt 1994): while mainstream parties respond to shifts in the mean voter position, Ezrow et al. (2011) found, niche parties across fifteen countries are most responsive to their partisan supporters. Niche parties are also punished at the polls for moderating their positions, while mainstream parties were not similarly penalised, suggesting that niche parties represent extremist ideological electorates (Adams et al. 2006). Again, we may expect niche party electorates to be more party-centred voters and mainstream party electorates more candidate-centred voters.

Hypothesis 4: The propensity to cast a personal vote is higher for voters of mainstream parties than for those of niche parties.

There are also important differences between districts. Most notably, candidates run more personalised campaigns in rural than in urban areas. In rural Austria, Eder, Jenny and Müller (2015) observe, candidates more fre-quently raise issues ignored by the party than in the urban centres; they also have more activists in their team who would not campaign for the party. The geographical distinction, they point out, is a proxy for differences in social relations and communication. In rural areas, social interaction is more per-sonal, facilitating a personal rapport with the target population (Baybeck and Huckfeldt 2002; Huckfeldt and Sprague 1995). Similar differences between rural and urban districts are reported in Canada (Cross and Young 2015) and Ireland (Marsh 2007).

Hypothesis 5: The propensity to cast a personal vote increases as the area a voter lives in grows more rural.

Finally, and also within the perspective of supply-side determinants, one could expect that candidates' qualities would affect personal voting. The supply of candidates is not uniform in all districts. Some voters are exposed to well-known figures running in their district. Others would only have less prominent politicians on their ballot. And that difference is not without consequence. Studies on personalisation have shown that the growing role of individual politicians is for the most important part due to the growing role of a handful of political leaders (Balmas et al. 2014). Poguntke and Webb (2005) refer to it as the presidentialisation of politics. Leaders are the ones triggering personal votes, the ones who are able to attract voters to vote for them and for their parties (Aarts, Blais and Schmitt 2011; Bittner 2011). Local candidates may also do it (Mattes and Milazzo 2014) but they tend to be dominated by leaders in attracting personal voters. In a recent study, Wauters and his colleagues (2016) have actually shown that when it comes to preference votes in the Belgian federal elections of 2014, there is even a trend of fewer voters casting preference votes when on the ballot there is no leader running. In such circumstances, more and more Belgian voters prefer to cast a list vote rather than to cast a vote for another, less prominent, candidate. Again, preference votes and personal votes are not identical. But it gives weight to the hypothesis that we would observe more personal voting in districts where party leaders are running than in other districts.

Hypothesis 6: The propensity to cast a personal vote is higher for voters supporting a list featuring the party leader.

THE EXTENT OF THE PARTY AND PERSONAL VOTE IN BELGIUM

Measuring the personal vote is a complex task. Most studies so far have focused on politicians' effort – during the campaign or over the legislative term – to build up a personal reputation that is strong and distinct from their party's image (see André, Depauw. and Shugart 2014, for a review). By contrast, measuring the personal vote at the level of voters has proven to be much more difficult. Some scholars have tried to measure it indirectly by comparing the aggregate electoral scores of candidates across districts (Swindle 2002) or across tiers in mixed-member electoral systems (Moser and Scheiner 2005). Better performances by some candidates compared to their co-partisans then provide some indication that they enjoy a personal vote. Opting for a more direct approach, a few studies have tried to measure the personal vote on the basis of survey data. Voters have, for instance, been asked to score the importance of particular candidates in their voting decision, to attribute sympathy scores to candidates or to directly indicate the relative importance of party and candidates in their vote choice (Marsh 2007; Karp et al. 2002). Although these questions are not perfect in disentangling the salience of candidate and party characteristics in voters' decision calculus, they have the distinct advantage of being straightforward and applicable in a wide range of institutional contexts.

Therefore, in this study, we measure the personal vote by directly asking individuals whether in their mind the party or the candidate was most decisive for their vote. Evidence from single transferable vote systems further suggests that this direct closed-ended question, better than open-ended questions, approximates inferences drawn from behaviour in the polling booth (Marsh 2007). In the 2014 PartiRep Voter Survey, respondents were invited to indicate, on an 11-point scale, 'which was most important in determining your vote choice, the candidate(s) or the party'. In the initial question wording, 0 equalled 'only the candidate is important' and 10 'only the party'. Because our principal aim is to identify the personal voters, for ease of interpretation, we reversed the scale in figure 12.2.

Figure 12.2 reports the distribution of respondents, indicating the considerable heterogeneity in this respect. The 11-point scale reflects that to many, if not to most, voters, both party and person matter. But there are clear differences where they put the emphasis. Those indicating values 0 to 5 feel that the party is most decisive, certainly more decisive than the candidate(s).

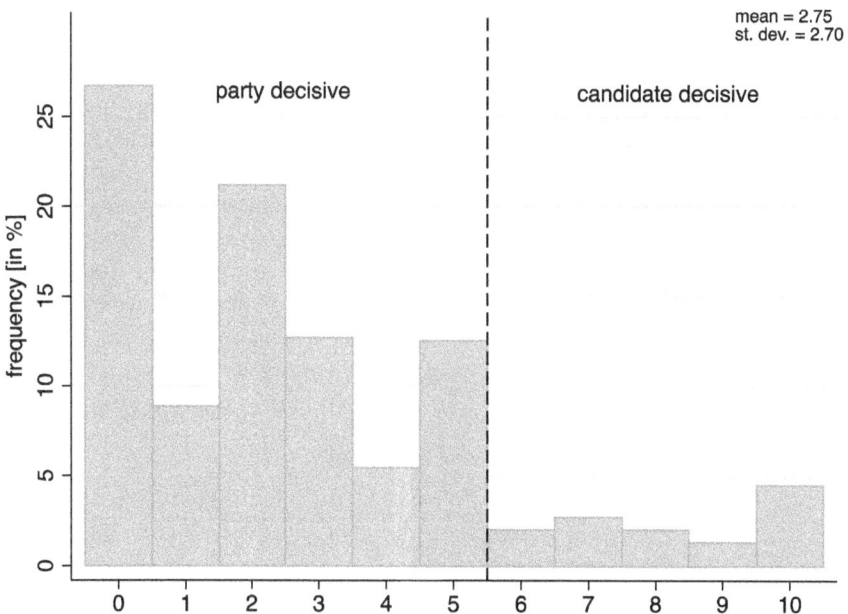

Figure 12.2. Distribution of the 11-point decisiveness scale

Note. st. dev.: Standard deviation.

They constitute by far the largest number: 87.9 per cent of the electorate. By contrast, those indicating values 6 to 10 think the candidate more decisive than the party. We use the more conservative definition of the personal vote, equating equal importance (i.e. values of 5) with a party-centred vote. Candidate-centred voters are a minority even in the context of the flexible list system used in electing parliamentarians in Belgium: 12.1 per cent of the voters are candidate-centred, the candidate outweighing in their mind the party list he or she ran on. While the number of candidate-centred voters is marginally larger in Flanders than in Wallonia, the difference is not statistically significant by any standard. Their number is roughly comparable to the 9 per cent candidate-centred voters in the Netherlands using a similar electoral system (van Holsteyn and Andeweg 2010). Yet it is distinctly lower than the 59 per cent of the Irish voters in the single-transferable-vote system (Marsh 2007).

The voter in Belgium has the option to either cast a list vote for a party or a preference vote for one or more candidates, provided they run under the same party label. This particular feature of the ballot structure allows us to make the distinction between such a preference vote and the personal vote. Table 12.1 cross-tabulates the two. Just under half of the voters are decidedly party-centred: they vote for the party list and the party is the most decisive factor in their decision. By contrast, 39 per cent cast a preference vote but considers the party more decisive than the candidate in their decision. Their preference vote does not amount to a personal vote in the strictest sense of the literature: that is, it is intertwined with, rather than independent from, the party label the candidate runs under (see Cain, Ferejohn and Fiorina 1987). A preference vote is also always a vote for the party and to a large number of voters the party continues to be the most important element in that particular equation.

Just over 10 per cent are decidedly candidate-centred: they support an individual candidate and consider that candidate the most important factor in their decision. Their vote constitutes a *direct* personal vote, in some sense irrespective of the party. There is also an *indirect* personal vote, when voters decide on the party because of the candidate(s) who run(s) under its label even if they do not run in their district. N-VA voters, for instance, frequently

Table 12.1. The extent of personal voting in Belgium

		Type of vote	
		List vote	Preference vote
Most decisive factor	Party	48.4	39.0
	Candidate	2.1	10.5

Note: List-wise deletion of observations with missing values on either the dependent or independent variables resulted in a final sample of 1,285 respondents.

Table 12.2. The share of personal and party voters per party

| | | Candidate decisive, % | | |
	Party decisive, %	Indirect personal vote	Direct personal vote	N
Flemish parties				
CD&V	83.1	3.1	13.9	130
Open VLD	74.5	0.9	24.5	106
SP.a	95.6	2.2	2.2	91
Groen	95.8	1.4	2.8	72
N-VA	90.8	3.1	6.1	263
VB	100.0	0.0	0.0	16
PVDA	95.0	0.0	5.0	20
LDD	0.0	25.0	75.0	4
Walloon parties				
cdH	77.4	2.7	19.8	107
MR	87.8	2.2	10.1	139
PS	85.9	1.6	12.5	192
Ecolo	90.2	0.0	9.8	61
FDF	100.0	0.0	0.0	12
PTB	93.0	2.3	4.7	43
PP	100.0	0.0	0.0	29

refer to its leader Bart De Wever as the decisive factor in their decision, but end up casting a list vote if they live in a constituency other than Antwerp where De Wever ran. Others referred to the help they got from a CD&V politician who ran for the Flemish Parliament. They cast a list vote for her party in the general election too. Taken together, about 2.1 per cent cast such an indirect personal vote. The indirect personal vote, table 12.2 confirms, is slightly more common among the N-VA and CD&V electorates, as the illustrations attest, but also among cdH voters, for instance. All in all, the direct personal vote is most pronounced in the traditional party families, with the notable exception of the SP.a. The electorates of the new regionalist, green, and far-left parties are by contrast more party-centred.

WHO CASTS A PERSONAL VOTE?

In the previous section, we have been able to evaluate the extent of the personal vote in Belgium, and to differentiate it from preference votes. The next step is to draw a more accurate picture of the main differences between voters casting a personal versus a party vote. The dependent variable, whether people vote for the party or for the candidate, is operationalised as a dichotomous indicator best modelled using logistic regression, although we first determined that OLS regression of the 11-point scale would yield very similar findings. The skewed nature of the variable, however, violates the assumption of normality and may thus reduce confidence in the OLS point estimates. The dichotomy is also more straightforward to grasp and is thus preferred. Key independent variables include the voter's party identification, time of the decision and standard demographic and attitudinal controls (gender, age, education and political sophistication). They further include indicators pertaining to the nature of the campaign, like party ideology, party type and the urban/rural character of the district. Table 12.3 reports the logistic regression parameter estimates and measures of model fit.

Before turning to the core of our argument, a few preliminary observations ought to be made. We find that standard demographic and attitudinal controls like gender, education or political sophistication do not have an effect. We do find an effect of age, however: the relationship, it seems, is curvilinear, candidate-centeredness being least pronounced in the younger and the older age cohorts and peaking at the age of 51. The finding in some sense contradicts the argument present in the literature on preference voting that especially older, but also younger, voters should prefer to vote for a candidate who shares their age-based group identity (André, Wauters and Pilet 2012; Bengtsson et al. 2014). The contrast only serves to underline the importance of the conceptual distinction between preference voting and the personal vote.

More central to our argument, we find that party identification has the expected effect. Non-partisans are more candidate-centred, confirming our first hypothesis. In both the bivariate and the multivariate specifications, the coefficient is negative and statistically significant. Those voters who have a strong partisan attachment, by contrast, are more party-centred and find the party the most decisive factor in their decision. The staunchest party identifiers have a probability of the candidate being decisive for their decision of only 9 per cent, a reduction by 7 per cent compared to non-partisans. This finding that the 'personal voters' who largely rely on candidate cues are more likely to be weak and non-partisans is certainly in line with the very definition of the personal vote.

Second, as suggested in our second hypothesis, we also find that people whose voting choice is resolved only in the later stages of the campaign are also more candidate-centred. People who have made their decision long before the campaign starts, decide more often on the basis of the party. The time of the decision, in sum, has an effect on the voting behaviour itself: candidate-centred voting requires information about the candidates that becomes available only during the course of the campaign. The main effect is positive and significant (Model 1). But, as expected, there is also evidence

Table 12.3. The determinants of personal voting

	Bivariate		Model 1		Model 2	
	b.	s.e.	b.	s.e.	b.	s.e.
Female	-0.253	(0.198)	-0.281	(0.220)	-0.259	(0.219)
Age	0.088	(0.036)*	0.098	(0.037)**	0.095	(0.037)**
Age²	-0.001	(0.000)*	-0.001	(0.000)**	-0.001	(0.000)*
Education	-0.001	(0.097)	-0.070	(0.104)	-0.075	(0.103)
Political knowledge	0.115	(0.062)#	0.122	(0.071)#	-0.110	(0.093)
Late deciders	0.635	(0.219)**	0.660	(0.251)**	-0.195	(0.371)
– * Political knowledge					0.361	(0.122)**
Left–right position	0.090	(0.039)*	0.148	(0.046)**	0.153	(0.045)***
Party identification	-0.181	(0.071)*	-0.158	(0.080)*	-0.157	(0.079)*
New party	-0.910	(0.217)***	-1.000	(0.210)***	-0.969	(0.208)***
Party leader on list	0.727	(0.206)***	0.942	(0.220)***	0.926	(0.223)***
Population density	-0.699	(0.217)**	-0.488	(0.209)*	-0.496	(0.209)*
Constant			-3.713	(1.065)***	-3.100	(1.099)**
N	1,285		1,285		1,285	
Pseudo log-likelihood			-401.8		-398.4	
LR(df)			87.59	(11)***	94.48	(12)***
Pseudo-R^2			0.10		0.11	

Note: Entries are the parameter estimates of logistic regression models as well as the models' likelihood ratio test (LR). The standard errors (s.e.) (in parentheses) are clustered by municipality.

#$p \leq 0.1$; *$p \leq 0.05$; **$p \leq 0.01$; ***$p \leq 0.001$, using two-tailed t-values.

of an interaction effect that strongly suggests that the personal vote is not more fickle. Model 2 demonstrates that the positive effect of the time of the decision is noticeable chiefly among the more sophisticated voters. The interaction term in Model 2 is positive and significant. For ease of interpretation, moreover, figure 12.3 plots the predicted probabilities of being candidate-centred for different values of political sophistication among the two groups of early and late deciders. While among the early deciders the impact of political sophistication on the probability of a candidate-centred vote is negligible, there emerges from the analysis a substantial number of sophisticated late deciders weighing all the information about candidates and voting not for the party, but for the candidate. Within the group of late deciders, figure 12.3 illustrates, sophisticates are over 16 percentage points more likely to decide on the basis of the candidate than non-sophisticated voters (26 per cent compared to 10 per cent).

Third, the evidence strongly suggests that the extent of personal vote-seeking on the part of candidates impacts voters' calculus. Extensive personalised campaigning has the ability to increase the information available to voters about candidates and thereby also voters' likelihood to decide on the basis of candidate cues. Personal campaigning in Belgium, as explained earlier, has been shown to be more frequent among right-wing as well as among mainstream parties. Indeed, we find that those voters supporting parties of

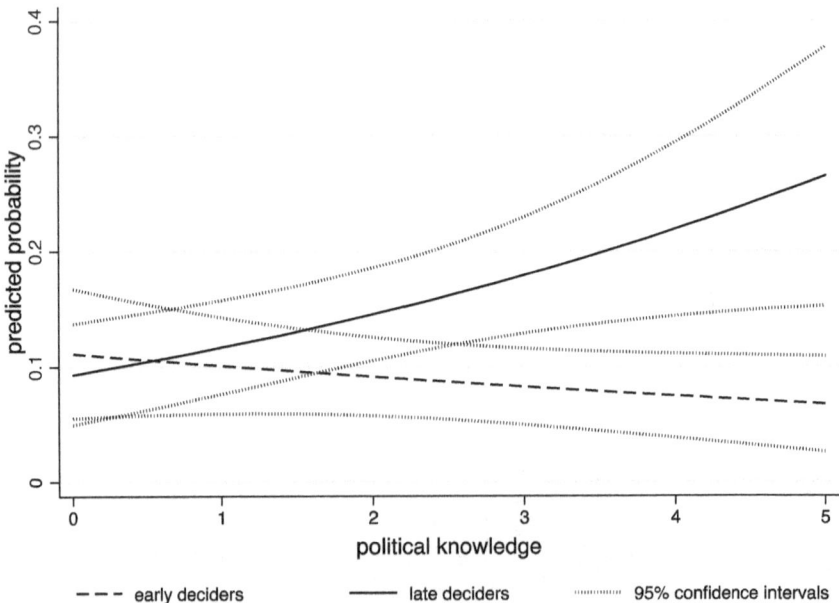

Figure 12.3. **The mediating effect of political knowledge**

the right are more candidate-centred, whereas supporters of the left are more party-centred, confirming our third hypothesis. The coefficient, table 12.3 attests, is positive and significant. If anything, controlling for alternative explanations in Models 1 and 2 only strengthens the effect of party ideology. Those on the far right of the political spectrum have a probability of 22 per cent to be candidate-centred, an increase by 16 per cent compared to those on the far left and one of the strongest effects found.

Mainstream party candidates also run more personalised campaigns than candidates running under a niche party's label. Again, the evidence strongly supports the view expressed by our fourth hypothesis that supporters of mainstream parties are also more candidate-centred, while those who vote for a niche party tend to be more party-centred. The coefficient in table 12.3 is negative and one of the most significant effects found. The probability of casting a personal vote is 17 per cent among mainstream party supporters and only 7 per cent among supporters of niche parties. The latter, as previous studies have pointed out, are more ideology-driven and less forgiving of candidates who in their personalised campaigns distance themselves from the party.

Finally, personalised campaigning tends to be more common in rural than in urban areas, supporting our fifth hypothesis. It is therefore reasonable that we find the personal vote is also larger in rural areas. The coefficient in table 12.3 is negative and significant, population density decreasing the propensity to cast a personal vote. Controlling for alternative explanations in Models 1 and 2 decreases the magnitude of the effect a little, but it continues to be significant at the conventional 5 per cent level. In the most densely populated urban centres, the voter's probability of deciding on the basis of the candidate is 8 per cent, but in the least populated areas his or her probability increases to 20 per cent, all things being equal. Taken together, the evidence strongly supports the view that when campaigning is most personalised, information available about the candidates will sway larger numbers of voters and prompt them to make a more candidate-centred, less party-centred, decision, thereby enlarging the magnitude of the personal vote.

We account for the personalised nature of the campaign in one final manner. In districts where the party leader heads the list in person, voters tend to be more candidate-centred. Personalised campaigning is also dependent on resources, the literature has argued, and extensive campaigns are frequently centred on the person of the party leader (Eder, Jenny and Müller 2015). This has led scholars to argue that by and large the growing trend towards the personalisation of politics is centralised on a handful of leaders in each country (Balmas et al. 2014; Karvonen 2010; see also the presidentialisation of politics, Poguntke and Webb 2007). To tap into this trend, we observe whether or not the leader of the party, for which the respondent votes, is on the ballot. In the district where the party leader is running, we find, his or her party's supporters are 13 percentage points more likely to find the candidate decisive than in the districts where the leader is not on the list (i.e. 23 per cent compared to 10 per cent). Again, these findings confirm our expectations (see hypothesis 6).

CONCLUSION

The personalisation of elections and of voting behaviour has been one of the rising themes in recent years in political science. Voters are said to be more and more motivated by candidates' traits in their decision how to vote. Belgium has been cited as a prime example of this evolution as the share of voters casting preference votes for specific candidates has been rising between 1919 and the early 2000s to peak around two-thirds of the electorate. However, we have demonstrated that assimilating preference votes to personal votes is highly misleading. While in the 2014 elections about half of the electorate in Belgium chose to cast a preference vote for at least one candidate, to many their decision as to which candidate to support was nested within their choice of party. Clearly, there is heterogeneity among voters in this regard. But the voters who decide on the basis of the party, we find, outnumber those who decide on the basis of the candidate about four to one. Predominantly, they pick a candidate from within the choice set of candidates running on their preferred party list. As such our findings lend support to Marsh's (2007) call to arms that closed-ended survey questions meaningfully capture the personal vote across different institutional contexts. Moreover, the magnitude of the personal vote we found in Belgium is in line with the literature, being decidedly smaller than in Ireland's STV (Marsh 2007) and in Finland's open-list system (Bengtsson et al. 2014).

Therefore, having shown that preference votes are clearly distinct from personal votes, this chapter has also tried to theorise which factors best differentiate those voters whose preference vote was primarily motivated by candidates from those led by party motives. Three sets of factors have been identified and shown to affect the personal vote in Belgium. First, weaker partisanship increases a voter's likelihood of casting a personal vote, firmly linking personal voting to the broader literature on partisan dealignment (Dalton 2013).

Second, we have identified a complex relationship between personal voting and political sophistication. Scholars disagree on the topic: some argue that mostly non-sophisticates vote for candidates (Lodge, McGraw and Stroh 1989); others say mostly sophisticated voters do (McGraw and Steenbergen 1995) and still others fail to find any effect (Hayes 2009). One reason, our findings suggest, is the heterogeneity among the electorate in this regard and its complex relationship identified with the timing of the decision. That is, among late deciders, politically sophisticated voters are more likely to vote for candidates than non-sophisticates – but not among early deciders.

Finally, the third set of factors is related to the nature of the campaign to which voters are exposed. First, more extensive personalised campaigning seems to increase voters' probability of casting a personal vote. Right-wing parties as well as mainstream parties have been shown in previous studies to run more intensive candidate-based campaigns. As a consequence, personal voters are more numerous in their electorate. In addition, it appears that candidates' visibility to voters is also important. Personal votes are more numerous when a prominent party leader is on the ballot in the voter's district.

What are the implications for party and candidate strategies? Whereas candidates seek (re)election, parties aim to maximise their seats in the legislature. As such, parties may benefit from candidates' personal vote-seeking, Crisp et al. (2013) argue, if these succeed in attracting non-partisan voters and thereby add to the party total. This is the reason why they reward personal vote-seeking with a higher position on the party list in the next election (see also André et al. 2017). After all, seat-maximising parties should be indifferent to the distribution of votes across its candidates, Bergman, Shugart and Watt (2013) agree, allowing *laissez-faire* intra-party competition. However, the ensuing equilibrium, our findings suggest, is not beneficial to the party. Co-partisan candidates have a strong incentive to compete for preference votes against one another first and foremost among the party's core supporters – if for no other reason than that they are easier to mobilise (see Scarrow 1994). By contrast, the share of the electorate that can be swayed by the candidates to cross party lines, our findings indicate, is small and difficult to get a hold of. Even though elections can be won or lost depending on a few percentage points, more often than not we should observe intensive personal campaigning on the part of candidates to little avail to the party (or even damaging the party record of cohesiveness). Political parties in the Netherlands, for instance, may have it right, actively dissuading candidates from running personal campaigns (see Andeweg 2005).

NOTE

1. For those voting on computer, the logic is slightly different. On a first screen they are supposed to tick which list they would like to vote for. Then, a second screen presents (only) the column with all candidates running for that list.

REFERENCES

Aarts, K., Blais, A. and Schmitt, H. (eds) (2011) *Political Leaders and Democratic Elections*, Oxford: Oxford University Press.

Adams, J., Clark, M., Ezrow, L. and Glasgow, G. (2006) 'Are Niche Parties Fundamentally Different from Mainstream Parties? The Causes and the Electoral Consequences of Western European Parties' Policy Shifts, 1976–1998', *American Journal of Political Science*, 50(3): 513–29.

Andeweg, R. B. (2005) 'The Netherlands: The Sanctity of Proportionality', in M. Gallagher and P. Mitchell (eds) *The Politics of Electoral Systems*, Oxford: Oxford University Press, 491–510.

André, A. and Depauw, S. (2016) 'District Magnitude and Home Styles of Representation in European Democracies', *West European Politics*, 36(5): 986–1006.

André, A., Depauw, S. and Beyens, S. (2015) 'Party Loyalty and Electoral Dealignment', *Party Politics*, 21(6): 970–81.

André, A., Depauw, S. and Martin, S. (2015) 'Electoral Systems and Legislators' Constituency Effort: The Mediating Effect of Electoral Vulnerability', *Comparative Political Studies*, 48(4): 464–96.

———. (2016) 'The Classification of Electoral Systems: Bringing Legislators Back in', *Electoral Studies*, 42: 42–53.

André, A., Depauw, S. and Shugart, M. S. (2014) 'The Effect of Electoral Institutions on Legislative Behavior', in S. Martin, T. Saalfeld and K. Strøm (eds) *The Oxford Handbook of Legislative Studies*, Oxford: Oxford University Press, 231–49.

André, A., Depauw, S., Shugart, M. S. and Chytilek, R. (2017) 'Party Nomination Strategies in Flexible-List Systems: Do Preference Votes Matter?' *Party Politics*, 23(25): 589–600. doi:10.1177/1354068815610974.

André, A., Wauters, B. and Pilet, J-B. (2012) 'It's Not Only about Lists: Explaining Preference Voting in Belgium', *Journal of Elections, Public Opinion & Parties*, 22(3): 293–313.

Balmas, M., Rahat, G., Sheafer, T. and Shenhav, S. R. (2014) 'Two Routes to Personalized Politics: Centralized and Decentralized Personalization', *Party Politics*, 20(1): 37–51.

Baybeck, B. and Huckfeldt, R. (2002) 'Urban Contexts, Spatially Dispersed Networks, and the Diffusion of Political Information', *Political Geography*, 21(2): 195–220.

Bengtsson, Å., Hansen, K. M., Hardarson, Ó. T., Narud, H. M. and Oscarsson, H. (2014) *The Nordic Voter: Myths of Exceptionalism*, Colchester: ECPR Press.

Bergman, M. E., Shugart, M. S. and Watt, K. A. (2013) 'Patterns of Intraparty Competition in Open-List & SNTV Systems', *Electoral Studies*, 32(2): 321–33.

Bittner, A. (2011) *Platform or Personality? The Role of Party Leaders in Elections*, Oxford: Oxford University Press.

Blumenstiel, J. E. and Plischke, T. (2015) 'Changing Motivations, Time of the Voting Decision, and Short-Term Volatility – the Dynamics of Voter Heterogeneity', *Electoral Studies*, 37: 28–40.

Bräuninger, T., Brunner, M. and Däubler, T. (2012) 'Personal Vote-Seeking in Flexible List Systems: How Electoral Incentives Shape Belgian MPs' Bill Initiation Behaviour', *European Journal of Political Research*, 51(5): 607–45.

Cain, B. E., Ferejohn, J. A. and Fiorina, M.P. (1987) *The Personal Vote: Constituency Service and Electoral Independence*, Cambridge, MA: Harvard University Press.

Canache, D., Mondak, J. J. and Cabrera, E. (2000) 'Voters and the Personal Vote: A Counterfactual Simulation', *Political Research Quarterly*, 53(3): 663–76.

Carey, J. M. and Shugart, M. S. (1995) 'Incentives to Cultivate a Personal Vote: A Rank Ordering of Electoral Formulas', *Electoral Studies*, 14(4): 417–39.

Coates, D. (1995) 'Measuring the "Personal Vote" of Members of Congress', *Public Choice*, 85(3–4): 227–48.

Crisp, B. F., Olivella, S., Malecki, M. and Sher, M. (2013) 'Vote-Earning Strategies in Flexible List Systems: Seats at the Price of Unity', *Electoral Studies*, 32(4): 658–69.

Cross, W. and Young, L. (2015) 'Personalization of Campaigns in an SMP System: The Canadian Case', *Electoral Studies*, 39: 306–15.

D'Alimonte, R. (1999) 'Party Behavior in a Polarized System: The Italian Communist Party and the Historic Compromise', in W. C. Müller and K. Strøm (eds) *Policy, Office, or Votes?* Cambridge: Cambridge University Press, 141–71.

Dalton, R. (2013) *The Apartisan American: Dealignment and Changing Electoral Politics*, Washington, DC: CQ Press.

Dalton, R. J. and Wattenberg, M. P. (eds) (2000) *Parties without Partisans: Political Change in Advanced Industrial Democracies*, Oxford: Oxford University Press.

Däubler, T., Bräuninger, T. and Brunner, M. (2016) 'Is Personal Vote-Seeking Behavior Effective?' *Legislative Studies Quarterly*, 41(2): 419–44.

De Winter, L. and Baudewyns, P. (2015) 'Candidate Centred Campaigning in a Party Centred Context: The Case of Belgium', *Electoral Studies*, 39: 295–305.

Dewachter, W. (2003) 'Elections, partis politiques et représentants. La quête d'une légitimité démocratique. 1919–2002', in E. Gubin, J-P. Nandrin, E. Gerard and E. Witte (eds) *Histoire de la Chambre des représentants en Belgique*, Brussels: Chambre des Représentants, 63–86.

Eder, N., Jenny, M. and Müller, W.C. (2015) 'Winning over Voters or Fighting Party Comrades? Personalized Constituency Campaigning in Austria', *Electoral Studies*, 39: 316–28.

Ezrow, L., De Vries, C., Steenbergen, M. and Edwards, E. (2011) 'Mean Voter Representation and Partisan Constituency Representation: Do Parties Respond to the Mean Voter Position or to Their Supporters?' *Party Politics*, 17(3): 275–301.

Fournier, P., Nadeau, R., Blais, A., Gidengil, E. and Nevitte, N. (2004) 'Time-of-Voting Decision and Susceptibility to Campaign Effects', *Electoral Studies*, 23(4): 661–81.

Giebler, H. and Wessels, B. (2013) 'Campaign Foci in European Parliamentary Elections: Determinants and Consequences', *Journal of Political Marketing*, 12(1): 53–76.

Gopoian, J. D. and Hadjiharalambous, S. (1994) 'Late-Deciding Voters in Presidential Elections', *Political Behavior*, 16(1): 55–78.

Hayes, D. (2009) 'Has Television Personalized Voting Behavior?' *Political Behavior*, 31(2): 231–60.

Huckfeldt, R. R. and Sprague, J. D. (1995) *Citizens, Politics, and Social Communication: Information and Influence in an Election Campaign*, Cambridge: Cambridge University Press.

Kam, C. J. (2009) *Party Discipline and Parliamentary Politics*, Cambridge: Cambridge University Press.

Karp, J., Vowles, J., Banducci, S. A. and Donovan, T. (2002) 'Strategic Voting, Party Activity, and Candidate Effects', *Electoral Studies*, 21: 1–22.

Karvonen, L. (2010) *The Personalisation of Politics: A Study of Parliamentary Democracies*, Colchester: ECPR Press.

Kitschelt, H. (1994) *The Transformation of European Social Democracy*, Cambridge: Cambridge University Press.

Kogen, L. and Gottfried, J. A. (2011) 'I Knew It All Along! Evaluating Time-of-Decision Measures in the 2008 U.S. Presidential Campaign', *Political Behavior*, 34(4): 719–36.

Lisi, M. and Santana-Pereira, J. (2014) 'Campaign Individualisation before and after the Bailout: A Comparison between Greece and Portugal', *South European Society and Politics*, 19(4): 541–59.

Lodge, M., McGraw, K. M. and Stroh, P. (1989) 'An Impression-Driven Model of Candidate Evaluation', *American Political Science Review*, 83(2): 399–419.

Marsh, M. (2007) 'Candidates or Parties? Objects of Electoral Choice in Ireland', *Party Politics*, 13(4): 500–527.

Mattes, K. and Milazzo, C. (2014) 'Pretty Faces, Marginal Races: Predicting Election Outcomes Using Trait Assessments of British Parliamentary Candidates', *Electoral Studies*, 34(1): 177–89.

McGraw, K. M. and Steenbergen, M. (1995) 'Pictures in the Head: Memory Representation of Political Candidates', in M. Lodge and K. M. McGraw (eds) *Political Judgment: Structure and Process*, Ann Arbor: University of Michigan Press, 15–42.

Moser, R. and Scheiner, E. (2005) 'Strategic Ticket Splitting and the Personal Vote in Mixed-Member Electoral Systems', *Legislative Studies Quarterly*, 30: 259–76.

Norris, P., Curtice, J., Sanders, D., Scammell, M. and Semetko, H. A. (eds) (1999) *On Message: Communicating the Campaign*, London: Sage.

Papp, Z. and Zorigt, B. (2016) 'Party-Directed Personalisation: The Role of Candidate Selection in Campaign Personalisation in Hungary', *East European Politics*, 32(4): 466–86.

Poguntke, T. and Webb, P. (eds) (2005) *The Presidentialization of Politics: A Comparative Study of Modern Democracies*, Oxford: Oxford University Press.

Scarrow, S. E. (1994) 'The "Paradox of Enrollment": Assessing the Costs and Benefits of Party Memberships', *European Journal of Political Research*, 25(1): 41–60.

Shugart, M. S. (2005) 'Comparative Electoral Systems Research: The Maturation of a Field and the New Challenges Ahead', in M. Gallagher and P. Mitchell (eds) *The Politics of Electoral Systems*, Oxford: Oxford University Press, 25–55.

Swindle, S. M. (2002) 'The Supply and Demand of the Personal Vote', *Party Politics*, 8: 279–300.

van Holsteyn, J. and Andeweg, R. B. (2010) 'Demoted Leaders and Exiled Candidates: Disentangling Party and Person in the Voter's Mind', *Electoral Studies*, 29(4): 628–35.

———. (2012) 'Tweede Orde Personalisering: Voorkeurstemmen in Nederland', *Res Publica*, 54(2): 163–91.

Wauters, B., Thijssen, P., Van Aelst, P. and Pilet, J-B. (2016) 'Centralized Personalization at the Expense of Decentralized Personalization. The Decline of Preferential Voting in Belgium (2003–2014)', *Party Politics*. doi:10.1177/13540688 16678882.

Wauters, B. and Weekers, K. (2008) 'Het gebruik van de voorkeurstem bij de federale parlementsverkiezingen van 10 juni 2007', *Res Publica*, 50(2): 49–88.

Wauters, B., Weekers, K. and Pilet, J-B. (2004) 'Het gebruik van de voorkeurstem bij de regionale en Europese parlementsverkiezingen van 13 juni 2004', *Res Publica*, 46(2–3): 377–411.

Zittel, T. (2015) 'Constituency Candidates in Comparative Perspective – How Personalized Are Constituency Campaigns, Why, and Does It Matter?' *Electoral Studies*, 39: 286–94.

Zittel, T. and Gschwend, T. (2008) 'Individualised Constituency Campaigns in Mixed-Member Electoral Systems: Candidates in the 2005 German Elections', *West European Politics*, 31(5): 978–1003.

Appendix

Operationalisation and summary statistics of the explanatory variables

Variable	Operationalisation	Summary statistics				
		N	min.	max.	mean	s.d.
Female	Coded '1' for women; '0' for men	1,285	0	1	0.51	0.50
Age	Measured in years	1,285	18	84	48.33	17.00
Education	Scale ranging from no education to university degree	1,285	0	5	2.90	1.21
Political knowledge	No. of correct answers on five political knowledge questions	1,285	0	5	2.25	1.40
Late deciders	Coded '1' for those who decided which party to vote for during the election campaign or on the day of the election; '0' for those who decided before the start of the campaign	1,285	0	1	0.55	0.50
Left-right position	A respondent's self-placement on an 11-point left-right scale	1,285	0	10	5.11	2.06
Party identification	Feeling of closeness to a party ranging from not at all close to very close	1,285	0	4	1.86	1.46

Variable	Operationalisation	Summary statistics				
		N	min.	max.	mean	s.d.
New party	Coded '0' for the traditional socialist (PS/SP.a), Christian democratic (cdH/CD&V) and liberal (MR/Open VLD) parties; '1' for all other parties	1,285	0	1	0.42	0.49
Party leader on list	Coded '1' if a respondent voted for a list that features the party leader; '0' if no party leader runs on that list	1,285	0	1	0.19	0.39
Population density	Decimal logarithm of a municipality's population density	1,285	1.47	3.52	2.68	0.42

Chapter 13

Preferential voting in local versus national elections: The role of proximity revisited

Peter Thijssen, Bram Wauters
and Patrick van Erkel

INTRODUCTION

Political personalisation refers to a shift over time in attention and/or power from collective actors to individual actors (Karvonen 2004; Mcallister 2009). Personalisation can take place in different arenas: in parties and government, in political news, among the electorate or in parliament (Rahat and Sheafer 2007). Yet, personalisation tendencies in one arena do not necessarily imply nor exclude the presence of this phenomenon in another arena. Belgium's flexible list system gives voters the opportunity to either cast a list vote, thereby supporting the whole party, or to mark a preference vote for one or several candidates within one list, thereby supporting one or more candidates (in addition to their party). As such, preferential voting in Belgium functions as a good indicator of personalisation among voters (Renwick and Pilet 2016; Wauters et al. 2017).

However, hitherto studies on personalisation and preferential voting usually assume that their explanations work similarly across different types of election levels. We will demonstrate that it makes sense to more systematically compare the factors driving preferential voting in both local and national elections. Such a systematic comparison is important because contrasting normative evaluations of electoral personalisation are often linked explicitly to both election levels. While in local elections electoral personalisation is often perceived positively, and preferential voting is considered as an indicator of a more democratised and responsive electoral system (Farrell and Mcallister 2006), at national level it is often perceived negatively because it may strengthen the position of individual politicians to the detriment of political parties (André et al. 2017). One possible explanation for this intriguing contrast is that personal acquaintances with some of the candidates on the ballot list is assumed to be widespread at local level, while it is rather exceptional at the national level (Wauters et al. 2012). Instead, at the national level personal knowledge is generally replaced by indirect mediatised knowledge which is more fickle, malleable and exclusive in the sense that only a few candidates get the bulk of the media attention. Hence, there is no need to support or even strengthen this personalisation logic at the national level, as power in the hands of one person is considered dangerous by many observers and politicians alike.

Next to the *locus* of the personalisation (local versus national elections), it is important to also take the *focus* of the personalisation into account. To what kind of politicians does the process of electoral personalisation applies? Politicians in general ('decentralised' or 'second-order' personalisation) or only a handful of top politicians, typically party leaders and ministers ('centralised' or 'first-order' personalisation, also labelled 'presidentialisation' (Balmas et al. 2014; Wauters et al. 2017; Van Aelst et al 2012). Again, both kinds of personalisation could occur simultaneously, separately or not at all. Hitherto, most research studying the characteristics of preferential voters in flexible list PR systems have used a dichotomous operationalisation of preferential voting; either citizens vote for one or more individual candidates or they cast a list vote endorsing the party. However, this operationalisation does not allow a proper distinction between centralised and decentralised personalisation. We can solve this problem by using another characteristic of the Belgian system, namely the fact that voters can cast multiple preferential votes. Consequently, we can have a very detailed image of the *focus* of the electoral personalisation in Belgium, because three forms of preferential voting can be distinguished: (1) centralised preferential voting (a preferential vote for the first candidate on the list or 'list puller'), (2) decentralised preferential voting (a preferential vote for (an)other candidate(s) than the list puller) and (3) a combination of the two (a preferential vote for list puller and for other candidate(s) on the list). A trichotomous operationalisation of preferential voting is particularly useful because it provides essential information to disentangle the double-barrelled character of the vote for the list puller in systems such as for example in Estonia and the Netherlands where voters only have one single preferential vote and no option to cast an undifferentiated list vote (Nagtzaam and van Erkel 2017). Moreover, recent longitudinal studies have established that different forms of preferential voting evolve in different ways over time (Wauters et al. 2017). While centralised preferential voting seems to be on the rise, decentralised preferential voting seems to decrease. Last but not least, using a trichotomous typology of preferential voting, one could investigate whether local elections are associated more strongly with decentralised personalisation (i.e. voting for candidates other than the list puller), while national elections are more about centralised personalisation (i.e. voting for list pullers and electoral leaders). This could be an additional explanation for the different normative evaluation of personalisation at the two levels. In sum, a trichotomous operationalisation of the dependent variable 'preferential voting' together with the integration of 'election level' as an independent variable can provide interesting insights for comparative research on electoral personalisation.

THE ROLE OF PROXIMITY

In the 1980s, Katz (1985: 87) rightfully stated that 'very little research has been done on intraparty preference voting'. Luckily things have changed for the better since then. In the following paragraphs we will give an overview of this recent work on motivations behind preferential voting. In this respect we are greatly inspired by the insightful systematisation proposed by André et al. (2012, 2013) who distinguish between: (1) *proximity* variables; socio-demographic variables that could be linked to (2) *political resources*, but at the same time these could also be used as a (3) source of *identification* and (4) *instrumental* factors related to the electoral opportunity structure. Yet, although these categories are extremely insightful, they are not mutually exclusive as some variables belong to several categories at the same time and their effects might go in opposite directions. Accordingly, it makes sense to look at possible interactions among the different categories. In this respect we give special attention to the interactions of the proximity logic with the other three logics.

To start with the proximity logic, it is generally assumed that candidates living in the neighbourhood of a voter are more accessible and better known and may therefore receive more preferential votes (Tavits 2010). Hence, one of the motivations for citizens to cast a preferential vote is personal knowledge. Thus, we can expect that once the proximity between candidates and voters is higher, voters will better know the candidates and may therefore be more inclined to cast a preferential vote, rather than a more anonymous list vote. There is some empirical proof substantiating the proximity argument. It is, for example, well known that more preferential votes are being cast in local electionss and relatively speaking more of these preferential votes are cast for other candidates than the list puller (André et al. 2013; Wauters et al. 2012). However, as far as we know no systematic study has rigorously compared proximity factors underlying preferential voting both in local and national elections.

Moreover, up till now proximity has been measured by indirect prox-ies such as party membership and interest group membership (André et al. 2012, 2013). The reasoning behind these proxies is that members of political associations have more occasions where they can meet political candidates personally. However, party membership also involves a strong identification with the party as such. Hence, in electoral systems where voters can either cast a party vote or a preferential vote for one or more candidates of that party, it is unclear what kind of vote a party member might prefer. A similar objection could be made with respect to interest group membership, as it is related to a specific issue one identifies with. In this respect, interest group membership might not only be indicative of proximity voting but also link up with identification voting. In sum, the effects of associational memberships may often be double-barrelled.

Alternatively, we argue that the level of elections (local versus national) might be a more direct measure of the psychological and geographical proximity of the candidates. While there is roughly one national representative for 50,000 Belgian citizens, a Belgian city with 50,000 inhabitants, for instance, has 37 local councillors. Moreover, because parties select candidates on their lists who are more or less evenly spread over the multimember voting district (Put and Maddens 2013), the geographical distance between voter and electoral candidate will be much smaller in local elections than in national/regional elections, making it more likely that voters know at least some candidates, and therefore increases the likelihood that they cast a preferential vote to support one of those candidates. Moreover, in a subjective evaluation of the most important reason for a local vote choice in Belgium, Marien et al. (2015) established that personal knowledge of a local candidate actually was the reason mentioned most often. Nevertheless, 'election level' has never been used in explanatory models. Hence, by using election level as a central independent variable, we can more rigorously test the explanatory effect of the proximity of candidates, given that this behavioural indicator may be more reliable than other proxies or than directly asking voters for their motivations. Of course, also with respect to 'election level' as a proxy for proximity, a reservation could be made as the effect of election level may be induced by other factors than purely by the proximity of the candidates. One could argue, for instance, that national elections are less ideological than local elections. Local elections may be more personalised because the issues involved are more service-oriented and therefore less partisan (Thijssen and Van Dooren 2016). Consequently, especially in local elections, personal knowledge of a candidate might stimulate voters to vote for that candidate even if his or her party is not really their most ideologically proximate one. However, we will control for this alternative ideological explanation by adding partisan affiliation as a fixed control in our explanatory models. Additionally, one may argue that a voter's wish to express ideological preferences does not prevent her to additionally reveal personal preferences as well. In this sense, the Belgian electoral system is a two-step rocket. Because candidates are fielded in separate party lists, voters first have to locate the correct party list to find that party's candidates.

In sum, given that both the psychological and geographical proximity is stronger in local elections, we expect voters in local elections to be more inclined to vote for individual candidates. Moreover, given that we expect more centralised personalisation in national elections and more decentralised personalisation in local elections, we expect proximity to have a stronger effect on the casting of a preferential vote for other candidates than the list puller and on the casting of a combined preferential vote (list puller and others), compared to a vote going exclusively to the list puller.

Hypothesis 1a: Voters are more likely to cast any kind of preferential vote in local elections than in national elections.

Hypothesis 1b: The proximity effect will be stronger for other candidates or a combined vote than for list pullers.

ALTERNATIVE EXPLANATORY LOGICS

Next to the proximity logic, André et al. (2012, 2013) introduce three additional logics to explain preferential voting. In this section, we discuss these three other explanatory categories for preferential voting and indicate how they might have different effects according to the election level. We contend that this is because the proximity logic cuts across the three explanatory logics and therefore different models for explaining the type of preferential vote apply to local and national elections.

The first explanatory logic for preferential voting, aside proximity, is the political resource logic. Previous research has shown that the traditional socio-demographic variables that stimulate political participation also lead to more preferential voting (André et al. 2012, 2013). Especially in electoral systems such as Belgium, one could argue that preferential voting is a more difficult form of political behaviour than voting for a party because a preferential vote implies an extra choice, and hence requires more political resources. Since candidates are nested in parties, the information needed to differentiate candidates is to some extent additional to the prior information needed to differentiate between parties. In this sense one could assume that voters with less formal education, the unemployed, the young and those with less political interest generally cast less-preferential votes, due to the fact that they have less political resources and are therefore inclined to cast a more 'easy' list vote.

A similar low-information heuristic may apply to the list puller. For casting a vote for the list puller, one does not necessarily need more information and more time than for casting a list vote. In a way, this could be an even easier vote than a list vote. Recent studies (Van Erkel and Thijssen 2016; Marcinkiewicz 2013) have pointed out that a vote for the list puller might be the simplest shortcut of them all, because it may be based on a primacy effect which simply assumes that parties will not give the top position of their list to someone who is not worth it. Anyhow, given the presidentialisation of the election campaigns (Van Aelst et al. 2008; Wauters et al. 2017), it may sometimes be easier to assess the personal characteristics of an electoral leader who is highly visible in the campaign than to evaluate the ideological or issue positions of a party. Hence, we expect a similar effect of the resources variables (variables such as level of education and political interest) on both a list vote and a vote for the list puller. In both cases, we expect these types of votes to be especially cast by citizens with fewer political resources.

Things probably look different with respect to personalised votes for other candidates on the list than the list puller. Because this kind of voting requires different information that is often not linked to the inter-party struggle, we expect that for this kind of votes more political resources are required, both in terms of motivation and knowledge. Thus, this type of votes will especially be cast by voters with more political resources. To test this expectation, we will first assess the effect of belonging to socio-demographic groups that traditionally possess more political resources, such as higher educated and older people. By subsequently adding political interest to the model, which is more directly related to the motivational component of political resources, we additionally get some insight in the importance of the knowledge component in the resources explanation of preferential votes for socio-demographic groups.

However, as we stated earlier, the proximity logic might cut across the resource logic. We expect that due to the higher proximity between citizens and candidates at the local level, the cost of political information is probably lower. Therefore, we expect that at the local level the effects of resource variables will be more limited as citizens can make up for their lack of political resources by personally knowing some local candidates. This could reduce the explanatory power of the resource logic. Based on these expectations we formulate the following hypotheses regarding the political resource explanatory factors:

Hypothesis 2a: Voters belonging to socio-demographic groups that generally have more political resources are more likely to cast a vote for other candidates or a combined vote than voters with less political resources who are more likely to cast a vote for the list or for the list puller.

Hypothesis 2b: Politically interested voters are more likely to cast a vote for other candidates or a combined vote than voters with less political resources who are more likely to cast a vote for the list or the list puller.

Hypothesis 2c: The effect of political resources on casting a vote for other candidates or a combined vote is stronger at the national level than at the local level.

Some of the socio-demographic characteristics are linked not only to the resource logic but also to a different explanatory model: the identification logic. One particular interesting socio-demographic variable in this respect is gender. In line with the general differences in institutionalised participation, we would expect female voters to be less inclined to cast a preferential vote than their male counterparts (Coffé and Bolzendahl 2010). Given the broader pattern of gender stereotyping, women still have less access to political resources. But, while André et al. (2012) found no significant gender effect based on *national* election data, André et al. (2013) even found an inverse effect based on *local* election data: female voters cast slightly more preferential votes than male voters. These findings are more or less confirmed in Dutch studies where women also vote more often for other candidates than the list puller (Van Holsteyn and Andeweg 2012). This effect could be explained by a countervailing identification logic. Generally speaking, female candidates may have less access to political resources, but this resource deficit can be offset by a strong identification with other females and an urge to substantiate this identification with a vote for one or more female candidates on the list (Thijssen and Jacobs 2004). Moreover, a symbolic vote that is based on identification with a gender group does not require advanced knowledge at the level of the candidates but can be based on a simple name recognition heuristic. This name recognition heuristic is less helpful for most other social groups – such as the young, who cannot gather information on age only from the ballot list – this trade-off between resources and identification might be rather specific for gender. Previous research indeed demonstrated that 'women votes' (i.e. women voting for women) do exist in the Belgian context, but the effect is rather small (Erzeel and Caluwaerts 2015; Marien et al. 2017; see also chapter 11). We do not see a reason why people should use the identity heuristic less at a particular election level, and therefore hypothesise that there are no differences in the use of preferential voting between women voting in national and in local elections.

Hypothesis 3a: Women are more likely to cast a preference vote than men.
Hypothesis 3b: Women voters are equally likely to cast a preference vote at the local and the national levels.

Finally, we look at the instrumental logic to explain preferential voting. The reasoning behind this logic is that voters do not want to spoil their vote and will usually be less inclined to cast a preference vote if this vote is unlikely to help their preferred candidate get elected. In other words, they are less inclined to cast a preferential vote when preferential votes have limited influence. Obviously, the chance to 'spoil' your vote on a list with a larger number of elected candidates is smaller, as on these lists candidates have a higher chance to get elected over their higher-positioned peers by means of preferential voting. Hence, André et al. (2012) see a proof for strategic considerations of the voters in the significant positive effect of party magnitude on preferential voting. However, in order to genuinely test whether the causal mechanism behind this effect is indeed instrumental, one needs to differentiate centralised and decentralised preferential votes. Only, when a higher party magnitude leads to more decentralised voting, this instrumental logic is really supported. Unfortunately, André et al. (2012) did not have the differentiated preferential voting variable at their disposal. Moreover, as with the resource logic, we can assume that this instrumental logic is cross-cut by the proximity logic. We can expect that the instrumental logic is probably less influential in local elections, given that local voting is largely driven by personal knowledge of the candidates. If one knows a candidate personally, one is inclined to support this candidate irrespective of the candidate's chances to become elected.

Hypothesis 4a: Citizens voting for lists with a small party magnitude are more likely to vote for the list puller or to cast a combined vote than citizens voting for lists with a higher party magnitude.

Hypothesis 4b: The negative effect of party magnitude on voting for the list puller or casting a combined vote is stronger on the national level than on the local level.

The instrumental logic could not be linked to party magnitude alone. Also, other, more institutional differences, for example, between the two regions in Belgium, could cause different voters to have different instrumental evaluations. The most visible difference is that, in local elections of the Walloon region of Belgium, the candidate with the most votes on the most popular list of the majority automatically becomes mayor. This system does not exist in the Flemish region of Belgium. Hence, given this institutional context, and following the instrumental logic, we would expect Walloon voters to be more prone to cast centralised preferential votes for the list puller at the local level than the Flemish voters.

Hypothesis 4c: Walloon voters in local elections are more likely to cast a preferential vote for the list puller than Flemish voters and voters in national elections.

DATA AND METHOD

As reported earlier, Belgium is a particularly interesting case to study the different shades of personalised voting because the electoral system allows voters to cast either a vote for the party in general or a vote for one or more candidates on one of the ordered lists. Furthermore, given that in the vast majority of the municipalities national parties are competing, one could argue that the Belgian local elections are fairly nationalised. Another indicator of the nationalisation of local elections is that almost all national politicians also compete in local elections (even about 80 per cent of national and regional MPs are also member of their local council [Rodenbach et al. 2013]). Consequently, the Belgian case can be identified as a least likely case to find differences between local and national elections. This logic is strengthened further by the fact that we selected the regional elections (Flanders/Wallonia) as our representative national elections. Hence, it makes sense to assume that if we find significant election level differences in this context, they will probably be even stronger at the federal level and other more likely cases.

For testing the hypotheses, we use a stacked dataset based on 2012 PartiRep Exit Poll and the 2014 PartiRep Voter Survey. Scholars may have largely refrained from a trichotomous categorisation of preferential voting because it may be too demanding for a respondent to recall this in a retrospective survey. However, this problem has been largely circumvented in our study because we use exit poll (local) and simulation ballot data (regional). In both cases respondents immediately had to indicate in a ballot similar to the real ballot as to how they voted and reported this to the interviewer directly (exit poll) or by phone very soon after the elections (simulation ballot). This is fairly important because we not only want a reliable report of the party they voted for but also want to know what kind of preferential vote was cast.

Given that we have a nominal dependent variable with four categories (list vote; vote list puller; vote other candidate; vote other candidate *and* list puller) we use a multinomial logistic regression. Additionally, we use clustered robust standard errors in order to account for the fact that citizens are nested in party lists. This way we can include party magnitude without underestimating the standard error. Other independent variables included are gender, education, age, employment (with dummies for being in manual labour and being unemployed), political interest,[1] a dummy for Walloon voters, and last but not least a dummy for the election level. Additionally, to account for the nested structure, we add fixed effects for the political parties (not depicted in tables).

RESULTS

Let us first look at the univariate distribution of our main dependent variable 'Type of vote'. As expected, we see in table 13.1 that in national elections exactly twice as many respondents cast a list vote for the party than in local elections (52 per cent versus 26 per cent). The figures correspond fairly well with the official election results for the forty municipalities included in the local election study (22.7 per cent list votes). With respect to the official result for the Flemish and the Walloon parliament (43.9 per cent list votes), the difference is more pronounced. A possible explanation for this discrepancy is the fact that some voters who have voted for a party as well as for one or more individual candidates have been erroneously catalogued as list voters. However, this does not seem to have fundamentally influenced our findings. Given that the local election study explicitly took into account this double vote choice, we could verify to what extent our results would change if these double votes were coded as party votes instead of preferential votes. This did not have a significant effect on the results of our regression models.

When we focus on the distributions of the type of preferential vote (second columns), we see that the proportion of preferential voters exclusively voting for the list puller is relatively low in local elections (24.7 per cent versus 28.7 per cent for national elections). While the list puller in local elections can profit from personal knowledge and centrality in the local election campaign, this is often not the case in national elections. The Belgian national election campaign mostly centres around the party leader who can be on the ballot list of only one electoral district. Nevertheless, the list puller scores relatively well in national elections. Is this a manifestation of a one-eyed king in the land of the blind as most of the other candidates on the ballot list are largely unknown to the voters?

Rather, the biggest differences can be observed for candidates other than the list puller. While many candidates in national elections are elected exclusively by virtue of the popularity of the list puller, in local elections the lesser gods on the lists matter much more. At local level and national level, respectively, 46.1 per cent and 39.0 per cent of the preferential votes exclusively go to other candidates than the list puller.

Taken together, we find, in general, support for hypothesis 1a stating that voters are more likely to cast *any* kind of preferential vote in local elections than in national elections. At the same time, these descriptives also give support to hypothesis 1b, which stated that proximity especially influences preferential votes for other candidates. Hence, these findings provide first evidence that decentralised personalisation occurs mainly at the local level.

In the following analysis, we will verify to what extent the descriptive results reported earlier uphold in a multivariate context. In table 13.2, we

Table 13.1.　Type of vote in local and national elections

Types of vote		Local elections			National elections		
List vote		26.1%		1,030	52.2%		686
Preferential vote	Only list puller	18.2%	24.7%	721	13.7%	28.7%	180
	List puller and other	21.6%	29.2%	854	15.5%	32.3%	203
	Only other	34.1%	46.1%	1,348	18.6%	39.0%	245
Total		100.0%		3,953	100.0%		1,314

Table 13.2.　Baseline multilevel multinomial logit model, reference category = list vote
(n = 4,433)

Variables	Only list puller	List puller and other candidate	Only other candidate
	B (S.E.)	B (S.E.)	B (S.E.)
Female	0.14 (0.10)	0.02 (0.08)	0.17 (0.09)[+]
Higher educated	0.08 (0.08)	0.22 (0.10)*	0.15 (0.08)[+]
Unemployed	0.16 (0.17)	−0.18 (0.22)	−0.12 (0.17)
Labour	0.02 (0.13)	0.02 (0.14)	−0.03 (0.13)
Age	−0.00 (0.00)	0.01 (0.00)***	−0.00 (0.00)
Local level	0.80 (0.22)***	0.94 (0.12)***	1.19 (0.13)***
Constant	−1.24 (0.37)***	−1.12 (0.23)***	−0.63 (0.23)**

Note: Pseudo-R^2 = 0.04; fixed party effects; robust standard errors (S.E.); ***p < 0.001; **p < 0.01; *p < 0.05; [+]p < 0.10.

present a baseline regression model that consists of the socio-demographic variables, as well as election level as explanatory variables. First, the results in this multivariate model confirm a robust effect of the 'election level'. In local elections, voters vote more often for individual candidates than for lists. Moreover, this effect is strong for all types of preferential voting, which again supports hypothesis 1a. Additionally, we find support for hypothesis 1b, as the effect 'election level' (and the proximity logic) is strongest for other candidates. When estimating the predicted probabilities, keeping all other variables at their mean, we find that the likelihood to vote for the list puller increases from 14.7 per cent (national level) to 17.5 per cent (local level), which is only a moderate effect. For the combined group, this increases from 16 per cent at the national level to 21.9 per cent at the local level, whereas for only other candidates, the increase from 19.1 per cent to 33.7 per cent is quite a strong effect. These findings give again clear support to hypotheses 1a and 1b.

Table 13.2 is also interesting for evaluating the resources and the identification component of socio-demographic variables. However, we cannot deny that overall the effects of the socio-demographic variables are rather modest. Only education level, age and gender have a significant effect on preferential voting. Nevertheless, these baseline effects could be modest because the underlying resource explanation is neutralised by a reverse identification explanation. As explained earlier, this notably could be the case for gender. Female voters traditionally have less access to political resources and consequently we expect them to cast less-preferential votes. On the other hand, many people valuing descriptive representation could identify with female candidates who can easily be recognised by their names. Hence, a negative resource effect for women voters could be overridden by a positive identification effect. The fact that the baseline effects for female voters in all models in table 13.2 are positive underscores this compensatory mechanism.

In order to further distinguish the identification and resource explanation, we look what happens when we add political interest to the model in table 13.3. It could be that the political resources component of these effects on preferential voting will be largely mediated by political interest. If a younger or less-educated voter is less inclined to cast a preferential vote, it could be because he or she is less interested in politics. Hence, if we add political interest in the model the effects could possibly shrink. At the same time, we also include two other variables mentioned in the hypotheses, that is region (Wallonia) and party magnitude.

The decline in effect is certainly true for education level, as the baseline significant positive effect of the higher educated on combined preferential voting decreases substantially in table 13.3. Yet, this is clearly not the case for 'age' as its effect does not change at all. Alternatively, one could argue that young people cast less preferential votes because they have less experience with elections and consequently it takes more effort to differentiate the

Table 13.3. Multilevel multinomial logit model, reference category = list vote (n = 4,433)

Variables	Only list puller B (S.E.)	List puller and other candidate B (S.E.)	Only other candidate B (S.E.)
Female	0.19 (0.10)[+]	0.16 (0.09)[+]	0.22 (0.09)*
Higher educated	0.04 (0.09)	0.07 (0.10)	0.11 (0.08)
Unemployed	0.10 (0.18)	−0.13 (0.22)	−0.08 (0.17)
Labour	−0.02 (0.13)	0.10 (0.15)	0.01 (0.13)
Age	−0.00 (0.00)	0.01 (0.00)***	−0.00 (0.00)
Political interest	0.010 (.02)	0.15 (0.02)***	0.05 (0.01)***
Wallonia	0.03 (0.36)	−0.05 (0.39)	−0.09 (0.32)
Party magnitude	0.07 (0.02)***	0.02 (0.01)	−0.02 (0.01)
Local level	0.44 (0.18)*	0.78 (0.13)***	1.28 (0.15)***
Constant	−1.60 (0.37)***	−1.95 (0.27)***	−0.83 (0.24)***

Note: Pseudo-R^2 = 0.06; fixed party effects; robust standard errors (s.e.); ***p < 0.001; **p < 0.01; *p < 0.05; [+]p < 0.10.

candidates. In this respect, it is logical that the direct effect stays intact after controlling for political interest.

Also in the case of female voters, adding political interest to the model has no compensatory effect. Rather, it only strengthens the positive effects of female voters on preferential voting. When controlling for the fact that female voters generally exhibit lower levels of political interest, their tendency to vote for individual candidates, especially those who are not on top of the list, becomes stronger (predicted probabilities increase from 28.5 to 31.1 per cent). Probably this suppressor effect can be explained by the fact that due to an identification with their under-represented own kind, many female voters vote for female candidates. In this case it is not surprising that we find an inverse effect for female voters because no particular political resources are required to identify the female candidates on a ballot list (Thijssen and Jacobs 2004).

With respect to the use of low-information heuristics, we also see an interesting direct effect of 'political interest' on preferential voting. In line with the resources explanation of hypothesis 2b, we see that politically interested voters are more inclined to vote for individual candidates, although this effect is only modest (predicted probabilities increase from 27.9 to 29 per cent between the lowest and highest categories). Moreover, this effect of political interest only applies to other candidates or the combined vote. We see no significant effect for preferential votes that exclusively go to the list puller. This finding points out that not all preferential votes require substantially more political resources than voting for a party. Because list pullers are highly visible in the election campaign, often there is an almost one-to-one relationship between party and list puller. Interestingly, the strongest effect for political interest can be found for the combined preferential voters who vote both for the list puller and for one or more other candidates (predicted probabilities increase from 10.8 to 33.1 per cent between the lowest and highest categories). If voters who are most politically interested cast a preferential vote, it will probably be a combined vote. In sum, table 13.3 gives support both to the resource model (but mostly only for political interest) and to the identity model (hypothesis 2b and hypothesis 3a), although these two models only impact the vote for other candidates and the combined vote, and not so much the vote for the list puller, where, as was expected, very similar mechanisms seem to play as for the list vote.

As said earlier, the interpretations for the effects that we just mentioned might be further substantiated if we look at interactions with proximity (election level). For example, earlier we argued that the negative age effect is caused by the fact that younger people have more difficulties in differentiating the candidates. However, it seems reasonable to assume that this effect would be more limited at the local level (hypothesis 2b). Indeed, if

Table 13.4. Multilevel multinomial logit model with interactions, reference category = list vote (*n* = 4,433)

	Only list puller	List puller and other candidate	Only other candidate
	B (S.E.)	B (S.E.)	B (S.E.)
Female	0.02 (0.17)	0.30 (0.19)	0.21 (0.17)
Higher educated	0.25 (0.18)	0.24 (0.20)	0.43 (0.18)*
Unemployed	−0.63 (0.43)	−0.08 (0.51)	−0.59 (0.46)
Labour	−0.41 (0.27)	−0.03 (0.35)	−0.11 (0.28)
Age	0.01 (0.01)	0.03 (0.01)***	0.01 (0.00)
Political interest	0.03 (0.04)	0.22 (0.04)***	0.05 (0.03)*
Party magnitude	0.07 (0.03)*	0.07 (0.03)*	0.02 (0.05)
Wallonia	0.87 (0.55)	0.26 (0.48)	0.53 (0.42)
Local level	1.37 (0.48)**	2.86 (0.59)***	2.48 (0.41)***
Female*Local level	0.24 (0.21)	−0.15 (0.22)	0.02 (0.20)
Higher educated*Local level	−0.30 (0.21)	−0.25 (0.23)	−0.44 (0.20)*
Unemployed*Local level	0.98 (0.48)*	0.04 (0.57)	0.69 (0.49)
Labour*Local level	0.53 (0.31)+	0.20 (0.39)	0.18 (0.31)
Age*Local level	−0.02 (0.01)*	−0.02 (0.01)***	−0.01 (0.01)**
Political interest*Local level	−0.02 (0.04)	−0.09 (0.05)+	−0.01 (0.03)
Party magnitude*Local level	0.00 (0.04)	−0.05 (0.03)+	−0.03 (0.04)
Wallonia*Local level	−0.84 (0.41)*	−0.30 (0.29)	−0.62 (0.29)*
Constant	−2.26 (0.52)***	−3.55 (0.55)***	−1.74 (0.39)***
Pseudo-R^2	0.059		

Note: Fixed party effects; robust standard errors (s.e.); ***p < 0.001; **p < 0.01; *p < 0.05; +p < 0.10.

we introduce an interaction between age and election level (table 13.4), we see the age effect disappearing at the local level for all the different forms of preferential voting. Older people only cast more preferential votes at the national level, notably preferential votes of the combined type, while this effect is not significant on the local level. This is not surprising because this seems to be the most sophisticated type of preferential voting. As expected we also find positive effects for political interest, notably for the combined preferential vote. However, here again, we expect the positive resources effect to be smaller at the local level because less resources are needed here. Again, this expectation is confirmed as political interest appears to be related significantly less with a combined preferential vote at local level. The proximity of the candidates at the local level seems to downplay the importance of political resources as a determinant of preferential voting. These findings allow us to support hypothesis 2b.

Furthermore, we expected to find no differences between election levels regarding the identity model (hypothesis 3b). Hence we should expect no significant interaction between gender and local levels. Table 13.4 indeed supports this.

Let us now look at the effects of the instrumental factors which could stimulate specific types of preferential voting. First, if the instrumental logic holds, one would expect that voters will be more inclined to cast a centralised preferential vote when the party magnitude is smaller. However, in this respect it is interesting to see (table 13.3) that there is a significant positive effect of party magnitude on the centralised and the combined form of preferential voting. It means that strong parties receive more preferential votes mainly because they have a popular list puller, and not because other candidates on the list obtain more votes. Therefore hypothesis 4a can be rejected. This suggests that voters do not seem to attach a lot of importance to instrumental factors influencing the chance that a candidate gets elected. This trend seems to be a little bit smaller at the local level. Yet in table 13.4 we see that party magnitude still has a positive effect for votes for the list puller at the local level. This means that hypothesis 4b is also not confirmed since it expected a stronger negative effect on centralised preferential voting at the local level.

Probably, this is related to the limited knowledge that citizens have of the structural context of preferential voting. This is also visible when we look at other structural differences. In local elections of the Walloon region of Belgium, the candidate with most votes on the most popular list automatically becomes mayor. This system does not exist in the Flemish region. Hence, we could expect that Walloon voters would be more prone to cast centralised preferential votes. However, also in this case we find no confirmation for this instrumental factor as we see that the interaction effect of Wallonia and local election is always negative. Moreover, we see that the effect on centralised preferential votes (votes exclusively for the list puller) is also significantly negative. In sum, neither hypothesis 4a, hypothesis 4b nor hypothesis 4c is confirmed by our results.

CONCLUSION AND DISCUSSION

This chapter studied which factors determine the type of preferential vote citizens cast in elections. Although we build on explanation logics as developed by André et al. (2012, 2013), we contribute to this literature by approaching the proximity logic in a new way, and by taking different features of preferential voting into account (centralised, decentralised and combined voting). Proximity is measured in a new way, by making a distinction based on the level on which elections are held, and by contending that the proximity argument cuts across the three other explanatory categories: political resources, identity and instrumental factors. Consequently, our argument is that between policy levels slightly different explanatory models apply. We also use a particular feature of the Belgian system to make a distinction between different types of preferential voting, differentiating between a preferential vote for the list puller, a preferential vote for other candidates or a combination of the two. This is in line with an important recent distinction in the personalisation literature, differentiating two types of personalisation: centralised and decentralised personalisation.

Based on our empirical analyses we reach two conclusions. First, we find support for three of the four explanatory logics. The *proximity logic* applies to all three types of preferential voting, meaning that at the local level people are more inclined to cast any type of preferential vote. However, we do find that this proximity logic is more applicable for citizens casting a combined vote or a preferential vote for candidates lower down the list compared to a preferential vote for the list puller. With regard to the *political resources model*, we find that this logic only applies to the combined vote and to preferential vote for candidates who are not the list puller. These are more cognitive demanding votes given that one needs information not only about the political party but also about at least some of its candidates. Interestingly, no distinction in political resources is found between voters who vote for the list puller and voters who cast a list vote. This confirms previous studies that have indicated that a vote for the list puller is generally not cognitively demanding and that this vote can aptly be conceived as an easy shortcut for making a voting decision (Marcinkiewicz 2013; Van Erkel and Thijssen 2016). Finally, some support is found for the *identity logic*, although again this logic only applies to decentralised or combined personalisation. The *instrumental logic* is not supported by our analyses. Although we find an effect of party magnitude, once we split it out by type of votes, the results counter the expectations that would be derived from this logic. When the party magnitude is higher, especially list pullers receive more votes, which is at odds with our expectations that voters for larger parties are more inclined to cast a preferential vote due to the fact that they have more impact on who gets elected. A second element of the effectiveness of preferential votes, their weight on the elected representatives, is not statistically significant. These all point to the fact that the instrumental logic only plays a minor role. We have no indication that citizens make a rational calculation based on the institutional setting, at least not with fairly marginal institutional differences.

The second conclusion of this chapter is that when studying the type of preferential voting, it is important to take election level into account. Our results indicate that not only are citizens more likely to cast a combined vote or a preferential vote for candidates who are not the list puller when their proximity to candidates is higher (such as in local elections), but the proximity logic also cuts across the political resource model logic. In other words, we find that a high proximity between voters and candidates can make up for a lack of political resources. Therefore, in local elections, voters with lower political knowledge can make up for this knowledge due to the fact that they (personally) know certain local candidates, and hence the political resource logic applies less to the local level, as it is overruled by the proximity logic.

Accordingly, these findings legitimate why normative assessments of electoral personalisation are usually more positive at local level than at the national level. After all, the most important implication of our study is that local elections are more democratic than national elections, to the extent that at the local level a more decentralised type of personalisation applies, compared to the more centralised personalisation logic at the national level. In addition, preferential voters in local elections are more representative for the general population, as they are not only cast by voters with the most political resources.

NOTE

1. Both studies used an 11-point scale to measure political interest. To increase comparability, we decided to use the question on interest in national politics from the local study, as we expect that the voters in the 2014 survey were also more likely thinking about national politics when answering the question.

REFERENCES

André, A., Wauters, B. and Pilet, J.-B. (2012) 'It's not only about lists: Explaining preference voting in Belgium', *Journal of Elections, Public Opinion and Parties*, 22(3): 293–313.

André, A., Depauw, S., Shugart, M. S. and Chytilek, R. (2017) 'Party nomination strategies in flexible-list systems: Do preference votes matter?' *Party Politics*, 23(5): 589–600. doi:1354068815610974.

André, A., Pilet, J.-B., Depauw, S. and Van Aelst, P. (2013) 'De partij, de leider of een "gewone" kandidaat? Het gebruik van de voorkeurstem bij de gemeenteraads-verkiezingen van 2012', in R. Dassonneville, M. Hooghe, S. Marien and J.-B. Pilet (eds) *De lokale kiezer: Het kiesgedrag bij de Belgische gemeenteraadsverkiezingen van oktober 2012*. Brussel: ASP, 119–42.

Balmas, M., Rahat, G., Sheafer, T. and Shenhav, S. R. (2014) 'Two routes to personalized politics centralized and decentralized personalization', *Party Politics*, 20(1): 37–51.

Coffé, H. and Bolzendahl, C. (2010) 'Same game, different rules? Gender differences in political participation', *Sex Roles*, 62(5–6): 318–33.

Erzeel, S. and Caluwaerts, D. (2015) 'Is it gender, ideology or resources? Individual-level determinants of preferential voting for male or female candidates', *Journal of Elections, Public Opinion and Parties*, 25(3): 265–83.

Farrell, D. M., and Mcallister, I. (2006) 'Voter satisfaction and electoral systems: Does preferential voting in candidate-centred systems make a difference?' *European Journal of Political Research*, 45(5): 723–49.

Karvonen, L. (2004) 'Preferential voting: Incidence and effects', *International Political Science Review*, 25(2): 203–26.

Katz, R. S. (1985) 'Intraparty preference voting', in B. Grofman and A. Lijphart (eds) *Electoral Laws and Their Political Consequences*. New York: Agathon Press, 85–103.

Marcinkiewicz, K. (2013) 'Electoral contexts that assist voter coordination: Ballot position effects in Poland', *Electoral Studies*, 33: 322–34.

Marien, S., Dassonneville, R. and Hooghe, M (2015) 'How second order are local elections? Voting motives and party preferences in Belgian municipal elections', *Local Government Studies*, 41(6): 898–916.

Marien, S., Schouteden, A. and Wauters, B. (2017) 'Voting for women in Belgium's flexible list system', *Politics & Gender*, 13(2): 305–35 (published FirstView).

Mcallister, I. (2009) 'The personalization of politics', in R. J. Dalton and H.-D. Klingemann (eds) *The Oxford Handbook of Political Science: The Oxford Handbook of Political Behaviour*. Oxford: Oxford University Press, 571–88.

Nagtzaam, M. and van Erkel, P. F. A. (2017) 'Preference votes without preference? Institutional effects on preference voting: an experiment', *Journal of Elections, Public Opinion and Parties*, 27(2): 172–91.

Put, G.-J. and Maddens, B. (2013) 'The selection of candidates for eligible positions on PR lists: The Belgian/Flemish federal elections 1999–2010', *Journal of Elections, Public Opinion and Parties*, 23(1): 49–65.

Rahat, G. and Sheafer, T. (2007) 'The personalization(s) of politics: Israel, 1949–2003', *Political Communication*, 24(1): 65–80.

Renwick, A. and Pilet, J.-B. (2016) *Faces on the Ballot: The Personalization of Electoral Systems in Europe*. Oxford: Oxford University Press.

Rodenbach, J., Steyvers, K. and Reynaert, H. (2013) 'Tussen Dorpsstraat en Wetstraat? Burgemeesters als stemmenkampioenen en cumulards?' in H. Reyneart and K. Steyvers (eds) *De verkiezingen van 14 oktober 2012. De kracht van verankering?* Brugge: Vanden Broele, 141–62.

Tavits, M. (2010) 'Effect of local ties on electoral success and parliamentary behaviour: The case of Estonia', *Party Politics*, 16(2): 215–35.

Thijssen, P. and Jacobs, K. (2004) 'Determinanten van voorkeurstemproporties bij (sub-) lokale verkiezingen: de Antwerpse districtraadsverkiezingen van 8 oktober 2000', *Res publica*, 4: 460–85.

Thijssen, P. and Van Dooren, W. (2016) 'Who you are/where you live: Do neighbourhood characteristics explain co-production?' *International Review of Administrative Sciences*, 82(1): 88–109.

Van Aelst, P., Sheafer, T. and Stanyer, J. (2012) 'The personalization of mediated political communication: A review of concepts, operationalizations and key findings', *Journalism*, 13(2): 203–20.

Van Aelst, P., Maddens, B., Noppe, J., and Fiers, S. (2008) 'Politicians in the news: Media or party logic? Media attention and electoral success in the Belgian election campaign of 2003', *European Journal of Communication*, 23(2): 193–210.

Van Erkel, P. F. A. and Thijssen, P. (2016) 'The first one wins: Distilling the primacy effect', *Electoral Studies*, 44: 245–54.

Van Holsteyn, J. J. M. and Andeweg, R. B. (2012) 'Tweede orde personalisering: voorkeurstemmen in Nederland', *Res Publica*, 54(2): 163–92.

Wauters, B., Verlet, D. and Ackaert, J. (2012) 'Giving more weight to preferential votes: Welcome or superfluous reform? The case of the local elections in Flanders (Belgium)', *Local Government Studies*, 38(1): 91–111.

Wauters, B., Thijssen, P., Van Aelst, P. and Pilet, J.-B. (2017, forthcoming) 'Centralized personalization at the expense of decentralized personalization. The decline of preferential voting in Belgium (2003–2014)', *Party Politics*. Online first: https://doi.org/10.1177/1354068816678882.

Index

Note: Page numbers in italics indicate either a figure or a table.

Contributors

Rudy B. Andeweg is a professor of Political Science at Leiden University and a member of the Royal Netherlands Academy of Arts and Sciences. His research interests include political legitimacy and representation.

Audrey André is a F.R.S.-FNRS postdoctoral researcher at the Centre d'étude de la vie politique (CEVIPOL) of the Université libre de Bruxelles. Her research focuses on the impact of electoral institutions on parties', legislators' and voters' behaviour. Key findings have been published in the *European Journal of Political Research*, *Electoral Studies*, *Comparative Political Studies*, *Party Politics*, *Acta Politica* and *West European Politics*.

Pierre Baudewyns is a professor of Political Science at the Université catholique de Louvain (UCLouvain, Belgium) and co-promotor of the Belgian National Election Study (French-speaking part). His main research interests are survey methodology and political behaviour.

Benjamin Biard is a F.R.S.-FNRS research fellow in political science at the Institute of Political Science Louvain-Europe. His main research interests include populism, the influence of populist parties on public policy and democracy. Benjamin is co-secretary of the Francophone Belgian Political Science Association (ABSP).

Didier Caluwaerts is an assistant professor of Public Policy at the Vrije Universiteit Brussel. His research deals with deliberative democracy and democratic innovations.

Ruth Dassonneville is an assistant professor in the Department of Political Science at Université de Montréal (Canada), where she holds the Canada Research Chair in Electoral Democracy. She is also a member of the Centre for the Study of Democratic Citizenship. Her main research interests are voting behaviour, dealignment and economic voting.

Marc Debus is a professor of Comparative Government at the University of Mannheim, Germany. His research interests include political institutions, in particular in multilevel systems, and their effects on political behaviour of voters and legislators, party competition, coalition politics and decision-making within parliaments and governments.

Sam Depauw is an assistant professor and postdoctoral researcher at the Vrije Universiteit Brussel. His research concentrates on legislative and electoral studies. He is co-editor of *Representing the People?* (Oxford UP 2014) and has published extensively on political representation and party discipline in *Political Behavior, West European Politics, Parliamentary Affairs, Electoral Studies, Journal of Legislative Studies* and *Party Politics.*

Kris Deschouwer is a research professor in the Department of Political Science of the Vrije Universiteit Brussel and central coordinator of the PartiRep project.

Lieven De Winter is a senior professor at the UCLouvain. His research focuses on the (comparative) analysis of government formation, legislatures, elections and political parties and political regionalism, mainly in Western Europe.

Jérémy Dodeigne is a assistant professor at the Universty de Namur. His research areas cover the study of elites' career patterns in multilevel systems, parliamentary behaviour, regional and federal studies, local politics and mixed methods research designs.

Silvia Erzeel is an assistant professor and postdoctoral researcher at the Political Science Department of the Vrije Universiteit Brussel. Her research interests include political representation, political parties, gender and ethnicity and comparative politics.

Marc Hooghe is a professor of Political Science at the University of Leuven, Belgium. He holds an Advanced Grant of the European Research Council to investigate the democratic linkage between citizens and the political system in Europe. He has published mainly on political participation, political trust and political socialisation.

Louise Hoon is a doctoral researcher at the Department of Political Science at the Vrije Universiteit Brussel and Université Libre de Bruxelles (ULB) and a PhD fellow of the Fonds voor Wetenschappelijk Onderzoek (FWO). Her doctoral research concerns Euroscepticism and party/voter realignment.

Vincent Jacquet is a research fellow in Political Science at the UCLouvain. His main research interests include democratic innovations, deliberative and participatory democracy and local politics.

Camille Kelbel is a PhD candidate and teaching assistant at the ULB. Her doctoral project focuses on candidate selection for European elections.

Sjifra de Leeuw is a PhD candidate in political communication at the Amsterdam School of Communication Research (University of Amsterdam). Before she was a student researchy assistant at the KU Leuven.

Christophe Lesschaeve is a PhD candidate in the Department of Political Science at the University of Antwerp, Belgium. His dissertation analyses the opinion congruence between political elites and voters in Belgium. His most recent work focuses on the differences in opinion congruence between lower and higher educated voters.

Sofie Marien is an assistant professor at the University of Leuven. Her research interests are focused on democratic legitimacy, democratic innovations and political equality.

Jean-Benoit Pilet is a professor of Political Science at ULB. He works on elections, electoral system, political parties and representation. He is the co-author of *Faces on the Ballot; The Personalization of Electoral Systems in Europe* (with Alan Renwick – Oxford UP 2016) and *The Politics of Political Party Leadership in Comparative Perspective* (with William Cross – Oxford UP 2015).

Min Reuchamps is a professor of Political Science at the UCLouvain. His teaching and research interests are federalism and multilevel governance as well as participatory and deliberative methods. He currently is the president of the Francophone Belgian Political Science Association (ABSP).

Benoît Rihoux is a full professor in Comparative Politics at the UCLouvain, where he chairs the Centre for political science and comparative politics. His substantive research interests comprise, among others, political parties, organisational change, social movements and gender and politics. He plays a leading role in the development of configurational comparative methods and QCA and coordinates the interdisciplinary COMPASS network in that field.

Giulia Sandri is an associate professor at the European School of Political and Social Sciences of the Catholic University of Lille. She was previously research fellow at Christ Church and at the Department of Politics and International Relations of the University of Oxford. Her main research interests are party politics, intra-party democracy and political behaviour.

Rüdiger Schmitt-Beck is a professor of Political Science and Political Sociology at the University of Mannheim and one of the principal investigators of the German Longitudinal Election Study GLES. His research interests focus on electoral behaviour and political communication.

Dave Sinardet is an associate professor in the Department of Political Science of the Vrije Universiteit Brussel. His work focuses on political communication and on the relation between identities and territorial politics.

Peter Thijssen is an associate professor at the Department of Political Science and member of the research group Media, Movements and Politics (M²P) at the University of Antwerp. His research focuses on public opinion, political participation and the politics of solidarity.

Jan W. van Deth was a professor of Political Science and International Comparative Social Research at the University of Mannheim and is project director at the Mannheim Centre for European Social Research. He published widely in the fields of political culture and participation, social change and comparative research methods.

Patrick van Erkel works at the Political Science Department at the University of Antwerp. He is also a member of the Research group M²P. His research focuses on electoral behaviour.

Emilie van Haute is an associate professor at the ULB and deputy director of the CEVIPOL. Her main research interests include party membership, intra-party dynamics, participation, elections and voting behaviour.

Virginie Van Ingelgom is a F.R.S.-FNRS research associate professor at the UCLouvain. Her research deals with the issue of legitimacy at both the national and the European levels, with the link between public policies and citizens' attitudes and behaviours, and with methodological issues concerning the use of qualitative comparative analysis.

Soetkin Verhaegen is a postdoctoral researcher at the Department of Political Science at Stockholm University. Her research focusses on public opinion about international and regional organisations and tackles questions about legitimacy, identity and participation.

Stefaan Walgrave is a professor of Political Science at the University of Antwerp. He leads the research group M^2P (www.m2p.be). His research interests are social movements, political participation, political communication and elections.

Bram Wauters is an associate professor at the Department of Political Sciences of the Ghent University, Belgium, where he leads the research group GASPAR. His research interests include political representation, elections and political parties, with special attention to diversity.